A *Journey* of
Love, Faith, Strength
and
Determination

D1479313

GROVER JACKSON, MARY FULLARD
AND E. CHRISTINE JACKSON

NEWMAN SPRINGS PUBLISHING
320 Broad Street
Red Bank, NJ 07701

First originally published by Newman Springs Publishing 2020

ISBN 978-1-64531-722-7 (Paperback)
ISBN 978-1-64801-575-5 (Hardcover)
ISBN 978-1-64531-723-4 (Digital)

Printed in the United States of America

To Gerod, my oldest son; Noah, my grandson; Sydney, my grand-daughter; and the next generation and beyond. A special tribute to Gerod who will never understand our past, present, or future. Yet he is an integral part of this book, if not in words, in every thought. To Noah and Sydney who are too young to understand today, someday will influence and change their generation for the good of mankind.

Contents

Acknowledgments

To my friend Mattie, a college classmate, who encouraged me to complete this project and offered priceless suggestions, I am eternally grateful. To E. Chris Jackson, my youngest sibling, who thought my choice of some words and events portrayal were too descriptive and provocative so she neutralized many of them. Mary F. Fullard, sibling number 6, whose research started and generated my interest in our family's ancestry. Finally, I extend my appreciation to Leola, my oldest sibling, who was strongly encouraged to participate in the writing of our history. Also, I'm very thankful to my sister Rosie, sibling number 2, who exercised love and a bit of reverse psychology in convincing Leola to participate in this project. To my other siblings, who, after much persuading, took the time to share their experiences and thoughts, and their life journey, I owe my all.

Introduction

This book is about a family that started with the creation of man. Then we drifted apart. Yet we traced our family of today back to 1827. Like most families, we were once one very close family, then people, place, time, and events changed and separated us. The idea for this book evolved over time. Friends and coworkers often said to me, "You should write a book," after they heard stories about my background and family. The stories consisted of the twists and turns of our large family of fourteen siblings and our parents. Some of the stories were about twelve people living in a two-bedroom shack, where early education was undeniably separate and irrefutably unequal.

Still others shared the same family stories just as the gospel writers Matthew, Mark, Luke, and John; four different writers told the same biblical stories from their viewpoint. However, the stories told by my siblings and me will only be recorded in the Jackson's epistle, this book entitled *A Journey of Love, Faith, Strength and Determination*. Our stories, like limbs on a tree, branch off in many directions: plowed other people's land, went from sharecropping to Wall Street, joined the US Peace Corps and served in Kenya, taught in Iran, and so many more stories that told of desolation, despair, bleakness, anguish, adventure, pride, happiness, and so much more.

At no point early on did I take the idea of writing a book seriously, although I remembered many, many details about my life experiences. Years later, I revisited the concept and suggested to each of my siblings that we should journalize our experiences from childhood through adulthood. I pledged that I would organize the content into a finished manuscript that they would be proud to read as a novel, share with friends, or perhaps one day, watch on the big screen. It took some prodding, but eventually, they were sold on my idea. The collection of stories is not a rags-to-riches story nor is it a feel-sorry-for-me one. Instead the stories are about a family of fourteen sisters and brothers. They share their intimate thoughts about one another and their mom and dad. Their stories shine light on their mother who motivated and encouraged them to make a difference in the world. They speak about their father's role in the family and how he impacted them. It was a real normal family. Well, perhaps not so normal, but it was certainly real.

During the period 1930–1958, our Jackson family experiences ranged from poverty, hopelessness, depression, oppression, suppression, optimism, and ecstasy. Some stories include raw emotions. Siblings share their personal experiences and feelings about each other and their family unit. Others chronicle the history of our extended family spanning nine generations to provide a background for our two-parent family. The fourteen Jackson children were born over a twenty-four year span of time. Our life's journey was anchored in a strong faith in God. Although we may have travelled separate paths and landed on different church pews with varying religious faiths, God, family, and country directed our journey, and we were led by caring and loving parents.

The genesis for much of the background material shared in this book came from research started by my sister Mary F. (Mamie, sibling 6) Fullard and was continued by yours truly (sibling 8), Grover. At the Bryant family reunion on Dad's side, held on July 14, 2007, in Elizabeth, New Jersey, Mamie presented a thorough report of the Bryant family tree from 1827–1930. She titled her research "A Journey of Love, Faith, and Strength." The title seemed very appropriate in describing our journey, but something was still missing. That missing piece of the puzzle turned out to be the glue that held the journey together. I surmised it was our *determination*, strength of character, strength of mind, strength of will, endurance, willpower, drive, and self-discipline. There was so much more under the umbrella of that one word that was missing. By adding that one word, it allowed us to focus on the big picture. She and I agreed to use her title and add—for emphasis—*determination* since it described our journey so appropriately. Her view of our ancestors was broad, but this book will focus specifically on the views of my siblings and our journeys. The time span will chronicle the fourteen siblings, who were born between February 1930 and February 1954, and our parents. Sadly, by the time we agreed to document our stories, six of our sisters and brothers had already passed. Their contributions to this effort will be posthumous. As I continue from where Mamie's research ended and mine started, I incorporated more details about our parents and their lineages. Both Dad and Mom went home to be with the Lord more than thirty-five years ago. The life principles they taught us are etched into our DNA as we are confronted, from time to time, with the good, the bad, and the ugly. We practice the good, learn from the bad, and use the ugly as teachable moments.

As confirmed by my sister's research, our earliest known ancestors, Bill Lewis Bryant Sr. and his wife, Phyllis (Thomas) Bryant; Dad's great-grandparents and Austin Givens and his wife Josephine (Porter) Givens, Mom's great-grandparents, were born into the system of slavery. Other relatives' names discussed herein were retrieved from lists in the government's archival historical records, known facts, and ancestry databases.

My parents spent years trying to make a living by farming. They tried both sharecropping and independent farming on rented land. They planted cotton, peanuts, and corn to generate cash. It was almost impossible to make a living farming, renting, and living on another person's land. The acreage we cultivated and farmed was small compared to modern plantation standards of using automated (tractor) equipment versus our manual (mule and human) process. My siblings and I grew to detest the farm work of picking cotton, shaking peanuts, and pulling corn, although there was nothing we, as kids, could do to change our situation. I can only imagine how our ancestors felt and what they experienced as they raised families while laboring as slaves in the fields on plantations. It took great strength, courage, and undying faith in God to toil in fields day in and day out. It took their uncompromising faith in Jesus hearing their cries as they sang the African-American spiritual "I Want Jesus to Walk with

Me" and other songs with similar themes. They likely prayed every minute to be freed from their oppression and misery. Fast-forward a hundred years and I know the line from Luther Barnes and the Red Budd Choir's song "Somehow Someway" which says, "We are going to make it to the other side," expressed my hopeful sentiments.

The foundation stories of my siblings contain bittersweet memories from their earliest experiences in Omaha (Stewart County), Georgia, a rural farming community. Omaha, Georgia, is on the state's western boundary, close by the Chattahoochee River. The river separates Georgia from Alabama. According to the 2015 United States census per capita income data, Stewart County remains one of the poorest counties in Georgia. It is ranked 140th out of Georgia's 159 counties. Data found in the same census report shows that there are nearly 1,900 households in the county. From an economic standpoint, not much has changed since slavery and our early years there.

As a family, we had food to eat most of the time, owned a few cows, chickens, pigs, and planted vegetables for our personal consumption. The family's income depended on peanuts and cotton planted, harvested, and sold commercially. The family cultivated land, planted, and harvested crops on rented farmland. The result never yielded a positive financial outcome for our family. Instead the experiences came with many challenges and sacrifices and without words to adequately express the family's plight.

Until the early 1960s, unless a family owned farmland, sharecropping was the primary source of employment with zero profit earned. Today farming in Stewart County, Georgia, is highly mechanized and much of the farmland has been converted into growing timber. My fourteen siblings, consisting of eight females and six males, were born in Stewart County, on land lived and worked by three generations of our extended family. Those generations' entire existence was living and farming on another person's land. With only a few exceptions, they never owned any land—not even a grain of soil—nor did they have any resources to acquire land of their own.

At the urging of Mom, Dad gave up farming and relocated to Camden, New Jersey. Before he made up his mind completely, five siblings—two brothers and three sisters—left Georgia, found jobs, and settled in various parts of New Jersey; some had even gotten married. In January 1958, my siblings who had already relocated to New Jersey purchased a one-way ticket from Omaha, Georgia, to Camden, New Jersey, for Dad to go seek work. With the financial help and sponsorship of my oldest siblings, we left Omaha, Georgia, on June 10, 1958—4 years, 110 days after the birth of the last sibling. We boarded and rode in the back of a Greyhound bus to Washington, DC. Beyond Washington; we sat on any available seat to Philadelphia, Pennsylvania, with Camden, New Jersey, as our destination. As the remaining nine youngest siblings, we traveled with Mom to our new home in Camden. Until then, none of the nine children, including me, had ever ventured more than fifty miles from our place of birth—Omaha, Georgia.

The family's northern migration wasn't the end to our economic and financial struggles. They both continued. The difference was that the family lived together or nearby as a family unit and worked together to solve the challenges thrown our way. Billy, sibling 3, our oldest brother who lived in Camden, made it possible for the family to secure housing. In 1959, he helped Mom and Dad purchase the home they owned and lived in until after Mom's death in 1984.

The move exposed us to educational opportunities that didn't exist for us in Stewart County. Through the years, ten of us attended and earned college degrees. Eight of the siblings earned degrees at New Jersey colleges and universities. Two sons earned their college degrees out of state at historically black colleges and universities (HBCUs). I was the first of ten siblings to earn a college degree and the first of five siblings to earn a graduate degree.

We were especially blessed and proud of our accomplishments, but no one was as proud as Mom. She never completed grammar school. While she may not have been educated in a formal classroom, she had knowledge and wisdom beyond textbooks and classrooms. She had practical knowledge and was well-versed on human behavior. She was the all-star coach behind the all-star team of our accomplishments. She was beyond her years in understanding and freely shared her insights with us. As was often the case, some of us, with years of education and degrees, were married and had families of our own before we realized the breadth and depth of Mom's wisdom. Mom specifically taught us to do our best always, to be the best we can be, to be as strong as we can, to be supportive of each other spiritually, socially, and financially. She insisted, with faith, we could overcome any weak links in the chains of our lives that were meant to constrain us, whether imagined or real.

Mom's formal classroom education ended in third grade, although her wisdom, experience, and common sense would match any graduate from an accredited college or university. She may not have been able to spell and articulate like a national spelling bee champion, but her perception was magical. Her grammar may not have earned a Nobel Prize for literature or a passing grade in today's classrooms, but she would have been able to teach both the teachers and students a lot about life and how to make this world a better place for all to survive.

Mom supported, motivated, encouraged, and challenged each of us to work and become outstanding in all our undertakings. She insisted that we should never ever accept mediocrity. She cherished each of our accomplishments. She understood and believed that her children had bright futures if they focused on achieving their goals. She stressed that we must never accept the shortcuts or the easy routes and never accept handouts. She firmly believed in work, earn our keep, always help, support family members, and help others in need. Each of us accepted Mom's challenge, overcame obstacles, made sacrifices, and kept our eyes on our long-term goals. Along the way, we all had setbacks and more than a few wake-up calls. We kept and honored her advice and legacy by assisting family members and others in need when spiritual, physical, and financial adversities presented themselves. In honor of Mom's life, we established a scholarship through her church. The scholarship was awarded to worthy college-bound students.

Dad was always present in our lives. Mom was the real driving force behind all of us. She was a firm and committed believer in following God's Word. Her fervent churchgoing ways, her persistent Bible readings, and her excellent demonstrations of doing were all characteristics extracted from God's teachings. Mom had only a few life principles. She taught us, preached to us, and demonstrated them for us by her actions, deeds, and sacrifices. Her principles were: (1) Trust and obey God and step out by faith. (2) We will not be alone because no man is an island unto himself. (3) Our rewards will be beyond our imagination, if we treat others the way we want to be treated. (4) Each of our experiences in life must have a purpose that is built on faith, character, and strength. Because of our mom's dedication, commitment, and personal sacrifices, our family thrived.

Our mom was a Proverbs-31 woman:

> The heart of her husband trusts in her, and he will have no lack of gain. She does him good, and not harm, all the days of her life. She opens her mouth with wisdom; and in her tongue, is the law of kindness. She looks well to the ways of her household and eats not the bread of idleness. Her children arise up, and call her blessed; her husband also, and he praises her. (Proverbs 31:2–3, 26–28, ESV)

This was our mom!

Chapter 1

The Journey Begins

My Great-Great-Grandparents

We grew up in Stewart County (Omaha), Georgia. It was just another place in the Deep South. It bordered on the Chattahoochee River, across from Alabama on the southwestern side of Georgia. The area was home to the Creek Indians long before the settlers (Irish) arrived and claimed their land. We experienced and encountered all the negative actions and attitudes by whites toward blacks. The Ku Klux Klan's (KKK) activities were quite prevalent. It was not uncommon to find dead black male bodies floating in creeks and ponds with both hands and feet bound. So to ignore the history of Omaha would be to omit and deny the existence of the people who once lived there; the Creek Indians, the former slave owners, settlers, my ancestors, and others.

Looking back, we lived in a place that was sheltered from the outside world and, in my mind, reality. It was also the place my great-great-grandparents were enslaved as validated by historical documents and oral history. Whether they were born there or brought on a slave ship, we don't know and will never know. What we know, as recorded in the historical documents, are the slave names and estimated date of births that enabled us to figure out their ages. We know the names of the plantations and the slave owners who settled there with their slaves. If it were not for a raid by the Creek Indians on Shepherd's Plantation, we would not have discovered historical documentation about the geographic area nor would we have records validating slaves' names and birthdates.

We were able to trace my mom's family back to (1827) and to Florence, an area less than five miles from my birthplace. They resided on property occupied by slave owners who, with the Georgia militia, had overtaken the Creek Native Americans' ancestral land. The slave owners and Creeks once lived peacefully together, but after the US declared independence from Britain, conflicts generated between the settlers and the Creeks. The hostility occurred after Georgia was enacted as a state and operated under its own rules of law. One particularly offensive law stipulated that Indians could live on the land but they could not hold title of ownership to the land. Settlers and their elected officials used such laws to steal the land from the Creek Indians. Conflicts arose and skirmishes increased between the settlers and indigenous people.[1] General Daniel Stewart, President Theodore Roosevelt's grandfather, served as an officer in both the Revolutionary War and the War of 1812. He fought and stabilized the territory for the white settlers. In 1830, as a tribute, Stewart County was named in his honor. My great-great grandfather, Austin Givens, was born three years before (in 1827) Stewart County was officially designated.[2]

The County's History

The subsequent actions of the Creek Indians helped to bridge the information gap between my generation and our ancestors. The Creek Native American culture was highly developed and played a role unknowingly in identifying my great-great-grandparents while they were slaves.

The Creek, Cherokee, and other Native American tribes occupied much of the southeastern territory long before the area became the United States. The Spanish traders, the first Europeans, encountered the Creek Indians in the mid-1600. There is archaeological evidence in and around Stewart County of their sophisticated civilization. Like the whites who came after them, tribal members owned and traded slaves who were purchased from the Spanish slave traders. For many years, the whites and Creeks prospered from the land, hunted, fished, and traded with one another peaceably. Until the early 1800s, some of the Creek leaders were themselves a mixed breed of Europeans and Native Americans. Many took on the culture of the Europeans who had tried to stifle them. As noted earlier, The Creek Indians inhabited a large portion of Southwest Georgia and Eastern Alabama, including the area now known as Stewart County.

Increasingly tired of the white territorial infringements and land taken away, on June 9, 1836, the Creek Indians invaded the Shepherd's Plantation in Florence (Stewart County, Georgia). Dr. Albert H. and his brother, Edward T. Shepherd, co-owned the Shepherd's Plantation.[3] To avoid the violence, Dr. Shepherd, his family, and slaves escaped and set up shelter in Lumpkin's (Stewart County, Georgia) courthouse.[4] James Fitzgerald rode to Fort McCreary with the grave news that the Shepherd's Plantation and others were under attack.[5] The whites lost twelve people in this engagement and seven people were wounded. The loss of the Indians was estimated at thirty killed and an unknown number of Indians wounded, but it was never fully verified.

Sources: National Register of Historic Places, Wikipedia, Georgia Plantations Works Project, Library of Congress. Data compiled by Janice Rice and Kim Torp

After several contrived treaties, some by their own interracial tribesmen and others by the whites, the US government forced the Creek Tribe to give up all rights to their ancestral land. Between 1836 and 1839, the Creeks and other Native Americans were forced to relocate to the Oklahoma territory by a treaty of law under Andrew Jackson's presidency. This included Creeks from Georgia and Alabama, the Cherokee, Chickasaw, Choctaw, and Seminole tribes from other surrounding states.

Flora Childs was the daughter of James Fitzgerald who owned the farmland where I was born.[6] The Jacksons rented land from her, farmed and lived on her property for many years, until we relocated to New Jersey on June 10, 1958. All but three Jackson siblings were born in Flora Childs' plantation quarters. Dr. Shepherd, owner of Shepherd's Plantation, died in 1837 from exposure to the elements.

In December 1837, during the settlement of Dr. Shepherd's estate, a list of his slaves and their values was revealed. Among his possessions was a young ten-year-old black slave named Austin Givens, valued at $450. This revelation gave us the name we had been searching for some time. It was the missing link needed to pin down my mother's side of the family. We had been unable to locate her origins anywhere in various historical records. We had researched ancestral databases for years. Finally, we had data that could verify my mom's ancestors and where in Georgia her family had originated.

The Family's Genealogy

My sister Mary Fullard (Mamie) has always been curious about our family's genealogy. As an adult, she drove our parents and others crazy with questions about our ancestors. Marie Woodward Flowers (Cousin Bae), the daughter of Lucy Bryant Woodward, my grandmother Hattie Worrell Jackson's sister, was the first person to give her a comprehensive understanding of our family's foundation. Cousin Bae did so in 1983 as they sat under an oak tree at a Bryant family reunion in Smith, Alabama. Cousin Bae stimulated Mamie's appetite and created a hunger to learn more about the family. Mamie appreciated the information shared and pursued the family's history more enthusiastically. She completed a thorough research of both Dad's and Mom's family trees. Later I supplemented her efforts by examining the historical records as reflected in ancestry websites.

The ancestry websites have handwritten copies of historical records containing names of people, places, and things. Her primary interest was to obtain our ancestors' names, dates of birth, any unknown relatives (missing family links), and places they lived. Since we were born in Georgia, we knew our ancestors were former slaves and worked for former slave owners. We had no written records of the family history up to that time. The history had been passed on by word-of-mouth and was usually incomplete. This made researching ancestry beyond my great grandparents not much better than shots in the dark. As Mamie imagined, accessing historical records to match names passed on verbally was not an easy task and creating a lineage tree proved extremely difficult. Various research sites were the starting points for discovering ancestors before the Civil War and proved to be accurate and very informative.

In the 1830 Census, white slave owners submitted the census data for blacks via a list of slaves they owned. The slaves were simply part of their households' items. Only the slave's age, gender, and color were maintained on the slave registry. There were no names, dates-of-birth references, or any indication of their relatives. In 1850, blacks were included in the census data, along with names they were commonly called. The names were not birth names, instead they were informal names by which the person responded to when called. For example, William Lewis (Bill) Bryant Jr. was commonly called William Lewis; so he appeared in the 1850 Census as William Lewis, not as William Lewis Bryant Jr. It was not until 1870 that the actual birth name for blacks appeared in the federal census.

Based on Mamie's research, from 1870 and beyond, the census form began to list the person's name, date of birth, and death. However, in general, due to the lack of specific information kept on blacks, dates of birth were noted on official records as "about" time frames. This is usually written as "Abt." Because of the data input and possibly storage limitations for Stewart County's records, death certificate information was not available before 1918.

With the evolution of the Internet, Mamie searched sites such as Ancestry.Com and other genealogical websites. Her prayers were answered. She located the early genealogy trees of both the Bryant (Bill and Phyllis), my father's family line, and Givens (Austin and Josephine), my mother's family tree. The United States initial recorded census began in 1790. In that census, blacks were recognized only as a quantity, not by a name. The earliest official census data for blacks in the US was available only after the 1850 Census. Black families' genealogical records before 1830 were passed down orally from individual family members. My family had no written records and those who may have had knowledge of earlier ancestors had passed away years earlier. Consequently, the earliest official census data about our family was not available until after the 1850 Census.

My Dad's Mother's Genealogy Tree[7]

With the passage of time, my family's oral ancestral history seemed all but lost. The individuals with any firsthand knowledge of the family's past were either dead or too feeble and frail to recount anything factual, insightful, or intimate about the family history. The only remaining hope rested in locating some written records of my paternal grandmother's family. We knew almost nothing about my paternal grandfather's family. There was certainly not enough linkage to build a family tree.

It took a great deal of time and lots of stamina just to gather the fundamental ancestral information. Mamie had the drive, the interest, and the skill set to not only perform the research but to collate the data as well. We now have documentation up to the ninth generation of the Bryant-Jackson and Givens-Jackson family ancestral trees.

Bill Lewis Bryant Sr. and Phyllis Thomas Bryant were my great-great-grandparents on my father's side. In my attempt to tell my own life story, I thought it would be meaningful to share some background information from whence I came. My siblings and I are the fifth generation since my forefathers and foremothers were born into slavery. For the most part, the stories told in this book are factual. However, with some of the details and experiences of my great-great-grandparents, I have taken the liberty to interject my educated opinions and imaginations.

My father's great-grandfather and great-grandmother were born in 1835 and 1840 respectively on an unknown plantation in Coffee County, Georgia. They were born into slavery as Bill Lewis Bryant Sr. and Phyllis Bryant, nee Thomas.

President Abraham Lincoln abolished slavery by the Emancipation Proclamation, an executive order that was issued on January 1, 1863. The Thirteenth Amendment of the US Constitution abolished slavery and involuntary servitude. It passed in the United States Senate on April 8, 1864, and in the house of representatives on January 31, 1865. The amendment was ratified on December 6, 1865, by three-fourths of the thirty-six states that made up the United States at that time.

Later Phyllis's brother, Andrew Thomas, and other emancipated slaves, who were seeking self-sufficiency, trusted that God would provide for them and migrated to Mineral Springs, Omaha, Georgia. Mineral Springs was 145 miles from the Coffee County Plantation. Their journey of faith included young children looking for a better life than the one they left behind in Coffee County. It was a one-way trip on foot. The philosopher Lao Tzu is credited with saying that the journey of a thousand miles begins with one step. As the Bryants continued their journey of faith and strength, destitute but free from slavery, I imagine that they thought and reflected on biblical stories that they had heard many, many times. God performed mighty miracles in times past. He separated the water in the Red Sea that allowed Moses and the Israelites to cross through on dry land as they were chased by their oppressors, the pharaoh and his Egyptian Army (Exodus 14:15–18). The Egyptian economy was built, maintained, and grew at the expense of Jewish slave labor just as black slave labor built the economy and maintained America's southern states. As the families continued walking, I'm sure that they rejoiced and had faith that God was real. They rejoiced, laughed, walked, and gave praise to the Almighty God who delivered them from the bondage of their white owners. I can envision them walking, heading to a better place that the Lord had shown them, while praising Him as Lord, as Savior, and as Deliverer of their answered prayers.

I imagine that they fellowshipped and sang songs like the old hymn "O they tell me of a home...far beyond the skies." They had no earthly home, only the promise of a home beyond the skies. I believe that they rejoiced and quoted Scripture that they had never read. Most slaves didn't even know how to read, but God printed His Word on their hearts and in their minds.

There are so many biblical analogies to imagine as I think about the Bryant's journey to the place where God would lead them, Omaha "Mineral Springs," Georgia. The biblical story of Joseph most appropriately comes to my mind. Joseph's brothers sold him to traveling traders who were on their way to Egypt. While in Egypt, Joseph was sold and imprisoned. But God raised him up and made him a mighty man. God allowed Joseph to forgive his brothers and save his family from famine. Joseph told his brothers, "As for you, you meant evil against me, but God meant it for good" (Genesis 50:20). Many years later, his ancestors became the great nation that God promised Abraham who was Joseph's great-great-grandfather. I can envision my forefathers accepting and using Joseph's words for their holy testimony as they talked about their former slave masters.

Bill and Phyllis and his family took up residence and settled in Omaha, Georgia, across the Chattahoochee River from Alabama. We do not know why they stopped in Omaha instead of crossing into Alabama. I am aware of no emergency. There was no need of a miracle to separate the waters over the Chattahoochee River as in the biblical story of Moses. Neither the pharaoh's army nor former slave owners chased or followed my forefathers from Coffee County to Stewart County in Omaha. The answer may be simply that Bill, Phyllis, and their family were just tired of walking.

The Daughter, Laura

The children of Bill and Phyllis Bryant grew up, married, and raised families of their own. Their children's names were: Bill Bryant Jr., George, Rene, Hector, Josie, Anna, Martha, Mary Lou, Lucy, and Laura.

My family line continued through Laura who married Frank Worrell, an emancipated slave who lived and farmed on the Fitzgerald's Plantation. Frank Worrell and Laura birthed eleven children, and Hattie was one of their daughters. Frank L. Jackson Sr. and Hattie (Worrell) Jackson, after their marriage, had ten children. My father, Frank L. Jackson Jr., was one of the ten children. He and my mother, Rosie Jackson, got married and had fourteen children. I was the eighth child born to them.

Some eighty-plus years after slavery, my siblings and I were born on the very same plantation where three generations of our Jackson ancestors had worked—as slaves and free people. Some of us knew my father's parents and spent quite a bit of time with them, but we know very little about my paternal grandfather's family. The Jacksons just weren't very chatty. My aunts would limit their conversations to subject matter that they wanted to talk about. If anyone deviated from their interests, they would shut down the communication. When they controlled the conversations, they would drill you with a series of questions until you were too exhausted to respond any longer or could not think of anything else to add. And under no circumstances were we as children allowed to question adults about anything. So, we did not even have word-of-mouth lessons about our relatives that the Jacksons did not freely share.

My father's parents, Frank Sr. (Grandpa) and Hattie (Grandma), had ten children, but I only knew six of them, two uncles and four aunts.[8] Grandpa and Grandma didn't live together, and I never understood why. I was always curious. But I knew better than to ask. During that time, children never asked such questions even if they wanted to know badly. If I, or any other child, had asked, the typical answer would have been a reprimand of "Boy! Hush your mouth!" I am not sure at what age we earned the right to question any adults on my father's side of the family. I can only say that by the time I started trying to uncover the family history at family gatherings, many of the adults who came, and their children, were ready to talk and share what they could recall or what they had heard.

Grandma Hattie lived with her youngest son's family, but she did not eat with them. She cooked her meals separately, then she ate and locked any remaining food in a 3' high × 4' wide × 3' deep trunk where she also kept her clothes and other worldly belongings. When we visited, Hattie graciously offered us treats selected from her trunk. The food had been stored in containers, although over time, some of it had become stale and was unsuitable to eat. Of course, storing clothes and food together alone rendered the food as undesirable to us. Aside from the storage issue, the food, particularly her bread, was not at all appetizing. She had been way too heavy-handed with the baking soda additive and one could almost smell it. Her bread tasted as if the baking soda was the main ingredient.

As a child, we had to be polite to all adults. So if we accepted the food, we walked outside and happily fed it to the yard animals that were not so discriminating about what they consumed. Although we were poor farm kids, we never got hungry enough to eat food from Grandma Hattie's trunk. There were other reasons beyond taste that made her food unappetizing. I was always very particular about both the food and the person who prepared it. I was poor, but I was discerning. My standards were high. Hattie dipped snuff, and I never ever knowingly ate food prepared by someone who dipped snuff. When I lowered that standard, the food had to have a skin or coating like baked sweet potatoes left in the skin or it had to be food prepared without a liquid. I avoided food prepared and touched by snuff dippers and others with unsanitary habits. Growing up, I was very, very picky about whose food I ate. I was not enticed to want to eat anything that Hattie offered. Two of my father's sisters also dipped snuff, and I made sure never to knowingly eat anything they cooked either. It helped that Mom generally forbade us to ever eat at anyone else's home, except our own. Most of the time, when we were offered food, we politely said, "No thanks" or "We are not hungry."

My grandpa lived with his oldest daughter (Alsie Mae) who was not married at that time. However, Aunt Alsie Mae had been married at one time and her only child was a grown son named Roosevelt. He is my oldest living cousin. At the writing of this book he is still living in Miami with his family. Grandpa's oldest son, my Uncle Grover, and my namesake, lived in Miami as well.

My great-uncle, Holt (Hope) Jackson, also lived on the Fitzgerald property less than one-half mile from us. He had mental and physical challenges, originating from birth. One challenge to him was a clubfoot. Some said his foot had been burned in a fire. Whether the condition was from a birth defect or from having been burned in a fire, it caused Uncle Holt to walk with a limp. As kids we had never known anyone else in our small community with such an ailment. This was long before we were taught to be empathetic and accepting of people with disabilities. He seldom ever visited our house during the years of my childhood. As a small child, we were afraid of him, if for no other reason than he was different. I remember that he lived alone. He did not mingle with the adults and never bothered with us kids. His strangeness in that way alone made him different. Our adult relatives called Uncle Holt crazy because of his anti-social behavior towards them. When we combined our imaginations, his clubfoot and limp with his lack of engagement with us kids, it was easy for us to accept that he must have been.

My father's sister Annie was admitted to a mental institution when she was very young. She spent her entire adult life in the Georgia State Mental Institution in Middleville, Georgia. Consequently, I never met her. Just as with Uncle Holt, we were told that she was crazy; beyond that, no one took the time to explain why she was there.

The Jacksons and my Aunt Lute's husband (Junior Hunter) were the only families who farmed and lived on the Fitzgerald's Plantation during the '40s and early '50s. Two Jackson brothers, two sisters, their families, and my grandparents lived less than a quarter of a mile apart. The Jackson siblings and cousins who stayed there included my father, Uncle Holt, Aunt Alsie, Aunt Eula (Lute), her husband, and eight children, three boys and five girls.

Aunt Lute dipped snuff and was as mean as a spitting cobra snake. This is how I saw her through my young eyes. She was quiet but acted and looked mean. I had to pass her house when I went to the well to draw water and was hesitant and almost afraid to speak to her. Usually from early morning until evening, her sole activity was to sit on her porch and spit saliva from the snuff that always seemed to be in her bottom lip. My other aunts, unlike Aunt Lute, were quite sociable and often carried on conversations described as small talk. In those days, children rarely started a conversation with an adult. The adult would make a statement or ask a question and the child would respond. There was no continuous dialogue between an adult and a child. When addressed by an adult, the appropriate response was always "yes, sir," "no, sir," or "yes, ma'am" or "no, ma'am." The adult would initiate any additional remarks to be made. There was zero tolerance for a child offering up an opinion or being perceived as misbehaving in the sense of acting grown. One of the principles of the day was that any adult could and would whip you with the instrument of their choice. They had permission to discipline anyone's child they perceived as being disrespectful or misbehaving. I don't believe that I was ever a disrespectful or disobedient child, but

I got more whippings than I deserved. It was my nature to take them in stride and move on.

My father's youngest sisters were twins. Aunt Ruth, nicknamed Doll, lived in Columbus, Georgia, and Aunt Naomi, nicknamed Byne, lived with her husband, Uncle Buddie, on his family-owned farm a few miles away. I have no memory of Aunt Doll ever living on a farm or farming. She and her husband moved to Columbus, Georgia, where I remember visiting them. Early in the 1950s, Aunt Doll's husband abandoned the family. Aunt Doll moved to New York City to live with her son, Sam. Aunt Byne and Uncle Buddie did not have any children, and after he died, she did not move from the family's farm. Long after Uncle Buddie passed away, she continued to live on their farm alone despite the absence of neighbors who were miles away. Aunt Byne lived her entire life not more than five miles from her birthplace near the Fitzgerald's Plantation quarters.

Although the two sisters, Doll and Byne, lived apart for more than sixty years, in different states, different environments, and climates, both lived to the ripe old age of ninety-six years old and died three weeks apart in November and December of 2003.

Marie and Melvin, Aunt Doll's daughter and son, were the first relatives on my father's side who attended and graduated from college. They, like me and my siblings, were just two generations away from slavery. Both Marie and Melvin taught school and retired as teachers. They were trailblazers for our family and set in motion an example for many of us to follow.

Marie, our first cousin, married George, our first cousin. As strange as this union appears, there was no incestuous relationship. The two were not related. Marie was the daughter of my father's sister Doll, and George was the son of my mother's youngest sister, Mary, nicknamed Mae.

My Maternal Family Tree

My great-great-grandparents, Austin Givens (1827) and Josephine Porter (1830), were slaves born on Shepherd's Plantation in Florence, Georgia, located in Stewart County. Josephine Porter's surname was derived from Sarah Porterhouse. Sarah was the daughter of Dr. Albert H. Shepherd. The Creek Indians invaded their property in June 1836. Among the slaves who escaped with Dr. Shepherd and his family were my Great-Grandfather Austin, age ten, and my Great-Great-Grandmother Josephine, age six. Josephine was the slave of Dr. Shepherd's daughter, Sarah Porterhouse Shepherd Flewellen.

Austin married Josephine Porter. Josephine gave birth to Madline Givens Davis. Madline gave birth to Josephine Davis. Josephine Davis Williams gave birth to Rosie L. Williams. Rosie L. Williams became my mother. Although this book addresses the accomplishments of my brothers, sisters, and me, we give tremendous attention to Rosie L. Jackson, our Mom, who we remember "in a happy way" as singer Shirley Caesar's song says.

The Daughter, Madline

My mother's lineage began in 1830. We were unable to trace any prior history for Josephine, except that she was born into slavery on Albert Shepherd's Plantation quarters along with her husband, Austin. Josephine Porter Givens' father's and mother's identities remain unknown. Historical documents stated that Josephine was the slave of Albert Shepherd's daughter whose married name was Porterhouse. Based on that bit of information, I assume Josephine chose the maiden name of Porter after her owner, a shorter version of Porterhouse. Josephine and Austin married and had eight children. Their children were Madline, Louise, Mary, Felix, Ellen, William, Gertrude, and Ophelia. At the age of twenty, in 1875, Madline married Addison Davis, who was thirty-six years old, and they were the parents of nine children.[9] The children were Josephine, (the oldest), Burl, Mary Queen, Emma, Brook, Henry, Ruth, Mary Lou, and Lawrence. My mother's family tree grew out of the Davis (Madline's and Addison's) line through their eldest daughter, Josephine Davis.

My maternal grandmother's (Josephine) first husband was named Joe Peterson. They had three children: Mattie, Lilla, and Robert Peterson. Joe Peterson passed away at an early age, and Josephine and her three children returned home to live with her parents, Addison and Madline Davis. Josephine's father, Addison, had issues with his granddaughter Mattie's skin complexion. According to historical written records and the family's oral history, he didn't accept Mattie in his home because he thought Mattie's skin color was too dark. So Mattie, at the age of twelve, still grieving over the loss of her father, was sent to live with her Great-Aunt Gertrude in New Jersey. I knew Aunt Mattie, and at one time, I lived in the same city where she lived. Her skin tone was more light brown than dark brown. I imagine it took a strong mental toughness for Aunt Mattie to overcome such negative feelings about physical traits that she could not control. Aunt Mattie was quiet and a very pleasant person to be around. She married and had a family and I knew her children. Despite being rejected by her grandfather, she lived a very normal and long life for more than eighty-two years. Hearing about Aunt Mattie's treatment was disconcerting. I couldn't make any sense of it or reconcile my great grandfather's thinking. Being unable to do so, I turned to and am interjecting excerpts from the inspirational thoughts of Roy Stockdill's *A Tribute to My Ancestors, Rhyming Relations: Genealogy in Verse* (1997) project.

> "They did not choose us, nor we them; we never knew them, nor they us; yet we are inextricably bound together for all eternity and there is no law in the universe, no metamorphosis physical or spiritual, that can ever alter this inalienable truth…We must learn from them, from their mistakes as well as their successes; from their tragedies as well as their triumphs; from their sins as well as their virtues; from their hopes as well as their fears…Remember that we, too, are the ancestors of those yet unborn and we should seek to leave for them a heritage of which they can be as proud as we are of that which my forebears bequeathed to us…We bless and thank our ancestors for the legacy of the good things they gave us, forgive them their errors and pray that

we will endeavor to use wisely the knowledge
which they handed down to us."

Approximately two years after her first husband's death,
Josephine married Gus Williams, whose wife had also died. Between
them they had seven children from their previous unions. Gus had
three boys and a girl (John, Ann, Eugene and Robert). Josephine
was a mother three young ones (Mattie, Lilla and a son also named
Robert (Bob)). They produced three more children during their
marriage (my mother, Rosie, George (Bud) and Mary (Mae)). As
we grew up in Stewart County, most of our aunts and uncles lived
nearby. Some, I did not get to meet until I was full grown. While
my mother spoke to my older siblings about all of her brothers and
sisters, she was probably all talked out by the time I came along;
because I never knew nor met two of my uncles, Eugene and Robert,
my Grandfather Gus' children.

Aunt Mattie, Aunt Lilla, and Uncle Eugene were Josephine's
children by her first husband, Joe Peterson. Eventually, my mother's
siblings moved away from Stewart County and settled throughout
New Jersey and in the Tampa, St. Petersburg areas of Florida. The
family's origin was Stewart County, Georgia, but many members
ventured to other states, seeking opportunities that didn't exist for
them in Georgia.

Uncle George died in 1944, at a young age, in Camden, New
Jersey, when I was less than two years old; and long before our entire
family moved there. I got to know Irving and Susie, his children,
when they visited us in the early 1950's in Georgia. They were the
only children we knew when we arrived in Camden, New Jersey. I
can recall Irving rescuing me from some bullies as I played basketball
on the Mickle Street playground, the summer we moved to Camden.
My oldest brother, Billy, lived with my uncle's wife, Aunt Mary
Frances Peterson, and her family when he first moved to Camden
from Georgia.

In 2010 and 2012, my brother George, cousins, friends, and I
organized and held two Omaha reunion events, supported by those
who were born, lived, and had family still in Omaha. The purpose

was to bring families back for a reunion with those whose family roots started in Omaha. We celebrated our past and renewed friendships. Since father time had changed much of our physical resemblances, our names were the only significant common denominator. The event concluded with a Sunday church services at Mount Moriah in 2010 and Saint Elmo in 2012, both churches we attended as youths.[10] We have had subsequent events and are planning another one for October 2017. It is important to mention here that the reunion events have been supported beyond our expectations. Many relatives have returned from various states to celebrate and fellowship with us. Some states represented are Massachusetts, New York, Pennsylvania, Michigan, Ohio, Virginia, Maryland, New Jersey, Florida, and others.

I invited Aunt Ann's daughters and her youngest son to the event.[11] They came from St. Petersburg, Florida. One of the best Thanksgiving Day's I ever had while growing up in Georgia was at Aunt Ann's house in 1950, on the outskirts of Lumpkin, Georgia. It was a warm family gathering. I remember having lots of fun, food, and a great fellowship with family. I ate turkey for the first time and a lot of sweet treats that my mom made to share. She brought sweet breads called tea biscuits and a pound cake, along with sweet potato pies. I really enjoyed spending time with relatives. It created a lasting memory for me of my mom and her sister's family having so much fun together.

While growing up, I knew very little about Mom's relatives, her extended family, or her uncles and aunts. As I got older though, I met and became close to several of her cousins, Aunt Mary's children. My sister Rose spent a fair amount of time at the home of Mom's sister, Aunt Lilla, and with her family. She, Rosie nicknamed Rose, remembered Aunt Mary and spent time at her home as she traveled to Tampa to Aunt Lilla's home. When she was in high school, she traveled between the homes of our aunts in Georgia and Florida. She stayed with Aunt Mary's family in Savannah where she changed trains on her way to Florida. She frequently traveled to Tampa to visit Aunt Lilla and her children, Rob and Honey. Rob was the first known family member, on either side of the family tree, to earn a college degree. He graduated from Bethune-Cookman University in the late 1940s. He was on the football team there. My sister Rose recalls being invited to his college homecoming activities. She was always willing to venture out and visit but having funds to pay for transportation was a problem. On occasions, our cousin Honey, Rob's sister, took their father's rail pass without his permission and sent it to Rose, my sister, for her transportation to Tampa. Rose had Mom's and Dad's permission to go, but she says she was an unknowing participant in the rail-pass scheme.

When we moved to New Jersey, I met many of my other cousins and Aunt Mary's children, including her daughters, Miriam and Shirley. They lived and grew up in Savannah, Georgia, but I did not become familiar with them until we moved to New Jersey. Miriam retired as a professor from Rutgers University and relocated to Hilton Head Island, South Carolina. My family and I spent time with Miriam and her husband during our annual visit to Hilton Head. I remember Mom and I visited Miriam at her home in (Levittown) Willingboro, New Jersey, during my Christmas recess while I was in college. It was my first meeting with Miriam and her husband, a Morehouse graduate. The next time I saw her was more than forty years later as my family and I vacationed on Hilton Head Island. It was then that I also had the pleasure of spending time with Shirley, her family, and Miriam's children.

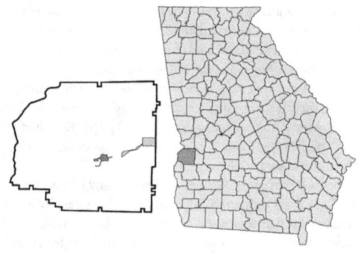

State of Georgia Map Showing Stewart County Location within the State.

Stewart County, GA, map with associated Landmarks, Omaha, Florence and Lumpkin. Daniel Stewart, President Theodore Roosevelt's grandfather.

The Battle of Shepherd Plantation between Creek
Indians, Settlers and Volunteer Solders

Lumpkin Courthouse and County Seat

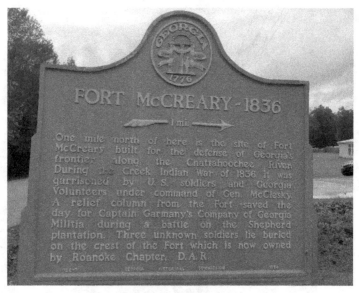

Fort Jones & Fort McCreary Road Marker
regarding the Creek Indians attack

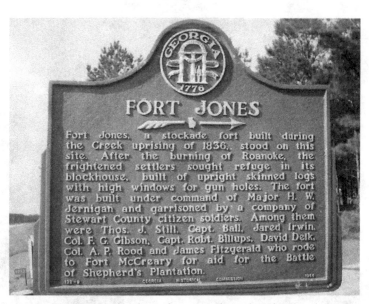

Fort Jones Road Marker regarding the Shepherd
Plantation's Creek Indian attach.

Frank & Hattie Jackson's Children Names

Name	Born	Married	Kids	Died
Grover F. Jackson (Bish)				
Stonewall Jackson, Sr.	4/1899	Yes	3	1982.
McKinley Jackson	1903	N/A	2	1930
Alsie Mae Jackson Cox	3/1898	Yes	1	N/A
Naomi Jackson Walton (Byne)	10/8/1908	Yes	0	1975
Ruth Jackson Neal (Doll)	10/9/1908	Yes	5	11/18/2003
Annie Laura Jackson	1911	No	0	12/20/2003
Frank L. Jackson, Jr. (Buddy)	8/1/1906	Yes	14	1968
Charlie B. Jackson (Friend)	12/12/1912	Yes	10	11/17/1985
Eula Jackson Hunter (Lute)	9/24/1904	Yes	8	2003
				1971

Father's Ancestor—Mother's Side

Name	Born	Married	Kids	Died
Bill Lewis Bryant, Sr. (Grandpa)	1835 (est.)	Yes	10	????
Phyllis Bryant, nee Thomas (Grandma)	1840 (est.)	Yes	10	1926
Frank Worrell	1850 (est.)	Yes	10	????
Laura Worrell, nee Bryants	1854 (est.)	Yes	10	1931
Frank Jackson, Sr. (Grandpa)	12/8/1874	Yes	10	10/1/1964
Hattie Jackson, nee Worrell (Bigma)	1877	Yes	10	12/1/1963

Frank & Rosalie (Williams) Jackson's Children Names

The Jackson Siblings Vital Record

Name	Born	Married	Kids	Died	Degrees / Year	Sibling #
Leola Pressley (Lee)	Feb. '30	Yes	5	N/A	BA '82	#1
Rosie Boyles (Rose)	Oct. '31	Yes	3	N/A	BA '84	#2
William C. Jackson (Billy)	7/27/1933	Yes	1	2/16/2013	Business Owner	#3
Charlie N. Jackson (Charles)	9/16/1935	Yes	3	12/13/1996	Business Owner	#4
Josephine Goggins (Jo)	5/12/1938	Yes	9	12/19/2009	N/A	#5
Mary Frances Fullard (Mamie)	Dec. '39	Yes	1	N/A	BA '75 Magna Cum Laude	#6
Geneva Williams (Tina)	Aug. '41	Yes	1	N/A	BA '78 / M. Lib. Sci. '03	#7
Grover Jackson (Junebug)	June '43	Yes	3	N/A	BS 67 / MBA '71	#8
Robert Jackson (Bob)	1/3/1945	No	None	9/15/1967	N/A	#9
George Jackson	Nov. '46	Yes	2	N/A	BS 73	#10
Otis D. Jackson (OJ)	June '48	Yes	None	N/A	BA 72	#11
Mary Lou Jackson (Sister)	12/31/1949	Yes	2	3/16/2010	BS '71 / M.Ed. '76	#12
Annie Louise Jackson (Ann)	6/10/1951	Yes	2	3/20/2003	BA '73 / M. Lib. Sci. '98	#13
Evelyn C. Jackson (Chris)	Feb. '54	Yes	1-Adopted	N/A	BA '76 / MBA '88	#14

Gus & Josephine Williams' Children Names

Name	Born	Married	Kids	Died
Roashie Williams (Gus/Josie Children)	11/2/1910	Yes	14	1/22/1984
Georgie Williams (Bud) (Gus/Josie Cildren)	1913	N/A	N/A	N/A
Mary Williams (Duke) (Gus/Josie Children)	1920	Yes	1	2/2/1991
Annie Williams (Gus Children)	1905	Yes	8	N/A
Eugene Williams (Gus Children)	N/A	N/A	N/A	N/A
Robert Williams (Gus Children)	1902	Yes	6	N/A
Mattie Peterson (Josie Children)	1897	Yes	N/A	8/1/1975
Lilla Peterson (Josie Children)	1903	Yes	2	N/A
Robert Peterson (Josie Children)	1909	Yes	2	N/A

Mother's Ancestor—Mother's Side

Name	Born	Married	Kids	Died
Austin Givings (Grandpa)	1827	Yes	10	????
Josephine Givings, nee Porter (Grandma)	1830	Yes	10	????
Addison Davis	1839	Yes	9	????
Madline Davis, nee Givings	1855	Yes	9	????
Augusta (Gus) Williams	1872	Yes	6	????
Josephine Williams, nee Davis	1877	Yes	6	1938

Family's Genealogy William Lewis & Phyllis Bryant and Austin & Josephine Givens, our great great grandfathers and great great grandmothers.

Family's Genealogy—Bryant, Worrell, & Jackson and Givens, Davis.

Madline, Mother's Grandmother and our Great Great Grandmother.

St. Elmo Baptist Church Daddy was chairman of deacons.

Aunt Ann Harris daughters Ruby, Edna and Alice. They relocated to St. Petersburg, FL is the early 1950's from Stewart County.

Chapter 2

The Journey Continues

Slave Owner's Family and Plantation

I heard a lot of talk about W. W. Fitzgerald while growing up. He was a merchant, farmer, judge, and a Confederate soldier. He served in the Georgia Legislature and as a justice in Georgia's inferior court. Florence (Flora) Fitzgerald Childs, his daughter and heir, ran the plantation during the time my father lived and farmed on land rented from her in Omaha, Georgia, my birthplace. Most of the Jackson siblings who were born prior to 1948 knew her. She exhibited all the hateful traits of the segregated South. She had absolutely no respect for blacks. She treated all black people, regardless of age or gender, as if they were her property and as if she was superior to them.

Most of the white landowners in Omaha were relatives either by birth or marriage, validated by the family names and personal association of those buried in the Fitzgerald's cemetery. The cemetery is a historical Stewart County site, located on the Fitzgerald's Plantation farm. Since many of the white residents in the area were relatives, there was very little need for another cemetery. The only other cemetery for whites that I knew about was in the woods behind the Mount Moriah Missionary Baptist Church property. It had not been used since the late 1870s and had not been maintained. After perusing the current cemetery conditions, I surmise that environmental conditions of land erosion and water table changes had, over time, prevented access to it.

Buried in the Fitzgerald cemetery are ninety-two documented Fitzgerald family members.[12] The first one was James Fitzgerald in 1880, Flora's grandfather. He is the same James Fitzgerald who, on June 9, 1836, rode to Fort McCreary to inform the pioneer settlers of the attack by the Creek Indians. The last burial on record at the family cemetery was Flora Childs' daughter Exa-Beall Childs Lennon Warner, who died on September 30, 1996, and son Ernest W. Childs Jr. on May 19, 1996. Other family members buried there that I knew are Flora (1957) and her daughters Mildred (1968) and Josephine (1983). I knew each of Flora's daughters. We interacted with them as children, living on the farmland they owned. They were blessed (except for the cultural nuances of the South) because they behaved nothing like their mother.

Our Farming Efforts

My father, Frank L. Jackson Jr., served the Fitzgerald's family. He rented and farmed land from the family that was the same land his ancestors had worked. Early on, and for a long time, my father was a very dedicated worker, along with his partner. Dad and his partner cultivated the land and were in step with each other. Correction! For every step my dad took, his partner took four; not that my dad was slow, his partner just took more steps. My father, by his own admission, always worked very hard and tried his very best to earn a living at farming, to make ends meet, however, he never did. My dad's partner never complained about working four times harder and always put in a full day's work. His partner never demanded anything and accepted what was given. His partner was his mule.

Not much had changed from the time his ancestors worked as slaves for their masters, the Fitzgerald's and other landlords. Only the names and times changed but not much else. Consequently, my siblings and I were destined to follow in our dad's footsteps until God intervened.

Our family was among the few independent farmers who farmed and never owned any land. The majority of those who were not landowners sharecropped or hired out as day laborers. As I reflect on my childhood farming experience, my family farmed and lived on the Fitzgerald's place seemingly just for the exercise. We worked hard and had great work ethics. However, we never had anything to show for our efforts—except nobody ever seemed to gain any weight. In those days, we were all of slight build. Funny how work seemed to have had that effect on individuals.

As a kid, living in Omaha, I recall our family moving five times between 1947–1953. During that time, we lived in four different residences. Whenever we moved, the routine would be the same: rented land, farmed independently, or sharecropped (one year)—both seemingly just for the exercise. Regardless of our status as an independent farmer or sharecropper, our financial well-being remained relatively unchanged. A simple definition of a *sharecropper* according to *Merriam-Webster's Learner's Dictionary* is, "A tenant farmer especially in the Southern United States who is provided with credit for seed, tools, living quarters, and food, who works the land, and who receives an agreed share of the value of the crop minus charges."

The definitions were virtually the same for both the sharecropper and the farmer who rented land. There was one exception. There were no out-of-pocket expenses for a sharecropper. The land-renting farmer, however, had a legal and financial obligation to pay out-of-pocket for the use of land, seeds, and other supplies. The net results were the same for both. The terms landowner, landlord, and supplier are used interchangeably herein because they were generally the same person or the same family. The landowner was always in control and colluded with the supplier on the price of seeds, fertilizer, equipment, and other items needed by an independent farmer. The landlord maintained the books under each scenario. The economic equations for both situations included living accommodations. The only discernable differences between a sharecropper and land-renting farmer was that the former was advanced a monthly recoverable cash draw. The land-renter had out-of-pocket expenses, and the risk associated with his indebtedness was greater. The sharecropper was generally promised 50 percent of the profits after all expenses; however, rarely—if ever—were those promises fulfilled.

The black farmer trusted the landowner for his family's survival. The only thing a farmer had to offer was labor. The black farmer never had the opportunity to verify the accounting entries. It was unthinkable that a black sharecropper questioned the landowner about finances. It is inconceivable that the landowner didn't overstate costs and understate the revenue. Even if a sharecropper was given the freedom to review the books, he wasn't educated on financial matters and wouldn't understand the financial details and the meaning of contracts. The sharecropper encountered a tough challenge trying to deal with a landowner and comprehend the intricacies of their financial arrangement. So, they resigned themselves to accept that the landowner was telling them the truth. In the end, the farmer either made enough for him and his family to survive on or he gave up after desperately trying.

The basic difference between the sharecropper and renter was bookkeeping duties. The supplier, grantor of credit, kept the ledger of indebtedness. The supplier controlled the supply and demand for *all* goods and services. The farmer, with help from county officials, reported the acreage for each crop planted. The supplier then calculated the amount of each product needed and the amount applied per acre. Although unwritten, the supplier also determined the value of the crops.

Revenue equaled the value of the crop times the amount of crop harvested. In our case, the crops were cotton and peanuts.[13] The landlord determined the amount owed to rent the land. The farmer generally paid this expense to the landowner directly. After the cost of the supplies were tallied, any remaining amount was given to the farmer. Any remaining amount was given to the farmer. The math was simple: (crop revenue)-(rent + supplies)=(amount for the farmer). After deducting all expenses, there may have been a marginal income for the farmer.

There was a lot of wiggle room for supplier's input assumptions in the sharecropper and rented land systems. The landowner extended credit to the farmer. At the end of the day, the landowner, supplier, and renting landlord could easily claim that the crops sold for less money than the farmer owed. If they had made such a claim, the farmer started the next year in the hole and broke. The consequence of no profits for the renter was the loss of all assets owned, the crops, animals, tools, etc. that collateralized his farming debt. The landowner and the supplier controlled the farm economy. They owned everything and always calculated the financial proceeds to their advantage. Some landowners were shameless enough to claim the sharecropper didn't earn enough to recover the cost of the crop.

As a sharecropper farmer, we worked the land. We were paid a two-dollar-wage per day for each person who worked. The profit sharing agreement was supposed to be 50-50 after expenses were deducted for crops grown, harvested, and sold. There were years when the landowner declared no profit or that there had been a breakeven harvest. My father, as a renter, paid the property owner a flat amount to rent a certain number of acres for a year, including the place we stayed. Blacks had been freed by an Act of Congress, but they were still involuntary servants by acts of the economic system for which they labored.

The county government administered the process to allocate the acres per crop to be cultivated. A county agent told us the exact number of acres of cotton and peanuts we could plant. How they arrived at the calculation is unknown. My father had signed the note to lease the land, by the acre, long before he knew the allotment of how many acres of cotton and peanuts he could plant. Usually after the best guess at the acreage, and sometimes after planting, a county agent came and measured the authorized acreage of cotton and peanuts to be planted. Acreage unauthorized that had been planted was plowed under, preventing harvesting and selling the products. The farmer told the supplier the acreage approved for planting and the supplier determined the amount of seeds and fertilizer required and delivered it.

Whether a farmer was a sharecropper or a lessee, he was always indebted and at the mercy of those who controlled the economic system. White county government agents controlled the allotment of how much a farmer could plant and harvest. Such constraints, applied sometimes after they were legally bound, prevented many small black farmers from either growing or escaping their menial existence. Everything used to operate the farm was controlled, including the animal stock quantities, i.e., mules, cows, and hogs. It was a catch-22 economic process that advantaged those in control of the land, supplies, and the accounting process. The odds were against the black farmer just based on economics. When that was coupled with our family situation, namely our Dad's mismanagement of our funds, it was a zero-sum predicament.

Since farming was built around an agriculture economy in the '40s and '50s, most farmers had large families that served as a source of farm labor. The children helped with chores. They planted and harvested crops. They also provided the labor required to maintain the farms. Farming was very hard work; and there were generally no days off, especially if there were farm animals involved. Cows had to be milked, cows, chickens, pigs and mules had to be fed. Everyone had an assigned job, even the youngest child. We each had chores to do, and we each did them or else there were often physical consequences. Each sibling had changing roles. We worked in the fields, cared for babies, and performed other household duties like fetching water from the well or firewood from the woodpile for the stove and fireplace. We never took a family vacation due primarily to the lack of money and the daily routines. There were always daily work chores that had to be done. If they were not done, the family, the farm, and the animals all suffered. Many of my ancestors raised families and labored 365 days a year on the Fitzgerald and Battle Plantations in Stewart County, Georgia, as did many others throughout the South.

Looking back over my life, the years I spent farming with my parents and siblings, the acreage cultivated was small by the standards of the plantations that preceded them. Regardless we disliked farming. There were very few upsides to our lifestyle as we worked in the fields, shook peanuts, pulled corn, and picked cotton.[14] However, having those chores taught us some great lessons about life, work, and survival. Surprisingly all the lessons I learned from performing many different hard chores and being responsible came in handy for me later in life.

The Moves and Locations

My father and his siblings lived less than a quarter of a mile apart on the Fitzgerald farm. The physical facilities consisted of framed buildings like other residences on nearby plantations. They were a cluster of framed buildings called the quarters.[15] The structures were positioned about twenty yards apart. They shared a seventy-five feet deep well to obtain drinking water. The Fitzgerald's place, where we stayed the longest, provided no additional conveniences or special comforts that were different than any of the other clustered buildings.

Mom and Dad moved to the Fitzgerald's Plantation in 1930 and lived there until 1948.[16] The births of their first ten children were on the Fitzgerald's Plantation. We moved across the creek (Hannahatchee Creek) late December of 1949 and farmed there in 1950. It was called that because there was a sizeable creek that separated the two sides of Omaha. It was also a method of identifying one from the other. Living across the creek was like another world compared to the place we moved from. We were not used to having modern conveniences. Considering all the places that we ever stayed in Omaha, it was the best-built house we lived in Stewart County. No one had ever lived in the house before we did. It was a four-room, three-bedroom house with a real kitchen. It had more rooms than any of the other places we stayed as a kid. Although it didn't have electricity, we were just fine with kerosene lamps and one with a mantle that emitted brighter light than the kerosene lamp, used only during special occasions. Otherwise we used the kerosene lamps for lighting, wood-burning stoves for cooking, and a wood-burning fireplace for heating.

This house across the creek was a dream come true. It was the closest we came to actually living on a real farm. The four rooms were an ideal fit for our family. There was a barn across the dirt road from the house with space for our mules, cows, and pigs. We even had, behind the house, a chicken coop with nests for the chickens to lay eggs, a place for them to safely roost at night away from foxes, weasels, and other chicken-eating animals. The land we cultivated for farming was in view of the house and a water pump was just steps away. It was perfect, and our family had never lived so comfortably.

The house was nice. Our newfound happiness ended when a creditor came after the harvest season and picked up all the animals and equipment that my father had on the property. He had used the animals and equipment as collateral to purchase farming supplies like seeds, fertilizer, and other materials needed to cultivate the land he rented. He had not paid the note despite all our tremendous farming efforts and the money we thought we had earned from the harvested crops. Earnings from our hard work were nowhere to be found. Mom said he had spent the money on women; but my view is there weren't enough events—places or women—in Omaha to spend any sizeable amount of money. Dad got shortchanged due to the economic system and his lack of basic financial knowledge.

1951–1952

On the road again, we moved to the Perkins' place, adjoining the Fitzgerald's Plantation. Since we had nothing, no mules to plow the land or equipment to cultivate it, we became sharecroppers. My brother Charles, Mom, Josephine, Mamie, Geneva, and I provided the labor. The landlord, Bradley Perkins, provided the property and all the resources required to farm. Everything that we had for farming and living, he provided them. These items were things like land, equipment, seeds, and fertilizer. Daddy just could not bear the idea of sharecropping after being an independent farmer, so he went to New Jersey to search for a place for us to live and for him to work when and if we moved there. By the time the crops were harvested and the sharecropper check was delivered, Dad had returned home. He had not worked the land that season, but he took complete control of the check. There must have been skimpy profits to share after all expenses were paid. We did not see any of the money from our hard work. So we moved again, this time to the Sawyer's Place. It was adjacent to the Fitzgerald's farm.

1952–1953

Our next stop was the Sawyer's Place. During the winter months, we always kept a fire in the fireplace 24-7. That had the two-fold purpose of heating our house and supplying general light to see. We did homework by the light from the wood-burning fireplace. Since it got dark at dusk during the winter months, a kerosene lamp was used in the kitchen as light for Mom to see as she cooked.

Staying in an unfamiliar place, we hated it when darkness came with a passion. All of us were afraid of the unknown darkness. We would take the kerosene lantern with us when we had to accompany a younger sibling to the outhouse. The outhouse was made of wood with a tin roof and a wooden door. It provided privacy. During the day, going to that building was just a necessary function. At night, there were shadows, sounds, and stirrings that kept our imaginations busy. It was a very dreaded place to go after dark. At some point, we got a urine pot for late-night usage, especially for the younger ones who could not control that aspect of their body functions. The pot also proved handy on cold and rainy nights for the rest of us.

Living on a farm in the 1940s and 1950s provided many around-the-campfire moments for the Jackson children. We were very naive and impressionable children, so the adults took advantage of those traits and relished in telling us ghost stories that they knew would scare us. Well, their objective was achieved for many days and nights after the stories were told. We were some frightened children at night, outside in the dark, with only the moon and stars shining down on us. The most frightening times seemed to have been when we walked down the road at night past the Fitzgerald's cemetery or an empty house. My knees would tremble, and I would almost go limp. If there was the least bit of wind, it added to the mystery and fear. When the wind blew and the trees moved back-and-forth, my hair seemingly rose up on my head. Of course, none of our reactions made any sense because we had seen these same sites (trees, barns, wells, burial grounds, and abandoned buildings) during the day. It was just that during the night, everything stationary or in motion took on a frightening and terrifying personality all of its own. There was no trepidation in going near these places when we could clearly see them. It was just that everything around us seemed scarier after hearing the adults exaggerate and accent with sound effects their eerie tales. Without our visual senses to penetrate the darkness, our imaginations overtook the reality of the world our other senses knew existed.

In 1953, we moved back to the Flora Fitzgerald Childs' quarters farm to a house where we had previously lived. This time, it was different. We no longer needed to use kerosene lamps. The house had been renovated, and electricity was added. There was a new tin roof. The floors that seemed 150 years old had been replaced with fresh-cut lumber, and now, there were fewer cracks and holes. Other than those physical changes, nothing else had changed. Alas! Our stay there was short-lived. Mrs. Flora Childs, the owner, felt the improvements were too good for us. We were upended so that a more seemingly deserving white family, the Cottons, could reside there. It was rare for a white family to move into a house where a black family had previously lived, but this house was dressed up. The Cotton family was poor like us, worked the fields themselves like us, and tried to survive just like us. An electric water pump was extended from the well to the house after we moved. They did not have to walk to the well to get water as we had to do. I surmise that this was their compensation for moving into a house vacated by blacks.

After we were told to move from the renovated house, we relocated to "the place."[17] It was just around the corner from the renovated house with electricity and a quarter of a mile away from the well. We moved by wagon, less than five hundred yards. It was just a location, not a house, and it certainly was not a home for me. It was just the place where we stayed from early 1953 to June 10, 1958, because we were unable to do better.

The place did not have electricity. All necessary heat was generated from wood that we had to cut, supply, and maintain all year long for cooking and heating. The water supply for our household and the animals' use was a quarter of a mile away. We did come upon an unintended benefit after having to move to make room for Mr. Clyde Cotton's family. The benefit was that we no longer had to manually draw water from the well. The reason is that there was a water faucet installed next to the well. The well was covered over after the installation of the electric water pump for the Cottons. As a result, we still had to walk a quarter of a mile to the well to get the pumped water but the overall process of getting water was somewhat easier.

The two-bedroom-and-kitchen house on the Fitzgerald's farm was the place where nine of my siblings and I stayed. It was built from logs. It had a tin roof and an add-on kitchen attached to the back of the main structure. It was built with rough-cut lumber used by most as firewood. The place sat about two feet off the ground with bricks lifting each corner at six feet intermittently apart for support to the structure. There were two fireplaces, one on each end of the structure. In the middle of the structure was an open porch with steps from the ground. The floors were not fit to walk on with bare feet. Mom covered the heavy traffic areas with cheap linoleum that covered an 8×10 area. Pieces of cardboard kept the cold air out and the warm air in during the winter months. During the daytime, any activities that took place underneath the place could be seen through the cracks in the boarded floor. For instance, chickens scratching or the movements of the dog and cat trying to create a cool place to rest during the hot summer months could easily be spied upon. Pets were never allowed inside the place.

Periodically, we shelled corn and took it to a grinding mill and converted it into cornmeal. We found use for the other corn parts in the crude imitation for a log cabin, I called the place. All four sides of our cabin had huge gaping holes. The gaps exposed us to the elements. Dirt freely blew in. During the fall and winter months, cold, chilled air easily penetrated this place. To minimize our exposure to the elements, we plugged the holes and cracks with left over corncobs which came in very handy for stopping up holes and big cracks because they were flexible and could easily be broken or cut. The corncobs were also very useful for starting a fire. Additionally, we used cardboard, newspapers, and anything else that could be used to insulate the cracks and holes in the place look alike log cabin where we stayed. Nothing went to waste. Whatever we planted and harvested, we also stored for consumption by our family and animals. George Washington Carver had nothing on us as we made use of whatever we had to survive, to live, and see another day.

I recall three of my older sisters and one of my younger sisters (Josephine, before she left, Mamie, Geneva, and Mary Lou) all slept in one bedroom. The entrance was across the covered open porch from the main room of the cabin.

There were five glass windows in the place. Two of the windows were in the front of the place with shutters on each side. We furnished the place with two regular-sized beds and a chiffonier in the girls' room. Wikipedia describes a chiffonier as "A closet-like piece of furniture that combines a long space for hanging clothes that is closely related to a wardrobe with a chest of drawers." Typically, the chiffonier wardrobe section runs down one side of the piece while the drawers occupy the other side. It may have two enclosing doors or have the drawer fronts exposed and a separate door for the hanging space. The chiffonier was first advertised in the *1908 Sears and Roebuck's Catalog*. It was described as a modern invention, having been in use only a short time. Four sisters slept in that room in two regular-sized beds. They slept in luxury with only two to a bed.

I slept in the master bedroom with Mom and Dad, along with three other younger brothers as well as two younger sisters. Located in the room were two double beds, a folding bed, and baby crib. All total, along with Mom and Dad, six children slept in this tiny room. The smaller and younger boys slept two at the head and two at the foot in the same double bed. The double beds had mattresses that were homemade with cotton from the field we planted and wild straw we cut to make brooms for sweeping. Each bed used opened metal springs that squeaked. There were twelve of us sleeping in a two-bedroom place with four beds, a folding cot, and a crib. There was no running water, no indoor plumbing, or even a well nearby. This was a tough way to survive, but we did.

The youngest children slept in the same room with Mom and Dad. There was no reason to wonder about this arrangement. The evidence came each year with the birth of a new sibling. My father was one busy man late at night. I would hear him strike up the bedspring's tune as he started the messing-around tune and beat. I grew tired of babies coming nearly every year. My sisters boldly verbalized their feelings about the new responsibilities that they would ultimately share. I only thought about it. Perhaps it was the issue of having to care for them and the dirty diapers or, should I say, rags. I had just about had enough of waste that babies generated. I handled, cleaned up, stepped in much waste from our farm animals each day, so I did not really care to deal with human waste too. Along with my sisters, I had become adept at using a stick to stir the pot to rinse the waste out of the makeshift diapers. The process was not too pleasant. It has been many years since that time, and I can still actually smell the waste even now. Perhaps the smell and the stirring process are embedded in my psyche. Even the dirty diapers from my three sons, during their infancies, did not mimic or displace the smell of the waste that I have retained in my mind. Furthermore, the makeshift diapers then were recycled compared to today's diapers which are disposable.

Mom worked at the Fort Benning, Georgia Army Base, from time to time to make up for some of our financial woes. She started out doing domestic work, cleaning homes for military families to fill the gap between planting and harvesting seasons. In the early 1950s, she stopped farming and began working in Fort Benning, Georgia, full-time. On cleaning day, the families stacked the newspapers to be discarded. Mom bought them home for us to read. These were the only newspapers we had access to, although they were at least a week old. Later we used the newspapers as toilet paper. Unlike today's environment, toilet paper was a luxury that we could not afford. Baby bottoms were protected. They were covered with diapers made of rags. Even the rags were better than the choices we had. Our choices were to use newspaper, pages from old *Sears Roebuck*, *Walterfield*, or *Spiegel* catalogs, tree leaves, pine straw, corncobs, leaves, grass, or nothing at all.

Lying in bed at night, we could see through the roof cracks to the sky and all its splendor. With the uncovered ceiling, we were treated to the acoustical noise from the rain beating on the tin roof. The sound was as though the roof was going to collapse. The noise of the rain pounding against the tin roof was unsettling and it frightened the younger children. The free-flowing water through the holes in the tin roof soaked our furnishings, beds, clothes containers, and anything that was not waterproofed. These things had to be repositioned or covered with paper or clothing. Buckets, tubs, cans, and any other available containers were strategically positioned to catch the rainwater.

It appeared that the larger the family got, the smaller the place we lived. The makeup of the family at this time consisted of Mom, Dad, and my seven sisters, three brothers, and me. There was a twenty-four-year age difference between the oldest and youngest child. Before I became a teenager, some of the older children had left to be on their own. The largest number of siblings that I lived with in the same house was eleven.

The place had two fireplaces with a brick chimney at opposite ends of it. In the middle was an opened covered porch. The porch looked like a room positioned in the middle that the builder failed to put a front and rear wall and doors around. The main room had three doors. The main door led from the porch. Another one opened into the main room and into the kitchen. The third door faced the front of the house. There were no steps to fill the gap of about three feet from the porch to the house. The same step-up gap existed from the ground to the porch. The kitchen seemed like an afterthought. It was positioned off the main room as an add-on. It had a wood-burning stove and a stovepipe that ran through the ceiling. There was no bathroom inside of the place. The outhouse was the only toilet option, not just for us but all blacks, and most whites, living on farms. It was usually located downwind about fifty yards from the house.

We were financially needy and lacking. In plain English, we were *po*, the alternative pronunciation of the word *poor* in our deep Southern accent. Conversely we were very proud, hardworking, and honest. We may have been uneducated by the world's standard at the time, but we never considered ourselves inferior to anyone. We never begged, borrowed, or stole. Well, anything of any value. In Scripture, David was accused of violating Jewish law for working, picking grain, and eating it on the Sabbath. However, we never walked through the grain field or picked grain no matter how hungry we got—on the Sabbath. As children, on weekdays, we may have walked through our neighbor's pecan orchards, watermelon patches, peaches, and other fruit tree orchards. We may have gorged on some of the produce because we were hungry and the nuts and fruits were too delectable to ignore. We may have even gotten punished for eating or for lying that we didn't eat the mouthwatering watermelons, peaches, pecans, and other produce available, but we always kept the Sabbath free of any of the hypothetical gorging explained above. So, we avoided sinning.

Mom always tried to make where we stayed comfortable. The yard was always neat. We brightened the place up by whitewashing the walls. I don't remember us ever painting anything, but we added color to it. Canyon Providence, now a Georgia State Park, known for its various colors of dirt, was only a wagon ride away.[18] So we gathered white dirt from the canyon and whitewashed or painted the walls white with white dirt.

Mrs. Flora showed no loyalty to our family. By this time, the Jacksons had lived on her farm for more than fifty years. My siblings were the third generation to live there since slavery. Escaping the economic system so common to our ancestors took more than hard work. It took personal fortitude, sacrifice, courage, and above all, a strong faith in God. Those traits were deeply rooted in my mom, and my brothers and sisters. They helped us to set new paths for our future.

As a little boy, I listened to my parents, relatives, neighbors, and other churchgoers as they sang old African-American spirituals both in the church and while working in the fields. These hymns expressed in song their struggles, not to man but rather to Jesus who they served. They often sang songs such as, "This world is not my home I'm just passing through…" To my ancestors, it was a belief and not just a song for entertainment. They worked, worshipped, and sang songs hoping, praying, and looking to Jesus for a better tomorrow. One such hymn was "I Want Jesus to Walk with Me." These are the words to that very simple hymn.

I want Jesus to walk with me (walk with me).
In my trials, Lord, I want Jesus to walk with me
    (walk with me).
When I am troubled, Lord, I want Jesus to walk
    with me (walk with me).
I want Jesus to walk with me (walk with me).
In my trials, Lord, I want Jesus to walk with me
    (walk with me).
When I am troubled, Lord, I want Jesus to walk
    with me (walk with me).
All along my pilgrim journey,
When my heart is almost breaking I want Jesus to
    walk with me (walk with me).
When my head is bowed in sorrow,
Lord, I want Jesus to walk with me (walk with me).

Others on the Move

As stated earlier, our grandpa did not live with my Grandmother Hattie.[19] He stayed with his oldest daughter who was not married at that time, but she had been. Her only child, an adult son, was away on active military duty. He served during the Korean conflict.

Grandma Hattie lived with my uncle, her youngest son Charlie, nicknamed Friend, and his wife and nine children, all in a two-room place with a kitchen. Frank Jr. (nicknamed Buddy), my father, duplicated the experience of living in the exact same place years later with twelve people—Mom, himself, and my ten siblings.

Uncle Friend later purchased a small farm with a loan granted under the GI Bill. He served in the US Navy during World War II. The farm he purchased was adjacent to Aunt Byne's family farm. While we did some independent farming, my parents never owned land while we lived in Georgia.

In 1953, we moved back to the Fitzgerald's quarters where we had resided years earlier. Thankfully, this two room place with a kitchen was my family's last move in Georgia before we migrated to New Jersey.

Bartering

Once a week, on Friday, a grocery truck we called the Store Man came through our rural area selling household products and food items. To earn cash, Mom, my older sisters, and I were hired out to perform day farm work in addition to the work we did on the land we rented and farmed. We could only do this when it was available and necessary. We picked wild and seasonal fruit, such as blackberries and plums, then sold or traded them for the Store Man's goods. Sometimes Mom would buy food on credit. Mostly, though, we would shell corn that we had stored in the barn for animal feed and for our consumption in the form of cornmeal to exchange and pay for groceries. At the time, we were truly poor. We made do with what we had and could afford. During the spring and summer months, Mom canned and made preserves from some of the wild-grown fruit we picked. We also exchanged some fresh fruit and canned goods for more needed items from the Store Man.

The Store Man's truck was enclosed and had shelves on two sides. The shelves were partitioned off to store cans, dry goods, and many of the things people living in the rural farming areas wanted and consumed. The Store Man carried foods like fresh mullet fish as well as salted fish that had been preserved. Sugar and slabs of bacon were made available for sale. He also had a wide variety of in season but not commonly found fruits such as grapes, oranges, apples, and bananas. Bananas were rare in our community. When this young country kid got the chance to eat one, I believed there was no better-tasting food on earth.

Flour was packaged in twenty-five-pound bags with printed designs on the sackcloth. The bag was sold as one piece with the excess materials stitched and stored inside the bag along with the flour. The packaging was pure non-televised marketing. The marketing companies intended to get the effect of providing more for less. The marketing campaigns were very well-thought-out and effective, just as the ones we see today—without the television. To this day, I am amazed at what and how much stuff was on that truck for people to purchase.

Wild plums and other kinds of (not available from the Store Man) fruit grew in our farm area. They were plentiful, and we gathered and ate as much as we could. During the summer, after peaches had ripened, growers came from Fort Valley with trucks loaded with them for sale. Mom bought some and made preserves and canned others for future use. Preserving fruit for later use came in handy. We were able to enjoy those peaches during the winter months when fresh fruit was scarce. During the summer months, we ate good. There were all kinds of fresh fruits like watermelons, peaches, berries, plums, and fresh vegetables such as okra, field peas, squash, tomatoes, and collard greens to pig out on.

When fresh vegetables were scarce, we had plenty of dried vegetables such as, black-eyed peas, beans, and sweet potatoes. We would secure a bag of dried black-eyed peas or beans and other dried vegetables, soak them overnight, and cook them the next day. The dried vegetables were hung in the crib house (barn) to keep them away from grain-eating insects. They were stored in the shell, and we would beat the contents in a bag, separating the dried vegetables from the shell. We then tossed the dried vegetables into the air, allowing the wind to separate the chaff from the dried vegetables.

We preserved and stored meat eaten during the fall and winter months in an old wooden shed and smoked it to cure and preserve it. As the weather turned cold, we would occasionally slaughter a pig and shared it with all the neighboring black farmers. This was a tradition and all who slaughtered pigs or hogs shared with other families. The black farmers helped each other through the kind deed of sharing. There were poor white farmers. But, during the 1940's–1950's in the south there was true discrimination. The races did not mix even for basic survival.

We soaked vegetables overnight and then cooked them with a piece of smoked pork bone or a slice of pork fat for seasoning. Among other purposes, we used the fireplace to heat the house. For snacks during the winter months, we baked sweet potatoes in the ashes of the fireplace. Other times, we roasted peanuts over the fire. We roasted peanuts and baked sweet potatoes in the kitchen oven as well, but it was easier baking and roasting over the fire. Roasting in the ashes was a quick way to get a delicious energy snack for the whole family to enjoy.

On occasions, Mom ran out of ingredients such as sugar, milk, eggs, and flour and would send us to a neighbor to borrow the missing items that she needed. We had no telephone to call in advance to ask. We just showed up, knocked on the door, and delivered the message. Usually the neighbor shared if they were able to do so.

Unlike cotton and peanuts raised and sold, we raised corn to feed, the animals, and ourselves. As previously discussed, all components of the corn were reused and recycled. We fed corn to our mules, cows, hogs, and chickens and ground it into meal for our households. Oftentimes we shucked and shelled extra corn, took it to the mill, and had it ground into meal. The rest, we sold for cash. The corncobs we used to fuel fires, hygiene, and other purposes. This was the way of life growing up in the 1940s and 1950s in Stewart County, Georgia. Our lives were not easy. Our experiences formed our characters, family values, and our respect for each other.

As noted earlier, I have thirteen siblings. There is a twenty-four-year spread between the oldest and youngest child. Some of us grew up in clusters and are closer to some than others in age. The twenty-four-year age gap means that many of us experienced each other and our parents at different phases of their lives. As the sibling stories that follow portray, we had disparate perspectives, and recalls of some of those shared experiences.

Fitzgerald Family Cemetery 92 family members buried there between 1861 to 1996 less than a quarter mile from the "Big House" residence.

Opened cotton bud ready for picking and one not yet opened.

A typical field of cotton like the ones we planted and harvested by hand.

A-typical "Framed house" usually Clustered together
like the ones on Fitzgerald farm. The house above
was Aunt Byne's & husband family farm.

The place electricity was installed, my birthplace and the "place" the Jacksons were told to move so a White farmer could live there.

'The Place' looks identical to this picture EXCEPT the place had a tin roof, sat higher off the ground, had huge holes and cracks that one could see through.

Canyon Providence where we obtain white dirt to white wash our walls.

Grandpa, Frank Jackson, Sr & Grandma Hattie Jackson.

Chapter 3

Sibling 1
The Journey Extended

The First Child's Story

Some days, I'm my mother's and my father's child named Leola. I am the very firstborn child of Frank L. and Rosie Jackson. I grew up with one sister and two brothers: Rosie, Billy, and Charles. I have enjoyed quite a bit over my eighty-eight years. Like each of my surviving siblings, I'm going to share as much as I can recall of my life below. Lately though, I have experienced a fading and fuzzy memory. You may have heard the joke that the memory is the first thing to go and I don't remember the second thing or anything else. Well, that's me. I don't remember much of my past other than it came and done gone! Nevertheless, I'm still here and can stand although not for very long periods of time. I sum my situation up as mind over meds. Even as an eighty-eight-year-old woman, I'm much better off than many much younger women than me. I can assure you of this, that I'm 100 percent better off than all the dead people because I'm still living. I'm alive. I have control and use of my five senses. The percentages of control, I don't know so don't ask. Age has certain privileges and I aim to exercise mine.

My mother said that my father was hoping for a male child to be the firstborn. As I grew, I often had questions that I wanted answered. One such question was why did my sister, who was less than two years younger than me, have such a beautiful grade of hair? Seemingly my hair would not grow more than an inch long. I often wondered if it was my father's wish for a male child that caused my hair to stunt its growth. My reason for wanting an answer to this ponder is that each time my mother combed and braided my sister's hair, I noticed that Rosie sat patiently and quietly until Mother was finished. When it was my turn for Mother to do my hair, she had a job on her hands to hold my head steady to braid it. I had a tender head, and my hair was very short. Mother used all the home remedies she was given to make my hair grow. She used strings to wrap the tiny braids. She applied all kinds of oil, even lard, hoping my hair would grow but to no avail. Because I was tender-headed, each time I saw Mother with a comb in her hand, my head began to ache.

Growing up with a sister and two brothers was good and bad. Being the oldest, I tried to do all the things my parents told me and my siblings to do. Otherwise I was held accountable and would be punished for things done or not done as required. Rosie was stubborn and refused to do her assigned tasks. She knew full well that if they weren't done, both of us would be punished; but that did not move her to fulfill her responsibilities. So I did our duties to avoid the chastisement by my parents. When my sister refused to do her chores such as clean the pots and pans, she knew and expected rebuke. To prepare for the punishment that was sure to come, she put on extra clothing as padding to soften the sting from the switches yanked from nearby tree branches. Her well-laid-out plan was soon discovered. One day, while well-padded, she fell asleep and forgot to do her chores. She was awakened with a carefully selected and pliable switch, landing squarely on her rear end. To her surprise, the switch became stuck in her undergarment padding. Her secret was now exposed. She was ordered to remove the extra garments. From that day forward, while we were children, at home together, we had some great days. Her chores were done as instructed.

By the time many of my younger siblings were born, I had moved to Jersey City, but we were close and are still close to this day. From the oldest to the youngest child, we were taught rule 1: to love and respect one another. If those rules were not followed, there would be dire consequences to pay. Our parents were not shy in using a tree switch, a belt, or both to ensure that rules were followed. The razor strap used by my father to punish his three oldest children was the same one he used years later to deliver justice to my younger siblings. During my childhood, both Dad and Mom punished us. Dad claimed he hated to beat us, but when he did, he struck us three or four times and uttered very few words. Mother had no limit on the words she uttered as she delivered her discipline. With each hit, she explained why she was beating us and dared us to ever do the same thing again. She had no preference for the tool she used to beat us. It could be a leather strap, belt, or a flexible switch from a tree.

Mother was a very wise person. She had a friend named Ms. Ella Mae who enjoyed young children. I don't remember her age, although I knew she was not an elderly person. Ms. Ella Mae's house was one of our favorite places to visit. When we visited with her, she allowed us to talk and ask questions about any subject and she would give us a reasonable response (this was not common for adults in our Georgia community). I enjoyed her company. On Saturdays, after we finished our chores, mopped the floors, and swept the dirty yard, we could visit her. A cousin lived across the road from Ms. Ella Mae with trees that blocked the view of her house. My cousin had six brothers, and she was the only girl. Since Saturday was the only day we could play, we knew our cousin's younger relatives would also be with her. Our parents had rules for us whenever we visited someone's house. One of them was, if we allow you to go to someone's home, do not leave there to go to anyone else's home without permission. Saturday came and we were supposed to go visit Ms. Ella Mae. Instead we went across the street to visit our cousin who always had some younger relatives visiting her around the same time. I knew the rules and begged my younger sister not to disobey. My begging fell on deaf ears.

After having violated the rules several times before, I went along with her, thinking we would play, go home, and no harm would be done. We left Ms. Ella Mae's house and went over to play with our cousins. In the meanwhile, Mother stopped by Ms. Ella Mae's house on her way home and we were not there as expected. We returned home by way of Ms. Ella Mae who never told us that Mother had stopped by looking for us. As we returned home, we thought we had covered our tracks because Mother couldn't have known that we had gone to our cousin's house. Upon returning home, we found Mother was all smiles. We had supposedly obeyed the rules and come home before sundown as we were told to do. Mother did not ask where we had been when we arrived home. She did not give us an inkling that she stopped by Ms. Ella Mae's house looking for us. After a bit, Mother inquired where we had been. My sister Rosie made up something, thinking she had pulled the wool over Mother's eyes. We both had miscalculated. We hadn't noticed that she had switches resting in the corner of the room waiting for us. I tried to do right. After that affair, I let it spill out that Rosie was the ringleader and troublemaker. From that day forward, I was no longer punished along with Rosie for wrongdoings when we were together. I wanted to be compliant, but Rosie refused to follow the instructions as given.

Another rule of my parents was don't talk to strangers and I didn't. Once I traveled from Omaha to Lumpkin to visit Aunt Ruth as I did from time to time. Father took me to meet the train and stayed until it arrived. I boarded and sat on an aisle seat by a man who sat next to the window. The man said to me, "I believe there is a man trying to get your attention." I was told by Father not to talk to strangers. So I kept my face looking straight ahead; I didn't look left or right. Little did I know the man was trying to help me. I later realized that the man wanted to tell me that my father was trying to get my attention. How ignorant I must have seemed, but I followed my parents' instructions! Can you imagine someone trying to carry on a conversation with you—a passenger on the seat next to him—and all he got was a frozen stare ahead like a statue? Well, it happened. Ironically same as today, train routes had names. For my encounter, on that day, the train service with stopovers in Omaha and Lumpkin was appropriately named the Butthead.

A few years later, I took the Butthead to Savannah from Omaha, then changed to the Silver Meteor to go to Newark, New Jersey. The Silver Meteor, a passenger train that ran between New York and Miami, Florida, was the first diesel-powered streamliner.[20] Today Amtrak operates Silver Service and Silver Star train services between New York and Florida. When I arrived in Newark, my mother's brother, Uncle Bob, and his girlfriend, Regenia Wallace, met me at the train station. They took me to their home in Jersey City. I lived with them for five years. Regenia was a wonderful person, and we got along well. Both she and her family treated me as if I was a blood relative. Later I moved into my Aunt Mae's house who is Mother's youngest sister. I stayed with her and family for seven years.

Later my nemesis, the troublemaker, sister Rosie, moved from South Jersey to Jersey City. We got a three-bedroom apartment together. Then Charles, our brother, moved in, and we shared the cost to make the rent easier on the three of us. Rosie was designated as the one who shopped for groceries and cooked the meals. She would spend less on food to allow the two of us to occasionally go to Club Nine in New York City. After several weeks, Charles sat down, looked at the meal prepared for dinner, and said, "Is this all my money can buy?" It was pig, pig, and more pig! It was pigtails on Monday, pig ears on Tuesday, pig feet on Wednesday, and anything pig that was cheap for the remainder of the week. Charles was not pleased with the pig meals that he was receiving.

I went to dance night in Club Nine with the money my sister saved out of the food budget. At the dance, I met a man on the dance floor who lived a couple of blocks from our apartment. We dated for a short while, then got married and gave birth to four children. Years later, my husband, Joe, drove the children and me, along with my niece, to South Carolina to meet his family. As we visited with his family in the country, Joe thought it would be a good time to teach me how to drive. During my very first driving lesson, I drove straight into a ditch on a country road.

Joe died at an early age. After his death, I did volunteer work for an association that helped the community's needy. Through the association, we helped to provide nourishment and clothes to such families. We assisted financially to help pay for nondiscretionary expenses such as gas for heating, electricity, and water bills. We also offered counseling and other needed services to community residents. The association, the Com-Bin-Nation, held an annual fund-raising event to support the needs of the community. During my years of volunteering, Com-Bin-Nation honored many local and national personalities of color who actively promoted and supported causes important to the black community. I was thrilled to see my sister Rosie selected and honored for the great work she did that helped to improve our local community.

Earlier during our time of sharing an apartment, Rosie, Charles, and I, were working just to make ends meet. Prior to getting married and raising a family, I worked as a factory worker. After our children got older, I entered college and graduated with my bachelor's degree from Saint Peter's University. Saint Peter's was founded in 1872 as a private coeducational Jesuit, Roman Catholic College located in Jersey City, New Jersey. For the next twenty years, I was employed by the Jersey City Board of Education, then as a social worker. I retired from full-time employment in 1979.

Silver Meteor Train (Leola Pressley) travelled to Newark, NJ.

Chapter 4

Sibling 2
Escape, Exploration, and Expedition

Early Years

I am Rosie, born to my parents, Frank and Rosie Jackson. I grew up with one older sister, Leola, and two younger brothers, Charles and Billy, but I was also around when younger siblings were added to the family. As farmers, my parents raised the basic crops of the day—corn, peanuts, cotton, and most of the food we ate. They left to work the fields before sunrise, returned for lunch, back to the  fields, and worked until sundown. As crops were planted and harvested, this was the daily routine five and a half days a week. Being too young to work in the fields, I showed an interest in cooking and Mother taught me how at a very young age. Out of necessity, she also taught me to wash dishes and clothes.

The older sister was supposed to oversee the younger siblings, making sure that household chores were done as instructed. My older sister didn't do as she was told. So, I completed them to avoid punishment for both of us. I made sure my parents' directives were followed. The beds were made. The dishes were washed. Babies' clothes were washed. I cared for the babies and made sure the house was kept clean always. Lee (Leola) was very soft and refused to obey my parents' commands. I made sure we did everything that was supposed to be done before they returned home from the fields. If the chores were not done, both my sister and I would be punished with a belt or a switch snatched from a tree branch. My older sister was afraid of almost everything such as bugs, spiders, worms, and almost any kind of insect. Being a bit devious, I went into the yard, picked up worms, and chased her with them. This was the first of many silly little things we as siblings did to entertain ourselves.

During certain times of the day, I drew water from the well and poured it into a pail/bucket or a large jug. I took it to my parents and other relatives who worked in the fields. The well served and provided water for the Jackson families. Our relatives consisted of five families. The well was located about a quarter of a mile from the farthest house. Water was pulled up from the well using a five-gallon bucket for all purposes: personal consumption, washing, drinking, cooking, and watering animals like our mules, cows, pigs, and chickens. The well was also the meeting place for the families. Often the well was the place where families decided which day of the week each family would wash their clothes. There was a special area setup for washing and all families used the same black pot that boiled the clothes for washing.[21] Today that pot is still among the family heirlooms and is in my brother Grover's garage. The prewash process included beating the dust out of certain pieces like sheets, blankets, and work clothes, called overalls, with a broom or large stick. To further loosen the dirt, clothes were boiled in that black pot. They were then handwashed, hand-rinsed, and hung out to dry. The clothesline was usually located on the side or rear of the house where each family lived. Washing clothes was almost a full day's job for my family.

Living in the Jackson's household was not peaches and cream. Everyone was expected to do their fair share of work. There was love, and it showed. My parents taught us to love one another and show love and respect to others. We were taught not to fight each other or anyone. If we did and Mother and Father found out, it was very bad news for the guilty parties. The love they taught and shared is with me today. I have the greatest love for each of my brothers and sisters. We have always had a loving and sharing relationship to address spiritual, financial, or any other needs. We have been there and will always be there to help and support each other.

I am very thankful that my parents did the best they could with the few resources they had to share. On holidays, namely Thanksgivings, Christmases, and New Years, we never had a turkey spread like some families living among us. We were happy and content with the little we had and never felt sorry for ourselves or jealous of what others had. On special holidays, Mother killed a chicken and she cooked it, opened some canned goods, and made a pie, cake, or both. She also made her specialty of butter rolls. They were so good. Then as we ate, she said, "Thank God for what we have." That was not exactly what I wanted to hear; I wanted more but was very appreciative for what we had. As I grew older and wiser, I learned and appreciated not just the food but the words she spoke. The love she shared made me who I am today.

High School Years

I attended high school in the city of Lumpkin, the county seat for Stewart County, Georgia, about twenty-five miles from Omaha. The only scheduled public transportation was a train. I don't remember if it ran daily or periodically during a week. The one thing I remember is that I returned home only when my parents had money for train fare. They paid for my boarding to attend Lumpkin High School, a public high school some twenty-five miles away. That was not a daily commute. So I lived with a family who used their home as a boarding house for farm girls who attended high school. I lived there with six other girls. Their parents picked them up on Friday evening and returned them on Sunday afternoon for classes on Monday.

One Friday afternoon, all the girls were picked up by their parents and taken home. I was left alone with a very noisy old property owner. I was out of food with very little money to buy any. I really wanted to go home but had only a few pennies—not enough money to pay the train fare home. As Jesse Jackson said many years later, "Keep hope alive." I took the few coins that I had and walked to the train station. As I arrived, I saw people I knew, and others I didn't, laughing and talking. So I pretended that I was happy laughing and speaking to people as I passed them. To be truthful, I was very afraid. I had only a few pennies which was not enough for the train fare, but I was determined to take the train home. I just did not know how I was going to pay. Finally, I heard the train whistle blow and I hoped for help, although I hadn't asked anyone nor would I. Time was running out; I looked in the sand while moving my feet backward and forward, pretending to have dropped some of my money in the sand. The train whistle blew again as it came around the curve. At that point, I cried real tears aloud until someone heard me. I needed financial help so I could get on the train. The Lord knew my hungry need. A young man I knew came over and gave me the money required to go home. "Keep hope alive," for God is good!

Another time, Mother's cousin came to town on a Friday after school had closed. I wanted to go home and saw that he was traveling alone. I ran over to him and asked if he would give me a ride home. He said, of course. Then he stated the amount that I would owe him. I responded, no problem, Mother would take care of the fare. I knew Mother didn't have funds to pay for my trip home or my return fare back to school. I knew before I asked or promised that Mother was going to pay him, but I wanted to go home; so I agreed that she would pay.

As he drove, I smiled and thought he came to town to pick up some items. He had not gone nor was he going out of his way. So why had he charged me, a high school student, for a trip that he was making anyway? He knew I was unable to pay nor were my parents able to do so. Then the thought left me; all I wanted to do was to get home. He would have to wait for a long time for payment. Many years later, he saw me and asked me about the money I owed him. My response was, "I thought Mother paid you! I am sure she forgot about it." My cousin died years later. He never collected the fee he charged to drop me off at home that day. In retrospect, I still don't understand how Mother supported me in boarding school, paid rent, or gave me money for food and other items I needed, but I know she always kept hope alive!

Mother's Dream

I finished high school and prepared for my future. Mother often talked about me leaving Georgia. She said, "Get out of Georgia. Get a job and help the family move to New Jersey." She had sisters who lived in Florida, New Jersey, and an aunt in Atlanta, Georgia, who sent her train fare to visit them from time to time. As she traveled, she met many of her relatives and kept in touch with them. The more she visited, the more she was convinced the family must leave Georgia and the failed farming ventures. During the Christmas season, her aunt in Atlanta, her sisters and aunt in New Jersey, and sisters in Florida sent the family fruit and clothing.

She reinforced her desire to leave Georgia and reminded me of Ben and Sarah Nelson. Ben and Sarah Nelson lived in Omaha, raised their family, and when the children were older, they left their parents and relocated to Ohio. A few years later, the children returned to Georgia and moved Ben and Sarah, their parents, to live with them in Ohio. I assumed Mother's eyes were opened as she visited relatives in cities outside of Steward County. Mother's relatives lived a better-quality lifestyle than she did. As she and I discussed my future, Mother repeated her earlier plea of my leaving Georgia soon, getting a job, and sending for the rest of the family. I promised her that I would do just that, whether single or married. It became my passion and priority to help my parents and family to relocate to New Jersey from Georgia.

Uncle Bud, mother's brother, died at a very young age. His wife, Aunt Mary, loved us and treated us like her own blood relatives and not as in-laws. Mother and Aunt Mary were very close, just like sisters. Mother wrote her a letter and asked if my brother Billy and I could live with her family. She replied, absolutely. My brother and I left Omaha in 1950 for Camden, New Jersey, to live with my deceased uncle's wife. I lived in New Jersey for more than sixty-six years. I raised a family there. I earned a college degree, taught secondary school, and retired there. Shortly after I retired, I relocated to Maryland, my current state of residence.

I lived in Camden for several years with Aunt Mary. It was my new home, so I joined New Mickle Street Baptist Church.[22] As a member, I got involved and enjoyed the church services and activities. Quite a few young people attended and participated in the church activities such as BYPU (Baptist Young Peoples Union). One of the BYPU's activities involved Bible verse memorization. On one occasion, as we recited Bible verses, a young man said, "You should do something..." He got mixed up, meant to say, "Honor your father and your mother, that your days may be long in the land that the Lord your God is giving you" (Exodus 20:12, ESV). That young man became a family friend for the rest of his life. He and my brother Billy married two sisters.

I joined the church choir and we visited other churches and sang from time to time. We visited a church in Florence, New Jersey. I was excited to be a member of the choir, traveling to and visiting other churches. During the visit, I was asked to bring greetings from New Mickle Baptist Church. My message had been written out in longhand. I had difficulties reading script. I stumbled, saying a little of this and a little of everything that was not on the paper. I do not remember if I was nervous or afraid or both. That was the first and last time I was asked to bring greetings from my church or any other one.

Several years passed, I relocated to Jersey City and lived with Mother's sister, my Aunt (Mary) Mae, and my oldest sister, Leola. After a few weeks in Jersey City, I interviewed for employment at a television-and-radio manufacturer. I got the job, and I thought the pay was great. I was now able to help Mother execute her plan to leave Omaha and Stewart County, Georgia.

Billy and I were very close and communicated freely on most matters. The United States was at war with North Korea, and Billy received a notice from the draft board to report for induction into the army. We planned to help the family relocate to New Jersey for a better life. Then I cried and cried. After I stopped crying, I decided if my brother goes into the army, I wanted to go as well. I told nobody about my plan—Mother, Aunt Mae, or anyone. I took a day off from work, went to Newark, and took the army entrance test, but I did not pass. God was so good; Billy didn't pass the test either. I told Mother and the family later what I had done. Their remarks were, "Suppose you had passed!" God is so good, He protects the needy, babies, and fools.

Planned Migration

After things settled down, Billy and I discussed with Father the timetable of the family's move to Camden. We sent him a ticket to come to Camden to stay for a few months. One weekend, I took a bus to Camden to visit with him and Billy to prepare a nice dinner for them. On the bus from Jersey City to Camden, I smiled all the way with excitement. I got off the bus, went to their apartment, and discovered Father had a bus ticket to leave the next day for Stewart County. Mother continued to write, saying, "Sarah was tired and wanted to leave Georgia."

I planned to use my car to transport the family from Georgia to New Jersey. I sent a few dollars for them to have for the trip. Mother planned to rent a trailer to hitch onto my car to carry their few items from Georgia. The weekend before the trip to Georgia, my brother Charles wrecked my car. He ran into a milk truck and milk spilled all over the street. In the '50s, '60s, and perhaps the early '70s, milk was delivered to individual homes in glass bottles. It was not as we had planned, but Mother's dream eventually came true. We all enjoyed having our family in relatively proximity for many years in New Jersey. "For my thoughts are not your thoughts, nor are your ways my ways—oracle of the Lord" (Isaiah 55:8).

Loving Mother

I believe if everyone had a mother like mine, the world would be a better place. She was my mother, a beautiful and kind person, and we talked about all subjects. To me, she was a Proverbs-31 woman.

She opened her mouth with wisdom. Her tongue spoke words of kindness. She worked hard to provide for us and planted good seeds in our life. Most importantly, she loved the Lord and was a good example that I followed. Both parents were Christians and loved the Lord, the living Lord and Savior. They took me to church and taught me the true value of love as Christ taught while on earth. The entire family went to church on Sundays and worshiped together.

My mother's religious denomination was African Methodist Episcopal (AME, Methodist) as were her parents. My father was of the Baptist faith as were his parents. As a child, I joined the Baptist Church. I wanted to join the AME Church but my father was against it. Although I joined the Baptist Church, I attended the Methodist Church and participated in all their programs and activities. As silly as this may sound, the primary reason my father didn't want me to join the Methodist Church was because he believed in water baptism. Although according to the Bible, one is not saved by water baptism rather by faith in Christ alone. The last program I participated in at Mother's church was an AME conference. Back then, my world was very small and my knowledge was limited. Bishops, elders, and preachers seemingly came from all over the world. I was on the program to say a poem. I knew the poem so well and upon being called to say it, I stood before the group and recited it very proudly. It was Psalm 23 and I knew it without reading it from the Bible. After finishing it, I said, "Oh!" Then I recited the poem that I learned for the program. I was eleven years old. Every minister who spoke during the conference mentioned my name and said how the Lord used me that evening.

My mother was the best mother anyone could ever hope or wish for. I thank my heavenly Father for giving her to me. I appreciate both my parents. I sometimes thought as I grew up, they were too strict. I realized many years later, their love was unconditional. Everything they did prepared me and protected me for life's challenges. They both now live in my heart and memory.

Our Relatives

I enjoyed my Tampa visits to see my uncle, aunt, and my cousins Honey and Rob, her brother. Honey's father was employed as a railroad train porter. I had just recently returned home from Tampa and was surprised by the invitation to return for Rob's homecoming game. Rob, a Bethune Cookman College football player, told his sister their homecoming game would be played against NC A&T Aggies in Tampa. Honey asked me if I would be allowed to return to Tampa, if she could get her father's pass for me to travel. Mother and Father agreed to let me go. Unbeknownst to me, my uncle and his immediate family were the only authorized travelers to use his pass. Honey sent me her father's pass for my visit to Tampa. I did not know that my cousin had stolen her father's railroad pass. I was very naive. I did not understand nor did I question her about why I had to be her, if anyone queried me on the train. So I went to Tampa to see my very first football game using a stolen railroad pass pretending to be Honey, my uncle's daughter.

During the game, I yelled each time Honey yelled. To be truthful, I had no clue why I yelled. I didn't understand the rules of the game. I clapped when the crowd clapped and ate popcorn when others ate popcorn. I was a naïve country girl out of her element pretending to be sophisticated.

While I am not trying to justify the theft of my uncle's train pass, my visits with my aunt, uncle, and cousins Honey and Rob in Tampa allowed me to meet other family members I had not known before. (I was introduced to another cousin who also played on the football team. Everyone called him Stovepipe. I don't know what his real name was.) It also helped me to meet Grandmother Itty's (Josephine's), sister (Mary), who lived in Savannah along with her husband and four children. Since I had to change trains in Savannah, on one of my trips, I took the opportunity to spend the night at Aunt Mary's home.

Grandmother Remembered

My mother's mom (Grandmother Itty or Josephine) had a very beautiful light-brown complexion, long black curly hair. She was short in stature, about 4'4" tall. She was very kind to me. She gave me great freedom as I visited her home. I got away with deeds that others did not dare to try; they knew it would be a punishable act. When she died, I lost all my freedom. I never knew a tree had so many branches until my Grandmother Itty passed.

It seemed Grandmother Itty and Grandfather Gus lived far away from us. Mother visited them at least twice a week, traveling through woods with no houses seen or in sight along the way. One day, as she was on her way to their house, Mother saw heavy dark smoke in the distant sky. At the time, she had no way of knowing it was her parents' house. After their house burned, Grandmother Itty and Grandfather Gus lived with us for a while.

I remember my grandmother as a pretty woman with a very beautiful smile. My Grandfather Gus might have been pleasant, but I never saw it. As I remember, in addition to not being very friendly, he rarely wore shoes, although he owned them. Upon visiting us, he would have his shoes tied together across his shoulder. I often wondered what happened when he went to church, had to walk through woods with thickets, or any kinds of thorny brushes or berry patches.

Education was very important to both Mother and Father. My father made sure homework was done and not left up to Mother. Even if she helped, he came home from working in the fields and reviewed the subject matter Mother and I had studied. He made sure homework was made a priority. He insisted that the lessons must be understood and retained. He ate dinner, pushed away from the table, and reached for his razor strap and placed it across his knee. I sat on his lap. He read and recited some words two or three times, then asked me to repeat them as he repeated them with me. He asked me to recite them, and both of us repeated them. He skipped around and if I forgot a word; he would reach for his razor strap.

In college, I took two reading classes and the professor asked each of us to write a paper on how we learned to read. My paper was very brief. The net of my paper stated that I learned by my father's razor strap. I remembered words forward, backward, skipped around, and wherever he pointed the pencil. I learned to read out of fear for the razor-strap beating. It instilled fear, although I learned the words. There had to be a better way! My father was not a man with any formal education, therefore, he did the best he could with what he knew—fear.

As I got older, I remember Father came after me to beat me about something. I said to myself, *I'm too old. I will not stand and let you beat me.* I was some distance away, saw him coming toward me with his strap, and I decided to make him work for his efforts. I ran and he chased me. I made a very careless mistake, slowed down, looked back to see how far behind he was, and as I turned, he grabbed me. Although he caught me, I knew he was too tired to do much beating.

Both parents were on the same page when it came to discipline. If I asked one for permission, the answer was the same for both parents. One of the traits I really loved about my parents is that they did not treat their children one way and the grandchildren another way. They did not spoil any of us children or grandchildren. Mother disciplined all of us in the same manner with love for both children and grandchildren. Mother talked more. Before or as she beat you, she told you the reason for your punishment, repeatedly. I believed it really hurt her emotionally. Mother was not a person to cuss or get angry. On an occasion when one of us did something she disapproved of, she lectured the guilty one. One of her sayings that I have heard, seemingly forever, went something like this, "You don't have a pot to piss in or a window to throw it out." And her point was *think*, don't do dumb things.

Reward and Punishment

Once a year, after the crops were harvested, it was time to discuss who needed shoes. Not all the kids were lucky enough to have new shoes bought. The rest of us got and wore hand-me-down shoes and clothes. There were no stores in our vicinity. Clothes and shoes were mail-ordered from a *Sears and Roebuck, Spiegel,* or *Walterfield's* mail-order catalogs. As shoes were ordered, my father believed in the theory of buying shoes two sizes larger than our actual foot size. Shoes too small were handed down to a sibling whose feet were smaller. If the shoes were too large and didn't fit, no problem, we stuffed the toes of the shoes with cotton. Those siblings whose feet had outgrown the shoes that they already owned received new shoes. The only siblings who got new shoes were those for whom a hand-me-down pair wasn't available. Those who were lucky to get new shoes got Daddy's favorite shoes—black-and-white oxfords. We hated those shoes. Ultimately, we resigned ourselves to the fact that we could do nothing without a voice and an ear to hear it.

To place the mail order for shoes, our feet were traced on a piece of paper. Then a catalog order for twice the size was placed. My father's theory of buying shoes was that a child's feet grows, therefore, he never bought shoes that fit or was the correct size. In fact, our feet did grow and I wore shoes too big for me, even if I stuffed them with cotton. It did not matter that cotton-stuffed shoes were uncomfortable. Neither was it relevant that the shoes would lose form and turn up at the toe area because they were too big. The key problem with my father's theory was that the shoes purchased were always cheap shoes and they wore out before our feet grew to fit them. One day, my father's sister came to the house to speak to him about those very large shoes that I was unable to keep on my feet. She said, "I'm tired of looking at my niece with shoes turned up at the toe, saying good morning and good evening."

Service Reaped Rewards

Mother made sure that as an adult, I was active in the community. From time to time, she would call and ask, "What are you doing for other people in need?" One day, I said to her, "Why me? You don't push others." She said, "I'm speaking to you."

I knew she was right, and it was just the nudge I needed to move off the square. I became a volunteer who helped to improve my community. Later I volunteered and served on Union's Human Rights Committee of Local 480 of radio and TV corporation.[23] Just by volunteering, I learned so much and traveled the state of New Jersey, fighting for both civil and human rights for all ethnicities. I fought for decent living conditions for migrant workers who came and harvested the seasonal vegetables and fruits. When we visited Camden, Mother prepared food and brought it to the centers for the volunteers. We worked and planned strategy during my time in South Jersey. I served as chairperson of the Local 480 Union Civil Rights Committee of the American Federation of Labor and Congress of Industrial Organizations (AFL-CIO) based at Emerson Radio Corporation (1950s). I met with many statesmen, elected officials such as the governor, mayors, and councilmen throughout the state to address the need for action against discriminatory labor practices and racial inequality.

We helped people to understand why they should vote and why they should support the elected officials. We made sure the elected officials who supported our causes were supported. I walked the streets many nights, passing out postcards saying, "I support you." They signed it, gave it back to me, and I mailed it. Mother called each week, checking up on me. The more she called, it appeared, the busier I got. I became the president of my block. We raised funds for the fire victims left homeless. I was a member of my community citizen advisory board. As a citizen advisory member, I met city officials and shared the community's concerns and reported back to the community. I organized the community to March on Trenton, New Jersey's state capitol. The elected officials did not even come out to greet us. During my years of activism, I became a lobbyist in Trenton, supported and participated in the March on Washington in 1964, and served on the local National Association for the Advancement of Colored People's Education Committee (NAACP). All the while, I maintained a personal spiritual life and a balanced family focus. Dr. Martin L. King Jr. met with our Union's Civil Rights Committees of AFL-CIO from New Jersey and New York City during a regional conference at Rutgers University.[24] The conference goals were to: (a) Combat offshore outsourcing, responsible for massive job losses. (b)

Fight racial segregation so we would have equal access to stores and public facilities.

Many years later, I invited Mother to my local NAACP recognition banquet.[25] I was honored and received an award. I was following her advice to contribute to society's solutions and not be the problem. She read the words on the award that said, "She feeds the hungry." She looked at me and said, "The hungry feeding the hungry."

I am happy to say Mother witnessed many of the honors I received. It was her faith and love for me that helped nurture me to make a difference in my New Jersey community. I never gave up; after retirement, I continued and helped with the shelters for the homeless. I did so until I relocated with my daughter to Maryland. I am now engaged in my local Maryland community. Mother didn't just encourage her own children; she motivated all who would listen to her. Mother's conversations stirred me to reach out to help others. My parents encouraged me to help make a better life for my family and those around me. My parents' discipline seemed very hard at times, but it was needed to help me to become who I am today.

Family "BLACK POT" stored in my garage.

New Mickle Baptist Church 1917-2017.

Rosie top left at AFL/CIO meeting with Martin
Luther King in Jersey City, NJ.

Rosie bottom right at Civil Rights Committee for Local 4 AFL/CIO.

Chapter 5

Sibling 6
Two-Parent Household Profile

The Preface

My brothers, sisters, and I grew up in a stable two-parent environment (stability in this context is a reference to longevity.) Our parents got married in 1929 when my mother was nineteen and my father was twenty-three years old.[26] They stayed together through thick and thin, for fifty-five years, until my mother passed. Their marriage produced fourteen children over a twenty-four-year span of time. From my insider's view, Mom and Daddy could not have been more different from one another. As a vested observer and participant in their family ties, their relationship could not be judged as highly qualitative. They rarely argued in front of us; but based on my experience, it was not a blissful bond. My intent here is not to analyze my parents' union but rather to share the interactions they had with us. As in any familial relationship, each of my parents played a role. I would characterize my mother as a loving generous caregiver, dependable provider, coach, cheerleader, and problem solver. She was easy to talk with; and at various points in our lives, each of us found it insightful when we sought her advice. She was dear to me. I remember her warmly. Daddy was a man of very few words. I have no positive analogies to adequately describe the role he played in our family. His actions resounded loudly though. Perhaps as I share my story below, you will more fully appreciate the shadow he casted and the unforgettable impact he had on us.

The Explosion of Children

I, Mary Frances, am the sixth child born to Frank Leonard and Rosie Jackson, in the Childs' quarters (Fitzgerald farm) in Omaha, Georgia. Mom and Daddy were farmers who both rented land and sharecropped at some point in their farm lives. Our three main farm crops were cotton, peanuts, and corn. Only the cotton and peanuts were planted, harvested, and sold as the primary commercial cash crop. The corn was kept for personal use and as food for a small number of farm animals we owned. As a farmer, Daddy rented land and farmed it as an independent farmer. Corn was sold and sometimes bartered to purchase food from the general store as our needs arose. On the Childs' quarters, we also grew products for our own consumption such as sweet potatoes, white potatoes, leafy vegetables, peas, beans, okra, tomatoes, watermelons, and a few other staples.

My grandpa, on Daddy's side of the family also lived in the Childs' quarters, along with my two aunts and an uncle. During this childhood stage, my life was good. We had plenty of food to eat and lived close to Grandpa whom I loved dearly, and he loved his grandchildren. He spent lots of quality time with us. He often took us to Sunday school, and, even though money was hard to come by, he gave each one of us a penny to put in the Sunday school collections and the church offerings.

Grandpa was a righteous and religious person. He was well-respected by all who knew him. We gained many life experiences when we were with him. One Saturday morning, Grandpa took us up to the big house, the residence of the landowner, Flora Childs.[27] He was collecting his pay for the work he had done for her. As was the custom, blacks did not go to the front door of a white person's house. There were only a few exceptions to this custom. Grandpa took us to the backdoor and called for Mrs. Flora. When she came to the backdoor, she threw two dimes to Grandpa that landed on the brick walkway in front of him. Grandpa picked them up and put them in his overalls' front pocket and we left. Even as a child, I knew it was not polite to throw anything to a person; and that experience, among many others, revealed to me what it meant to be black living in the South.

When she spoke to Grandpa, Mrs. Flora called him Uncle Frank. She really confused me by doing that. As I got older, I learned more of the social norms of the South. Young black men or women were called by their given Christian name. Whites never used a prefix of Mr., Mrs., or Ms. when they called our name. As an older person, whites reverted to calling us uncle or aunt, a term of debasement. The Childs' had a granddaughter named Jenny who lived in Tennessee; and upon visiting her grandmother, Mrs. Flora Childs asked Mom to let Josephine and me play with Jenny. We played with Jenny on the front steps, but we were not allowed to enter the Childs' house. Jenny, Josephine, and I called each by our first names until she turned about twelve years old. According to the customs of the day, thereafter, we had to address her as Ms. Jenny, although she may have been younger than either of us.

Years later, Jenny's grandmother, Mrs. Flora Childs, became ill. She was bedridden and suffered pain for several years. We could hear her crying out throughout the quarters, begging God to ease her pain. One day, she sent for Grandpa to pray for her. As you may recall, Mrs. Flora Childs was the woman who threw the dimes to Grandpa on the brick walkway. Despite her previous actions, he accepted the invitation to go to the big house to pray for Mrs. Flora and was let in by her daughter, Josephine. Grandpa said, when he dropped on his knees to pray for Mrs. Flora, he was unable to speak to the Lord on her behalf. Our black neighbors, far and near, rejoiced upon hearing this news. They suggested it was God's punishment to Mrs. Flora for her cruel deeds and mistreatment of us and blacks in general.

Activities for socializing during my youth were very limited. There was a public movie theater. Blacks and whites had separate entrances and sat in different sections. Blacks had to sit in the balcony called the buzzard's nest. Buzzards are vultures and are black bird scavengers that eat scraps and the remains of dead animals that other more ferocious animals may have left behind. As I reflect, the designation of buzzard's nest said it all about what the Southern ruling white class thought of blacks.

The church was the center of black life, both socially and spiritually. All our activities involved the church. There were church-sponsored fish fries. The women of the church got together, pan-fried large quantities of fish, and sandwiched pieces of it between two slices of white bread and sold it for a fee. Another activity was selling boxed suppers with chicken, potato salad, collard greens, cake, and a slice of white (light) bread. The purpose of each of these activities was to raise money for the church. I was so happy one day as Daddy bought home a boxed supper. It was a treat that he did not often provide. If ever we asked Daddy for money or anything, he would say, "I not got no money." While he did not have much, he had some. In my child's eye, he always had money to buy tobacco. He always had money to treat a female churchgoer to a fish sandwich during the church-sponsored fish fries. In our household, Daddy was an authoritarian and a man of few words; but in public, he joked and laughed and was downright friendly. He seemed to be the life of the party.

We did not have electricity when we lived in the quarters. One day, Daddy purchased a battery-operated Silvertone radio from Sears and Roebuck. The radio was always near a window. To obtain reception, Daddy strung the antenna out the window and attached it to a pole. The children were not allowed to touch it. Daddy used the radio only for his entertainment. It was not shared. He listened to boxing matches, especially Joe Lewis; baseball, especially the Dodgers; the baseball game of the week; Amos and Andy; the news; spirituals on Sunday morning; and a few other shows or events. When the radio was on, we had to be very quiet so Daddy's focus on the radio broadcast would not be disturbed.

We stayed on the Childs' quarters until 1947. Then we moved to a place we called over the creek to the Carter's place. It was approximately ten miles from the Childs' place and across a creek. The Childs' place, the Sawyer' place, and the Bradley Perkins' place were adjoining places. When we moved to the Carter's place, we thought we had arrived. The house had three bedrooms, a front and back porch with doors to access them, and a side door. The only thing that was missing was electricity and indoor plumbing. Instead of drawing water from a well, as we previously had done, we had a pump located outside the fenced-in yard. There was a red barn across the road from the house and a chicken coop in the rear of the house and nests for chickens to lay eggs. We had animals: several mules, milk cows, pigs, and a lot of land for farming. Living there was a fun time and we enjoyed it beyond words to describe it. There was a cave that we played in. We loved to roam the woods, seeking to snack on the varied and plentiful wild fruits that grew there.

Other than farming, there were very few nonfarming jobs. However, as the economy grew after WWII, a few jobs were created in timber harvesting. So in 1947, my oldest brother, Billy, got a job working for Brit Alexander at his sawmill. Billy was fourteen years old. He labored for long hours. However, much to his dismay, he was not allowed to pick up his own paycheck. Billy watched enviously as other young men such as our neighbor James Booth picked up their own checks. They had earned the money and could spend it as they and their parents saw fit, but Billy had no say in what to do with his pay. Billy was kind-spirited. If given a chance, he would have certainly shared and helped the family with expenses; however, Daddy interceded and picked up Billy's check from Brit's sawmill. Daddy was not the type of person who would explain his actions, so he never discussed what he did with Billy's money.

Billy quietly seethed about the way Daddy treated him. He looked for ways to leave Georgia and get away from home. One day, our Aunt Mary Peterson, by way of marriage to Mom's brother, George, visited us. She lived in Camden, New Jersey. Billy pleaded with Aunt Mary to allow him to go live with her. He needed separation and relief from Daddy's domineering influence. Several months after she returned to Camden, she sent for Billy. Billy went to visit her and did not return to Omaha again until eight years and four babies later.

I guess I was in a fog and not very attentive when I was a child because when I was nine years old, on June 3, 1948, I was awakened to the cry of another baby, sibling 11. I did not even know my mother was pregnant. To my surprise, I was introduced to another brother. This one was named Otis David, the eleventh child of Frank and Rosie Jackson. I did not know the lady who arrived at our place several weeks earlier was a midwife; neither did I know that midwives delivered babies. She was called Aunt Lucie. I hated her because she was mean. She chewed and spit out a lot of tobacco. One day, she threatened to spit tobacco into our eyes. She kept us out of our house and made us play in the backyard. After having a baby, it was customary for mothers to stay in bed for nine days. During Mom's stay in bed, Aunt Lucie cooked and watched over us. Daddy never expended his energy to do housework or to take care of us.

After a while Rosie (Rose), our sister, sibling 2, returned temporarily from Jersey City, New Jersey, and spared us from Aunt Lucie. She began to take care of us while Mom fully recuperated. She took over and performed the motherly role. Since it was summer, we harvested fruits and vegetables and Rose canned them so we had food for the winter months.

Rose made sure that we performed our chores. We swept the yard, gathered eggs from the chickens, and handwashed diapers. The diapers were colored rags, made from old sheets and pillow cases. Those diapers were nasty. There were no such conveniences as disposable diapers during this time. There were many reasons why we never wanted to see another baby in our household. One main reason was surely that we hated handwashing the poop out of those diapers. It was a despicable task. It was just an awful time for me. I secretly resented Mom having more babies. On December 31, 1949, Mary Lou, sibling 12, was born two months premature.

I was ten years old, and I was given more chores. Josephine, Geneva, and I were assigned the task of washing for the entire family. The chore of washing was an entire day's affair. We often had to miss school to complete the task. We had to pump water from a well and fill a huge black pot over a fire to heat the water (Aunt Byne kept that black water pot for us, and when Grover moved to Stone Mountain, Georgia, she told him about it. He now has the pot in his garage). We sorted the clothes and boiled the like-colored clothes in the black pot. Then we washed, rinsed, wrung out, and hung the clothes on a line to sun-dry. The process of washing and drying clothes was a completely outdoor affair. Such responsibilities were life on a farm for a child during that time. We always had work to do. There was housework, fieldwork, schoolwork, and going to church which, due to its frequency, felt like work as well.

We worked in the fields at planting and harvesting times and anytime in between those two events. Farm work was never completed. It could never be put off for a later day. If one had animals, they had to be cared for and fed daily. Crops planted in the fields had to be cultivated at specific intervals or the crop's yield would suffer.

Farming was very hard work. In Omaha, Georgia, the heat was unbearable. Picking cotton from sunup until sundown was physical punishment as we dealt with the painful aspects of harvesting. Cotton picking was no picnic. One had to bend over to pick the cotton from the buds. The cotton had to be deposited in bags. To move to the next cottonbush, I had to pull the weighted bag of cotton along. Along the rows of cotton, one got continuously stuck and scratched. The whole process took a great deal of endurance.

During the summer months, vegetables and fruits were plentiful, especially watermelons. We worked for every meal we ate. We harvested and processed fresh vegetables. The peas were shelled. The beans were plucked. Corn was pulled from its stalk and the kernels from its husk. To prepare for the off-season, Mom canned many of our fruits and vegetables to ensure that we always had food available. We did not eat a whole lot of meat. We had fresh meat usually in late fall, after harvest, when families slaughtered an animal. Most of our meat was canned, cured by smoking it, or salted down for later use.

During the time we lived across the creek, Mom developed tooth issues from having kids. She stayed in bed for days in agony from her aching teeth. She sent us out into the woods to look for a plant called rabbit tobacco, used as a homegrown cure for many ailments. Mom took dried rabbit tobacco leaves, rolled joints, and smoked them to relieve the toothache (it was the only time I ever witnessed Mom smoke anything). Daddy never offered to take Mom to a dentist or any other medical facility for treatment. He had a gold crown-capped tooth in his mouth and no such teeth issues. The rabbit tobacco only provided Mom temporary relief. She finally wrote to her sister Aunt Mae in Jersey City, asked for money, and got the infected teeth abstracted.

The Unexpected Transition

Early in the morning on January 4, 1951, before we went to school, a huge truck with the name of Singer Company on it drove into our yard.[28] It backed up to our barn. To our dismay, the driver and his passenger loaded every animal we owned onto the truck. We later learned that they took the stock to settle a $1,500-debt for the purchase of seed, fertilizer, and for cash expended to produce the crops for the year 1950. The statement on the bill of sale included the following:

> My entire crop of cotton, hay, cottonseed, peanuts, corn, peas and beans now planted and to be planted.
> Two mules—weighing about 1,000 lbs. each one was seven years old and the other one about twelve years old
> Two mixed breeds "milch" cows, weighing 700 lbs. each, one heifer calf about three months old
> Two mixed breed brood sows weighing about 250 lbs. each, one barrow hog weighing 300 lbs.
> Six Shoats (weaned pigs) weighing about 50 lbs. each
> One Nissan, (a two-horse wagon) and other plowing tools and equipment.

Before the truck drove off, Daddy was handed the original promissory note he signed on January 6, 1950, marked "PAID IN FULL," signed and dated, "1/4/51-The Singer Co. by SS Singer."

That day, we lost animals that had been in our family for a very long time. They were part of our family. We had named many of them. The seven-year-old mare mule was named Cora. The twelve-year-old was named Shirley. Both mules had been with us longer than I could remember. The cows were named Alice and Red. I had milked those cows many times before I went to school. We poured the milk into a churn to settle. Cream would come to the top and we churned it until we had butter. The butter was then removed. We had buttermilk from those cows that we drank and cooked with to make our weekly ration of biscuits and corn bread.

Upon returning home from school, the Singer Company had taken all we owned. Daddy told us that we had to move since we had nothing to farm with or any money to purchase anything. He said we would move to the Bradley Perkins' place and sharecrop for a year. Charles, then sixteen, was the oldest male in the house, followed by Josephine, age thirteen, and me, Mamie, age eleven. We would lead our sharecropping efforts on the Bradley Perkins farm. At the end of 1951, Daddy said we would move to New Jersey. He said he would go to New Jersey to work and we would follow shortly thereafter. We got excited about that news. Charles, Mom, Josephine, and I worked those fields. I was anxiously looking forward to leaving for New Jersey very soon. Every two weeks, Mom worked at the Bradley Perkins' house and was paid $5 for a day's work. I worked in the fields. During lunch, I left the fields to serve lunch at the Bradley Perkins' house, washed dishes, then went back to the fields and worked until the end of the day. For my domestic services, I earned 50¢ a day and was paid $5 every two weeks. I was able to eat while I cleaned up the kitchen. The money really helped Mom with expenses.

After working all year, it was time to settle with Bradley Perkins. The principle of sharecropping was to share the profits 50-50 after expenses were paid. Daddy was still in New Jersey, preparing a way for us to move there. So Mom and our sister Rose, who had come to visit, stood at the mailstop to meet the postwoman. They were awaiting the sharecropping settlement check so they could pay bills and go Christmas shopping. Upon the postwoman's arrival, to our surprise, Daddy popped out of the vehicle. In those days, in our rural community, if you were known to the mailperson and needed a ride, you were welcomed to ride along. There was no public transportation and there were long distances to travel. Without explanation, Daddy had returned home. He confiscated our sharecropper's settlement check. He took the money, although he had not worked a day in the fields all year. Charles had worked all year long, with nothing to show for it, and was very disappointed and frustrated by this event.

In May 1951, on a Friday evening, Charles quit working early from the fields to attend the prom at Omaha Training School. Someone told Bradley that Charles left the fields before dusk, so he dropped by our house. Mom said she expected him to come by based on her knowledge and years of experience of living among and working for whites. Bradley asked for Charles, and her response was, "What do you want with him?" He said that he wanted to talk with Charles. Mom said to Bradley, "You can talk to me. I'm his mother."

Of course, he knew that. It had gotten back to mom that Bradley wanted to beat Charles for leaving the fields early to prepare for the prom that evening. So she pressed him on why he wanted to see Charles. Then she told him, "Mr. Bradley, you can talk to me, I'm his mother. You never had a black child by a black woman, if you did, the child wouldn't be a black child." Flushed, Bradley took off in his truck and stopped at Grandpa's place. Bradley said, "Uncle Frank, you need to go talk with Rosie, she is crazy."

Mom was not afraid of anyone and would say exactly what needed to be said without any show of anger. After that encounter, Mom said she went to the fields late—on purpose—the next day. She wanted to discourage Bradley from any inclinations he had to discipline Charles. He got the message. After the initial encounter, Bradley went out of his way to acknowledge and greet Mom as he passed each day.

In 1951, Charles was the oldest sibling living at home. He decided that was his last year of farming, then Charles left for the bright lights of Jersey City. After he left home, the oldest siblings living with our parents were females: Josephine, age fourteen; me, age thirteen; and Geneva, age eleven. So in 1952, Daddy returned to farming by himself as the only plow-hand in the family. He no longer had much beyond the very basic tools to cultivate the farmland. I do not know where he got the credit and/or money to restart his efforts, unless he used the money Charles and Mom earned sharecropping on the Bradley Perkins place. He never shared those insights with us. However, I do know that from then on, he worked us for long hours, allotting us little personal time while we cultivated other people's land for little pay.

On June 10, 1951, Annie, sibling 13, was born. Annie was the only one of the fourteen siblings born in a hospital. Annie was a very beautiful baby, and Daddy named her Lizzie Mae. Mom was bedridden after Annie was born. Rose again came back to Omaha to take care of the children while Mom recovered. Rose did not like the name Lizzie Mae and expressed her dislike of the name, saying Lizzie Mae was an old name for such a beautiful baby and told Mom to name the beautiful baby Annie Louise. She also suggested she be nicknamed Dolly.

In January of 1952, we moved to the Sawyer's place. The excitement of moving to New Jersey had faded and was dissipating like a vapor. Daddy was not a stable provider. To supplement our income, Mom, Josephine, and I worked on other people's farms to earn money. Even though we did the work, Daddy collected the money and we never saw any of it nor learned what became of it. However, there was not much we could say or do as fourteen and thirteen-year-old girls. At the end of 1952, we were on the road again; this time, back to the Childs' quarters, the place we moved from in 1947. This time, the old house had been renovated and it had electricity. It still didn't measure up to the home across the creek that was about ten miles away. Early in 1953, after the move, Mom made an announcement. She said that she had hoed her last row of cotton and peanuts. Going forward, she would work full-time in Fort Benning doing domestic work. Daddy would be responsible for his own farming.

No-Frill Life

Everything was scarce to us during these times. To save on soap, water, and clothes, we generally bathed weekly. During the summer, however, to manage the Georgia heat, we sometimes took baths more often. Taking a bath gave us clean bodies, but it rarely provided enduring comfort from the sweltering heat and humidity.

To stay cool, at night, we sat on the porch. This usually resulted in a relaxed gathering of neighbors and friends along the porch that stretched across the front of our tiny house. As we attempted to enjoy the little bit of pleasantry that the Georgia sundown provided, we created other challenges. We tried to fight off the droves of mosquitos that crept closer to us in the stale night air by burning rags in an old iron pot that sat nearby. The smoke was stifling and did little to ward off the mosquitoes and it certainly made it very difficult to breathe.

As we sat outside, there must have been something in the smoke because the adult men began to tell us terrifying, petrifying, and spine-chilling ghost stories or lies as we called them. There were many, but several that I recall most are about headless horses that met people only at night on their way to church and a light always traveled and appeared without a person carrying it. Another one was about travelers passing an empty house at night. The travelers heard chains rattling inside the old empty house. Finally in a version of the latter tale, travelers passed cemeteries at night and heard frightening noises. The lies of headless horses, chains, and bright lights frightened the dickens out of us children. The tales had lasting affects because long after they were told, we were too frightened to pass empty houses and cemeteries during the night, whether we were alone or with other playmates. Oftentimes we were unable to sleep and certainly did not want to go outside in the dark. Doing so caused trepidation and fear as the hairs rose up on the back of my neck.

Our two-bedroom house at the Childs' quarters did not have a bathroom. In fact, we lived in three different houses when I was a child and none of them ever had an indoor bathroom. We always had outhouses. This was a small wooden single-room facility just outside of the house with a bench across the back and a hole cut in the center that served as the toilet seat and no running water. It had a single purpose: to be the place to dispose of our body waste. We did not have toilet paper. To clean our bottoms, among other things, we used newspaper, corncobs, and, the corn husk from ears of corn. Sometimes we used tree leaves for the same purpose. The corn by-products were also an alternative food source for our cows and mules.

When we had guests for dinner, they ate well. If the main meal was chicken, the guests were given the leg, wing, thigh, and breast portions. We ate what was left over, for example, the liver, gizzard, feet, neck, and back. To this day, I do not eat those parts of the chicken. Similarly the better parts of the pig were fed to visitors. Just like the leftover parts of the chicken, I do not eat pork products that include pig feet, intestines, liver, or any other non-appetizing parts of a pig.

We moved four times but lived in just three different places that I can remember while we lived in Omaha. The reason black folks, like us, moved around to work as sharecroppers from one plantation to another was because we thought if one plantation owner had treated us badly, the next plantation owner would treat us better. What we never knew or thought about was all the white landowners—putting it mildly—were playing the keys on the same piano. We were no longer self-sufficient with our own tools or farm stock. Since my older siblings had left home, we had fewer family members available to labor in the fields, and the returns from sharecropping grew more and more meager.

To my complete disappointment, Josephine told me, in the fall of 1953, that Mom was pregnant again. I was so sad I began to cry. I declared that Mom was not pregnant. She said she was not going to have any more children. Well, whether by surprise or planned, in February 1954, Evelyn Christine, nicknamed Chris, was sibling 14. I got to name the fourteenth child born to my parents. That privilege was likely a tactic by Mom to pacify me.

The Rebellion

Josephine and Geneva resented that Mom was having babies seemly every year. They refused to do anything to help around the house. I have never been confrontational, so I picked up the slack and did their work. Whatever Mom told me to do, I did it.

Josephine and Geneva were feeling overburdened, having to care for our younger siblings and constrained by Daddy who would not allow us to go anyplace. He prohibited us from going to school's socials or anyplace with friends. No matter the request, his answer to us was always no, laced with a bit of profanity. After being tired of Daddy rejecting every request we made for personal freedom or enjoyment, Josephine gave me an ultimatum. "Either you rebel against Daddy's directives about going to the dance or I'll beat your behind." She spoke firmly, "The choice is yours, who do you want the whipping from, Daddy or me? This is what we are going to do. We will take extra clothes and store them outside and when we return home, we will put them on. When Daddy beats us for disobeying him, we will be prepared."

We did exactly as Josephine planned. We went to the dance. We put on the extra clothes before we came into the house. As expected, Daddy beat us. But we had padded ourselves with extra layers of clothing and thus shielded ourselves from some of the pain causing blows. In the end, we had a great time at the dance and had no regrets for our actions.

After Christine's birth, Mom went back to Fort Benning to work. Her pay was our only reliable source of income for food. The fruits of our labor from farming were not being realized. Mom bought ground beef and V8 juice. We cooked the ground beef and mixed it with V8 juice as a meat sauce. I remember this mixture— distastefully. I don't like V8 juice today because of it. Daddy's financial and familial contributions were slim, and I also remember that he was the first to sit at the table and usually was the first to eat. It often bothered me that he also demanded that we cook him loaves of bread to accompany his meals.

Each day, before Mom left for work, she would designate one of us to stay home with the smaller kids. That meant that one of us had to take turns staying home from school. Josephine's attitude was becoming increasingly rebellious. She let it be known to Geneva and me that she was not staying home with the children. Geneva followed Josephine's lead and refused to miss school. On their day to stay home to watch our younger siblings, they got dressed, got on the bus, and left me to tend to them. I was afraid to tell Mom what Josephine and Geneva were doing. I was sure that if I did, they would beat me. Daddy was around, but his caring for the kids never seemed to be a consideration.

Early Education in Georgia

My early education in Georgia was provided in a church.[29] We had only one teacher. She taught all grade levels and did not have a college degree. The eleventh grade was the highest level of achievement in our community until the early 1950s. My sister Rose completed high school in Lumpkin, Georgia, as a boarding student. Rose's expenses for living or boarding at school were paid by Mom and Daddy.

Each day, before we walked to school, we got up and did our chores which were: feeding the chickens, gathering eggs, spending about thirty minutes churning the milk for butter, milking the cows, feeding the hogs, and finally, walking to meet up with other black children walking to school. Upon reaching school, we made a fire in the potbelly stove, sang a song, and saluted the American flag and recited the Pledge of Allegiance to our country. The teacher was dedicated and tried to help the students to reach their highest scholastic potential. On Friday, each student had to either recite a poem or a Bible verse. After our Friday's program, we cleaned up and left the building clean and ready for Sunday morning services.

The white children rode the yellow school bus, even the poor white family that lived next door to us. As the bus passed us, it was standard practice for the children to open the windows, spit out the windows at us, and call us the N-word.

Before building the consolidated schools, we attended Omaha Training School that ended at the eleventh grade.[30] The Omaha school for blacks was regionalized and consolidated with the elementary school. Later a junior high and high school were built in Lumpkin, Georgia, for us. We were given a used school bus several years before the Lumpkin schools opened. Our bus driver was named Mr. Moses Cracker. A new bus was purchased for the white students to be transported to their schools. So we were assigned their hand-me-down bus for use after the junior and high schools opened for black students. Now we had two buses; one bus was for transporting students to Omaha Elementary and Junior High, and the second bus, driven by Cousin James Williams, transported the upper-class students some twenty miles away to Lumpkin High School. Even though we had new buildings, we were relegated to the old used yellow school buses, no longer good enough to use for the white students.

Family Life

While living over the creek, George, our brother and sibling 10, swallowed some chemical that was called potash, meaning lye. It was a poisonous and toxic chemical substance. The chemical contained acid used around the farm and not meant for human consumption. The chemical burned his tongue and the skin it touched. Since there were no internal symptoms (injuries), we assumed he spit it out immediately after his intake. Yet our family was very distraught, hysterical, distressed, troubled, and worried that George would die from the intake of poison. Although his mouth may have been in a bit of discomfort, he never showed it. George was three years old and seemed completely unaware of the danger. He laughed and played while the family stressed out.

As we grew older, the dream of moving to New Jersey seemed distant. Daddy continued to farm and make all sorts of promises. One such promise involved Mr. Aaron Walton. In 1954, Mr. Aaron Walton, who had grown too old to farm, offered Daddy the opportunity to farm his land for a split of the profits earned. Daddy came to us because he needed bodies to chop the cotton and harvest both the cotton and peanut crops. He said that he and Grover (who was eleven years old) would handle the plowing and planting. He offered and promised us—Josephine, Geneva, and me—that if we worked the land, he would give us the profits from Mr. Walton's farm. So we worked the land on both farms, our rented land, and Mr. Walton's land. We did not want to do it, but we were sucked in by the idea of earning money. We would be able to spend it on things that we wanted to buy. We were so excited and dreamed of the school clothes we would be able to buy. We could have discretionary things like all the other children in our school.

After the harvest, Mr. Walton came by and settled the financial matters with Daddy. He gave him our share of the profits. I had fretted all summer about an Ivy League skirt and the Penny loafers that I wanted. I dreamed of going to school with my new outfits to make the girls jealous and to show them that I too could afford new outfits. We worked two farms, and it was difficult but worth it for the rewards promised. Upon seeing Mr. Walton, we were elated and could not wait for Daddy to come and give us our earnings. He came in with the money, but Daddy never made any mention of it. Nor did he offer us a dime. This incident exhausted any remaining tolerance Josephine had for staying home. She became even more determined to leave the Omaha area and get away from Daddy!

Josephine plotted to get as far away from Daddy's empty promises as she could possibly go. A lifeline was thrown to her in 1955. Billy returned to Georgia for a visit. It had been eight years since he had left at the age of fourteen. He was now twenty-two years old. In desperation, Josephine expressed her frustrations to Billy. He understood and was sympathetic since he too had been a victim of Daddy's money-handling tactics and empty promises. Billy bought Josephine a one-way Greyhound bus ticket to New Jersey. She would now be free of Daddy's oversight. To get Mom's buy-in, Billy promised that Josephine would finish high school.

Gleefully Josephine left Omaha in 1955 when she was seventeen years old. She had grown tired of taking care of our younger siblings, picking cotton, and harvesting peanuts. She was the fifth child to leave home and settle in New Jersey. Josephine settled in Jersey City with her oldest sisters, Leola and Rose. By now, they both had married and had young children. Ironically Josephine began to experience her newfound freedom from Daddy by babysitting for them during the day as they worked. In reverence to Mom, she enrolled in Snyder High night school to pursue her high school diploma.

Josephine's departure left me (sixteen years old at the time), Geneva, and Grover home to take over the farming responsibilities.

George and the other children were still too young to toil in the fields. Geneva really had a tough time, working in the sun. She could not take the heat or the hot sun barreling down on her. She would grow weak and tired and was unable to function. Daddy was not one to do too much farm work himself, but he wanted to make sure it got done. So like overseers in times past, to impress upon us the need to complete the fieldwork, he would go into the woods and get a switch and try to beat Geneva into compliance. In empathy for her situation, I would help Geneva with the fieldwork to minimize her beatings. This way of handling the situation brought my desire to be a caretaker to the forefront. Daddy's way of trying to increase productivity levels riled Geneva and brought out her sense of defiance.

Grover was now the oldest male still at home. Although the trigger for it was unclear, Daddy started taking his aggression out on Grover. Grover never let his thoughts betray him. He did not talk much about what he was thinking or feeling. If he wanted to do something, he did it. If he did not want to do it, he did not do it. One afternoon, while standing near the woodpile, Daddy commanded Grover to chop some wood. Grover's immediate response must not have been quick enough for Daddy. He picked up a stick, and Grover started to run. Daddy threw the stick with his full force and hit Grover on his left eye socket bone. Only God prevented that stick from piercing his eye and blinding him. Grover bears that scar to this day. Mom was not pleased.

Country Religion Practices

In our rural Omaha community, black churches set a specific time of the year when one could join the church or give the preacher your hand to accept Christ and be baptized. This time was called the revival meeting time. The revival period occurred the first two weeks in August. During this time, there was praying and singing only. The following week, after more praying and singing, the preachers ended with the second Sunday services and baptisms.

During the revival meeting, sinners called nonchurch members had to pray to seek God. They were not allowed to mingle with other family members. If the person/sinner ate or interacted with family members or others during that two-week time frame prior to the revival meeting and then joined the church, their actions were deemed not genuine. They were judged as not having religion and could not be baptized. If a person was judged not ready, they had to wait until the following year to try again.

When I was eleven, nearing twelve years old, Mom said, "Jesus was baptized at the age of twelve." Her statement was a hint that perhaps it was time for me to seek Jesus and to be baptized. As the revival commenced, I started to seek Jesus. During revival time, evening meals were prepared early. The family sat around and talked until it was time to eat, which was roughly around 4:00 p.m., before heading to the evening church services. The sinner was me who was requesting the baptism. My normal routine was too fast, so I needed to pray and seek Jesus in solitude. I stayed in the rear of our house, meaning to pray, as the family sat on the front porch; still hunger pangs and the smell of the food got the best of me. Out of weakness, I gave into temptation, snuck in the house through the backdoor, and ate as much food as I could. I was sure that no one would ever find out that food was missing. I was mostly concerned that my mom would not find out.

At the appropriate time during the service, I gave the preacher my hand and joined the church. Daddy was a chairman of the deacon board, not at our church but another church in the community. After we returned from church, Daddy asked me if I was sure and ready to join the church. He asked if God had forgiven my sins. Based on his interrogation, I sensed that he knew that I had eaten. He decided I was not ready to join the church. He said it was wrong for me to give the preacher my hand. He judged me as not having religion and informed me that I would not be baptized that year.

Daddy proclaimed that I could not go back to the mourner's bench until the next year. The mourner's bench was the front row of the church. Some sat there for a short time and others sat there for many years. No matter what one's actions were, the adults had to be convinced by those actions and words that you had religion and were saved. I sat on the mourner's bench for three years and decided the third time was going to be my charm. So I isolated myself a week before the next revival meeting. I did not eat. I did not talk with anyone. I was going to come off the mourner's bench this time. The second night of the revival, I came off the bench, singing what I thought they wanted to hear. I jumped up, singing the lyrics, "I got Jesus all in my soul, and I'm not ashamed to tell the world everywhere I go." That did it! I was baptized the second Sunday of September 1951.

Aside from my failed revival experiences, in my early childhood, I was known for getting religion when inclement weather hit our area. When real dark clouds arose and thunder roared while lightning flashed across our small community, it made me very frightened. Adults used to claim that such storms came out of Saint Peter's mud hole and they were very dangerous. At the young age of eleven or twelve, I had no clue what they meant but experiencing violent atmospheric conditions scared me beyond belief. Those storms frightened me, and with each one, I got more religion. I can honestly say they scared the hell out of me.

During the second week of August, the guest minister preached and church members had the responsibility for housing and feeding them. As years passed, the size of our family grew. We did not have the resources, space, or food required to support guests, but the pastor and his guest preacher for the revival services often stayed with us. Despite our significant family size, we sacrificed sleeping quarters, food, and so much more.

The only fresh meat we had available was alive and running around in our yard. To prepare a meal for the preachers, we, as children, had to run the chicken down, catch it, kill it, and pluck its feathers. Mom cooked it and other side dishes to make a complete meal. Then we watched the preachers eat it. Even if we killed four chickens, there wasn't enough to feed a family our size. When preachers visited, we only got to smell the food cooking. We only got to eat the leftovers, less appetizing parts, for instance, chicken feet, necks, gizzards, liver, and backs. The best parts of the chicken were finger-licking good for the preacher. We licked our fingers from the homemade gravy Mom made for us. She took the grease from the fried chicken and browned some flour, added water, seasoned it with salt, pepper, and chicken parts consisted of the neck, back, feet, gizzards, and liver. We poured it over rice or just sopped it with a biscuit.

Billy once shared his childhood experience when the preacher visited for dinner. While the ministers ate their meal, he made them comfortable by generating a small breeze, and to ward off flies, one of the children would be required to stand nearby and fan them. Fanning was necessary because we did not have the protection of a screened-in porch nor was there electricity. On one day, Billy fanned. The preachers ate heartily until only a single piece of chicken remained. As one of the preachers reached for the last piece of chicken, Billy, who was hungry, reached for it at the same time. Billy had, no doubt, watched them eat as his mouth watered and his stomach growled for that last piece of chicken. Being a child and doing what Billy did to the preacher got him the worse whipping of his life.

Northern Migration of Jacksons

In 1957, Rose returned to Georgia from New Jersey for a visit. It was decided then that after I graduated from high school in June 1958, the entire family would relocate to Camden, New Jersey. Daddy left again ahead of us to find employment to pave the way for our move. We had yearned for this to occur. This time, it was really going to happen. We were leaving Omaha for good.

After the decision was made that we would migrate to Camden, Mom's initial excitement wore off and she became somewhat apprehensive. I was the oldest of the nine children still left at home. Recognizing that reality, Mom started to verbalize some of her concerns. She talked to me about needing my help once we moved. She would say things like, "I need you to help me raise these children. I don't want my children getting in trouble and going to jail. I can't trust your father to help me."

I would be finished with high school by the time we moved. My siblings would still be attending classes. They would automatically be demoted one grade. It seemed that being put back a year in school occurred to all students from Southern states when they relocated to New Jersey. The reasoning behind this was that the Southern school systems were thought to be inferior to New Jersey's educational system. Thus after enrollment, it would take a year longer for students from the South to graduate.

On Saturday, May 7, 1958, I attended a community baseball game in Omaha. On my way home, I checked with the post office to see if any mail had been sent to us. It was not unusual to intercept the mail at the post office before the mail carrier left to make their mail deliveries.[31] I checked, and we did have a significant delivery.[32] Anxiously I hitched a ride home on the back of a pickup truck owned by Philip Crayton, our neighbor, who married our second cousin. He let me off at Grandpa's place. Mom was relaxing on the swing on Grandpa's porch.

I kept the mail delivery a secret from Mom until we got to our place about a quarter mile away. I handed Mom the envelope with the money order she had been anticipating for months. Upon opening the mail, she screamed so loud that Grandpa and my aunts, Lute and Alsie, came running, thinking that something devastating had happened. Wasting absolutely no time, and because she was so excited, the next day, Mom went to church and said goodbye to relatives and friends.

Our trip was financed by a loan from the Seaboard Loan Company office in Jersey City, New Jersey. Josephine signed for the loan, and Mom's sister Mary (Mae) cosigned it.

We were leaving Omaha for good and would be moving to Camden, New Jersey. Mom and I went to Lumpkin, Georgia, Stewart County's county seat, and cashed the money orders that following Monday. We went to the courthouse, obtained each child's birth certificate, Mom's marriage license, and any other documents we would need after we relocated to Camden.

Mom went shopping to buy food for our trip. We packed our meager belongings in cardboard boxes, pillowcases, sheets, and cheap suitcases. Then on Tuesday, June 10, 1958, which was Annie's birthday, Philip Crayton took Mom and the nine of us, who were still at home, to Columbus, Georgia, to board an 11:00 a.m. Greyhound bus for Philadelphia, Pennsylvania.[33] Philadelphia was a big city, just across the bridge from Camden which would be our destination.

On the bus, Mom and I sat on the same row of seats and shared the task of holding Chris. Chris was four years old. She could travel for free, at her age, if she did not occupy a seat. Geneva shared a seat with Mary Lou and Annie, Grover, George, Bob, and Otis sat on the long back seat that extended across the back of the bus. Because it was prior to the mid-'60s in the South, we all sat in the back of the bus. Segregation rules did not allow blacks to ride in the front of public transportation. Grover, who always marched to his own beat, acted as if he didn't know us until it was time to eat the chicken Mom had packed for us.

It took a very strong will, survival instinct, and faith to do the same thing, day after day for seemingly a lifetime, and not see a positive change or have anything to show for it. This was exactly my experience for the first eighteen years of my life and many more for my mom and Daddy. To take their minds off the pain, boredom, and despair, older people sang Negro spirituals. Some told humorous stories and still others just hummed the blues. My favorite thing to do was hum the blues. I liked artists such as Johnny Lee Hooker, B. B. King, Muddy Waters, Jimmy Smith, and many, many others; but my very favorite song, while working in the hot fields, was "Trouble in Mind" written (1926) and recorded by Richard M. Jones. The lyrics are in the public domain. A few lines of the lyrics include, "Trouble in mind, babe, I'm blue, but I won't be blue always. Yes, the sun gonna shine, in my backdoor someday."

I gained energy from those words. I visualized places I had only dreamed about. I thought about what they were like, and I thought I might even go to those places someday. I was energized just from the thought that someday, life would be different for me and the hot Georgia field would only be a blip in my rearview mirror.

There were many days when I felt very low in spirit. Then I would hear a train whistle passing in the distance. That whistle made me long to go where the train was going. I guess I was not alone because some of the older people used to sing out, "A train going my way, this just ain't my day." To this day, I love to travel by train. It brings back the wistfulness I had as a child after hearing the trains whistle as they passed and left me behind.

Settling In

After our thirty-hour trip, we arrived at the Greyhound bus terminal in Philadelphia. Billy and his friend John Saunders picked us up and drove us to a three-story house at 310 Stevens Street. It was situated in downtown Camden. It was a row house, connected on both sides by other houses. It was on a busy street with lots of people and cars about. Inside we had no beds, so we had to sleep on the floor until Billy could purchase beds and mattresses. The next morning, I began to explore our new surroundings. I climbed the stairs to the third floor, and as I looked out the window, I noticed a huge hole in the shabby building we called our new home. To acclimate us to city living, Billy laid down the rules that we, as country children, must now obey to stay out of trouble. The main rule was that we could sit on the house stoop or steps but we could not go to or stand on the corner. He let us know that only people who are up to no good stood on the corners.

I had envisioned Camden to be much different than it was. In my mind's eye, it was going to be pristine. From my first impression, it was far from sparkling clean. I looked out and saw trash on the sidewalks as though it had been carelessly strewn about. It seemed that there was filthiness all around. I thought in Omaha, we did not have much, but we kept what we had clean. We swept the yard so that it was neat, and we burned our trash rather than let it lay about. What a culture shock Camden had turned out to be. We stayed at Stevens Street from June 10, 1958, until November 1958. By Thanksgiving of 1958, we had moved on South Seventh Street.

Shortly after we arrived, Rose came to Camden and convinced Mom to let me go back to Jersey City with her. She was going to help me find a job. I went to Jersey City and got a factory job producing sacks for pork rolls, but that didn't work out well. I did not have money to send home to Mom to help with expenditures. After

I spent one year in Jersey City, Mom called and said, "Billy and I are coming to pick you up, pack your bags. I need your help in raising these children." So I was ready when Mom and Billy arrived to take me back to Camden. By then, we had moved and settled into a residence at 812 Florence Street where I remained until I got married.

Money was short until I found a job. The tension was noticeable in our house. My brother George begged me not to let us get on welfare. Daddy didn't mind the idea of getting public assistance. He was very open to the idea of receiving a handout. At Christmas time, someone told Daddy to go and ask the committee person, one who was connected to the political establishment, for help. He did, and on Christmas Eve, a committee person knocked on our front door. He had a food-basket offering and some toys for us. Mom listened to him patiently, and smiling gratefully, she told him he could leave the food but he was to keep the toys.

Mom never wanted to accept handouts. She used to drill into each of us the need to earn what we received. She would make us hold out our hands and she would say, "See your hands! They are made to work. Do not accept handouts. Work and take care of yourself. You can help those in need, but God blessed you with health and strength. So use your talents and skills to take care of yourself and never look for or accept a handout from others."

I never had to look for a job on my own before I returned to Camden. I had no discernable skills. Apart from farming, the only work I had ever done in Georgia was domestic work. Mom occasionally took me with her to Fort Benning to clean an army officer's home when the family needed help, and in Jersey City, Rose helped me get the pork roll factory job.

A Special Someone

I was fortunate. When I came back to Camden, a good family friend, Ms. Mamie Foster, God bless her soul, helped me get a job in the West Jersey Hospital's laundry. Mom and I were partners again. I took the money I earned and gave it to her to help with my younger siblings. We used it to buy food, pay for the boys' haircuts, and take care of other necessities.

While I worked at West Jersey Hospital, I met Carl Fullard. We dated for two years. During that time, Carl visited and became comfortable with my family. He introduced us to Vienna sausages, bologna, lunchmeat, and Kool-Aid. All my younger sisters and brothers loved him. When Carl visited, he rarely came empty-handed. In the evening, to get some private time with me, Carl gave my siblings each five or ten cents to go to the corner store for hand-dipped ice cream or candy. When they returned, he stayed and watched television with us. Mom enjoyed his company too.

Daddy stayed mostly to himself. At sundown, Daddy went upstairs and dressed for bed. His nightclothes consisted of long johns with a flap that snapped in the back. The snap made it easy to go to the bathroom quickly without disrobing the entire top part of his long johns. I don't know if he had frequent urination problems at that time in his life, but every half-hour or so, Daddy would walk from his room to the bathroom. He walked so that his presence was known, almost deliberate and ominous. Until Carl finally met him, he thought Daddy was a huge person, much like the giant in the *Jack and the Beanstalk* story.

Great Strides

After a two-year courtship with my family, Carl and I got engaged. Mom was happy for me. She gave me her blessing. She took me aside and said, "Mamie, you have been very loyal, and I will help you with your wedding." Shortly before we married in 1962, Grover graduated from high school. After a lot of hard work and effort, he was accepted at Johnson C. Smith University in Charlotte, North Carolina. He was to be the first child in our family to attend college.[34] Mom was so proud of him. She turned to me and said, "I know I promised to help you with your wedding, but Grover is going to college. That takes priority over your wedding. I have got to help him." That was the way Mom was. She always looked to first resolve the most important issues at hand. She focused her problem-solving skills on solving important issues. She did what she thought was important and fair.

I got married in September 1962. While I was on my honeymoon, Grover prepared to leave for college. He needed some basic things to take with him. Carl and I received some sheets, pillows, pillowcases, and towels as wedding gifts. They had been left with Mom pending our return. To send Grover on his way with what he required for college, Mom sorted through our gifts and gave him the sheets and other basic things he needed for college. Mom was very practical. There was not much money available to give him or to buy things for him. So Mom did what was best. She was truthful. When we returned home from our honeymoon, she told us what she had done. What was I supposed to say? Nothing! It was for the greater good.

Grover started a trend in our family by going to Johnson C. Smith University (JCSU). Thereafter, George graduated from high school and went to Rutgers part-time. Ultimately though, he graduated from Hampton University. Mary Lou followed and graduated from Rider College. Otis was accepted and attended Shaw University. He went there for a short time, returned home, and graduated from Glassboro State College. Annie followed Mary Lou and graduated from Rider College as well. Christine, a short while later, the last of the fourteen Jackson children, graduated from Douglas College.

Daddy had a job with the Camden Sanitation Department, but he refused to give the children his tax information so that they could qualify to get student loans and any other financial aid for college. They each had to work around this challenge. Daddy was afraid of debt. He said he did not want to owe anybody. This was mildly interesting because after we got to New Jersey, due to his delinquent payments, we were often without electricity, heat, and phone service. He rarely paid any bills.

Just around the corner from our house, on Ninth Street there was a corner store owned by Mr. and Mrs. Young. In the mid-1960s and 1970s, corner stores were comparable to today's Wawa. Wawa Inc. is a chain of convenience stores combined with gas stations located along the East Coast of the United States. They operate in Pennsylvania, New Jersey, Delaware, Maryland, Virginia, and

Florida. Mr. and Mrs. Young sold luncheon meat, bread, sandwiches, soda, milk, and assorted other convenience products. The owners knew all their customers and their family members. One day, while visiting my mom, I struck up a conversation with Mr. Young. He told me that Daddy told him that his children had finished school. They all had good jobs. Daddy surmised that if each one of them gave him five dollars per week, he would never have to work again. That was Daddy. He was always trying to figure out how he could get money, and consequently, he never seemed to have any money to share with others.

We had been trained by the best. When each of us gained employment, we committed to make Mom comfortable. We did not want her to ever feel threatened again about not having a roof over her head. Grover started paying the property taxes. Otis and the rest of us contributed spending money and became responsible for paying the household bills.

Mom never studied past third grade in Omaha, but she understood the value of education. To Mom's disappointment, although she promised she would complete high school when she came north, Josephine dropped out and never earned her high school diploma. Josephine was capable, but life's other choices got in her way. Seven of us sisters graduated from both high school and college; Josephine was the only sister to not graduate high school. While she did not complete high school, Josephine married and had nine children. She created a close-knit and loving family in New Jersey. Many years later, she and her family settled in Baltimore, Maryland. There she began working at a private school. Over time, she got many promotions and increased responsibilities. At the time she passed away, she was head of food services and well-loved by students and was respected by the school's administration. I add this simply to say that the lack of a high school diploma did not stifle her drive to do well by her own initiative. Three of my six brothers also did not complete high school. Billy and Charles initially worked for other firms, but they ventured out to own small businesses at various points in their lives. Robert (Bob) never earned a high school diploma. He was constrained with learning disabilities and health challenges throughout his short life.

Mom was so excited and beside herself. She had never dreamed that she would have children graduating from college so soon after we had come north. She began to brag to her friends. She just could not imagine that she would have one child to attend college, let alone have six, at the time to graduate. Mom's friends would say they got tired of her bragging, but they began to appreciate where she came from and what she had gone through, and they started to rejoice with her.

Before Chris graduated from high school, I got a job at RCA under the race for the moon project. When the project ended, I was laid off. I was still in my twenties. Carl and I were raising our son, Derrick. I started contemplating going to college. Camden County College (CCC) had just opened. I enrolled in CCC. I thoroughly enjoyed the educational experience there. I made the dean's list my first semester in college. Each semester I attended CCC, I made the dean's list or the president's list. After the two-year CCC curriculum, I earned an associate degree. I transferred to Glassboro State College and graduated from Glassboro State with a GPA of 3.99. I, Mary Fullard, graduated magna cum laude from Glassboro State College in the 1970s with a BA degree in education. I taught school for a while. I went on to do social work for the Camden County Child Care Office. I ran the training office for thirty-five years. We were a resource to childcare professionals, parents, early childhood and public school teachers. This profession suited my caregiver tendencies. I never expected, growing up in Georgia, to achieve the positions and responsibilities that I earned. Life was good. We were never defined by our meager circumstances while living in Omaha, Georgia.[35] I thank God and Mom who never settled for the status quo. She pushed us to want more, to reach for more, and to always work for more. Ultimately my chosen direction was aligned with and influenced by the poem that I have loved since I was a child, "A House by the Side of the Road" by Sam Walter Foss. The last stanza of it reads:

> Let me live in my house by the side of the road
> It's here the race of men go by.

They are good, they are bad, they are weak, they
    are strong,
Wise, foolish—so am I;
Then why should I sit in the scorner's seat,
Or hurl the cynic's ban?
Let me live in my house by the side of the road
And be a friend to man.

Reaching Out

After Grover graduated from Johnson C. Smith University (JCSU), he joined the US Peace Corps and went to Kenya, East Africa. We were all so proud that Grover had graduated, and we bragged about him being in Africa; but everyone could not appreciate Grover's effort to serve others in this way. One day, one of our cousins, Charles Davis Jr., who had moved from Omaha to a Philadelphia suburb, came to Camden for a visit. He asked, "Where is Grover?" When we told him that he was in Kenya his response was, "Couldn't Grover find anything better to do than go to Africa and swing from tree to tree?"

During this time, there was a weekly Tarzan series broadcasting on the television. In it, Tarzan was a man-child character who was raised by apes in Africa. He learned the ways of the apes and jumped from tree to tree as he came to the rescue of someone in distress in each episode of the television series. Our cousin had confused the serious work that Grover was doing in Kenya with the caricature of African life as presented on television.

The first time I noticed weakness in Mom was when George got drafted into the army. The Vietnam War was at its peak. George was the only one of her six boys to serve in the military. Mom was concerned about George going to Vietnam and the possibility of getting killed. She sent me over to Antioch Church to see a psyche—a war fortune-teller—with specific instructions to ask if George would be sent to Vietnam and be killed. Mom had a faith lapse. She allowed Satan to divert her focus from the Word of God. "My help comes from the Lord, who made heaven and earth" (Psalm 121:2, ESV) and "So faith comes from hearing, and hearing through the word of Christ" (Romans 10:17, ESV). That was the very first time I saw her weak and without confidence. "And I am sure of this, that he who began a good work in you will bring it to completion at the day of Jesus Christ" (Philippians 1:6, ESV).

Looking back, Mom experienced a lack of trust and faith in God that many of us go through. This was a real-life experience of breaking under pressure and stress, but God picked Mom up and carried her through the trials and put her back on solid ground and firm footing. Later she said she never believed in fortune-tellers. When Mom took her focus off God, the world crept in and redirected her thoughts and actions that resulted in ungodly deeds. "Rejoice always, pray without ceasing, give thanks in all circumstances; for this is the will of God in Christ Jesus for you" (1 Thessalonians 5:16–18, ESV). George did not go to Vietnam. He was stationed in Germany, and from Europe, he came back to the USA. After his tour of duty, he was discharged. God reassured Mom that He was still God. She needed to trust Him and believe in Him, not some ungodly phony person claiming to be someone with powers.

Mom and I were partners for a very long time. I never lived more than thirty minutes away from her. She liked to travel. From time to time, she would call me up and say, "I'm going to Ohio to visit some cousins." Mom had friends and family all over this country, and when she wanted to travel, we sponsored her trips by way of cruises or whatever mode of transportation she wanted to use. She had a traveling partner—Mrs. Fallings.[36] The two women attended both of Grover's graduations at JCSU and Atlanta University where he earned a Master of Business Administration (MBA) degree. We appreciated Mom for raising and teaching us lasting values. We loved her deeply and wanted to return in kind all that she had done to support and shape us.

Daddy was a homebody and rarely traveled anywhere overnight. From time to time, as Mom traveled, she asked me to check in and make sure Daddy had something to eat. I always did as she asked. I either stopped in with food or I cooked it at 812 Florence Street where I stopped to visit with him frequently.

Final Transitional Move

Mom passed away in her sleep on Sunday, January 20, 1984. She had packed to go visit Grover and his family. They were living in Stone Mountain, Georgia. He sent her a plane ticket, and she was ready to travel.

I was devastated at her surprised death, refused to accept and believe it. I kept saying, "Mom didn't call me." So I kept pretending that she was still alive. In early February of 1984, I had a dream about Mom still living at 812 Florence Street. In the dream, my sister Josephine visited and Mom hugged her but not me. I asked Mom why she had not hugged me too. She gave me a very disapproving look. That dream bothered me. I could not let it go. I mentioned the dream to my husband, Carl. He had been studying dreams. He advised me that Mom was telling me to let her go. By not accepting her death, I was not allowing her to transition and begin her afterlife. I never dreamed about Mom in that way again.

President Jimmy Carter's Kindness

After Mom passed away, I found four sheets of paper in the family Bible. It contained a slither of information about Mom's family history. On one sheet of paper, Mom had written, "I don't know much about my Grandfather Davis' side of the family. My Mother told me that Grandpa Davis' (Addison Davis) niece was married to Bishop Johnson and they lived in Plains, GA." This tucked away trinket of information provided by Mom gave me enough of a lead to trace some of our ancestors to their slave owners and the war between the Creek Indians and the Georgia Militia in 1836 in Roanoke, Georgia.

Over the years, I combed databases for Bishop Johnson without success. I researched alphabetically each county in Georgia, looking for information about Bishop Johnson, a distant relative. Then in the fall of 2011, on a Saturday evening, I hit pay dirt upon searching Webster County on Google.

On the Webster County homepage, it read:

> Education in Webster County has progressed from numerous one-room segregated schools to today's modern multiracial elementary, middle and high schools. In the late 1920s William Dexter Johnson, the bishop of five Midwestern states in the African Methodist Episcopal Church (AME Church), founded the Johnson Home Industrial School as a private African American college, which later became a grammar and high school.
>
> The school flourished for many years until Johnson's death in 1936. Bishop Johnson, father of composer Hall Johnson, was from the Archery community, near Plains in nearby Sumter County. The 39th U. S. President, Jimmy Carter, has described Johnson as a pioneering Black leader who transformed Carter's life.

On display at the Jimmy Carter Presidential Library in Atlanta is an exhibit of Bishop Johnson with the quote from President Carter.[37] "Except for my own parents, the people who most deeply affected my early life were Bishop Johnson, Rachel Clark, my Uncle Buddy, Julia Coleman, and Willis Wright. Two of them were White."[38]

President Carter also stated in his book, *Jimmy Carter: An Hour Before Daylight Memories of a Rural Boyhood,* published by Simon & Schuster, (2011):

> Even before I was an adult and able to understand the difficulty of overcoming racial barriers, I looked on Bishop Johnson as an extraordinary example of success in life. He had come from a tiny rural place, set his sights high, obtained a good education, and then risen to the top of his chosen profession. Of no less importance to me,

he retained his close ties with Archery and the people who lived there. I still go by his relatively modest grave on occasion and wonder how much my own ambitions were kindled by these early impressions.

According to the Historic Markers Across Georgia website, a historical marker is a plaque or sign erected at historically significant locations, facilities, or buildings. There are "Historic Markers Across Georgia. There is a marker located at Archery on Bishop Johnson's Circle and one on Old Plains Highway in honor of Bishop Johnson that reads, "This rural community of Archery, established in 1800's, consisted of a train stop, houses of railroad employees, the St. Mark African Methodist Episcopal (AME) Church, a school of Black youth, and a store.[39] The community was named for Sublime Order of Archery, a relief organization of the A.M.E. Church that assisted the southern Black families. Two permanent White families, the Watsons and the Carters, lived here. Edward Herman Watson was the Seaboard Railroad section foreman and James Early Carter, Sr., was the father of Jimmy Carter, 39th President of the United States who spent his youth here. The other 25 families were African-American."

William Decker Johnson, Bishop of the A.M.E. Church, became the most prominent person in Archery.[40] He came here with the purpose of establishing a school for Black youth lacking the resources for an Education. The Johnson Home Industrial College opened its doors in 1912 and offered technical classes aiding students in obtaining jobs. This school offered male and female students primary, high school, collegiate, and vocational classes. Bishop Johnson's efforts for the cause of education had many faithful supporters who helped the school to flourish. Bishop Johnson is buried in the St. Mark A. M.E. Church cemetery.

During my exploration of Bishop Johnson, I learned that he had a son, Hall Johnson. Hall's mother and grandmother had been slaves. He learned to sing and appreciate Negro spirituals from both. Hall taught himself how to play the violin and became a noted violinist, composer, director, and arranger. Throughout Hall's career, he took pride in preserving spirituals as they had been performed during slavery times.[41]

HONOREE

ROSALIE BOYLES

Rosalie Boyles, nee Jackson is the wife of Chester Boyles, Jr., and the mother of three children: Sharon, Chester and Seresa.

She was born under the sign of Libra, the scale of justice. Rose has spent most of her life using the scale as a springboard for all of her humanitarian deeds.

Integrity and the thoughts of the heart are her yardstick in her dealings with fellow human beings and their rights, for the rights of humans to such an extent that she's know as a "Crusader" in the areas of equal human rights.

Rose is a quiet woman - so much so that one hardly knows she is around - but when a distress signal is sent out, there is confidence and self-mastery. If ever there was an example of one following the "Commandments of Christ" to "feed the hungry, clothe the poor and heal the sick," it is Rose.

She served for many years as chairman of Emerson Radio & T.V Company's Human - Rights Committee enabling many of the employees and their children to further and/or better their education.

Rosalie is twice president emeritas of her block association, where she worked tirelessly to raise funds for fire victims left homeless. Her voluntary work in the community is unending. She is a past member of the Citizen Advisory Board of Jersey City. She is the organizer of the Stevens Avenue Block Assn. Some of her other accomplishments are aiding the needy with baskets of food, formed a committee to insure removal of abandoned houses for the safety of the neighborhood children. Other activities: Bingo Committee (St. Paul's R. C. Church) Mother's Guild, Lobbyist in Trenton, March on Trenton, March on Washington, Poor People's March and member of the N.A.A.C.P Education Committee.

Enjoy yourselves, enjoy your lives by living them to the fullest for God, and one another. We thank him for our presence here tonight.

Honoree for serve and commitment to her community.

Dad's & Mom's Marriage License dated 9-15-29 (copy issued 6-16-58).

The Fitzgerald (Childs) Residence we called it 'The Big House.

BILL OF SALE—PERSONAL PROPERTY   Gammage Print Shop, Americus, Ga.

GEORGIA, Stewart County.

In order to secure the payment of one   certain promissory note , payable to the order of The Singer Co. SINGER A SINGER, and signed by   Frank L. Jackson, Jr.

and all other notes, as well as any renewals of such note or notes, drafts, or other indebtedness, which the grantor may now owe or may hereafter owe grantee, whether as maker, surety or endorser, not to exceed $ 1500.00 before the surrender and cancellation of this conveyance, I the said grantor do hereby sell, alien and convey to the grantee, the   the following described property, to-wit:

> One black mare mule, weight 1000 lbs., 7 years old.
> One black mare mule, weight 1000 lbs., 12 years old.
>
> Two mixed breed milch cows, average weight about 700 lbs.
> One heifer calf about three months old.
>
> Two mixed breed brood sows, weight 250 lbs. each.
> One black barrow hog weighting about 300 lbs.
> Six shoats, weight about 50 lbs. each.
> One Nisson make two horse wagon. All other plow tools,
> plows, and other equipments owned by me.
>
> My entire crop of Cotton, hay, cottonseed, peanuts,
> corn, peas, and beans now planted and to be planted
> on the Carter place on Lots of land 249 and 250
> in the 22nd district of Stewart County Georgia.
>
> This bill of sale given for the purchase of seed,
> fertilizer and for cash to produce the above crops
> for the year 1950.

Paid in full 1/4/51 the Singer Co.

The Singer Co.

TO HAVE AND TO HOLD unto the said SINGER A SINGER, its successors and assigns, as security as aforesaid in Fee Simple forever.

I warrant the title of said property against the lawful claims of all persons whomsoever and here and now declare that there are no other liens or encumbrances of any kind whatsoever against said property, but that I own the same in my own right unconditionally.

There shall be no abatement of said debt on account of the death, loss, damage or destruction of said property by fire, theft or otherwise, whether due to my fault or not, I assuming all risk thereof.

In the event I should default in the payment of any of the indebtedness above described when due, SINGER A SINGER, its successors or any person to whom the note hereby secured may be transferred, is authorized and empowered to immediately take charge of all of the above described property, sell the same at the prevailing market price at private sale or advertise the same to be sold either on the premises where located, or

before the courthouse door in   Lumpkin   after three or ten days' notice, which ad-

Loan for farming seeds & supplies that led us into sharecropping.

Mount Moriah Baptist, our home church and first public school.

Omaha Training School, the county's first Provided
school for Blacks in Ohaha, now a private home.

Omaha Old Post Office.

Omaha Post Office today.

Philip Crayton drove us to the Greyhound Bus Station on 6-10-19583

JCSU's Biddle Hall administration buildingfrom the west gate.

Omaha establish in 1891 as posted sign states.

Mom & Mrs. Fallings, Mom's traveling partner.

Bishop Johnson pictured & exhibited at President
Jimmy Carter Presidential Library.

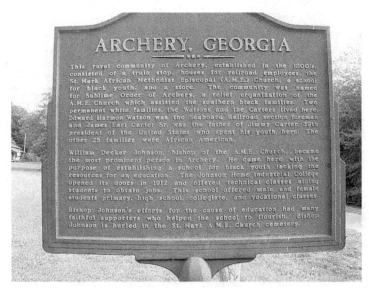

Road marker recognizing Bishop Johnson contribution
and significant to te people and area.

St. Mark A.M.E Church in Plains, GA (Archery)
foundered and pastored by Bishop Johnson.

The old Singer Company building located in Lumpkin,
across from the Stewart County Courthouse.

Chapter 6

Sibling 7
Geneva's Memories

How We Lived

My story will be a bit scattered. It's the way my mind works. I remember snippets and snapshots in time. For instance, I recall that my parents bought our shoes from *Sears & Roebuck* and *Spiegel* catalogues. My parents, especially Dad, were experts on measuring our feet. He placed our feet on a piece of white paper. Then he drew the outline of our foot and sent it off to the catalogue stores. Almost assuredly, the shoes would come back too small.

Growing up in rural Georgia, one thing we did, habitually, every Sunday we attended Sunday school. We went every Sunday—rain or shine. We walked two miles on a dusty and sometimes wet and sloshy red clay backroad to church. When the road was wet, the red clay would clump together and gummy up our shoes. Sunday school was a priority for all the children in our house. My grandfather also attended. I remember clearly that he unsparingly gave each of us a penny to put in the collection plate. Grandpa was a very quiet person, well-respected, and loved by all his grandchildren. He passed at ninety years of age, six years after we moved to Camden, New Jersey.

Once a year, if we were lucky, my parents ordered clothes for us from a catalogue called *Waterfield's*. It was a company based out of Chicago, Illinois. For Easter, I got my first pair of black patent leather shoes with a small (not pump) heel on them. I was so excited! I wanted to put my beautiful new shoes on full display. Easter morning could not come fast enough. I went to church, and I recited my speech that I had learned especially for the occasion. All the children were expected to either recite a poem, a piece of scripture, or deliver something they memorized solely to praise the fact that it was resurrection Sunday.

As it turned out, the shoes were made of cheap see-through plastic. As my luck would have it, it rained that Easter. The wet red clay dirt road was not my friend. Completely covered with rain and wet dirt, my shoes were destroyed before I returned home from church. One of my aunts saw my shoes and said to me, "Why do you have those shoes on? You can't walk in them." To my dismay, she was right. My shoes, about which I had been so proud, were torn up before the sun went down.

This was very unusual, but one Easter, everyone went to church, except for me. I didn't have any new shoes to wear and why I could stay home escapes my memory. I am sure that it had absolutely nothing to do with not having anything new to wear. My parents did not seem to be troubled by those kinds of things so imagine living in the woods with no other human nearby while everyone else is at church. I can't remember how I kept busy, except I always had work to do.

There were plenty of pecan trees where we lived. The owner, Mrs. Flora Childs, didn't want any of us renters picking the pecans up for consumption. She'd rather the pigs eat them than us harvesting them for consumption. Despite her meanness, when the high winds came and blew them to the ground, we would go and pick some of them off the ground for eating. My mother sent a few of them to our relatives in the north. This is a tradition my brother Grover, who lives in Georgia, still upholds. He buys them and sell as a fund-raiser for his college class endowment. Though he does not pick them off the ground or trees. There were various kinds of pecans, soft-shell and hard. We loved the soft-shell because they cracked easily. We had lots of fun on the farm when there wasn't hard work to do.

We lived in a house closest to the big house, the residence of Flora Childs. She had lots of chickens. She had chickens of all colors, white-feathered and brown-speckled and black. As a child, I would clean her chicken coop for money. She would give me five or ten cents to clean five coops. After I got paid, I would spend the money on candy in her store where she sold small items. I would get home and be so excited about the candy. Then I would have to share with all my sisters and brothers.

One day, Flora Childs got sick and sent word for my grandfather to come pray for her. In those days, whites would call on an old godly black man to pray for them when they were old, got sick, and afraid. She was so mean that my grandfather said, when he got on his knees to pray for her, he couldn't. Grandpa was a religious man, but he said the words wouldn't come out of his mouth. We never forgot that story. When I grew up and later reflected on that situation, it was curious. Regardless of status, whites in the South treated black men with no respect at all. Yet they valued their prayers.

As the seventh of fourteen children, life was not easy for me growing up in the Southwest Georgia farming community called Omaha.[42] I had difficulties handling the scorching heat working in the fields. The farming community of Omaha was a very small rural town and nothing of consequence was located there. It was situated on the banks of the Chattahoochee River, approximately thirty miles south of Columbus, Georgia, and twenty-three miles north of Eufaula, Alabama. All three towns are located on the banks of the Chattahoochee. It was estimated that 250 families lived in the radius of Omaha.

I personally hated farm life. The sun was too hot, and I felt I could never do any worthwhile work. In fact, most days, I sat under a shade tree. Consequently I was always in trouble with my father during harvest season. Picking cotton and shaking peanuts were no joke. Every day I went to the field, I got hollered at. I was about seven or eight years old, and I knew this was not the life for me.

In those days, one began work around 5:00 a.m. Before school, we milked the cows and took them to the pasture to graze for the day. After school, we went to the pasture, got the cows, and put them in the barn. The next day, the whole process started all over again for seven days a week. We also raised our own chickens and hogs. Occasionally Mom planned our holiday meals weeks—and sometimes months—in advance. If chicken meat was going to be the meat of choice, especially a mature rooster or older hen, she had us catch it and put the chicken in a coop. It was then fed corn and cornmeal only. This was a way of cleansing the chicken.

Being Chased

Adults were good at killing the chickens. One day, I had to kill a chicken. I put a string around its neck and chopped its head off with an axe as most children did. Most of the time, it took three children; one held the chicken by the feet, placed it on the chopping block that was used to cut wood. Another sibling took a stick and held the neck flat on the chopping block, and the third sibling chopped the chicken's head off. Many times, the holder, in fear, would let go of the chicken before the process was completed. The chicken would scurry off. Then we had to chase it down. This took a considerable amount of time. The chicken, with its body separated from the head, hopped around for a period as we watched. If the chicken, with its head removed, hopped in the direction of either one of us, we ran in fear. It was a terribly frightening experience. So we learned from our mistakes. We tied the chicken's feet with a string before we went through the above process. If the chicken was let go, we could retrieve it easy. Mom killed chickens in a more merciful manner. She simply held the chicken with her left arm and would break the chicken's neck with her right hand. There was no blood, but there was still our emotional trauma of seeing a chicken jump around with its head dangling while still attached to the body.

I was horrible at working in the fields, so when my sister Annie was born, my mother said, "Geneva, I need you to babysit her." The rest of the family went to the fields, and I took care of Annie, Otis, and Mary Lou who were very young at the time. I was alone for hours with my younger siblings. I was afraid; however, I had to do what my parents told me to do. Annie was such a beautiful baby. I treated her like she was a doll. She had curly hair, and I loved to comb it. I bathed her, and she never cried.

When Annie became sick with pneumonia, I was blamed for not properly taking care of her. I was nine years old. I didn't know anything about diagnosing sickness and I had no idea what caused Annie to get sick, and I certainly didn't know how to cure her illness. The accusation hurt me deeply. I never told anyone how much that really bothered me.

My dad and I always had disagreements. He was a very controlling person. Before doing things I was directed to do, I often asked questions. He never liked to answer my or any of his children's questions.

He seemed to resent the audacity that any of us would even query him. Honestly, I think it was a genetic Jackson trait. My recall is that Daddy's sisters never warmed to questions, particularly from children. It seemed to be taken as a personal affront to have a conversation with a child, let alone answer questions posed by one. Anyway one day, after a disagreement with my father, I went to school and planned not to ever return home. I got off the bus at my friend's house instead. My friend's family never knew why I wanted to spend the night. I stayed for two nights. I didn't plan to return home ever. Mom wrote me a note and sent it to school by my older sister Mamie. Mom said if I came home, Dad would not beat me. So I begrudgingly returned.

Mamie was the next oldest child to me. She always obeyed the rules but not me. If I didn't like something, you knew it. My attitude, though not outwardly expressed, was that children can think as well as adults. I resisted saying that aloud because I did not want to get whipped. When I got older and had my daughter, Dad told her that I was a horrible person as a young child.

I loved playing and roaming in the woods and climbing trees. I would follow a stream for miles. That was quite a time for me. One day, while climbing a tree, I saw a snake looking up at me. I leaped from that tree and never went back to that tree in the woods again.

My mother had a first cousin who didn't have children. He and his wife would come get me and take me to their home in Columbus, Georgia. Those times were enjoyable.

We moved to New Jersey when I was fifteen years old on June 10, 1958. It was Annie's birthday. I completed high school in Camden. All my siblings, except Christine who migrated to Camden from Omaha that day, graduated from Camden High School. Grover, George, Otis, Mary Lou, and Annie attended and graduated from Camden High School. Christine attended and graduated from Camden Cathedral Academy. Bob (Robert) did not complete secondary school due to medical and learning disability issues. Both Billy and Charles saw no benefits or rewards to working as a farm hand. They quit school and moved to New Jersey without ever returning to school. They were owners and operators of their own small businesses at the time they passed away.

My brother Billy's friend John came to our home every Saturday; and before leaving, he always laughed at my family napping. Someone was napping each time or would take a nap sometime before he left. Growing up in a big family was fun most of the time. When we were young, we entertained ourselves by singing songs, reciting poetry, dancing, or acting out. One of the funny things that I did was to put on a long dress and clean house with a head rag on my head. I looked like Aunt Jemima from the pancake box. Another thing we thought was funny and a bit strange, at the same time, was that Grover slept with a cover over his head in both winter and summer. We never knew why he did that. Perhaps he did it to keep out the light or maybe he did it to be alone.

Of all my siblings growing up, I remember my dearest sister Mary Lou the most. She was a very bright child. She spent much of her pastime reading books; sometimes she read all night long. Each morning, she had a new story to tell us. She had a great imagination. She would tell us how she had traveled to various countries such as Paris, France, and throughout the continent of Africa. Our mother would look at her and crack up laughing, but Mary would say that she was serious. She really meant that she had traveled to various places through reading and visualization.

Dreamer, Traveler, and Educator

Shortly after graduating from high school in the '60s, I got married. My dad did not attend my wedding, Mamie's, nor Mary Lou's. In fact, I don't recall that he attended any of his children's weddings. He said that weddings made him sad. Well, in my case, it was all right because the union did not endure. It did, however, produce my vivacious daughter, Chyrisse. She's married, and I have a wonderful son-in-law, William Patrick Mosely II, and two terrific grandsons, William Patrick III and Julian Derrick.[43]

My sister Mary grew up to be an educator. After college, she married a native of Ghana. They moved to Cleveland, Ohio, and resided in the Shaker Heights section of the city. He was attending graduate school there. Annie, Chris, and I went to visit her there. She gave us a tour of the Cleveland Museum. Then we visited with her friend Kathy in Ann Arbor, Michigan. Kathy had previously worked with Mary. We also went to Canada, and I enjoyed going there and seeing all the beautiful flowers.

Betty, who was my best friend in high school, married a career State Department diplomat. She traveled all over the world. They lived in Abidjan, Ivory Coast, and Haiti for a while. I visited them in both countries. Mary accompanied me on my trip to Haiti. She turned her imaginary childhood escapades of imagining being in faraway lands into a reality when she became an adult. She became a world traveler. Her marriage did not last. Shortly after she divorced, she took a job in Iran and taught English and business education to the Iranians secretaries.[44] After the monarchy of the Shah of Iran was overthrown, there was a great deal of confusion and turmoil in the country. Some Americans were taken as hostages. For several weeks, we were concerned that Mary would not get out safely. She was on the last plane to leave the country before it fell to the Muslim Fundamentalists.

I was invited to go to Istanbul with Mary but was unable to do so because I worked that summer. Admittedly I have always regretted not going. Traveling with Mary Lou was a treat as she was a great tour guide. She was always enthusiastic about the town, museum, store, or whatever she was showing at the time. I went to Boston to visit her and she showed me all aspects of the city. She provided insights that were not commonly known. Whenever we visited her in the DC metro area, she couldn't wait for us to settle. She was always ready to take us on a tour of wherever she resided at the time. She had copiously reviewed the weekend newspaper sections concerning events and things to do. She was excited about showing us what the town had to offer. Sadly Mary is no longer with us, but her spirit is everlasting.

The Pursued Career

After careers in cosmetology, retail, and other jobs, I attended Glassboro State College and graduated with a Bachelor of Arts degree in elementary and early childhood education. I returned several years later and became a certified media specialist. I was offered and accepted a position as a classroom elementary school teacher. I continued my education toward a master's degree; and although I had completed all the classroom requirements, I didn't complete my written thesis. I moved from a classroom teacher after twenty years and continued as a media specialist. I retired from the City of Camden Board of Education in 2013 after thirty-three years in education.

I am a member of the Alpha Kappa Alpha Inc. Sorority. I serve on the scholarship committee, along with being involved with many other people. I have been a member of the Ferry Avenue Methodist Church for many years and serve on various committees including the trustee board, nominating committee, pastor parish relations, and the United Methodist Homes Committee. I was also a Girl Scout leader.

Camden High School where six of the Jackson sibling graduated.

Geneva's daughterChyrisse, Will , Julian and Patrick her grandsons.

Camden woman witness to terror

Teacher tells of Iran stay

By STEVE ROYER
Courier-Post Staff

Rifle and mortar fire roused Mary Jackson from a sound sleep.

Stirring in her bed, she looked out the window and couldn't believe what she saw.

It seemed as if every person on the street had a weapon and was firing on the office building next to her high-rise apartment.

"I was really scared," she said. "I thought to myself 'Is this going to be the end?'"

The scene Miss Jackson witnessed was that of Ayatollah Ruhollah Khomeini's followers fighting for control of the Agriculture Ministry building in downtown Tehran.

"The whole scene was crazy as hell," she said Wednesday from the safety of her parents' South Camden home. "I kept thinking we were going to be next. That they would just keep firing and never stop."

Miss Jackson finally arrived home Monday after a month of trying to leave the battle-torn country. She had been in Iran since September 1977 teaching English to women in an English-speaking school.

In the beginning, life in Iran was pleasant, she said. There was teaching at the school during the day and dancing at the discos at night.

"You could always sense the political tension, but there were no public expressions of violence in Tehran until last fall."

Continued on Page 4—Col. 1

Courier-Post Photo by Steven Geuvein

ROSIE LEE JACKSON gives her daughter, Mary, a welcome-home kiss. Miss Jackson, who taught secretarial skills to Iranian women, says she feared for her life during her last days in the country.

Teacher tells story of Iran stay.

Chapter 7

Unabridged Gap

Way of Life

efore I went to school, if in fact I went to school, I had to take breakfast to Dad and others who worked in the fields. I was seven years old. Black farmers' kids only went to school after they completed their farm chores. So there were many days I never made it to school. Older children worked in the fields. Younger ones took care of their smaller siblings as the family worked in the fields during the spring and fall harvest. By age ten, I was a farm semipro. I just had not quite graduated to the big league of deciding when and what to plant, but I had mastered plowing the fields. After I took breakfast to Dad, who had been out in the fields already, he would tell me to plow while he ate his breakfast. Even with no previous experience, except seeing him break ground, I was expected to do so flawlessly. Little did I know that I was auditioning for the job of a plow-hand and would regret it for years to come! Instead of tilling rows, I plowed whole fields all day until the plowing was completed. We had no tractor. I was behind a mule.

And without divine intervention, sadly that would have been my career, my life's destiny.

As I look back, I don't know whether to consider plowing at that age as a blessing or curse but doing so taught me valuable lessons. Even at the age of ten, I knew there had to be a better way of making a living. I knew nothing about earning a livelihood, but I believed there had to be a better way to earn one. My dad worked hard at farming without success or any tangible benefits for his efforts. I recall having a tireless conversation with me, myself, and I. I asked myself, *Are the Jacksons different from all the other families who farmed?* I asked but myself never answered the question and me just remained stoic and didn't even ponder or query, *Are you talking to me?* I was disquieted by my lack of a response. I just did not see a future in following in my father's footsteps.

During lull times on the farm, the white farmer who moved into the house we vacated would ask my parents if I could play with his boy. How funny! I only played at their house and never in public places. Upon seeing one another in Omaha, we were like strangers who had never met. We were taught to say "yes, sir!" and "no, sir!" even to children younger or not much older than we were. That was how things were in Stewart (Omaha) County, Georgia, in the 1940s and 1950s.

All the crops were harvested by the middle of November. We had harvested enough to feed the few animals—chicken, pigs, mules, and cattle—until the next fall season. Mom canned enough vegetables during the summer to last the entire winter and into the early spring. If we ran short on items such as canned or smoked meats, we killed a chicken usually for Sunday dinner or when we had guests like the preacher. We purchased, as needed, nonperishable foods like floor, grits, rice, and sugar. Our neighbors shared as did we. We cared that every family had enough food to get through to another day. Mom bartered with the mobile store man. She traded goods we produced for goods he sold.

We owned a few cows, but they did not yield enough milk to support the family requirements for butter and milk. We never slaughtered a calf for food and only occasionally slaughtered a pig.

Instead Dad sold the animals for cash to pay bills he created. The family was always in survival mode. We sold almost every animal born into our family instead of building a herd for food and milk. I was never told and was certainly too young to know why, but we were always in a financial crisis mode. After crops were harvested and sold, Dad never had money for simple items like a new pair of shoes, dress pants, socks, or anything else for that matter. If we were lucky, we got one pair of very cheap shoes and an outfit that we wore only on Sundays. The shoes were so cheap that if they got wet, the soles separated from the base of the shoe. To rectify that, so that we would still have shoes to wear, we punched holes through the outer front and side of the shoe base and sole with an icepick. Then we connected the base and sole with haywire to keep the sole from flopping as we walked. It was pitiful. We had little to look forward to as a reward for all the work we did during the year. Mom tried her best to buy each kid something around Easter, if she had worked enough day jobs (as a domestic) at the military base in Fort Benning.

The place we moved to across the creek was a dream come true. It consisted of a very nice house with four rooms. It was an ideal fit for the Jackson family. There were only eight siblings living at home at that time. The single house was surrounded by farmland. The other places we stayed provided cover from the elements and were unfit to be called a house. This house had a barn that was across the dirt road from it. The barn had space for the mules, cows, and pigs. We even had a chicken coop with nests built for the chickens to lay eggs. Another extremely nice addition to the chicken coop was a place for the chickens to safely roost at night, away from the cagey foxes, weasels, and other chicken-eating animals. The entire farmland was in view of the house. It had many conveniences including water. We simply stepped outside and a water pump was steps away, however, our stay at that house lasted only a year. Based on the multiple times we moved, we were homeless long before the phrase was coined. I don't think I ever heard Mom or Dad discuss being homeless, but I felt it. It took almost eight more years before it was seriously addressed.

We were on a physical and spiritual journey. It would take a steady hand and an abundance of faith to get on the right path. My mother was the guidepost and the steady hand. She worked in the fields, cleaned houses for military personnel by day, and met my daddy's needs (desires) at night and boy, did she pray.

Mom never complained about anything such as work, lack of resources, family, or her personal needs. She just did the things necessary to maintain the family. She did not talk about it with the younger siblings, but she was laying the groundwork for a better life for the family. She lived by faith, trusted God to bring about the reality of a new life for our family. She trusted God's Word. She believed He would extend His blessing, grace, and mercy to our family. The precedent for us was biblical, and the example was Joseph, son of Jacob and Rachel, in the book of Genesis. God delivers those who trust and believes in His name. It took faith to start our expedition, vitality to continue it, and confidence, conviction, and assurance to sustain it. We, like Joseph, relied on God's promises. Without His direction, the Jackson clan would not have overcome the challenges presented to us.

Why the Huge Family?

During the '40s and '50s, American family sizes were larger than any other time in our history. American social scientists have analyzed the data contributing to the increase. I'm no sociologist. I cannot give you the macrofactors for why that occurred, but I witnessed the Jackson contribution to this trend as early as 1946. My brother George was born in November of that year. I was just three and a half years old. George was the tenth Jackson sibling.

Now that I am an adult, my reflective evaluation of the Jackson contribution to the increase in family size leading up to and through the period 1940s–1950s follows. My parents birthed a child each month of the year except March and April for the period 1930–1954. Four children were born after George. Perhaps Mom and Daddy were trying to fill in the missing two months' (March and April) gap. Since we shared a bedroom when I was a child, they certainly tried often enough to do so. If they had just held off on striking up the musical bedsprings band, it would have given me a bit longer rest period between rinsing mess out of rags being used as diapers. Try as they might have to fill in those two missing months, the last four offspring were born on months other siblings had already claimed.

The last four siblings were born during months accounted for: February, June, and December. Otis (sibling 11) and Annie (13) infringed on my space of June, and Mary Lou (12) trespassed Mamie's (6) birth space of December. In the latter, scenario they even doubled up on the first name, Mary. To allow for some individuality, they gave them a distinctive middle name. The final opportunity to have births in at least eleven months also came up shy as Christine was born in February. The most significant data point in my analysis is that the first and last siblings' birthdates were the same month of February, just two days and twenty-four years apart.

To complete my evaluation of the Jackson trend analysis, I conclude with the following: five times, my mom birthed a child every other year—1933, 1935, 1941, 1943, 1949, 1951—and four times gave birth every year—1930 and 1931, 1938 and 1939, 1945 and 1946, 1948 and 1949. There was one data anomaly. There was a three-year lapse between the birth of my last siblings: Annie in 1951 and Christine in 1954.

Finally, please note the births by month and date for each sibling below:

- January—Robert, Wednesday
- February—Leola, Saturday, the oldest; and Christine, Saturday, the youngest sister; born the same month, just two days apart and on Saturday
- May—Josephine, Thursday
- June—Otis, Thursday; Annie, Sunday; and Grover, Wednesday
- July—Billy, Thursday
- August—Geneva, Wednesday
- September—Charles, Monday
- October—Rosie, Monday

- November—George, Tuesday
- December—Mary Francis, Sunday; and Mary Lou, Saturday. Both Marys were born a week and ten years apart.

There were no siblings born in the months of March or April. None came into the Jackson clan on a Friday either. Assuming a nine-month pregnancy and birth, except for one who was premature, June through August were great months to mess around as the Ray Charles song says, "Do the mess around." The first two weeks in August were reserved for church prayer and revival meetings. The way I figure, there was still time for my parents to rest. There was little fieldwork to be done because harvesting didn't begin until late September through early November.

Living on a farm, I learned very early that regular sexual activity between husband and wife and between animals usually resulted in an offspring. I was young but not dumb and knew where and how babies were conceived. It didn't come from kissing. I never saw my parents do much of that. We were taught to keep and raise female pigs and cows so when they became mature, we would have them impregnated or serviced by a male animal. Very few farmers kept a male animal for breeding unless they had many animals to be bred. It didn't make economic sense to keep and feed a male animal for breeding purpose for just a few female animals. We would take the female cow and pig to a farmer owning a male bull or hog to have the female serviced or impregnated. We saw domesticated animals having sex daily. It was a way of life.

I didn't mind more animals, but I resented more babies. It was a struggle to feed the children already born, why continue to have more? As a young child, this just didn't seem right! It seemed like babies arrived faster than planting and harvesting crops. Why? What was the purpose? They came and we would have to take care of them. I didn't ask for more babies, so why do I have to take care of them and still do chores? I got tired of chopping wood, feeding hogs, tending the cows and the mule(s). I know that we needed water for drinking, bathing, and cooking. What I did not know was why I had to be the one to go to the well and draw water and carry it almost a half-mile.

Anything to do with diapers turned my stomach and made me sick. The smell of the dirty baby rags was awful.

When it was time to wash clothes, it was my duty to draw water from a seventy-five-feet deep well and put it in a five-gallon tin bucket. I had to fill up two to three washing tubs and a thirty-gallon round black cast-iron pot with water for boiling the clothes to wash them. Then draw water to rinse them. It was a hard job for a child not yet eight. Every child growing up on a farm back then had chores to do. There was very little time to play; and while playing was what every child wanted to do, work always came first. I was not a happy child growing up. I felt that I was entitled to some time on my own.

The one thing my parents thought I was entitled to was being whipped with a leather strap or a switch. I got my share of beatings, whether justified or not. Most of the time, it was because I said what was on my mind. Talking back or mumbling was not condoned. As I grew older and realized that a spanking was coming, I grew smarter and put on extra clothing to soften the impact of the blows. It worked for a while with my mother until she realized I was faking fear and pretending to be crying. She got smarter and decided to wait until I went to bed and caught me with very few clothes on and believe me, I felt the entire impact of the whipping.

One Plus One Doesn't Equal Two

The Jacksons were one of the few families who stayed on the same land our ancestors resided on during and immediately after slavery. We remained on the quarters from 1930–1958, except for three years. We moved off and back onto the Fitzgerald's Plantation (within the quarters) multiple times. The last time we moved back, we lived in the same house where many of my siblings and I were born. During my fourteen years of living in Omaha, we moved five times. We rented land and farmed as an independent farmer, except for one year when we sharecropped. Some of the moves were to the Carter place over the creek, the Perkins' Plantation, and the Sawyer place; then we moved back to the Childs' quarters where our ancestors lived and farmed.[45]

Farmers living and working in Stewart County during the 1930s–1950s shared the misery of the Great Depression, WWII, and the Korean conflict with the rest of the country. I am not sure how much those world events affected the various supplies that we needed but food was in short supply. The family had no money to spend on food, clothes, or anything else for much of my fourteen years there.

The experience for black males in Stewart County seemed to be much worse than for women and very small children. This was typical of many Southern towns. White men respected no black males either young or old. Most blacks knew not to disrespect a white person by talking back to them. We had been taught from an early age to not reveal that we were equal or, in any way, on the same level as whites. Just portraying confidence around a white person could be misconstrued as being disrespectful and could lead to bad results for any black man.

My first cousin's brother-in-law had a confrontation with some white men. Shortly thereafter, he was found floating in a creek with bricks tied to his ankles. He was just sixteen years old. There were several instances of other young black men mysteriously found dead. There were never any investigations of these suspicious deaths. The people who committed those hideous acts were undoubtedly landowners, suppliers, and members of the white families who we saw daily and with whom we worked the fields.

When we lived on Bradley's place, the overseer of the farm once threatened to beat my brother Charles because he stopped work early to attend his school prom. At age sixteen, my brother was self-assured. He was unafraid to stick up for himself. He did not allow anyone to abuse him, not my dad nor anyone else. Several years earlier, my sisters Leola and Rose moved to New Jersey. I am not sure who encouraged Charles to leave Georgia to avoid a confrontation with an overseer, but he left Omaha for Jersey City between late 1951 and early 1952. A black man's life was worthless to the social elites in Stewart County, Georgia, during our young lives and at this period in history.

The Creek referenced as "over the creek" five
miles from the town called Omaha.

Chapter 8

Family, Foundation, Focus, and Future

Mom Remembered

As a career, I was predestined to walk in my father's footsteps—behind a mule. He was a dirt farmer. His father was one. His father and his family had been dirt farmers since slavery. There was nothing that indicated my future would be any different, except Mom's vision. Mom never sat us down and said, "Children, this is my dream for your life." She simply taught us to love one another. She didn't just mean to care about my siblings. She was using a biblical reference to love and serve mankind. She instilled in us to be respectful of others, even if we were disrespected. Mom never preached the Bible to us. She lived it. The Holy Bible was her guidebook on life and eternity.

Upon being asked for money, Mom had a saying, "This ain't 'gimmy' Georgia," meaning nothing will be given. It must be earned. Mom was a very proud and loving mother. She worked and earned the money she was paid and taught each of us to do the same. Her message was never look for a handout. Never depend or expect something for nothing. As farmers, the entire family was assigned chores, worked as laborers in the fields, or took care of younger siblings and cooked. Every child over age six was assigned a job and expected to perform it. There were dire consequences for not doing so.

Mom instructed us to be role models. She demonstrated strong ethics and taught them to us. In every job that she performed, she performed it as if *God* physically stood there watching. Thus as Scripture states, He lives inside each and all believers who accepted His Son, Jesus Christ, as Lord and Savior. She always worked and never expected anything from anyone that had not been earned. She led by examples and never ever did she complain about her condition and situation. Mom rarely got upset about anything. This is not to suggest that she was satisfied with her living. She clearly desired a better standard of living.

She challenged each one of her fourteen children to seek a better and more purposeful and prosperous life. She drilled into us to help each other in good times and in bad. She stressed that we should never forget that someone helped us. So we must go and do likewise. She never stopped helping, whether it was strangers, family members, or friends. Helping others was her motto. My mom's unique life principles demonstrated how a loving family of faith, strength, and unity could achieve dreams beyond anyone's imagination. None of us set out saying Mom wanted me to do this or do that. That was not the case. She led mostly by example. We followed her lead, paid attention. We were mindful of her lessons, and her teachings became rooted into our fabric to strive for a higher status and be of service to one another.

Earlier I may have implied that the Jackson children were to be seen, not heard. This suggests that we had no ability to impact decision-making in our favor. Well, that is not wholly true. The siblings agreed among themselves to never eat the food of certain relatives or friends. Mom totally agreed. This was a voluntary pact which assured you that the agreement was never broken. We never ate or ever wanted to eat at the home of relatives, friends, or associates who dipped snuff or chewed tobacco. Just the thought that a drip could fall into the food during preparation or when it was done turned my stomach. Tobacco-product (snuff) users carried a can, usually a sixteen-ounce one to spit in while they were indoors. Outdoors, they spat on the ground, and everyone would know that a snuff-dipping spitting person had been there and left their signature of brown tobacco markings on the pathways. Two of our aunts (Daddy's sisters) dipped snuff, and when either of them offered food or snacks, we agreed to the two ways to decline. It was appropriate to say either "no thanks" or "I'm not hungry."

Mom didn't smoke, dip snuff, drink, or curse. Well, let me just say, she was not a curser. There was a term she used when she was truly annoyed with something we had done. It took a lot out of her just to say it, but she said it occasionally. It was a simple saying that went something like this, "You don't have a pot to 'piss' in nor a window to throw it out of." Case closed; we knew she was highly upset when that phrase was uttered! This was mild by today's standards; after all, as I think back to those days, I don't recall smokers or snuff users ever running out of their tobacco supply. We had many meatless meals, and my father always had his smoking tobacco (was it a coincidence or my father showing the family where his priorities were?). Both men and women dipped snuff. I don't recall any older women smoking cigarettes. Younger women who had left the community and returned for visits smoked cigarettes. Mostly I saw only men smoking cigarettes. Pre-rolled cigarettes were available, but they were generally cost prohibitive for struggling farmers. So, they bought loose tobacco and cigarette paper and rolled their own cigarettes (just as I had seen in 1950s western movies). From my very young and impressionable perspective, the man's process for creating a cigarette was always the same. Some smokers were quite good. They carefully dumped the tobacco onto the cigarette paper while the paper was held in the left hand. Then they rolled the paper around the tobacco and licked the paper seams to paste the seams together. They would use their right hand to put the tobacco back into their shirt or pants pocket, if right-handed, otherwise the reverse would apply.

The term *snuff* is not too common today. Chewing tobacco is more common and is sometimes used by old-school baseball players instead of pumpkin seeds or bubble gum. The definitions of both snuff and chewing tobacco as defined by Wikipedia follows:

> Dipping tobacco which is a type of snuff is a finely ground or shredded, moistened smokeless tobacco product. It is commonly and idi-

omatically known by various terms, namely as dip and sometimes as rub. Dipping tobacco is used by placing a lump, pinch, or dip of tobacco between one's lip and the gum. The act of using it is called dipping. Typically, before dipping, the act of "packing" is performed, where the user places the "can" in between their thumb and middle finger, then flicks their index finger onto the lid of the can.

Chewing tobacco is a type of smokeless tobacco product consumed by placing a portion of the tobacco between the cheek and gum or upper lip teeth and chewing. Unlike dipping (snuff) tobacco, it is not ground and must be manually crushed with the teeth to release flavor and nicotine. Unwanted juices are then expectorated (spat). In the United States, snuff is less readily available and typically is found only in specialty tobacco shops or online. Nasal snuff is subject to the warning label found on other smokeless tobacco products, "WARNING: This product is not a safe alternative to cigarettes," and the warning must appear on the packaging.

"I Remember Mama" expresses my message about my mom. Shirley Caesar's song brings out my deepest feelings about Mom and her legacy. She departed this life in 1984, yet I remember Mom as if it was yesterday. Mom could ask me for anything and I would find a way to give it to her. She very rarely ever asked for anything. I tear up just thinking about her. She died in her sleep, of a heart attack, in January 1984 after packing to come and spend time with my family and me. My wife had given birth to our youngest son. We asked Mom to come and babysit for us while my wife and I participated in a company recognition event in Phoenix, Arizona. I sent her a plane ticket, and she was so excited for the invitation to come and see her thirty-third grandchild.

As a music lover, a song oftentimes expresses the message better than any words. Shirley Caesar's gospel song entitled "I Remember Mama" expresses my sentiments about my mom.

This is what the song says:

> I remember Mama in a happy way.
> I remember Mama, and the love that she gave
> kneeling by her bed side
> I can still hear Mama say,
> The people are depending on you...
> Don't you let them down
> I remember Mama in a happy way
> We went to school with holes in our shoes
> We didn't have much,
> But the Lord saw us through
> Ma kept the family together
> I remember Mama in a happy way
> She packed our lunch in an old greasy bag
> It might've seemed empty,
> But it was more than others had
> It had a lot of love way down deep inside (yes it
> did)
> And I remember Mama in a happy way
> I remember Mama in a happy way
> Now Mama is sleeping in the bosom of Jesus
> Christ (yeah)
> Somehow, I know she's smiling, she's smiling on
> us right now
> One day I'll see her again, how happy I will be
> (yeah yeah)
> And I remember Mama in a happy way (yeah
> yeah)
> I remember Mama in a happy way
> My brothers and sisters, they're living far apart
> although
> Mama's gone, she's right here in our hearts

We're all gonna pull together and stay in the holy
    place
I remember Mama in a happy way
I remember Mama in a happy way

Early School Experiences

In Stewart (Omaha) County during the 1940s–1950s, school and church for blacks were held in the same building, a black-community church. The positive aspect of that arrangement was that we truly attended neighborhood schools. Almost everything else about that accommodation was third world in nature and was totally unacceptable. We had to gather wood for a potbelly stove, the white students didn't. The textbooks were hand-me-downs from the white schools, often with missing and torn pages. Our teachers had attended college, but they may not all have completed the requirements to earn a college degree. It is very likely that they had no certification to teach. Still in the black schools, the teachers taught all grade levels. So if there were one hundred children eligible for grades 1–8 and two teachers, one would teach grades 1–4 and the other teacher would teach grades 5–8. All the grades for that teacher were in the same classroom together.

President Jimmy Carter, in his book titled *An Hour Before Daylight: Memories of a Rural Boyhood*, wrote:

> Black children in our part of the (Sumter) county had classes in more than a dozen churches or private homes, often with all grades crowded into a single room. They were usually furnished with chairs of various sizes, a blackboard, and textbooks considered too dilapidated for use by White students. The County School Board was strict on mandatory attendance for White children, but quite flexible for Blacks, as if their education above an elementary level was not important.

157

This division of the two races was supposed to meet the US Supreme Court's mandate of separate but equal.

President Jimmy Carter wrote:

> There were gross abuses of the "separate but equal" principles laid down by the U.S. Supreme Court in 1896 that prevailed at the time, but most people chose to ignore them. In the mid-1950s, almost two decades after I left home, the Atlanta newspapers and civil-rights leaders began to challenge these discriminatory practices, but most of the distinguished lawyers and respected religious leaders in the South defended them as justified under the U.S. Constitution and the mandates of God Almighty.

While we stayed at the Fitzgerald's place, Mount Moriah Baptist Church, our family church, was the only school we knew in the early '50s. We went to this site six days a week, Sunday through Friday. During the week, our school was a single-room facility. All of us stayed in the same room, regardless of our age, throughout elementary school. We also met weekly on Sunday at Mount Moriah Church for Bible study; and once a month, on the second Sunday, we attended worship services. Grandpa, deacons, or others who knew the Bible, even Daddy, taught weekly Bible study. Worship service was once a month because we could not afford a resident minister. Mount Moriah had a traveling preacher who covered a forty-mile or so radius to deliver service to similarly situated churches. He came on Saturday to be ready for Sunday service. Church members would board and feed him during his monthly visits.

In 1949, when we moved across the creek or over the creek, we attended yet another school. It was held at Mount Zion Baptist Church, up the road and around the bend from our home. Consistent with our prior experience, we attended a community-based school. The only expense the county incurred for our education was a low teacher salary. The church building was free as were the textbooks.

They were used torn books with missing pages, inherited from the white school.

Mount Zion Baptist Church sat next to a very deep drop-off (abyss), caused by soil erosion, on a road that had an estimated ninety-degree curve away from the abyss. Otherwise the traveler would crash straight into the soil-eroded gorge. It appeared to be expanding toward both the church and the road. The abyss looked to be more than one hundred feet deep and more than 75 yards wide at its mouth and 250 yards in length or further on a downward slope as it disappeared into the woods behind the church building. Today we would probably be concerned about the safety of this location. There was no rail or fence that prevented a careless driver from accidently going overboard. Thank God it never happened. Most of the farmers traveled by wagon pulled by a mule or they walked. Only a handful of people who lived in the area owned vehicles. There was zero chance of a mule going overboard. The mules were very stubborn and could sense danger and would never go close to the abyss.

One year, as I remember, we lived over the creek and attended school in the one-room Mount Zion Baptist Church building. The county school board issued some government surplus goods to schools such as apples, oranges, and orange juice that were delivered at different intervals over time. They gave us the apples seemingly during the fall. They were packed in a bushel bag. The teacher gave us one apple a day and put the rest in the church closet until they were all gone or spoiled. The closet door didn't have a lock, so the contents were easily accessible by intruders or prankish boys. I was barely seven years old. After school and on weekends, the older boys entered the unlocked church, reached into the closet, and helped themselves to the fruit. They got plenty and shared it with all who wanted some. The fragrance of fruit was very tantalizing. We knew it was wrong. We were mischievous. And we could not resist the temptation of biting into one of those delicious apples. Even in a church, we accepted the stolen goods. The devil had a hand in making us do it in as much as our justification was that the fruit was intended for us anyway.

Fast-forward to 1950, all the church schools had been consolidated into Omaha Training School. Black students were given a hand-me-down yellow school bus from the white school. I remember one teacher, Cousin Mattie. She was the wife of Mom's first cousin, Henry. She struck fear in each of us. She punished us on hearsay about things other children told her or for breaking the rules she had established, whether right or wrong. For example, if Cousin Mattie gave a student permission to go to the outhouse for a toilet break and that child did not return based on the time she allocated, that student was punished. It didn't matter the reason. In those days, having a stomach virus, called the rotgut, was a common occurrence due to the types of food we ate. The rotgut produced stomach cramps which sent children running full speed to an outhouse. It could take a while to recover from such cramps; however, it didn't matter, Cousin Mattie would light up that child's backside when he/she returned for staying past the time she had allotted.

I think that Cousin Mattie, our teacher, punished me more than my mom or dad. She didn't accept excuses. Farm children had chores to do before and after school. Time did not always allow for us to spend as much time on our assignments as we needed. If she called on a student to spell a word or do a math problem on the blackboard and the student was unable to do so, that student got punished with her favorite tool—the switch of her choice. If she softened or empathized with you and gave you a grace period during class and you were still not able to perform the task satisfactorily, you really got abused.

Cousin Mattie beat me for writing a note to a girl. The girl was her niece, and the note wasn't even written during class time. I became convinced that Cousin Mattie was judge, jury, and executioner when she caught us communicating with the girls. It was like she tried to ward us off from developing relationships with girls. I don't remember much of what I learned while she taught me, even though I do recall that she was a lay-the-wood-on-the-backside teacher. I did not appreciate her approach to discipline one bit. Nevertheless, I survived physically, unharmed, and I don't think I was affected emotionally either.

Around third or fourth grade, all the black children's classes, previously held in churches, were combined and consolidated into the Omaha Training School, a larger community school. The consolidation of schools required transportation. We were privileged to ride to school in a hand-me-down yellow school bus, passed down to us by the county school system. They had bought new shiny yellow buses for the white school children. The entire time we lived in Stewart County, black schools were never issued one new shiny yellow school bus.

Every day, the new shiny school bus passed our old faded-yellow hand-me-down school bus. The buses were going to different schools in different directions. The shiny new yellow bus transported the whites to the whites-only school. And our old faded well-worn bus transported us to the blacks-only school. Occasionally our old hand-me-down bus had mechanical breakdowns, and although we were stranded on the country roads, in the middle of nowhere, the shiny new school bus rolled on by us as if we weren't even there.

It was not until the federal suit *Brown v. The Board of Education* that we experienced and noticed any change in our education process. The supreme court ruled unanimously that segregating children by race in public schools was "inherently unequal" and violated the Fourteenth Amendment. The establishment was slow to comply with the new law of the land. Blacks in our area continued to be supplied with hand-me-down buses and well-worn books. However, we were finally assigned to an actual place, built and used, for the sole purpose of education. We were elated to get a schoolhouse. Our new schoolhouse was located on land about two miles from Omaha. It was about three miles from where we stayed and less than three miles from the Chattahoochee River which separated Georgia from Alabama.

From early childhood, attending school was a priority for the Jackson siblings. While we were too young to understand the significance of our education, we attended school regularly. We looked forward to the opportunity to go to school. We were not deterred, even if we were sick. Our attitude was that we could either be sick at home or sick at school; such sickness was not transferable, so we made the best of the time. We nourished the opportunity to be schooled regardless of inclement conditions like tremendous downpours of rain. We found ways to stagger our time to perform farm duties during planting and harvest seasons to learn as much as we could. We overcame barriers daily. Perhaps love for school stemmed from Mom and our teachers who instilled in us that no one could take learning away from us once it became ingrained in us. We were energized to learn. Additionally we enjoyed socializing with people, and school was a place to be around people our age.

When we began busing to the consolidated school, a new teacher entered my world, Mr. Martin, or Professor Martin as we called him. He taught grades 5–9, and he impacted my education the most. He challenged me and made learning fun and exciting. He created an atmosphere and an attitude that every student could achieve his/her life's goals by focusing and working toward those goals. Professor Martin knew how to motivate the students.[46] One tactic he used was very effective. He assigned the younger students in the lower grades to do the classwork of those in the higher grades. He used me to do math problems in higher grades. Math was always easier to me than other subjects. It just required me to use basic logic. Professor Martin's psychology was to motivate me and challenge the older students. I cherished the opportunity and studied harder so I would never disappoint him when he called upon me. It also motivated the students in the higher grades not to let the younger students do their class-level work if they couldn't also do it. Both the younger and older students studied a bit more. This accomplished exactly what Professor Martin desired. He was one of the few people I reminisced about after we relocated to New Jersey in the late 1950s.

He was a loving and caring person. He motivated students to believe they could do whatever they set their minds to do, no matter how difficult the task seemed. Professor Martin discovered each student's strength. He used it to motivate them to do things they previously thought were not possible to do. He got students to apply common sense skills they used daily to solve complex problems. He taught and stressed that a person's skin color and background had no impact on one's character, even if his family worked as farmers and possessed no material things. He singled out black people who had achieved greatness and who had done extraordinary tasks and used them as examples for us. He talked about their backgrounds and their successes to prove the point that we could do the same and even surpass their accomplishments. I didn't realize it then, but Mr. Martin was instilling in us many life principles.

One life principle that was hammered into our minds by Professor Martin and my parents was, don't be influenced by troublemakers. Don't ever be brought down to their level. Troublemakers picked fights because they were show-offs and bullies. Mr. Martin called them unmotivated people, not interested in doing better for themselves. Well, during my tenure with Professor Martin, I came to appreciate the meaning of the saying a lesson learned is a lesson earned. The experience will stay with me forever.

As a sixth grader, I got into some big trouble. I was standing in line to board our hand-me-down bus after school. Some of the children began pushing and shoving each other, better known as harmless roughhousing. There was a lot of jockeying for position. It became a bit rowdy. So the principal tried to re-establish order using a strap. In those days, corporal punishment to a child was normal when initiated by black people of authority. This meant that almost any adult in our community, namely parents, teachers, principals, adult neighbors, and adult relatives, could administer discipline. The strap he used was a thick slice of an old heavy rubber pulley belt. It was made of the same material used to make auto tires without the steel wiring. It was firm yet very pliable. As the jostling for position continued, the children pushed me out of the line. My instinct was to try to re-establish my position. So I tried to get back in line. Before I knew it, the principal wacked me across my back with the strap. I was totally stunned, and my immediate reaction was to thrust my books at him, hitting him in the chest. It was an impulsive reaction to the sting of being hit. I reacted to the pain without thinking. Each child stopped moving in their tracks and the world stood still! They were shocked. Everyone seemed traumatized, including the principal and me. There were dire consequences that would result from my action. No one had to tell me—I just knew, and every one of my classmates also knew!

I was afraid to go home. There is an old saying, don't commit a crime if you don't want to do the time. After I arrived home, I sheepishly told Mom what happened at school. I told her before I could return to school, she or Dad had to go see the principal with me. That night, my mom gave me a real thumping. That evening, with the thrashing at school and the whipping from Mom, I was sore all over my body. Now it is sixty-five years later, and I still have a vivid memory of the sharp stinging pain from the principal's blow. I was not a troublemaker, although I had been involved in a few scuffles with children from time to time. Generally, I ran from fights instead of toward them. I learned that day that trouble can find you. When that occurs, the best approach is to assess the situation quickly and respond with a level-headed plan of action to soften the personal impacts or consequences.

Encounter with Bullies

Before leaving Georgia, I completed ninth grade and was promoted to tenth grade. When I registered for class in the Camden City School District, the school district assigned me to repeat ninth grade. This was done without any testing or evaluation. This happened to my sisters and brothers too. So it was the district's standard procedure. Maybe the administrators thought a New Jersey education was one grade level superior to that in Georgia.

Our initial residence was located on Steven Street, near downtown Camden. There was a lot to dislike about living on Steven Street; be that as it may, more than anything else, I hated having to attend Pyne Poynt Junior High School. Although at that time, I had only visited it to register. Let me explain why. Several weeks after we arrived in Camden, I went to the playground to shoot basketball hoops. While I was on the court, some boys my age came to the playground. As I took shots with my basketball, they asked to play as well and I agreed. They chose teams and left me out. They wanted to play with my basketball but not with me. I objected and said if I cannot play, nobody plays. I was unaware they had recently been released from the Jamesburg, New Jersey, reform jail for juveniles.

The lead bully asked me, "Do you want to settle it?"

Being straight from the country, I totally misunderstood and answered, "Yes." He wanted to fight, and I did not understand the magnitude of the answer that I had just uttered. Before I knew it, he hit me multiple times and continued the pounding. As soon as I could escape, I ran to my cousin Irving's house with the bully chasing me. He lived several blocks away. My cousin was born and lived in Camden. More importantly, he was a big person, weighing more than both the bully and me together. We walked back to the playground to get my basketball. He knew the jailbird and his friends and told them to leave me alone. Then I went home to Steven Street several blocks away. That experience revealed a previously undeveloped skill. From that encounter, I discovered that I could run a distance with a bit of speed and endurance. Later when I went to high school, I put my running skills to use in athletic competitions. I joined the track-and-field team. I ran the half-mile and mile in track-and-field and cross-country events.

As school began in Camden in the fall of 1958, the school-aged Jackson children had individual challenges and learning curves. The playground bully haunted me. I reported to Pyne Poynt to enroll. I had never attended a school with more than several hundred students. Pyne Poynt's campus was huge and appeared to be about five times the student capacity of any school I had ever attended. There were no school buses, shiny nor worn, to pick up students from their homes and drop them off at school. The walking distance from our home on Steven Street to school was nearly three miles.

The juveniles and I enrolled for school at the same time. They succeeded in intimidating me each time they saw me. They repeatedly warned that we will "finish this after school." I took their threats seriously, and I took no chances. I delayed leaving school after dismissal. When I was sure everyone had gone, I left for home using indirect routes to avoid them. I took no chances of them hiding out and waiting for me, so I played it safe. I was lonely all the time when I went to Pyne Poynt Junior High School. With no friends,

I was frightened and felt very isolated. None of my siblings or parents knew about my situation. I was determined to work it out by myself. Because I was fearful, I do not think I learned a thing during the entire time I attended Pyne Poynt. Just three months earlier, I had completed ninth grade. Now three months later, I was repeating ninth grade, dealing with distractions that I had never thought about or anticipated. Until my Pyne Poynt nightmare, I looked forward to going to school. School had mostly been a pleasant and stimulating experience for me.

Pyne Poynt was the first and only integrated school that I had ever attended. The bullying from the mean-spirited juveniles made my life miserable. I adapted easily to the other aspects of the school. We sat alphabetically at desks, left to right, in the classroom with perhaps five rows across and six rows deep. This was like my Omaha classroom arrangement. There was no classroom adjustment needed. I felt very comfortable with both students and teachers. Only a few people suggested that my Southern dialect was a bit strange; still they didn't make a big deal about it. Mom taught us that some people may look and talk differently but they were no better or worse than we were. The most obvious difference about Pyne Poynt versus my Omaha schools was that most of the teachers were white. The ethnicity of students appeared to be a balanced mixture of blacks, Jewish, Irish, Italian, Polish, and Latino. Camden had two public junior high schools and two high schools. The Catholic Church offered a junior high and high school option for any ethnicity able to pay. In Georgia, our schools had only black students and black teachers.

My nightmare of being bullied lasted about five months (from the late summer extending into the fall). We moved in November of 1958 to Morgan Village, 777 South Seventh Street. Our move from the urban ghetto of Steven Street to a mixed neighborhood was a dream come true. It was a quiet family-friendly city neighborhood. We were among several black families who fit into the stable neighborhood. It was comprised of families who were of primarily Jewish, Polish and Italian descent. Regardless of skin color, we all played together on the school grounds, just two blocks away, without conflict or incident. My younger sisters and the neighbor's children played hopscotch and jump rope. Our new home was at the corner of Florence and Seventh Street. It adjoined a local neighborhood grocery shop owned and run by Mr. Fine, a Jewish man. Most of the neighborhood shopped at Mr. Fine's store, especially for fresh meats. There were very few supermarkets in those days and there were none in our neighborhood.

The best news of all was that our new home meant that I was going to a new school on the opposite side of town. I was finally away from the bullies who struck fear in me as I attended Pyne Poynt Junior High. I attended my second school in three months. It was named Hatch Junior High School. The change of scenery made an amazing impact on me, both socially and psychologically. I made friends. I have been out of school for nearly six decades and still communicate with some of my classmates from Hatch Junior High School.

I have only fond memories of my classmates at Hatch Junior High School and Camden High School. I have no recollection of any student being bullied, insulted, harassed, or beaten during my entire secondary school years, after my initial very aggravating introduction to public school in Camden. There were no troublemakers who were rude or ugly to anyone. We got along as friends and cared for each other. We shared lunches and money with those who needed a dime or quarter to pay for lunch. Everyone was very friendly, and we enjoyed the time we spent together. This camaraderie extended to the children who lived in the neighborhood and went to Catholic school. Our schools competed in sports, so we got to spend time with them in a school environment as well. We shared a mutual respect and could relate to each as religious moral people with strong family values.

Both Hatch Junior High and Camden High School were in the Parkside section of Camden. The schools were about three miles southeast from our new home and less than a half-mile apart. Because of the stable neighborhoods, most of us knew each other from junior high through high school and many had known one another since elementary school. Most of us who attended Hatch Junior High and Camden High schools lived in the South Camden neighborhoods of: Morgan Village, Centerville, Whitman Park, Parkside, and other parts of the city assigned to those two schools. We walked to school instead of paying for public transportation. We used our few pennies to buy lunch. Occasionally a parent—not mine because they never learned to drive or owned a vehicle—would give us a ride to school. My brother Billy occasionally gave a few of us a ride. Otherwise the walking convoy of students started in Morgan Village, joined by those from Centerville, Liberty Park, and Whitman Park, and we ended at one of the schools in Parkside. We reversed the sequence and repeated the trip after school.

I attended Hatch from December to June and only remember three teachers: Mr. Bates, my homeroom and shop teacher, the music teacher, and Mrs. Nimmo, my English teacher. She was the wife of the pastor of Kaighn Avenue Baptist Church in the neighborhood. She and Mr. Bates both were black, very good, tough and demanding teachers. Just when I thought I had left her behind at Hatch, she transferred to Camden High; and since I could select some of my own classes in high school, I avoided her class like the plague. I didn't realize until years later that she was the exact English teacher I needed.

I was promoted to tenth grade and attended Camden High School (also called the High or CHS). High school was an enjoyable learning environment. Teachers were paid to teach and that was what they did. Discipline was never an issue; if it was, the assistant principal or principal handled it. Students served as hall monitors, and we followed the rules. We knew the consequences for violating the freedom we were given. Anyone who abused and violated the rules jeopardized his/her freedom. This resulted in a suspension or afterschool detention or a paddle on the rear for boys. I have no idea what happened when and if girls broke the rules. It was not an issue during my high school years.

I was always on my best behavior during my three years of high school, and I had perfect attendance. I was a model student. I was never in trouble. I was punished once for being late for class without an excuse. I was given and served two hours of detention to be served over a two-day period. I told the truth as to why I was late for class, but the teacher didn't believe me. I suppose she had heard that excuse one too many times. The truth on that day served no purpose. I was just one of 1,600 students in a sea of unknowns. I accepted the punishment without protest and no reaction. I had matured since the time we lined up to board an old hand-me-down yellow school bus in Georgia. During detention, I sat in a classroom after school with the windows and shades down. We had to sit upright without talking. We could not sleep or leave the room for a bathroom break for an entire hour after school. The detention sessions were monitored by a teacher for strict compliance; violation of the rules resulted in more hours of detention. The toughest part of the punishment was that I missed track practice. I was confined indoors, and my friends were laughing and talking outside, enjoying themselves.

I have one very clear memory of interacting with my younger sisters and brothers. I tired of doing dishes given my school activities. So I paid one of my sisters fifty cents to wash dishes for me for the entire week. Fast-forward almost sixty years, I can't stand leaving an unclean dish, pot, or pan overnight in the sink.

I don't remember much about my siblings between the summer of 1958 and high school graduation in June of 1962. In late summer of 1962, I was off to college and spent very little time at home or around family until the summer. Even then, I worked summer jobs and gave little or no thought to my younger siblings. Although we grew up together in the same household, my siblings and I stayed busy and saw each other as we passed coming and going. I have a vague memory of sibling 13, Ms. Ann, having volunteered as a candy striper (hospital volunteer). We were adults before I really sat down and got to know my younger siblings.

I got involved in school activities, but I have no meaningful recall of encountering any of my siblings while I was at Camden High. Both Geneva (sibling 7) and I attended Camden High and overlapped by a year. She was a senior during my sophomore year. George (sibling 10) and I overlapped high school. I was a senior during his sophomore year. I only remember him from high school by his being on the cross-country team. Otherwise we did not mingle while at school.

During 1959, the family found a house for sale and bought it. It was just a block from our Seventh Street address between Eighth and Ninth Streets on the same block as H. B. Wilson Elementary School. It was an ideal location since five siblings attended that elementary school. As youth, they played basketball, stickball, and gathered for social events in H. B. Wilson's schoolyard.

I still have my 1962 Camden High School Yearbook. After fifty-six years, it's in mint condition. I have very fond memories of my high school experience, the teachers, and most of the students. Some of us Camden High students have remained in close contact over the years. We graduated from the same junior high and high school class and attended the same college together.[47] We graduated from Johnson C. Smith University. We have known each other since my family moved to Morgan Village, November 1958. The family's move radically changed my life. The move impacted me almost as much as the family's move from Georgia. It allowed me to transfer from Pyne Poynt Junior High—my worst nightmare—to a calm normal school environment. One friend still lives in South Jersey. He has kept me up-to-date on the news from Camden. Four of my closest friends were my college classmates. We are spread out and live in Rochester, New York, Pontiac, Michigan, Richmond, Virginia, and I live in Georgia. It is amazing that we are, today, still best friends.

After high school graduation, I never looked back but I didn't forget either. I attended Camden High School class of 1962's fortieth class reunion. It was the first time I had attended my alma mater's high school reunion. I enjoyed the dinner, classmates, and the social. We discussed activities for our forty-fifth reunion. An outcome of that effort was that an alumnae board was incorporated and its officers were appointed. I became the CEO. We solicited donations from classmates and sponsored $1,000 annual scholarships for over ten years thereafter. The Camden High School administration provided student recommendations based on academic achievements, extracurricular activities, essays, and college plans. The scholarships didn't pay much of their college expenses, however, they were an encouragement to pursue college for a better life. At the CHS class's fiftieth reunion, we still had more than $1,500 in the bank. I requested scholarship application candidates from CHS, but none were sent. They stopped submitting candidates. The board agreed to use the funds to help defray the cost of some of our classmates whose health were failing or who were on fixed incomes so that they could attend Camden High School's fiftieth class reunion.

He motivated his students to performed beyond
what was expected of them.

Steve, Margo, Lorraine & I met in Jr. High And were
together through College at the same time.

Chapter 9

Stepping Back—Planting Seeds
that Moved Me Forward

A Day Remembered

June 10, 1958, was our move day. After many promises, met with several disappointments, our move day was finally realized. The time for our departure had come. We were moving north.

My two sisters, Mamie and Geneva, who were a couple of years older than me, helped Mom prepare for our extended trip to Philadelphia, Pennsylvania. Philadelphia was not our destination. It was the stop closest to where we were headed, i.e., Camden, New Jersey. Mom and my sisters had cooked plenty to eat. They wrapped the food and stored it in shoeboxes and brown paper bags. The boxes contained enough fried chicken and pound cake to feed us when we got hungry and to appease us when we became antsy. Grease and butter residue stained the sides of each box as it dripped from the prepared meals.

Philip Crayton, our neighbor, agreed to drive us to the Greyhound bus terminal in Columbus. The Crayton family owned seven hundred acres of land adjacent to the Fitzgerald's quarters. He and two of his brothers lived there with their families and farmed the land. It seemed like it took forever for Philip to come pick us up. It was time for me to say goodbye to that old two-room place with a makeshift kitchen and a tin roof that leaked. Too many of us had stayed there for too many years. Through the years, up to thirteen of us Jacksons had lived in the place at the same time. When Philip finally arrived, we exploded with excitement. We loaded our boxes, bags, pillowcases, and sheets and ourselves in the back of his pickup truck. Mom, Mamie, and Christine sat in the cab with Philip. We were elated and ready to leave the place and Omaha, Georgia, forever. We gave little or no thought to what our future lives would be like in Camden. We were just ready to leave and be on our one-way trip to our new beginnings. We arrived at the terminal early, if for no other reason than Philip drove exceedingly fast. He had a heavy foot. At the bus station, we, nine of us—ages four to eighteen—and Mom sat in the colored-only section. We were near the colored-only restrooms and a colored-only drinking water faucet. We waited anxiously for the time to board. In Southern states, if a bus was carrying white passengers, blacks had to sit at the rear of the bus. It was the law.

Prior to our one-way trip by Greyhound bus, our normal mode of transportation was a mule pulling an open-air convertible wagon or we walked. The Greyhound bus was the only commercial bus that any of the siblings had ever boarded. The bus had tinted windows, air-conditioning, and cushioned reclining seats. Just being on such a bus was enough to excite my siblings and me. It was very comfortable compared to riding in a wagon on bumpy dirt roads and trails. We were country children. This ride was nothing like our daily yellow hand-me-down school bus rides. The roads were not the typical red dusty Georgia clay which were sometimes too muddy to travel. Nor were they like the backroads that were lined with trees, uneven, and rugged. We were traveling on traffic-filled concrete-paved smooth multilane highways that sometimes crossed over and under one another. The landscape was new to all my siblings and me.

As we arrived in the big cities, the bus driver announced them and the next city to follow. Our first stop was Atlanta, Georgia. The next one was Charlotte, North Carolina. It was followed by Richmond, Virginia. We stopped and changed buses in Washington, DC, with Baltimore, Maryland, being next. It was the last stop before Philadelphia. I tried hard to stay awake, still sleep was overtaking me. I was exhausted and can only clearly remember the driver announcing our arrivals in Atlanta, Washington, Baltimore, and Philadelphia.

We no longer had to sit in the back of the bus when we left DC. My anticipation peaked when we left Baltimore and the driver said, "The next stop and final destination is Philadelphia." I had no idea about the distance between Baltimore and Philadelphia. This led me to imagine that we were close, although it seemed like it took forever to arrive there.

I was really spellbound at seeing very tall buildings when we reached the cities. On the farm, aside from the main plantation homes, we saw mostly single-story huts that the workers lived in. Occasionally some of the farms had two-story barns. Of course, Columbus, Georgia, had multistory buildings, however, there was no comparison to the twenty-five-plus-storied buildings that we saw in Baltimore and Philadelphia. The further north we drove, seemingly the taller the buildings and wider the highways. Long bridges, stretching over wide rivers, kept my eyes focused on the views outside the bus window. It appeared that we would never get across the bridges. Driving under a body of water through tunnels puzzled and amazed me. I couldn't fathom how it was done. I had never traveled more than fifty miles from my birthplace. The bus passed through cities, and I saw buildings that I had read about. I never dreamed that I would really see or pass through them.

Finally after a thirty-two-hour trip, Mom and the nine of us arrived at the Greyhound bus terminal in Philadelphia. The one-way journey had been completed without incident. The Philadelphia bus station was located underground in a huge building with buses coming and going. Mom directed each of us to gather our meager belongings, consisting of cardboard boxes as suitcases, boxes wrapped in bed sheets, and some of our clothes thrown into pillowcases. Whenever we went out to someplace new, Mom told us to act our best, look our best, and act like we had been there before. This situation wasn't new to her. We had just left the cotton fields several days before when suddenly, Mom told us there was no reason that we had to appear to still be there. The way she wanted us to act was easier said than done! We were awestruck.

I was fourteen years old at the time and I could not explain my actions. My problem was that as we rode on the bus and at the

Greyhound bus terminal, I was embarrassed to be associated with my siblings. I wanted to distance myself from them. I wished I could hide. I never intentionally drew attention to myself. I always tried to avoid it. I had no explanations for why I felt and acted in such a manner. In Omaha, it was okay that we looked like country farmers because we were. In the city of Philadelphia, it occurred to me that we had moved on and left that life behind us; however, we had not yet done so visually and mentally. With our pillowcases, things tied up in bedsheets and pillowcases and cardboard boxes tagging behind our Mom, we looked just like sharecroppers' kids straight off the farm. Until my brother Billy came to pick us up, I disassociated myself from the rest of the family at the bus station. We looked like country bumpkin farm hands.

My oldest brother, Billy, and his closest friend, John, met us at the bus station and transported us to our new home in Camden. Billy was sixteen years old when he left Georgia to live with Aunt Mary Frances Peterson in Camden. He was now twenty-five years old. Some of his siblings had not seen him since he left Georgia. Robert (Bob), George, and Otis were too young to remember him. Mary Lou was a baby, and Annie and Chris (Evelyn Christine) were born years after he left. Billy made both personal and financial sacrifices to help us as did Rosie, Josephine, Leola, and Charles. Because of their sacrifices, we were able to migrate from Stewart County, Georgia, to Camden, New Jersey, to start a new and better life.

The names and ages of the Jackson clan who departed Stewart County, (Omaha) Georgia, on June 10, 1958, and were given a new beginning in Camden, New Jersey, were: Mary Francis, eighteen; Geneva, seventeen; Grover, fourteen; Bob, thirteen; George, twelve; Otis, ten; Mary Lou, nine; Annie, seven; and Chris, four. Mom was forty-eight years old and led our ragtag group. Our older siblings' ages were: Leola, twenty-eight; Rosie, twenty-seven; Charles, twenty-three; and Josephine, twenty. They relocated to Jersey City, New Jersey, years earlier. Both Rosie and Charles were married and had children. Billy was twenty-five years old and unmarried and neither were Leola and Josephine at the time. Billy was our primary sponsor after we arrived. He provided shelter for us. He lived with us, provided transportation, and helped us financially until he got married in the spring of 1968. Daddy was fifty-two. He had traveled to Camden six months earlier to prepare for our arrival. It was not clear what preparations he had made. He did not have a steady job and did not get one until six months after we arrived. Eventually he landed a job with Camden's Sanitation Department.

Our move north was the fulfillment of Mom's prayers, sustained by God's grace, and endowed with strength from life's journey of faith. The faith that is described in the Bible, "Now faith is the assurance of things hoped for, the conviction of things not seen" (Hebrews 11:1, ESV), describes the actions of faith by those who believed God and trusted Him. Mom believed and trusted God. She taught us to do the same. Therefore, the journey of faith and strength started with Mom and still lives, as her legacy, in the heart of each of her children.

After we arrived in Camden, some of my excitement and anticipation wore off. We were in downtown Camden, perhaps five blocks from Camden City Hall. Billy had arranged for us to stay at 310 Steven Street. It was a three-storied brick house located several doors from three bars that served alcohol by the drink and sold it by the bottle. At the intersection of Steven and Fourth Street, there were four commercial establishments, one on each corner. Three of the four establishments were liquor stores.

All of this was new and different for all of us. We could go outside but were not allowed to roam freely. There were no other children to play with. Concerned for our safety and well-being, Mom and Billy warned us not to leave the stoop in front of the house until we became more familiar with our surroundings. They specifically meant that we could play outside but were confined to the space in front of our new residence. There was plenty of sales traffic in and out of the liquor stores at the intersection of Steven and Fourth Street. The house was less than fifty feet from the corner of those stores. The customer traffic consisted of both females and males, and every opening minute brought a steady stream of customers to the bars. Some of the men had processed hairstyles and dressed differently than the men we were accustomed to seeing in Omaha. I was unfamiliar with this strange and new culture. Some men even dressed, spoke, and acted effeminately. It was not the ideal place to live, but it was our home on June 10, 1958, for several months after escaping the bleakness and desperation of Stewart County, Georgia.

The Migrants

To make ends meet, the older children tried to help Mom as best we could. At age fifteen, I was not old enough to legally work but I had a skillset that was easily employable. As a result, I hired myself out as a migrant worker, along with other local children and adults in need of money. During the rest of that summer, before sunrise, we jumped on the back of a flatbed truck and headed to various farms in South Jersey. We picked vegetables and fruits like tomatoes, peaches, and blueberries. I was not afraid to work, just didn't like riding in the back of a flatbed truck. We looked exactly like who and what we were—migrant workers. I was outright embarrassed just as I was at the Greyhound bus depot when we arrived from Georgia in the summer of 1958. Going to the farms in the morning was not so bad because we boarded the truck before the sun came up when there were very few people on the roads. Our return trip home, however, was in the peak of evening traffic, mostly on New Jersey Route 73 and Route 70. It seemed that people peered at us as we passed by. In Georgia, we lived in the country, cultivated the land as farmers, and we looked and acted like farmers. Now I lived in the city and looked like a stereotypical migrant worker. Most of the migrant workers were black and Latino. Since I was not filled up with pride, falling was not an issue (biblical passage, "Pride goes before destruction, and a haughty spirit before a fall"). Loosely translated, pride comes before a fall (Proverbs 16:18, KJV). I swallowed my pride and did what I had to do to earn money.

I especially enjoyed picking blueberries. As a child, in Stewart County, we used to walk through the swamps, searched for, found, and ate all the gooseberries, a close relative to blueberries, we could find. So I felt very comfortable picking them. I got paid and ate more than I picked for pay.

Tomato farming was significant in South Jersey with the Campbell Soup Company being only a few miles away in downtown Camden. I picked tomatoes and enjoyed eating my share of them for lunch as well. I never had money to buy lunch as a migrant worker, so I took some salt and pepper with me every day that I went to pick tomatoes. During the lunch break, I took out my salt and pepper, found a big red tomato, wiped it clean on my clothing, then took a big delicious bite. I seasoned it with salt and pepper as needed. It was succulent. After a brief pause to eat, I was ready to fill as many bushel baskets as I could. Both jobs of picking blueberries and tomatoes were short-lived. Although the work was available, getting to the farm locations was an issue. Most migrant work was seasonal which lasted for a short time. Laborers showed up for work until they earned the amount of money they needed, then they stopped coming to the pickup spot. This resulted in the laborer contractor being unable to find enough workers to justify making the round trip, to Camden, each day.

Playing Sports

Growing up on the farm, there was no opportunity for us to play organized sports. In Camden, there were many opportunities to participate in sports, both in school and in the community. I played summer league baseball for the local park league. Those were some fun times. I hit the ball and ran around the bases, seemingly with lightning speed. Fast running was one of my best attributes, and, looking back to those days, I remember that I played offense and defense quite well. The players were between fourteen and sixteen years old. Most were rising-star sophomores and juniors in high school.

The pitchers in the summer park leagues were just average. I was a contact hitter. It was almost impossible to throw me out on ground balls due to my speed. I usually outran the throw from the fielder to first base. On defense, I played centerfield. If a ball was hit into the air there, I was guaranteed to catch it. Centerfield was my comfort zone. It was very difficult to hit a ball over my head there. My deficiency was my throwing arm. I just didn't have the arm strength to throw well. Just as my strength was to outrun throws, my weakness was that I could not hold the runners on the bag. They were not afraid to tag up and run. I presented no threat since I lacked velocity on my throw to the next base. I also played fast-pitch softball in a church summer league, along with Billy and his friend John. I enjoyed playing softball with the older guys and again, I held my own in hitting and fielding.

I loved all sports with baseball being my most cherished one. My favorite team was the Dodgers. Living in Georgia, I never dreamed of seeing a professional baseball game in person, especially the Dodgers. Billy surprised us one Friday evening and took Bob, George, Otis, and me to see a Phillies vs. Dodgers game at Connie Mack Stadium in Philadelphia. My love for the Dodgers' blue was cemented for life. The Dodgers moved to Los Angeles in 1957, a year before we arrived in Camden.

At the age of thirteen, still living in Omaha, I was a dreamer with no sense of reality. I was very naive! I wrote a letter to Walter O'Malley, the owner of the Dodgers at that time, and told him I loved the Dodgers. In addition, I told him that I came from a big and poor family. I also told him that I was a big Dodger fan and I wanted to play baseball for them. Reflecting now about my naivete, I had no idea what I expected Mr. O'Malley to do.

During the broadcast of Dodgers' games, the announcer advertised a Dodgers' directory that included individual players, team pictures, as well as their top farm prospects. I put fifty cents in the letter to pay for a *Dodger Team and Farm System Directory*. After receiving the book, I worshiped it. I knew every player on the team and the best prospect in the farm system. The Dodgers were in Brooklyn and moved to Los Angeles in 1957. I stayed up late listening to the Dodgers games from Los Angeles. Although the radio had a very faint signal, I strained to hear the broadcast, and with my book in hand, I studied the players.

Liking the Dodgers seemed natural. It was the first team that had a player I could identify with in the name of Jackie Robinson. He allowed me to dream and believe that a child like me, of humble beginnings and background, had a chance to succeed. I convinced myself that becoming a professional baseball player was a possibility for anyone who had some ability, a positive work ethic, and determination. I truly believed I could develop into a professional baseball player. The only doubt I had was my arm strength and my ability to throw back to the infield which was a major requirement as an outfielder.

As the New York Mets were preparing for their initial season in 1962, the team held several local tryouts. They were held on the Camden High School baseball fields. Lots of boys between the age of sixteen and thirty showed up for the tryouts. From all appearances, I was the smallest person in size and weight who showed up to participate. I was 5'7" and 160 pounds soaking wet! Nevertheless, I got the opportunity to tryout.

As I watched the others before me try out, I observed the pitcher's speed and velocity. I estimated it to be about eighty-seven to ninety mph. I began to think about the hardest throwing pitcher that I had faced in high school. I reminded myself that high school pitchers just didn't compare to major league pitchers. This pitcher looked to be in his late twenties and he really had control, speed, and velocity. In fact, he frightened me. While I sat, waiting for my turn, I convinced myself that this was going to be a difficult task. Finally the moment of truth arrived. It was my turn at the plate. I couldn't back down or back out. Taking stock of my athletic characteristics, I reminded myself that I was a very nimble guy and my primary goal was to get a hit. I battled him by fouling off a few pitches. Ultimately I hit a ground ball to the shortstop. I beat out his throw to first base. I thought my performance, while not outstanding, was adequate, but I was not invited to a follow-up at the Mets tryout camp. The absence of a subsequent invite signaled the end of my professional baseball dream. As I grew older, I realized that desire alone was not enough. I became more realistic as I matured, recognizing that a college degree could enable me to do the other things I also longed to do.

The Process

Day after day and night after night, I would sit in my room. Well, it was my room now that Billy had gotten married and moved out. I had the radio on, but I was in deep thought. By now, Dad was employed by the city of Camden as a sanitation engineer, a trash collector. I did not want to end up like my Dad. I could not imagine getting up at 4:00 a.m., with the temperature being minus degrees, picking up garbage and trash. I never believed I deserved better. I just believed I could do better.

Facilitator Mom

Not long after we arrived in Camden, Mom started doing domestic work several days a week for a family who lacked for nothing. The family owned a medium-sized business that manufactured aluminum products. I don't know who introduced her to them, but I just know they were very wealthy and kind. They planted vegetable gardens. We worked the gardens for them, and they allowed us to share the harvest. We always enjoyed fresh vegetables while Mom worked for them. Additionally their youngest son gave her stylish new and very expensive jackets and sweaters to give to us. He was not condescending. He shared the clothes with the attitude that, "They are too small for me now. If you can use them, you are welcome to them." I was the main recipient of his generosity; and in high school, I was well-dressed, and no one knew the clothes were given to me. Of course, it didn't matter that the clothes were hand-me-downs. I could not have been more blessed. Instead of spending the little money I earned on clothes, I saved for school and other necessary expenditures.

Mom taught all of us by her examples. She walked eight blocks daily from our house to the bus stop. She waited for the bus to get to work regardless of the weather conditions. Throughout her commute, she faced the seasonal elements all year round. During the summer, the heat and humidity were sweltering. This was before climate change, so we got pounded with mounds of snow throughout the winter; and when there was no snow, the rest of the winter produced bone-chilling cold temperatures. It bothered me that she had to work so hard, but at age sixteen, I had no means of providing ways for her not to have to work. Generally when I worked,

I shared money that I earned with her. That was my priority. She was so appreciative and grateful to receive it. I never thought that it was ever enough. I did not hang out on the streets or spend money earned frivolously. Usually I stayed home in my room, read books, and listened to music, day and night, and never disturbed anyone.

As a tenth grader, I started working for Dr. Geyer, one of Mom's clients. I started out working once a month. It gradually increased to every Saturday. Initially he saw me as just a young child and gave me instructions on what to do when cleaning the grounds around his house. He was unaware that I had a lifetime of experience working on a farm. He quickly learned that I had done more in a day than most city children had done in their lifetime. I did all that I had time to do like clear brushes and remove poison ivy from the around the house. After a while, I became creative with his landscaping. I was good and did things to make his lawn and flower beds standout. Ultimately I beautified the landscape and planted and maintained his flowers so that they looked exquisite. I never took any shortcuts. I learned on the farm, and Mom taught us to do our best and to do a day's work for a day's pay.

I did not have any means of transportation. So I took the public service bus to Haddonfield and Dr. or Mrs. Geyer met me and drove me to their home. They prepared lunch for me, and around 5:00 p.m., they drove me back to Haddonfield where I caught the bus back to Camden. During our summer break, they employed me to maintain the flowers around his office building. He also introduced me to his neighbor who was retired, and I assisted him with his yard. Whatever the amount they paid me, I took it home and gave most of it to Mom.

Dr. Geyer was an encourager. We often talked about life and college, although he knew I had limited exposure to the real world. I learned a lot from him as a friend and employer. His only daughter, Joan, was two or three years older than me when she graduated from Cherry Hill High School. She entered nursing school. She met and married a University of Pennsylvania medical student at Dr. and Mrs. Geyer's home. They gave me a small role in the ceremony as an usher, exposing me to their friends and other professional people.

As I entered high school, the guidance counselors never asked or advised me about my future. They didn't give me an option about the subjects to study, for example, college prep or general business subjects. I had recently arrived in Camden from the fields of Georgia. If I had been asked to make a choice, my family would not have been able to advise me properly. The counselors likely steered me to a curriculum to prepare me for the labor market. I excelled in the curriculum assigned to me such as bookkeeping, typing, and general clerical-type subjects. Of course, there were other basic courses I had to take as well.

As I got closer to high school graduation, Dr. Geyer asked me what college I planned to attend. The high school curriculum I was assigned and matriculated was not designed for college attendance. Therefore, I had no clue where or what college would accept me and how I would pay.

I knew from my days on the farm, a seed must first be planted before it could yield a harvest. Dr. Geyer and others had started my fires burning. I now knew that I wanted to go to college. As classmates talked about colleges, I too participated in the conversations. I mentioned that I was looking at Howard, Temple, and a few others. The fact of the matter is that I did not even know how to write an essay to complete the college application. I had written book reports, but they were different than writing an essay on a college application. This was all new territory for me. The reality of life is that it took preparation and money and I had neither. I had the aptitude, just not the preparation. I had not taken the courses necessary for college enrollment. No colleges offered scholarships to students who were not prepared to attend.

I had people who believed in me and supported me: my Mom, Billy, and all my other siblings. Billy lived in Camden for more than twelve years and never finished high school; nevertheless, he had lots of common sense and knew people who could help me. In those twelve years, he had associated and become friends with many people. I had never completed a college application or written an essay required for college admission. I told Billy, and one Sunday afternoon, he introduced me to Mr. Baker, his friend, who attended Howard University.

Mr. Baker shared things about college that nobody talked about. He cleared up the notion that the college preparation curriculum was the only study track to gain college admission. He stressed the road to college was personal. Some of the smartest individuals he met had outstanding grades coming out of high school, however, they lacked discipline, lost focus, and failed at their initial attempt to matriculate in a college or university. He stressed, as Mom had done, that each of us will be challenged by failure. The difference between those who succeed or fail is the nature of their response to the situation. His and her point was, don't focus on failure, rather focus on recovery and don't repeat the same mistakes that you made previously; instead learn from those mistakes.

Mr. Baker taught me there was life beyond high school graduation. I could have a great future with the right dedication, attitude, and focus. If I had the will and ability, I could achieve beyond what some had expected of me. He said that I determined my destiny and my future. It was mine alone. He confirmed in our conversation that I must continue my journey on the road less traveled. He said, just by thinking I could go to college started the journey. Now there were boxes to be checked off: (a) I must do a self-examination and prioritize the purpose, events, and length of my journey, (b) my commitment to complete the process, (c) what will happen when my faith gets tested such as who would I turn to and why?

The biggest question and issue before me was, did I have the determination to finish the journey? The lyrics from a song written by Billie Holiday and Arthur Herzog Jr. in 1939, "Mama may have, Papa may have, but God bless the child who has his own…That's got his own." The point was, once I walked out of my parents' front door, my focus must be on navigating all the hazards that would be incurred on the road less traveled. There would be decisions about which my family could and should pray to help me, even though it must be my ultimate determination to overcome all barriers. The journey was going to be lonely at times, and I would be challenged to the core. I would have to persevere, knowing that the distractions would be conquered if I focused on my purpose.

I was on my journey of faith. I needed strength, push, and determination. Those were supplied to me through the love and support of my family. By now, I had everyone in my family excited that I was pursuing college. Even when odds were beyond the reality of the dream, my family encouraged me. Some of my siblings had nothing more to offer me beyond prayers. By now, the older ones, except Billy, were married with families of their own. They didn't have two wooden nickels to throw my way to help me pay for college if I was accepted. I had the will, just not the way. Mom assured me, God would make a way!

So I began to think positively that if a college accepted me for admission, the funds would be provided, although I had no idea from whom, where, or how. My faith was strengthened through Scriptures, Romans 8:28, "And we know that for those who love God all things work together for good, for those who are called according to his purpose." Others had already prayed for me long before I knew. It had been designed that I would be the first of my parents' children to attend and graduate from college, despite my having to apply and be accepted by a school.

I sent away for college bulletins from Northeastern in Boston, Howard University in Washington, DC, and Temple University in Philadelphia. I knew a few people who graduated from Camden High School who attended Johnson C. Smith University (JSCU or Smith) in Charlotte, North Carolina. I had never heard of it. So what? The entire college process was new to me. I received an application from Johnson C. Smith University, and Mr. Baker wrote a draft essay for me to complete. I finished the essay, filled out the rest of the application, and mailed it.

JCSU accepted me on probation. I had a lot of catching up to do pertaining to the three Rs—Reading, Riting, and Rithmetic. Apparently my brain just had not been trained the correct way, and I hadn't been required to put any emphasis on writing skills. Math was a lot easier and logical to do than reading a passage and summarizing the author's intent. Writing turned out to be a challenge, primarily due to how I pronounced, wrote, and spelled words. Before you laugh me off the planet, I did poorly on many written papers due to my diction. An example, the word *made*, I spelled it as *maded*. There were other reoccurring errors. I just could not get my brain to accept simple stuff. In school, I didn't pick up an understanding of the basic principles of grammar and sentence structure. Since I had taken only classes that prepared me to enter the workforce, less emphasis was on thinking and more on doing clerical transactions.

The Friends

Dr. and Mrs. Geyer were truly my friends. Mom asked him for a $1,200 loan for my first year's tuition, room and board, and he granted her the request. As it turned out, he never accepted repayment. I never counted on him nor would I have ever asked him. What was I thinking? Dr. Geyer was always on my side with words of encouragement. Mom was also always there for all of us. I appreciated her love, help, and the confidence she had in me. She was very proud of us, and it showed when she talked with friends about us.

Dr. Geyer was a man before his time. He made it possible for me to pursue my dream. He never gave me advice. We just talked. I was able to glean wisdom and learn without him telling me anything. He made suggestions and he asked me direct questions, all for pointing me in the right direction. I learned a great deal from him. I will always fondly remember him as a very dear friend. Dr. Geyer was a University of Pennsylvania graduate and physician with a heart of gold.

He was kind, generous, and gracious, but nothing about him was ostentatious or elitist. He was engaging. He was a common man who went to work every day. He was the first person I visited during the Christmas recess after I arrived home from my first year of college, and I went to visit the Geyers again later that summer. Each time, they welcomed me. They prepared a snack. We sat and just talked about my college experience.

My first year as a student at Johnson C. Smith was full of self-esteem, and I felt like nothing could stop me. I was a serious student. I took German as my foreign language, biology, college math, English, and several easy subjects to balance out my class load. The core college subjects were a challenge, and I struggled; nevertheless I did well. I also joined the track-and-field team—a mistake yet doing so taught me a lesson.

During my sophomore year, I had hoped to take a few classes in my major. Well, I did not! I was struggling through courses like sociology. The subject was simple. The professor made it very difficult. As a result, I failed it and ended up repeating the course. Statistics was another class that challenged me. Again the subject was not difficult, but my poor study habits and the dispassionate teacher's delivery each collided to make me a casualty in that class also.

To be honest, it wasn't just the courses. I also got distracted with nonacademic pursuits. When the dust settled and grades were recorded and posted, the administration advised me to take a break until I refocused on the reasons why I had enrolled in the university in the first place. I should have put more emphasis on being a student; instead I started to take the whole experience for granted. I succeeded my freshman year, although I was studying less. So I assumed that I would overcome any challenges I faced. Track-and-field practice and meet began to absorb a great deal of my time. Now I had almost eight months to think and reprioritize my time. After falling prey to the challenge of sociology and statistics, I took the time off, not by choice rather by command, and I regrouped. The time off humbled me, and upon returning in the spring semester of 1965, I was a bit more mature. I took the administration's advice, came back with my mind made up to overcome any odds. During the time away, I began to more fully appreciate the benefits of having a college degree. I had motivating factors. They included: working factory-type jobs, waiting for a bus on cold lonely nights to commute to or from those jobs, and lacking a social life. I was unhappy with myself. Each factor played a significant role in my rejuvenation and desire to earn my college degree from JCSU.

I needed the time away from JCSU. Upon returning, after my semester suspension, I was motivated and passed those subjects that I had failed earlier (taught by the same professors). All the noise around me dissipated, and I recalled my conversation with Mr. Baker on being challenged by failure. I was ready to rededicate myself and focus on my recovery. I would not repeat the same mistakes.

Interesting People

I have met many celebrities in my lifetime. I wasn't into taking selfies to brag about it later. Of course, in the 1960s, selfies did not exist. The process of photographing anything would not have produced immediate results. It would have taken several weeks thereafter to have the film developed, but I survived. If I had wanted a picture with any one of the celebrities, I am sure they would have accommodated me. As the recording by Brooke Benton entitled "Looking Back" says, "I'll never make that same mistake again." I would have taken pictures to show family and friends.

After I turned seventeen and obtained my New Jersey State driver's license, my brother Billy allowed me to take his car for a drive. I picked up Steve, a friend, a classmate, and a star basketball player on Camden High's basketball team. We drove through the city and ended up in the Camden County Park. The car was a 1954 Chevrolet Bellaire, stick shift, manual transmission. Steve didn't know how to drive a stick shift, so he asked me to teach him. I stopped in the county park and gave him some brief instructions, then switched to the passenger seat and allowed him to try a hand at starting to drive. I continued to direct him on the steps required to shift gears as he drove through the park.

It never dawned on me that a driver's license or permit was needed to drive on public property. After a short while, a police officer approached us. I imagine he had been observing us. He asked us our purpose for being in the park. I told him that we were just riding around. He asked for our driver's licenses. Steve didn't have a driver's license nor a driver's permit and did not know how to drive. At that time, in New Jersey, a driver's permit could be obtained at sixteen after passing a written test. Even after that, a driver with a permit was not allowed to drive without a licensed driver also in the car. I never asked Steve if he had a permit before allowing him to get behind the wheel. It was at that moment that I realized the trouble I had gotten myself into. A mild panic began to come over me. I could be jailed or issued a ticket for letting an unlicensed driver handle my brother's car.

The policeman asked a few questions about my family. I answered him. I told him the car belonged to my brother. He knew Billy. That was my free ticket to stay out of jail or be ticketed. We conversed a bit more. The officer was Arnold Raymond Cream, a detective and a policeman, with the City of Camden Police Department. I learned his birth name and that his daughter was in my high school class. I also learned that his pseudo name was Jersey Joe Walcott, the professional boxer.

I had listened to his fights on the radio while growing up in Georgia. The entire family used to sit around Daddy's portable radio, listening to the fights with Joe Lewis, Jersey Joe, Sugar Ray, and many other greats. I met the great Jersey Joe. I was very impressed, even under the strained circumstances. I met a person that I had admired for so many years. Listening to fights and other radio programs was one of the few family home entertainments that we enjoyed with Dad while growing up in Stewart County.

In the end, due mainly to his familiarity with Billy, I did not get arrested nor was I issued a ticket. Both Steve and I were given a warning to avoid driving without a license. I switched positions with Steve and we left the park to find other opportunities to pursue. I remain a fan of Jersey Joe and was awed by meeting one of my idols in person.

I showed great potential as a runner in high school cross-country and track. I was the second-best distance runner on my high school team and successfully competed against the area's best runners as a miler on my track-and-field team. As a result, I was the third-best runner in all South Jersey.

In college, it was a new and different experience. We competed against some of the world's fastest, most experienced, and best track stars enrolled in college. Most of the athletes on college teams had been recruited and were on scholarships. They had notoriety as sprinters, hurdlers, and relay racers. I was a walk-on and a distance runner who did not even run a four-minute mile. I got very little attention. No one knew other than my teammates.

During the spring of 1963, our team was invited to partici-pate in an invitational track-and-field meet. The schools that par-ticipated had world-class student athletes. Bob Hayes, one of the fastest track specialists, a future Olympian, from Florida A and M University (FAMU) was one such athlete. Aside from FAMU, other historically black colleges and universities represented included Morgan State, North Carolina Central, North Carolina A and T, SC State, Delaware State, and Virginia State. I watched and participated against athletes that I had only heard about and seen from a distance at the University of Pennsylvania Relays (Penn Relays). I did not know any of the runners personally but soon got an introduction and ran against some of them.

Johnson C. Smith did not have a squad of specialized runners. In any event, the track coach looked around and said that he wanted me to run as part of the sprint medley relay. It consisted of four ath-letes running distances of 440, 220, 220, and 880 yards. He needed someone to run the first leg—440 yards—and he chose me. I was not a sprinter. Yet he chose me to race 440 yards against some of the world's best sprinters. The second leg was 220 yards and a pure sprint. Well, I had my day in the sun, and I ran the first leg of 440 yards as fast as I could. Bob Hayes ran the second leg, of 220 yards for FAMU.

The competition was head and shoulders better than me and I knew it. I just wanted to finish before the next runner, Bob Hayes, completed the first 220 yards of the second leg. I did indeed. If I had not, I would have been laughed off the bus on our return trip to Charlotte with the rest of the JCSU team. I have no idea what my time was for the 440. My only motivation was getting off the track field without embarrassing myself. As expected, I was far back in the pack, yet I finished before Bob Hayes completed his 220-yard leg of the medley. Doing so was a victory. JCSU did not win the sprint medley relay race but just being on the same track with those elite runners was a big deal, a personal victory. It was an experience I will cherish for life. It had been less than five years before that race when I realized my ability to run. I discovered it quite by accident and out of a necessity. The necessity was that during the summer of 1958, I sprinted away from a jailbird troublemaker who wanted to use me as a punching bag during my first summer in Camden.

Some of those college athletes against whom we competed later represented the United States in the 1964 Summer Olympics in Mexico City. Bob Hayes won two gold medals. Following that, in the 1968 Tokyo Summer Olympics, he won gold medals for the one-hundred-meter dash and the four-hundred-meter relay. After retiring from track-and-field, Bob Hayes became a professional football player and exceled as a pro bowl wide receiver with the Dallas Cowboys.

A few years later, after hanging up my track shoes, Vince Matthews, a freshman from New York City (NYC), enrolled at JCSU and quickly became well-known. We became friends. He made a name for both himself and for the university as a natural runner. He won two Olympic gold medals, one at the 1968 Mexico City Summer Olympics where he ran the first leg on the 4×400 meters relay team. He and his American teammates set the world record of 2.56.16 for that event. The record lasted for twenty-four years. He earned his second Olympic gold medal at the 1972 Munich Summer Olympics where he competed and won the individual four hundred meters race with a winning time of 44.66 seconds.

Upon completing my first year of graduate school, I visited my dear friend Dr. Geyer at his home in Cherry Hill, New Jersey. During my visit, he mentioned he had a new neighbor that he wanted me to meet. He never mentioned the name of the new neighbor or anything about him. We walked across the road to the neighbor's house. Lo and behold, his neighbor was Muhammad Ali. He was lying on the floor watching television. After my introduction to him, he treated me like a friend that he had known for a lifetime. He was very respectful and cordial. He offered me some refreshments, and we talked casually for quite some time.

Of all the personalities I have met, Muhammad Ali is the one who stood out the most. He lived up to his reputation as being a real person. He demonstrated and affirmed my basic belief that it doesn't cost anything to be cordial.

GROVER JACKSON, MARY FULLARD AND E. CHRISTINE JACKSON

The Alumni Dance

During my years as a JCSU student, the JCSU-NAA sponsored a summer fund-raising dance in New York City (NYC). The summer of 1964, I borrowed Billy's new car, drove it from Camden to NYC, and attended the dance. Quite a few of my college friends and track teammates also attended. Up to that time, I had never tasted any alcoholic beverages. I used to laugh at those who did. Liquor had a unique effect on people who consumed it. Over the years, I had observed some of the changes in personality and slips of the tongue after having a few drinks. Some of these observations had been of my dad. Friends in college who were not used to drinking displayed some of those same traits after a few drinks. For reasons I cannot explain, I promised out of stupidity, I would drink with them at the dance. I assumed that a couple of shots of liquor wouldn't be harmful.

I swallowed several straight shots of Chivas Regal liquor. I did not know it would knock me out. In hindsight, I am mindful of the song by the Tams, "What Kind of Fool Do You Think I Am." Well, let me just say, that Friday evening, I was a fool by any definition. I got sloppy drunk and woke up in a strange bed in a strange home. It was the home of the parents of a young female schoolmate who lived in NYC. She was a true friend when she took me to her parents' home, and they treated me as a son. The schoolmate was a transfer student from a nearby college who was from NYC. We became friends a year earlier during the Thanksgiving holiday break when students who lived beyond normal driving distances to go home stayed on campus.

After waking up the next morning, I had the worst headache I ever had and was so very thirsty. I didn't remember anything about the previous evening. I wanted to know how I got to my friend's home and where my brother's car was. I was most embarrassed. After several shots and being totally drunk, my friends said I acted like a buffoon. I started yelling out, "Where is SA (initials), I want SA!" SA are the initials of a female college student whom I had only a casual talking relationship. I had wished for a deeper emotional tie. I had hoped the relationship would grow over the summer. Obviously I made a complete fool of myself. I shamed her and my friends.

She was from South Carolina and spent the summer of 1964 with her aunt on Staten Island. After that Friday evening's incident and my suspension from school, the relationship died and there was no known medical treatment to revive it. I was sick from Friday evening through Sunday which seemed like weeks. Despite my ignorance, God protected me and I drove my brother's car back to Camden in time for him to report to for work on Monday morning. I recovered, although my headache lasted for several days longer. I learned several lessons the hard way. The first lesson was *never* drink alcoholic beverages. The second lesson was never drink alcoholic beverages, and if stupid enough to do so, *never* drink water after being drunk before eating food. Drinking water while drunk without eating food usually extends one's drunkenness. I had an entire semester to think about this incident, about my friend, and what I wanted out of life. I had earned, because of my poor JCSU grades, an extended leave beyond the summer. I had an entire summer and the fall semester of 1964 to digest the lessons I failed to learn as a sophomore college student. Poor study habits coupled with that infamous night of drunkenness didn't help. They were a hindrance. Given a second chance, I assured myself that my study habits would improve and my mistakes would be corrected.

Drinking has never been something I enjoyed doing. For the rest of my JCSU college life and in corporate America, I watched others make fools of themselves. If I drank, it was sparingly. My glass was more chaser than liquor. Since 1973, I have totally abstained from alcoholic beverages due to my personal religious convictions and healthy lifestyle and my firm belief that no good results can come from consuming alcohol.

Jobs and Doubts

During the summer and fall of 1964, I found work in Jersey City. I lived with my brother Charles and his family. Between June and January, I worked two different jobs. The first job was at a zipper factory in Newark. I kept the production going by distributing the fabric necessary to fill the orders. I matched colors, quantities, and lengths. As orders came in, I gave them to my female coworkers for completion. I collected the finished goods and verified that each order was correct and submitted it to be packaged and shipped. I worked from 8:30 a.m. to 4:30 p.m. five days a week. It took three buses and a short walk from Broad Street in Newark to the factory. Public service buses ran with regularity from Jersey City to Newark and all the surrounding communities. The bus was very convenient, affordable, and reliable and was the primary mode of transportation for most people who lived in the area.

I quickly learned my way around the factory. One situation, however, frightened and flustered me beyond belief. One afternoon, as I walked through the building, I stopped in the bathroom as I had done many times before. I opened a stall door and closed it behind me. I sat down to relieve myself of discomfort. Seconds later, the main bathroom door swung open again. This time, I heard the click of a woman's heels against the hard tile floors. My heart started beating. No, it was pounding like it was trying to escape my body cavity. I quickly realized the enormity of my error while keeping as calm as I possibly could in this situation. In fear, I raised my feet off the floor so I wouldn't be seen. A few minutes later, the heels clicked out of the bathroom just as they had entered. Without completing the act that led me to the bathroom, I immediately prepared myself for an escape. After I surveyed the area to ensure that I would not be seen, I rushed out. My heart still pounding, I looked at the door and it was affirmed that I had entered the women's bathroom. How had I made such an error? I noticed, for the first time, there were two ladies' restrooms back-to-back. Since the workforce was mostly female, that arrangement was a practical accommodation. The men's restroom was immediately past the two women's rooms. This presented yet another lesson learned. Always look twice and read before wandering into a public bathroom facility. The bathroom could have an unexpected occupant.

My second and final job during my academic suspension was in Bayonne, at a corrugated box factory. The boxes and displays met peak holiday demands and other specialized requirements. Therefore, the plant ran three full-time shifts, and due to the demands, I worked overtime and double shifts. I worked overtime as often as I could to earn the money needed for the next college semester. The tuition would be about $600. I worked the 3:00 p.m. to 11:00 p.m. shift, five days a week. At that time, the pay was exceptional for unskilled labor. It was 25¢ per hour with a differential for the second shift and time and a half for overtime. It was a male-only shop, so I did not have to be on alert for restroom mix-ups.

The workforce was primarily Italian and Polish middle-aged men who worked well together. They took time to show me the correct procedures or the art of the job. My duties were to keep the presses running by having the material for the next job at the press and ready for processing. I pulled my load and earned their respect while clearly waiting to see the end of this job. I returned to Charlotte and JCSU to continue my educational journey in January 1965.

Kindness

In high school and college, I was a sociable person but on the quiet side. There were young ladies I liked, however, I was too shy or afraid of rejection to approach them. I had a sense of humor and I used my quick wit to start conversations despite never being the life of any party. I usually stood around, talked, and observed others. At college socials, I went alone and met my friends there. I dated a few females who ended up just being friends. They were fun to go to a movie and spend time with on campus. On the few occasions that I had an emotional attachment, the desired person did not feel that way about me. I never showed or expressed a desire for a long-term relationship with anyone. It was great protection to avoid getting hurt or heartbroken. I was the happy-go-lucky person who everyone liked as a nice boy. I hid my true emotions. Portions of the song "Smiling Faces Sometimes" written by Norman Whitfield and Barrett Strong and originally recorded by the Temptations in 1971 described me perfectly:

> Smiling faces, Smiling Faces, sometimes they
> don't tell the truth.
> Smiling faces, smiling faces tell lies and I got
> proof.

The truth is in the eye 'cause the eyes don't lie,
    amen.
Remember, a smile is just a frown turned upside
    down my friend.
So, hear me when I'm saying

At the beginning of the 1964 spring semester, a friend from Paterson, New Jersey, told me a freshman young lady liked me. My interest spiked. I played it cool. After all, I was a sophomore and she was a freshman. After I discovered who she was and who she dated, I had second thoughts. She was dating one of my friends from NYC and a member of the track team. I also learned that he was being unfaithful to her. He was sharing his affections with a young lady who lived off campus in the city of Charlotte. The freshman turned out to be a very attractive young lady. She was sweet, very kind, and she cared for me. After agonizing, I stepped up and accepted her affections. After a few months though, I broke off the relationship. It was just a game for me to see if I could really change a woman's affection from someone else to me. Later I regretted my actions and felt horrible for my actions. She deserved better. That act of meanness haunted me, and I deeply regretted it for many years.

An Acquaintance

Before I even considered staying with Charles and his family during my academic suspension from JCSU, I got an agreement on the monthly cost for my room and board. I always paid in cash, in advance, for the entire month. I had witnessed the negative implications of not paying bills down through the years with Daddy settling our family debts. So I took that responsibility seriously. Charles was family, but I did not want to be a burden to him. The impact of the Singer Company's debt collection in 1951 of our animals and farm tools, many years ago, still lingered on in my mind.[48]

I had many relatives who lived in Jersey City. Additionally I knew JCSU graduates and friends who were natives to the area. My closest friend at the time was a six-foot-eight male JCSU college basketball player who had graduated and worked as a social worker in Jersey City. Jersey City was home for him, and we frequently enjoyed each other's company. As people saw us together, he at six feet eight and I at five feet seven, people called us Mutt and Jeff. I knew his family and his brothers were tall as well. He always wanted me to meet some of the young ladies he knew and grew up with in Jersey City. Being a bit old-fashioned, I preferred to go it alone. Since we socialized together, I knew sooner or later I would be cornered. Finally we were at his home, and, either planned or accidently, he introduced me to a young lady. I never followed up or called her. Years later, she became his wife. It was not meant to be for me after all.

During the time I lived with Charles, he managed a Pep Boys, a full-service tire and automotive aftermarket chain store, in Bayonne, New Jersey. One day, in June 1964, I borrowed his car to go job hunting. I returned to his store just before closing time. As he closed and prepared the bank deposits, he introduced me to a very attractive young woman he had hired as a cashier for the summer. As we left the store, the young woman headed toward the bus stop. I asked her where she lived and offered her a ride home. She accepted. I dropped Charles off at his home and proceeded to take her home. I had finally met someone my age, and I hoped to see her again. I looked forward to getting to know her.

"Just one look and I fell so hard in love with you…" are words from the song sung by Doris Troy entitled "Just One Look." It was that first look at her that took my breath away, and it was that last look that I will always remember. Was this love at first sight? It really felt like it. I experienced a very strong emotional and physical attraction to her, and I aimed to spend time with her. As the summer passed and fall arrived, I spent every moment possible either with her, talking to her on the phone, or thinking about her. I spent as much time with her as her schedule allowed, mostly during weekends. I do not know why. Perhaps it was her warm caring attitude that made her so personable. Maybe it was her innocent looks. Regardless of the reasons, I caught a fever and there was no cure. She was adorable to have as a friend, and the time I spent with her was beyond any words that I could describe. I really liked and enjoyed spending quality time with her. She was very intelligent and approachable. While I never discussed being girlfriend and boyfriend, I thoroughly enjoyed her company and the thought of a serious kinship crossed my mind; nevertheless, I did not want to rush the relationship. I was never one who lacked confidence in any way. The joy of being with her gave me pleasure. She gave me a sense of happiness, appreciation, and inspiration. I did not have to impress her. The joy that I had, the world didn't give to me. It came from being with her, talking with her, and just thinking about her.

She was a very special woman to me, and I adored her and everything about her. Yet I felt I had nothing to offer her. At the time we met, neither one of us had reached the age of twenty-one. I had a desire to fulfill her life, but how? I wanted to provide her with happiness in life, not things. She seemed happy and wasn't looking or expecting anything more. However, I wanted to be more to her, but more of what, when, and how? She was a student at Jersey City State College, pursuing a college education. I did not want to be a distraction to her as I had been to myself. I wanted her to complete her goal. At that time, I had absolutely nothing to offer her other than my genuine friendship. She was the first young woman that I met during my stay in Jersey City. She was the only child of a single mother, Ms. Edwina as I called her.

We used to have some very meaningful conversations over a cup of tea. Ms. Edwina was a soft-spoken woman. I enjoyed spending time talking with her, although it was her daughter that I was there to spend time with. I headed back to North Carolina and college in late January 1965 for the spring semester, the school term 1964–1965. I kept in touch with my dear friend and looked forward to seeing her often. Upon completing her degree at Jersey City State, she moved in with her Uncle Sonny and his wife, Estelle. They lived in Elizabeth, New Jersey. Although he treated me kindly, I always felt that he did not trust me with his niece. We spent evenings and weekends alone in Jersey City. I treated her very respectfully as the classy lady she was. In all the years I knew her, we never did anything that I am ashamed of or would not do publicly. I had very strong feelings for her and always treated her in the highest regard. We were both young, and

I cared for her in a very special manner. Strange as it may seem, I never even kissed her or attempted to kiss her. Surely I wanted to and certainly could have many, many times. I wanted the moment of kissing her to be very meaningful, not just physical passion. Call me lame, old-fashioned, afraid, or any other name, but it thrilled me to be with her. Just holding her hand and feeling the warmth of her blood pulsating in my hands left me with a major high. It stimulated my senses. The story didn't end there because there were miles to go before I slept.

Upon returning to Smith for the 1965 spring semester, my work-aid assignment was in the campus post office, and I did so until I graduated in May 1967. As the campus mailperson, I got to know every student on campus by name (this was long before e-mails, texts, smartphones, or social media). As a game, I paid especially close attention to their mail. I could tell if an envelope was from their relatives or a special friend just by their body language. Their facial expression and the regularity of the mail told me a lot about the sender. Based on from whom and from where the mail came, I learned a very valuable lesson. If a female student expected mail, usually it was not from home. I could tell by body language or facial expression whether it was from a very, very special friend, like a boyfriend. I would raise a mental eyebrow if I knew she already had a boyfriend on or near campus. I learned both the job and students well. I enjoyed working in the campus post office. It sharpened my observation skills and heightened my senses to be able to read people. These were inherent abilities that would serve me well in other phases of my life.

During my four and a half years as a JCSU student, I can say I got to know many students, not just their names. However, I only knew three women that I can call *true* and *special* friends. I worked with two of them in the campus post office. I had known the other one since junior high school. They will always be my genuine special friends.

A Life-Changing Speech

As I continued my journey of faith and strength, I was reminded of JFK's inaugural speech that captivated my attention as a junior in high school. I glued a silhouette of President Kennedy in my year-book, along with this quote.[49] The quote as it appeared, "And so, my fellow Americans: ask not what your country can do for you, but rather ask what you can do for your country. My fellow citizens of the world: ask not what America will do for you, but what together we can do for the freedom of man." After that speech, I was motivated to make a difference, whether for me, my family, my country, or the world.

I was reminded of President Kennedy's speech and quote in the spring of 1966. The US Peace Corps sent a Smith graduate, a Returned Peace Corps Volunteer (RPCV), to campus on a recruiting trip. The Smith graduate had served as a PCV in West Africa. She completed her tour of duty and hoped to recruit others to do as she had done. I knew her. She was a senior my freshman year. Her Peace Corps experience got my attention. I took the application and promised to complete it. It was nearly about twenty-five pages. As I read it and reviewed the questions, I became curious. I thought I had everything! No, I was a lot more positive and really had everything to gain and nothing to lose. I spent a lot of time thinking about it. The day after I completed the documentation requested for the application, I handed it in to the PCV. My attitude was, I would wait and see. The RPCV submitted my application to the Peace Corps in Washington. After a short while, I was accepted.

I still had a year to complete my degree. Acceptance into the Peace Corps and being assigned a tour of duty required a success-ful completion of a multiphased training program. I was selected to attend phase 1. I spent the summer evaluating the Peace Corps, and they were doing the same for me. The sole purpose was to determine if I had what it took to serve, work independently and unsupervised in Kenya, East Africa.

Before the summer training started, there were a few administrative things I had to complete. I had to pass a physical examination and had some minor dental work done at the US taxpayers' expense. Having completed my junior year of college, I took my very first plane ride via North West Orient (now defunct) from Philadelphia to the Midwest industrial town of Milwaukee, Wisconsin. Upon completing a successful phase-1 training, I returned to college and completed my requirements for graduation.

I was not obligated to serve or join the Peace Corps. It offered me an opportunity to travel and see places that I ordinarily wouldn't see. I teamed and spent the summer with college students from across America representing Stanford, Berkley, UCLA, Harvard, University of Nebraska, Texas College, and other universities. We met on the campus of University of Wisconsin at Milwaukee, and the experience was electrifying and insightful. The participants were bright-eyed and very idealistic about making a difference by changing the world for the better. We spent a fair amount of time on buses and began to know each other very well. We visited dairy farmers around the state of Wisconsin. We stayed two weeks on the University of Wisconsin-Madison main campus for lectures, presentations, and demonstrations by professors on best practice dairy-farming techniques. We then traveled by bus to North Carolina due to an airline strike and spent a week living and working with black tobacco farmers. The summer of 1966 was the most fulfilling summer of my life. It planted the seeds of what was to come, and I experienced tremendous personal growth.

I returned to Smith in the fall of 1966 to finish my senior year of college. We continued the Peace Corps Advance Training Program (PC-ATP) in December of 1966 during the college Christmas recess. We met for a week of training in Tuskegee, Alabama. We traveled from Montgomery to a wooded area, some ten miles from Tuskegee, and never did get to see Tuskegee, the city or school. When we arrived in Montgomery on Sunday evening, the temperature was eighteen degrees. Fifty young men from Maine to California, students from UConn, University of Maine, and other schools, rode on the back of uncovered trucks about forty miles to the Tuskegee site. None of us were dressed or prepared for such harsh conditions. Imagine the temperature, already eighteen degrees, and riding on the back of an open truck at fifty miles an hour. Many of us were frozen stiff. We could hardly get off the truck after arriving at the site. The wind-chill factor felt like it was in minus degrees with the combination of the frigid night air and the cold wind penetrating our bodies as the uncovered truck traveled at fifty miles per hour.

We arrived at the Tuskegee camp well after 9:00 p.m. It was a very dark location. To find a place to sleep, we had to use Coleman lanterns. Our only option was to choose the best cabin we could find in the darkness, crawl into our sleeping bags, and hope that sleep would find its way into our eyes. It was an 18' × 18' feet concrete slab base. It was made entirely of plastic on all sides, including the roof. The next morning, as each of us arose from our sleeping bags, we saw our living quarters for the first time. After breakfast, we inspected our individual abodes and made any necessary repairs. Some of the cabins had real personalities and were very creatively designed, although they were not very practical for cold-weather survival. The facility's living quarters were designed for summer living, but we were there for a week's stay during the dead of winter. Each of us inspected the living space and made repairs for potential intrusions of precipitation or the impact of low temperatures. We then built, rebuilt, redesigned, and reoccupied them according to our own imaginations. Other Peace Corps volunteers in training had previously constructed the cabins. They had trained and lived in the camp, for six weeks the previous summer, before they left for Kenya on a two-year tour of duty.

At the Tuskegee campsite, we continued our preparation for a tour as a PCV in Kenya. The preparation included developing skills or exercising our existing farm skills. Having farmed early Monday morning, we met for breakfast in the central facility where language training and group sessions took place. We spent most of the week in language training. We had group and individual sessions with a psychologist. The group sessions were designed to see how well each of us adjusted under pressure. It was a prescreening exercise, involving trash-talking in a controlled environment, and ultimately, it would be one reason that only thirty-five of the sixty-five volunteers who started the program made it to Kenya. It was all about being able to adapt and adjust to other people and cultures. After all, we would represent the United States of America as ambassadors.

The temperature never rose above twenty degrees during the entire week we were there. The shower facilities were centrally located. To have heated water, someone had to build a fire and wait perhaps an hour or two for the water to warm. We had a dilemma. Our choices were to get up in twenty-degree temperatures, take a cold shower, or build a fire to heat one hundred gallons of water so we all could take a hot shower. We surmised that one of us would have to rise very early to build a fire to heat that quantity of water. Neither of the options were good. In the end, we chose not to shower. We washed and brushed our teeth using ice water. Our stay ended just as it had begun—very cold. It was time to pack up and return home. None of us had ever unpacked our bags. We left as we came, riding on the back of an old US Air Force flatbed truck without any covering. It could not have gotten any worse; nonetheless, we all endured and returned home for Christmas before we went back to college for our final semester.

Graduation

After several years, I adjusted to normal college life and focused on studying. I overcame the big hiccup that almost destroyed my dreams. I was very focused for the final stretch. I had completed the requirements for my college degree. So I took additional and related courses that specialized in my major which was economics. A degree in economics was the closest I got to a business major at Smith. After taking the fewest economics classes possible, I still earned a degree in economics. The business management course options piqued my interest more. So I took classes in accounting, business law, taxes, banking, finance, and real estate. These subjects were more sensible and logical and easy for me to grasp. I found them stimulating. They were practical and I could see and relate to their real-world applications and implications. The subject matter was less theoretical. Finally this was what I thought college would be like.

If I wanted to see the fruit on the other side of the mountain, I had to make the climb first. My second-year struggles with sociology, biology, geometry, German, and statistics were on the slippery slopes of the mountain, and they appeared to be my downfall. Happily, to this end, I successfully navigated those slopes and reached the summit. Let me confess, Mr. Baker, my brother Billy's friend who helped me with my college essay, was correct when he said that college requires discipline and focus. His theory was tested. I was accepted at JCSU as a probationary entrant. I did not impress the college with my sophomore effort. I was suspended and subsequently was given a second chance. I needed a wake-up call and, boy, did I get one! I had the aptitude, the will, and the support system to attend and earn a college degree. I was the first child in my family to do so. I was determined not to let myself down or to disappoint my family. The time away from JCSU allowed me to mature, refocus, and make the necessary adjustments to succeed. Once I accepted the responsibility for my success or failure, I earned As, with a splatter of Bs, without much effort in my last two years of school.

Choice of Door: 1 or 2

My next options, after graduation, were very limited. I had not yet considered attending graduate school, and I had no job offers. What would I do after graduation? There were two options: to either choose from behind door 1 or choose from behind door 2. Unlike the game shows, I knew what was behind each door. The option behind door 1 was go to Kenya as a Peace Corps volunteer (PCV) if chosen. Regardless of the outcome, the Peace Corps training had already been a great experience. Since the government had invested sizable resources to prepare me to serve as a goodwill ambassador, I wanted to complete the assignment. Some who signed up for the Peace Corps did so because their states of residence were running out of noncollege-age men to draft, especially California. All of us, trained to serve as Peace Corps volunteers, were still subject to the draft. The option behind door 2 was to be drafted and, most likely, be sent to Vietnam. I loved my country despite the option behind door 2 not being a good one for me at that time.

Ultimately I was blessed and selected to go to Kenya as a PCV. None of the thirty-five PCVs, who served as a PCV in Kenya, was obligated to stay in the Peace Corps program. In the mid-'60s, the Vietnam War was going strong and men were drafted to serve in the military. We had the option of serving in the military, typi-

cally in army artillery division. We were young idealists with varying thoughts about the war and sought another way to serve. Every
male, upon turning age eighteen, was required to register with his
local selective service board. Avoiding the draft was not my primary
motivation for joining the Peace Corps. I believed that serving my
country, and mankind for the greater good, far outweighed war. I was
aware that Peace Corps service did not substitute for military service.
Joining the Peace Corps did not exempt any of us from military duty.
All of us who trained to serve as Peace Corps volunteers were subject
to the draft. As volunteers, we hedged our bets that the war would be
over before our tours of duty were completed.

The Vietnam War had not ended. In fact, it had escalated
before we returned home. Some returning volunteers were drafted
and served honorably as I would have, if I had been drafted. When I
returned from my Kenyan assignment, I was more mature. I understood life more. I had grown to appreciate that I can control some
events, others are out of my hands, and others are in the hands of
God. Above all, I had partaken in many cultural exchanges with
different ethnicities in various places. Some of my experiences were
positive and growth-inspiring. Others were surprising. And one
or two incidences were downright uncomfortable. Each of those
encounters made me realize that my sweet home country had some
blotches and some evolving to do, but I knew, for sure, that America
was number 1 and was second to none. I felt that my representation
of America as PCV had a hand in making and keeping it great. I felt
that my representation of America as PCV had a hand in making
and keeping it great.

The Draft Process

Every American male was required to register with the Selective
Service System (SSS) at the age of eighteen. I registered and was issued
a registration certificate, required by law, on June 28, 1961. My SSS
number was 28-9-43-219.[50] On the back of the registration was the
following: address and location of the local board, which was 9 for
New Jersey, Fourth Floor, US Post Office, Market and Fourth Street,

Camden, New Jersey. Other details included on the card were color of eyes, hair color, height, and weight. As shown from the address, a lot has changed since then. That was the era before zip codes were implemented.

The draft was for real. The law carried a fine up to $10,000 or imprisonment up to five years or both for alteration, forging, or changes in any manner to the SSS card. The law also required the card to be in my possession always and to notify the local board in writing: (1) of every change of address, physical condition and occupation, marital status, family changes, dependency, and military status, and (2) of any other fact which might change my classification.

A few years later, congress changed the SSS of the United States. During my college years, the Selective Service drafted young men into the army unless the draftee was a full-time college student or had a deferment. On December 1, 1969, instead of the draft, the SSS of the United States conducted, for the first time, two lotteries that determined the order of call to military service for the Vietnam War for men born between 1944–1950. Days of the year, including February 29, were written on slips of paper. The slips were placed in separate plastic capsules, mixed in a shoebox, and were dumped into a deep glass jar/capsule and drawn from the jar one at a time. The first number drawn was 258 for September 14. So all registrants with that birthday were assigned lottery 1. The second number drawn was 115 for April 24, and so forth. All men of draft age, born between 1944–1950, who had the same birthdate were called to serve at once. My birth year, 1943, was outside of the draft lottery interval 1944-1950. So, I was no longer required to serve in the military.

Counting Down

As in baseball, it was the ninth inning; the group of sixty-five that started in the Peace Corps training program was down to forty-five. There was no finite number of us to go to Kenya. It was a matter of prerequisites like temperament, mental and physical fitness. I met the criteria and requirements. Now it was down to who would be chosen to go. There was one final screen. Peer recruits and the Peace

Corps staff were required to decide who would go to Kenya. Those of us who remained had personal input based on personal interactions, observations, and knowledge of who deserved to serve in Kenya's development. The process was very subjective. Nevertheless, it was the best process we had for selecting who would go. However, the psychologist's input was probably the tiebreaker and carried the most weight. It boiled down to one's ability to get along with people. In summary, if one of us had issues with a peer, then he/she would have difficulty adjusting in a foreign country, Kenya with its people, environment, food, culture, and other unknowns.

Like a relief pitcher, it was the bottom of the ninth inning. The game was tied and it was up to the teammates to win the game. The preparation had been completed and out of my hands. Each of us did our part. Who would go or who would stay was out of my hands. I was committed to go, and I was ready to go. I was excited and looked forward to leaving America on a two-year assignment and to be exposed to new experiences, different cultures, people, and all that came with being a PCV. I tried to imagine my feeling of being in Africa. I wanted to be exposed to people who looked like people I knew but spoke a different language and lived in a country that was eight thousand miles from the place I called home. After much consideration, the decision was made in early August 1967. Thirty-five of the forty-five young men who completed PC-ATP took off as a team to serve two years in Kenya.

The journey started in the summer of 1966, more than a year before, with sixty-five idealistic young men who dreamed of changing the world. Thirty-five young American men were chosen to go: three blacks and thirty-two whites. Fifty-four percent of the original group of sixty-five was assigned to Kenya as Peace Corps Volunteers. On April 12, 1967, the US State Department issued me a US passport with stamped visas in anticipation and with the assurance that I would be going to Kenya, if selected. It read:

> I, the undersigned Secretary of State of
> The United States of America hereby request all
> whom it may concern to permit the citizen(s) of

the United States named herein to pass without
delay or hindrance and in case of need to give
said citizen(s) all lawful aid and protection.
Signed by the US Secretary of State,
Dean Rusk.

Reality of Leaving America

When I left America for Kenya on my PCV assignment, I really
did not leave any deep-rooted relationships other than family. I had
been trying to cultivate one. I wished it would grow very deeply and
have sturdy roots over a lifetime. I never knowingly invested in a
relationship that I felt would yield a negative return. My unique
most-guarded assets, my emotions, were far too valuable, fragile, and
precious to me.

I discussed the PCV adventure, the excitement, and the desire
to serve in Kenya with my treasured friend from Jersey City. We
never discussed our future together, but I always dreamed that she
would be in my life. If she had asked me not to go to Kenya, I would
have known exactly how she felt about me. She didn't because we
were two of a kind. We never pushed one another to do what the
other one wanted. To us, love was not selfish and did not insist on
having its own way. She understood that the Peace Corps service
was something I just had to do. While I was in Kenya, she would
always be in my thoughts. Perhaps I should have anticipated her concerns, feelings, hopes, and desires. I should have, at least, discussed
them; but on the contrary, I didn't. Was I immature, selfish, or was I
just plain clueless? In truth, I was leaving the country and I did not
want to lose her. We would communicate regularly. I promised that
I would return. I hoped that she would wait for me and would have
faith that I would do as I promised.

Could it be that I was afraid or too immature to verbally invest
my sentimental capital in a relationship with a two-year absence? I
felt mentally and emotionally committed, but I did not dare verbalize
that commitment. Perhaps I was afraid to ask for hers because I was
unsure of her response. I was the only person she was seeing at the

time. Leaving my safe abode, my home in America, and all familial relationships were very difficult. I did not want to add a broken heart to the equation. It would be too much to bear. If I got too emotionally attached, would I be distraught and unable to do my job eight thousand miles away in Kenya? The apprehension, anticipation, and the unexpected threw me a bit off kilter. Bottom line, I wanted both: to stay in America and be with her and go to Kenya and perform my duties. In the end, I took the risk of going and hoping that she would wait until I kept my promise to return.

Up, Up, and Away

On August 15, 1967, we left America by way of New York's Kennedy International Airport on board a KLM chartered flight to Nairobi, Kenya. Our all-male Kenya-bound agricultural group shared the flight with other volunteers, educators, males, and females bound for Senegal and Cameroon. We enjoyed their company to Amsterdam. There they changed airplanes bound for West Africa and we continued the KLM chartered to Kenya with stops in Beirut and Addis Abba before reaching Nairobi, Kenya.

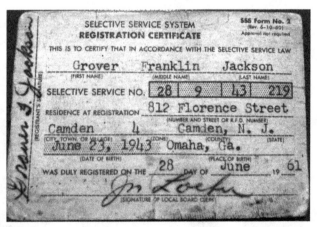

A glued silhouete of President Kennedy in my
CHS yearbook alone with this quote.

My SSS Card issued shortly after my 18th birthday; like my SS Card
it includes a middle name that doesn't exit on my bith certificate.

Chapter 10

Kenya's Experiences

Nakuru, Kenya

I arrived in Nakuru, Kenya, August 1967.[51] The city had a population about fifty thousand. It was located approximately 97 miles northwest of Nairobi and sets about 1.15 miles above sea level and within the Great Rift Valley. Nakuru derived its name from Nakurro or Maasai, meaning a dusty place. It is located between Lake Nakuru National Park, known for its pink flamingos, and to the South is the Menengai Crater. It is 7,800 miles from New York City as the sign at its highest peak stated. The economy of Nakuru was largely dependent on the rich agricultural land areas. Its rolling hills and valleys were ideal for crops grown when I was there. Some of the crops were coffee, sisal, pyrethrum, corn, and wheat. Some other economic staples were dairy products such as milk and butter. The biggest economic contributor to Nakuru was tourism due to Lake Nakuru, its volcanic landscapes, and its natural habitat for iconic pink flamingos.

Upon arriving for my new job assignment, I met the Peace Corps volunteers that I was replacing. They took the time and introduced me to my new environment and some of the people that I would be interacting with on a regular basis, namely farmers, other PVCs, British expatriates, Germans, Dutch, and other Americans who were living in Nakuru at that time.

The Assignment

Kenya gained its independence from Britain on December 12, 1963. Prior to the transition of power, a little over 55,000 whites controlled the East African country of more than 18.4 million Africans. Kenya was one of the last East African colonies to be ruled by Britain. Before its independence, Europeans owned and cultivated the fertile Rift Valley farmland. The Kenyan government purchased the farms from the Britain expatriates. Some of the new Kenyan farm owners had previously worked for the expatriates before becoming independent. After Kenya gained its independence, some of the expatriates stayed and became Kenyan citizens and continued farming.[52] However, many were unwilling to live in Africa under a majority-rule government.[53] So they migrated further south to Rhodesia, now Zimbabwe. Rhodesia was a white-minority-ruled government, a British colony, until April 14, 1980, when it too came under native African leadership.

As a PCV, I shared with the new farmers the basic details on the how and why of successful farming.[54] My work area covered nearly seventy-five Kenyan farmers and more than fifty thousand acres. From time to time, we attended locally sponsored government farm seminars that demonstrated successful farm practices. We also visited government-owned and operated farms to highlight best practices farm principles for cash crops and dairy animals.

As a PCV goodwill ambassador, I solicited peer farmers to tell about their experiences and share the successful principles they used. The experiences shared by fellow countrymen meant a lot more to the farmers than anything we offered. I was a messenger who bought Kenyan farmers together. Some of their successes were minor. Nevertheless, they provided positive input that made the farmers very proud of the fact that they had contributed. It was one small stride for the local farmer and a giant stride for Kenyan farmers. They realized, right away, that successful farming led to small advances that ultimately led to sound management practices. Their realization was supported by written plans that were well-documented and executed. My assigned work location was upcountry in Nakuru, located in the middle of the Rift Valley. It had splendid vistas of the countryside.

Letter to Mom (September 4, 1967)

Dear Mom,

We have just finished in-country training and I am glad to leave away from there to do some actual work. Up to now, we have been eating, sleeping, and going on field trips. This is my chance to prove myself. Just this morning, I met our Kenyan District Agricultural Officer and received my job assignment. Of all the different jobs, I think mine is the most interesting and best one. I will be doing large scale farm extension work. I will be working in and out of an office with land surveyors, map drawers, and farm layout teams. I will be recommending to them what to plant, where, and why based on Kenya's longterm strategy for land use. The final decision will be decided on by the land owners.

The climate here is ideal, with temperatures very rarely getting below 45 Degrees Fahrenheit. We are about 7,000 feet above sea level. There are plenty of hills and valleys here in the Nakuru District. At times, I will travel up to 9,000 feet above sea level and travel more than 50 miles a day riding a Triumph motorcycle. The area in Nakuru where I will be living is 6,000 feet above sea level or about 1.5 miles above the sea. After all, this is the Rift Valley, a large escarpment that runs through all nine East African countries which are: Ethiopia, Kenya, Uganda, Rwanda, Burundi, Zambia, Tanzania, Malawi and Mozambique resulting in some of the most scenic views seen by mankind. I get to see some of them each day as well as cross the equator. The equator is just an imaginary line that separates the northern and southern hemispheres. That is as much geography and science I need to discuss for this letter.

As for living quarters, I do not have any yet. I will be leaving here on tomorrow, Monday, September 4. The date above is for Monday since I will not mail it until tomorrow. Last Wednesday, an Englishman invited me to his home for dinner. He works for the Kenyan government and we will be working in the same office, but not doing the same work.

Last night, I met a journalist who wanted to discuss the "Negro" problem in America. He is a Kenyan who I do not care for or think very much of because he is the very person who writes negative articles about the Peace Corps volunteers of which I am one. Without talking to any of us he generalized and said that we were here on a paid vacation. If I was on a paid vacation, I certainly would need more than one hundred dollars a month to live on.

Tell Christine, Annie and all others that the television stations here are up to date. They have some of the same television programs you see back in the states, especially the night programs. You just name it, and, they have it. Almost everything you can see, we can see also. However, I do not have a television and will not purchase one and even if I did, there is no guarantee that I will have electricity to operate it. I really like the Kenya radio station here, and am unpacking my battery powered radio on tomorrow, I will purchase a tape recorder to tape music. I bought tapes some time ago and both the radio and tape recorder use batteries. I am going to purchase a camera around Christmas that will cost about two hundred and fifty Kenyan Shillings which is thirty-six dollars in US currency.

I will not hire a cook because I am too particular about my foods. I will cook for myself. Yesterday I washed my clothes for the first time, all by hand in a bucket which was fun. I have seen everything here except an automatic washer.

I am still passing as an African, it does not pay all the times especially when I am trying to get a ride to town. Only Africans will stop to give me a ride unless I am with a White Peace Corps Volunteer (PCV), then Europeans and Asians will stop as well. They think I am his servant and upon learning otherwise, they want to invite me home for dinner. Go figure!

I am going to get another language instructor. The Peace Corps will pay any expenses incurred. I am still planning to live off twenty-five dollars a month. However, I still must buy cooking supplies, and right now, I do not know if I will have electricity. There is a chance I will and a chance I will not have electricity.

Always,
Your Beloved Son
Grover

As I became more accustomed to the country, I realized that being stationed in the heart of Nakuru literally put me out of touch with home and family. In an emergency, the options to contact me were limited. The only mailing address was Peace Corps, Washington, DC, by way of the US Embassy in Kenya. In a real emergency, a call was made to the US State Department in Washington, DC. The emergency information would then be transferred to the US Embassy in Kenya to an in-country Kenyan representative, and then to my

Peace Corps supervisor. The supervisor would drive as many hours as necessary to find me and communicate the nature of the emergency. There was no guarantee that I would be at my residence or reachable within any reasonable amount of time. I could have been out visiting my local contacts or performing my field assignments. I had a family emergency a month to the day, on September 15, 1967, after I arrived and settled in Nakuru.

Returning Home

Bob (Robert), sibling 9, died on September 15, 1967. It was tough dealing with a death in the family so many miles away. It was a total shock. He had not shown any physical signs of being ill. Upon leaving for my PCV assignment, I said goodbye. I told him, confidently, I would see him in a couple of years. It never even occurred to me that those would be the last words I spoke to him.

My Peace Corps supervisor drove, with my plane ticket in hand, ninety-seven miles from Nairobi to tell me to return to America for my brother's funeral. Shaken, I packed a suitcase, and he drove me back to the Nairobi airport. I had a lonely eight-thousand-mile flight back to the US to be with my family after Bob's death. It had been slightly more than a month since I left America and said farewell to him.

Bob was a very special person. He was a loner, quiet, and easygoing. He had a wry dry sense of humor. He could deliver a zinger, jokingly critical of a sibling, and you wouldn't even realize that he had done it until sometime later. He was small and thin in stature. He had learning disabilities that caused him to be slow mentally in a school environment. So he never graduated from high school. He was born with a hole in his heart. His health issues and conditioning were not discovered until our arrival in Camden. I'm uncertain if he ever visited a doctor in Stewart County. Aside from bouts with asthma attacks, Bob never suffered physically. He functioned normally without issues and traveled about on his own without any assistance. He and Gustin, my youngest son, were born on January 3, thirty-eight years apart. Bob was twenty-two years old when he passed away.

The only way I handled his death was to be home with the family around me. Bob was the first sibling to pass. It was tough getting through the grief, thus I had to pull myself together, regroup, and move on with my life. It was not easy for me to do. I cannot explain my reasoning, but I had to grieve quietly and alone. I never saw his body and I did not attend his wake or funeral, so after a week at home with the family, I returned to Kenya and resumed my PCV assignment.

The next immediate family member's death happened seventeen years later, on January 22, 1984. This one stung deeply into my core and hurt beyond any describable words that I could say. Since 1967, six siblings—three were sisters and three were brothers—along with both parents have died.

A Costly Incident

In June 1968, I had a flare-up of gout and bunions or vice versa or both. The problem stemmed from wearing ill-fitted shoes when I was a child. Growing up, I wore shoes too small and very tight out of necessity. Because we were poor, all my siblings did the same. My gout condition started long before I arrived in Kenya. I suffered tremendous foot pain years earlier in junior high school. It became more aggravated in Kenya, perhaps from walking and kick-starting my motorcycle. After a few months, I was unable to put enough pressure on either foot to start my motorcycle. Obviously I had issues that had to be dealt with. The pain was so agonizing, even a light breeze on my feet was unbearable. The suffering became increasingly acute as time passed. I finally saw a podiatrist who recommended surgery to resolve the problem. He performed the surgery in Nairobi. Being unable to ride a motorcycle, I spent almost two months recuperating in Nairobi.

During my recuperation, I was assigned and worked on a United Nations Economic Farm Impact Study project. The project was not the focus of the next experience I will share. I got myself into a rather sticky situation and almost didn't get out of it alive. While on the UN assignment, I was given a small jeep for transportation until my feet healed. During my stay in Nairobi, I stayed with my Peace Corps supervisor.

One day, while at work, I struck up a conversation with a young Kenyan from the Kikuyu tribe. As we talked, the conversation led to how she got to work and what part of Nairobi she lived in. Eventually I offered her a ride home. She and my Peace Corps supervisor lived in the same neighborhood. Giving her a ride saved her hours of time. Public transportation in Nairobi wasn't very good or reliable. Perhaps to say thank you, she invited me into her apartment for chai (Swahili) which is tea. Chai along with *kahawa*, Swahili for coffee, are social drinks. I accepted her invitation. It was an English custom, twice daily, to take a tea and biscuit break. The breaks were usually between 10:30 a.m. and 4:00 p.m. Culturally it would have been an insult for me to refuse her invitation. After all, I was there not only to do a job but to be an American goodwill ambassador as well. We entered her apartment, and she continued to the kitchen to prepare the tea (it was a peculiarity to me that many Kenyans, Europeans, Asians, and Africans used milk instead of water to make tea or coffee. They would boil the milk, tea, or coffee and sugar together).

While the tea was brewing, she briefly left and went to her bedroom. I overheard a commotion involving her and a male. They were engaged in a spirited conversation. Approximately ten minutes later, she brought me the cup of tea and then left again for her bedroom. The commotion resumed. Voices had raised, and the tone was heated.

Many small Kenyan apartments consisted of a living room, kitchen, and bedroom and a small entranceway. The bedroom was usually located on the other side of the kitchen with the living room nearest the entrance. Her apartment was no different than all the others. I heard the young Kenyan and male speaking in a combination of Swahili and English in the bedroom, and it wasn't a normal or pleasant-sounding conversation. I was getting very uncomfortable. Then I heard her say very clearly, "No, let him alone, I invited him in for chai."

His response, "I will teach this American a lesson." And then there was a bit of scuffling and the talking got louder and his voice got angrier. I sat in the living room, as calmly as I could, under the circumstances. Then I became edgy, nervous, jittery, anxious, and stressed. I didn't know what to do. I began hoping for the best but expecting the worst. In those days, neither the police nor the general public carried guns, therefore, I had no fear of being injured or killed by gunshot in Kenya.

Seconds later, the male emerged from the bedroom coming toward me with the young lady hanging onto him, trying to take something away from him. I got up, forgetting the chai that was on the coffee table. It was time for me to leave without a confrontation and hopefully unharmed. I said to him, whom I had never met, "Mister, if you let me go this time, you will never see me again."

He didn't like or accept that option. So I grabbed the instrument and tried unsuccessfully to take it away. Then I asked her to hold the instrument and him until I could make my getaway. I maneuvered the three of us around the coffee table until my back was against the living room entrance door. I opened the door, tried to make an escape while all the time asking her to hold firmly onto the instrument so I could get out and run to my vehicle. She tried unsuccessfully to keep him inside. I took a chance and ran to the vehicle and tried to start it before he got there. Keep in mind, it had not been that long ago that I ran track and I still believed I had breakaway speed.

I briefly forgot that I was recovering from foot surgery. My attempt to create a comfortable lead failed. When I reached the car, I was fidgeting and was unable to get the key into the jeep ignition to start it. By the time I did, he was banging on the windshield with an iron pipe. It was three to four feet long and about an inch in diameter. He screamed, "Get out, get out, I'm going to teach you a lesson. I'm going to teach you a lesson!"

With my heart pounding, I thought, *How will I be able to explain the damage to the vehicle?* And more importantly, *What if I'm injured!* I stopped trying to start the jeep. Instead I started begging, saying, "Mister, if you let me go this time, you will never see me again." I repeatedly begged and pleaded, saying, "Mister, let me go, you will never see me again." It worked. He let me go, and I left with my heart beating beyond any rate I had ever experienced from either fear or running track.

The next morning, I awoke with the realization that the encounter happened. It was not just a bad dream. Upon seeing me at work, she was embarrassed and apologized for the encounter. I was just happy that I had lived to tell the story. I never offered or gave her a ride and never visited her place again. To my knowledge, I kept my promise and never saw her companion again and I do not believe that he ever set eyes me. Bottom line, this was one time the Temptations song "Ain't Too Proud to Beg" proved true.

My mother used to say that anyone could be a hero, even the dead and buried. There are lots of them. She emphasized, a man is not a man because of his brute strength. He's one because he uses his head. As children, we used to come home bleeding from scratches and bruises. As she cleaned us up, she drilled into us, it's okay to walk away or run away from a confrontation, if necessary. "A man walks away and only a fool would stay and fight." She would exclaim and ask, "What good would come from fighting?"

On that day, I remembered to avoid confrontation at all cost. There was nothing to be gained. On that day, in addition to thinking about being physically harmed and the vehicle damaged, I also kept in mind that I was a guest of the Kenyan government and a representative of the United States of America. I had nothing to gain and everything to lose to prove what? On that day, I took my mother's advice. I took the high road and lived to see another day. I have seen many days, months, and years evolve with my pride and ego still intact.

Volunteers and Others

There were up to ten American PCVs in or near Nakuru when I arrived. Several of them did the same job that I was assigned to do, although they did not have the same coverage area. Other PVCs were educators, mainly teachers, that I befriended and with whom I shared social events. Included in the group were Canadians, Germans, and other foreigners, expatriates, and Kenyan locals. Several of the American PCV tours of duty had expired and they were returning home. One of the PCVs, was an attorney from Chicago. He was a bit older than those of us who had just arrived. He was very sociable and had a great sense of humor. He also loved to play chess. While our tours overlapped, we played chess every time we met. It was a game I enjoyed. I came very close to winning several times, although I never did win a match. I will never know if he was very good or if I was just mediocre. We didn't outwardly compete. Skill levels did not matter. Playing chess helped to pass the time away, especially on rainy days.

I replaced one of the two PCVs assigned to work with the Kenyan farmers in Nakuru. One was black; and although he called Detroit his home, he was like me—born in the South, specifically in Greenville, Alabama. The other PCV was a native of Chicago. They both were intellectuals and stimulating to be around. One was a talker and the other one was a thinker; both were great conversationalists. About the only place we could get to on a motorcycle, during the rainy season, was the home of an American couple. On rainy days, traveling on a motorcycle on muddy dirt roads was not ideal or easy.[55] In fact, it was almost impossible. The mud gripped the tires and clogged up the motorcycle fenders. The couple lived in the city of Nakuru. Their home turned out to be our home away from home until they returned to the States. I missed them enormously when they left. They were genuine and great company. Additionally we enjoyed great meals at their house. The young American couple was from Minnesota, and they had one child, a toddler, whom we enjoyed and entertained. It was a delight to go to their home in Nakuru because we knew we would have a great time of fellowshipping, conversing, and solving the world's problems. It did not hurt that we also feasted on hardy American meals. Being new to Kenya, I had an open invitation to visit, along with the other volunteers, and we exercised it often. The lady of the house allowed us to buy food or give her money to buy food stuffs that we liked. I sensed that she only accepted our money to make us feel like we were contributing and not being freeloaders.

She was from a wealthy family and appreciated our company. She even insisted that we stay over many nights as we allowed darkness to slip up on us. She was home with their son all day and welcomed our company. She was the only married American woman that I knew who lived in Nakuru, and she was an only child to her parents. Both she and her husband were very hospitable. We entertained her in conversation about subjects she wanted to discuss. She was insightful and spoke about issues that most men just ignored. She was a classy lady, very attractive, and smart. Having her family as friends really helped me to adjust quickly to my new environment.

The PCV I replaced joined the Peace Corps straight out of college like most of us. I lived in the same house he occupied after he returned to the States. He was a talker, very intelligent, and while the other PCV (attorney) and I played chess, he and the wife of the American diplomat solved the world's problems. It was mutually beneficial for all of us to be together. While we enjoyed our Kenyan associates and spent time together, our discussions were not always culturally relevant. So it was always refreshing to get together, among friends, without the worry of making culturally nuanced blunders.

The PCV I replaced in Kenya returned to Detroit and was drafted into the army and served in combat in Vietnam. I ran into him, some thirty years after our Peace Corps tour, in the Atlanta Airport as we were traveling between cities. I recognized him by his gait and his physical build. I was completely sure it was the former PCV I had replaced. I called out his name, figuring if it was not him, there would be no harm done. I spoke his name loudly enough for him to hear, and he turned around. As one who has a pretty good memory of people, places, and things, I was quite sure that I knew the walk, remembered his size, and other details. He shared his journey since our Kenya days. He became a very successful corporate attorney for a very large oil company and was now retired. He also shared with me that he had served in the public education sector in Southern California.

At that brief meeting at the airport, for no apparent reason, we did not exchange telephone or any other contact information. In 2016, I decided to write this book and thought about my friend and tried to locate him without any initial success. Finally I got serious about locating him and found him in Burbank, California. Last summer, he came to Atlanta for a visit. We got together and toured the Carter Library, then agreed we would keep the lines of communication open. I promised to visit him this year after the Alaska Cruise and did.

My wife and I, on our return trip from the Johnson C. Smith Class of '67 Alaskan Cruise, continued on a second trip to Burbank, California, to visit her sister. At that time, I visited with my former PCV friend. We agreed to return to Kenya together in 2019 as I had already planned to do. Instead of going on a tour, we plan to rent a vehicle and drive around the areas where we worked and resided.

As we drove around Los Angeles, Hollywood, and Burbank, my friend and I laughed at some of the conversations we had with various individuals while serving in Kenya. One was the Kenya Peace Corps director who was a black African American. I knew him before we left for Kenya and before he was named the Peace Corps director for Kenya. He used to joke with us as new PCVs and would say, "Why did you come all the way to Africa to shovel snow?" The term *shovel snow* referred to us dating white Americans and other non-African women. We didn't just date white American women, we socialized with all races and colors: Asians, South-African blacks, Ugandans, British, Canadian, and European women living and working in Kenya as volunteers like us.

We were young and idealistic. We were in Kenya to serve and to complete the Peace Corps' mission. We were focused on our mission, and we rarely considered the country, origin, or color of the other volunteers with whom we worked. Neither did the women with whom we socialized. We met at my home, at parties in Nairobi, and at the beach as young people often do. We enjoyed the interactions and fellowship. The conversations were stimulating. We discussed our limited worldview of our cultures, and the sharing was insightful. It just boiled down to single people of the same age, living away from home, more than likely, for the first extended period since college.

We validated Maslow's 1943 psychological hierarchy of needs theory. Maslow's theory was that human behavior was developed as he/she moved through different stages of needs. Needs were stacked in a pyramidal or hierarchical manner from bottom to top. He called these needs physiological, safety, love and belonging (social), esteem, and self-actualization. According to Maslow, for one to be the most complete person, the needs at each stage of the hierarchy had to be satisfied from lower to higher. For instance, if basic or physiological needs for food, housing, healthcare, etc. could not be satisfied, then the next stage of safety needs, i.e., morality, employment, feeling of worth, etc. would perhaps be lacking. This would affect family or other relationships, identified by the need for love, trust, and inspiration. Even in Kenya, there were more single women than single men. We were great company for each other. One such female, assigned to the American Embassy, wanted to establish a serious relationship, but I had some unfinished business in the USA and I could not betray a trust. Recently I visited friends in Washington, DC, who spent a tour of duty in Nairobi during my Peace Corps years. I spent many weekends at their Nairobi home. During my visit, our Detroit PCV friend's name came up in a conversation. I was able to share that he had retired as a legal counsel for an oil company and was living in Southern California.

Who was the American in Nakuru and what was his duty? He was assigned to the United States Agency of International Development (USAID). He had a definite job; nevertheless, what was it? I didn't know and am unsure if anyone else knew. I ate at his home many times and he never discussed his USAID assignment with me, and I didn't ask. For all I knew, he could have been a CIA agent or another clandestine US government agent in Kenya. All I remember was he talked about how fast the Porsche he owned could go from zero to sixty. Such a car in Kenya was rare and impractical in our setting. The Porsche seated only two people. Repairs and maintenance, I assumed, had to be done in Nairobi, situated nearly one hundred miles away.

The British expatriates were older and very private. However, they were hospitable and would often socialize with us. Some ran the major businesses in Nakuru. Others were farmers. I got to know and worked with some of them. They lived on the same land they farmed and owned before Kenya's independence. They were great assets to me and to the Kenyan farmers whom I assisted. They had many years of experience farming, and they shared their knowledge freely with the new repatriated Kenyans who became farmers.

During the time I was in Kenya, specifically Nakuru, I don't recall any businesses owned by Kenyans. The key industry products were foreign-owned and run by expatriates, Asians, or the Kenyan government. That was understandable, being that Kenya was a new country that had only earned independence in 1963 which was just four years earlier. The Asians had a lock on all the consumer retail products and services and provided excellent support. My landlord, an Asian lawyer, ran a farm; and in all my dealings with him, he was very fair as were all the shop owners that I dealt with in Nakuru. The US Peace Corps contracted an Asian-owned motorcycle shop in Nakuru that maintained my motorcycle. The owner hired very talented mechanics, and I had good business relationships with them.

I have some friends who are Kenyans and live in the same area where I was assigned and worked. One such friend attended a seminary in Atlanta where I live. He also attended First Baptist Atlanta Church and a Bible study class that I coordinated. He is very talented and has a doctorate in theology. He advised me that he very much wanted to return to Kenya to open a ministry. In 2011, with the support of some church members, we incorporated a not-for-profit 501(c)3 to help achieve his ministerial objectives. The long-term plan to help him become self-sufficient is to establish a chicken farm to fund the ministry by selling eggs.

A Hitchhiking Tip

Occasionally I went to Kenya's capital city, Nairobi, which is ninety-seven miles away from Nakuru. I could not use my motorcycle. It was primarily for PCV business and local transportation. We could use it to commute to see other PCVs or attend social gatherings in nearby communities; then again, driving it to Nairobi for personal weekend trips or taking it on long vacations would have been frowned upon. Initially I tried to hitchhike. I was completely unsuccessful in that effort. There was no safety concern in hitchhiking. However, there was a real issue of getting Asians, Europeans, and middle and upper-class native Kenyans to stop for black hitchhikers. For unknown reasons, very few, if any, would give a black Kenyan or me a ride. Since I am dark complexioned, I could pass as a Kenyan. Consequently when I traveled alone, hitchhiking was an unsuccessful adventure for me. Of course, I could have used a limousine service but I was on a tight budget. Then too, a limousine may have appeared to be too extravagant. Limousine was simply the name of the service. It was not fancy or expensive. The cost to travel from and to Nairobi one way in a limousine at the time was less than seven shillings or one dollar.

After many attempts, I realized the problem and decided to take a different approach. My new approach was to travel and hitchhike with a white PCV companion. It worked perfectly! I observed that drivers stopped readily and picked up white PCVs. If the white PCV was perceived as the primary hitchhiker, then I could enter the vehicle as well. The drivers automatically assumed that I was his servant, so it was okay for me to ride along. Once in the car, we struck up conversations. They learned that I too was an American PCV and I became accepted. My fellow PCVs and I were then all invited over for a meals and fellowship. Just like that, color was no longer an issue.

Living in Nakuru

I lived initially in a small guesthouse located on a coffee farm overlooking the Menengai Crater.[56] Six months into my assignment, I moved to a larger house[57] and shared it with a German volunteer from Frankfurt, West Germany. It was located about a mile from my original guesthouse and faced acres of coffee plants growing at the foot of the Menengai Crater.[58] Only the field of coffee plants separated the house and the crater, about two miles away. The house had three bedrooms. The huge master bedroom faced the crater. It was a typical British house, surrounded by an array of flowering plants. They emitted wonderful fragrances and came in various colors and sizes, and they overlooked the natural landscape provided by the view of the crater.

My housemate, Rolf, and I both arrived in Nakuru about the same time.[59] He came as a replacement for two other German volunteers who were returning home to West Germany. His assignment was to build a community healthcare facility, furnish it. Then turn it over to the Kenyans. The work location assignment was in the Baringo District, some seventy-five miles northeast of Nakuru. He spent several days a week at the development facility before he returned home. Baringo District was an undeveloped restricted area in Northern Kenya that required a government-issued permit to travel and work there. A four-wheel vehicle was a necessity because the roads were treacherous during Kenya's rainy season. Rolf was issued a Land Rover for his work assignment that permitted him to come home on weekends. When he was home, we ate breakfast on the porch, usually something light, cheese, crackers, coffee, and something sweet. Just eating on the porch was worth a lifetime of memories simply because the spectacular view was priceless. We conversed about our week's work experiences. To keep up with what was going on back in the States, I read old news from *The International Tribune*. He read German newspapers. One observation was that things and occurrences that appeared unique and newsworthy a few months earlier were now just normal occurrences.

The larger house was ideal. It was furnished with a wood-burning stove and indoor plumbing but no electricity. It was a great setup. I did all the cooking, although Rolf helped. Food cooked had to be eaten or thrown out. We owned a refrigerator that was powered by paraffin which is a substance used to make candles. The refrigerator provided ice to keep our drinking water cool. We collected rainwater for all our usage in a five-hundred-gallon container that flowed using gravity.[60] We used it for all purposes: drinking, cooking, and personal hygiene. The water we drank and cooked with was boiled on the wood-burning cooking stove. For showering, we simply built a fire under the hot water tank. It got hot, and it lasted several days. With a bit of manual effort, we were able to enjoy all the comforts of royalty. We never ran out of water due to a lack of rain. If we had, there was a water faucet about a half-mile away that the farm residents used. I hired a local Kenyan to provide wood and wash our clothes, and he constantly offered his services to cook for us, although I preferred to do my own cooking. Things I learned while growing up in Georgia were not lost on me. In fact, many similarities from my childhood often crossed my mind.

Under the master bedroom floor was a beehive. I was unaware of it. Then one day, as I was playing with my black Labrador retriever in our front yard, I saw a huge number of bees flying about. They seemed to be coming from underneath the house. There was no access to the hive from the outside, so I decided to take up some of the flooring. I moved my bed and discovered a cutout directly where the hive was located. Obviously the bees had been there for many years and the previous owner knew and collected honey. I was not brave enough to lift the cutout, so I asked the Kenyan who washed our clothes how to scatter the bees so that I could collect the honeycomb. He advised me to use smoke. I had no way to generate the amount of smoke needed to scatter the bees, so I went to the farm supply store and bought some smoke bombs. I used the smoke bombs to disperse the bees and collected the honeycomb. I gave the honeycomb to the Kenyan and asked him to share it with the neighbors.

We had plenty of people visit our new house on the weekends. Mostly they were PCVs who wanted to eat out, catch a movie, or just socialize. We took minisafaris on our motorcycles just to see places like Thomson Falls, a 243-foot scenic waterfall.[61] Thomson Falls was located two miles from the town of Nyahururu, at almost 8,000 feet above sea level, and was in the center of Kenya. It was about thirty miles from home. It was a very popular and picturesque attraction. It was always an enjoyable sight to see regardless of how many times I visited. Another very popular site was at the top of the Menengai Crater that overlooked our house.[62] The crater had a panoramic view of landmarks and landmasses that I could see for miles around me.

My Living Allowance

As PCVs, we were given one hundred dollars each month for our living expenses. It covered our food and other personal expenses. While in Kenya we lived on our allowance and still managed to take two fantastic vacations to Zanzibar and Mount Kenya and beyond.[63] My allowance was deposited on the first of every month into Barclay's Bank. Cash was withdrawn to pay rent and other expenditures. I shopped for food, cooked, and ate well without breaking the bank. Every other month or two, a group of us met in Nairobi for the weekend. An ex-Peace Corps staff member, who was a friend back in the States, lived in Nairobi. When I visited Nairobi, he and his wife provided me with free sleeping quarters in their home. He had been a PCV years earlier in Tanzania. He accepted a position with the US Department of State at the American Embassy in Nairobi, Kenya, as a USAID diplomat.

My Kenya Exploits

My housemate and I often visited Lake Nakuru Kenya National Game Park in his assigned Land Rover. The park was best known as the habitat for seemingly millions of pink flamingos. It was also one of our favorite places to visit. We spent hours bird-watching and in awe at the vast number of bird species in their natural habitat. Many other animals migrated and roamed in and out of the park, namely lions, elephants, wildebeests, water buffaloes, antelopes, and many other wildlife creatures. Most tourists went to the park, including us, to see members of the big five: elephants, lions, cheetahs, rhinoceroses, and leopards. Unfortunately we never saw a leopard at Lake Nakuru, and the only leopard I saw in Africa was in the Serengeti, National Park in Tanzania but never at Lake Nakuru.

During our eight-day December 1968 Christmas safari, however, we saw the big five and many other species. Rolf, six other PCVs, and I left Nakuru with a full itinerary with stops planned in Nairobi, Amboseli Game Park, Arusha, Tanzania, Serengeti Plains, and the Ngorongoro Crater.[64] Our journey terminated at the apex of Mount Kilimanjaro on Christmas Day.

Before our climb of Mount Kilimanjaro, we drove through the vast plains of the Serengeti.[65] We stepped out onto Olduvai Gorge and touched the soil and admired the elegance of it. At the time, I was driving and we drove through herds of animals like gazelles, zebras, wildebeests, and many others.[66] While we observed the natural beauty of the animals and the vastness of the plains, a gazelle ran in front of the Land Rover. I hit and wounded it. It was unavoidable, but still, I was devastated about hitting it. Though I was filled with regret, I had to put the accident aside and move on. In the natural scheme of things, I knew that hyenas, wild dogs, lions, or some other animals or fowl would feast on the wounded gazelle after killing it.

We arrived at Ngorongoro Crater Lodge and Hotel after driving 112 miles from Arusha.[67] We set up our tents on the camping grounds. Our next goal was to build a fire to cook and to primarily keep animals away. A water buffalo came very close to observe before wandering off into the night. The first day of our trip was worth the two years of service alone. After eating dinner, we turned in and woke up early for breakfast and began our descent down the wall into the crater. The estimate of the crater wall is two thousand feet deep and its floor covers 100 square miles. Now that is massive.

The Vacation

As we climbed our way up Kilimanjaro, at fourteen thousand feet, we observed a female Caucasian dressed in a white pantsuit walking ahead of the four Africans. They were carrying her belongings. I shook my head in dismay at the portrayal that she was leading them. Anyone who spent more than a day in East Africa knew those Africans climbed that mountain often and did so with sometimes fifty lbs. and more on their heads. The image struck us as being very odd. We knew those Africans were used to the altitude, and it had little or no effect on them. Outsiders, however, were gasping and struggling for air to breathe. We laughed and joked that even in the heart of Africa, on Mount Kilimanjaro, the stereotypical image of white colonialism was on display for all to see.

Amboseli National Park was the most impressive sight, on a sunny day, with Mount Kilimanjaro as its backdrop. It was sheer splendor. We could see the magnificent snowcapped peak of the mountain in the distance. There were clouds hanging below the mountain peak. Wild animals were in the foreground in their natural habitats. It was a sight to behold. It just didn't get any better than that. We spent two or three hours waiting to get pictures of such splendor but we were unsuccessful, so we captured the images in our minds to view whenever we reminisced. Sometimes the written word just does not give it justice, and Amboseli, Kilimanjaro, Serengeti were such places I am unable to describe with words. Try to imagine the following:

- Climbing Mount Kilimanjaro, a 19,340 feet mountain.
- Driving through the Serengeti Plains and witnessing the vastness of it on a self-guided tour and seeing the Serengeti Plains spanning approximately 18,650 square miles in both Tanzania and Kenya
- Visiting Olduvai Gorge, a steep-sided ravine that stretches some thirty miles through the Eastern Serengeti Plains near Arusha, Tanzania, that some claim to be the most important paleoanthropological sites in the world. I personally viewed it as just another historical site and could say I visited it.
- Admiring Amboseli National Park with its five-thousand-square-mile ecosystem spreading across the Kenya/Tanzania border with Mount Kilimanjaro hovering high above into the clouds. As a backdrop, it provided for some outstanding photographs of the Maasai people, the animals, many species of birds, and scenery.
- Living the dream of being there and experiencing the Ngorongoro Crater, a breathtaking natural wonder, volcanic crater, two thousand feet depth, the twelve miles (across) width, and more than one hundred square miles in area. The breathtaking drive down the narrow single and narrow lane road that an errant move by the driver could prove to be certain death.

It was all the above and much more. I was living the dream of a lifetime. Now a half-century later, I can bring back bittersweet memories of my PCV travels.

Just ten years earlier, I was living in Stewart County, Georgia, and the only difference in my life versus many of the Kenyans' lives were hope and sacrifice by those who made it possible for me to help change lives and to be changed. Moving forward to a few years later and eight thousand miles removed, it made a world of difference in my life, my development, and my experience. I cherished the experience and will for the rest of my life. I have shared my story with many people and hope that the stories, along with the background, will inspire others to look up, look out, and be inspired. Each of us can make a difference around the world right from our current location. We can also venture out, do good deeds, and plant seeds that will change lives for good.

On Thursday, December 26, 1968, we returned from a climb of Africa's tallest mountain, Mount Kilimanjaro. I had fulfilled a dream and accomplished a mission that I would remember for the rest of my life. As we relaxed by the swimming pool at the YMCA in Moshi, Tanzania, where we next boarded, I tried to relive each moment I had experienced in the days prior.[68] I savored each day of the safari and our mountain climb. I was very much aware that in less than eight months, all of us would have completed our two-year tour of duty. We would be performing some other duty(s), perhaps in another foreign land, not of our own choosing. The draft was still active. Like the PCV who I replaced, we could still be sent to Vietnam.

Prior to jumping into the pool, I captured a clear picture of Mount Kilimanjaro.[69] The pool water reflected the majestic mountain and its crest. The image was so vivid that it was difficult to distinguish the pool reflection of the mountain from the mountain itself. Many thoughts raced through my mind that morning. I had just completed an eight-day safari. I had been on Africa's tallest mountain less than twenty-four hours earlier. It didn't matter that I had stopped just short of fifty yards before reaching the apex. The climb was a two-day walk to the last hut, just one hundred yards from the summit at 19,341 feet.[70] We arrived at the last hut on the second day, just before dark. We prepared our evening meal, rested, and started our ascent up the slope. The summit, although less than one hundred yards straight up from 19,000 feet, was not an easy climb. Freezing temperatures, high altitude resulting in thin air, and lack of oxygen made the climb very challenging. The last one-hundred-yard climb started at 3:00 a.m., so climbers could reach the apex at sunrise, between 6:30 a.m. and 7:00 a.m. Due to the thin air, steep slopes, cold temperature, and our insufficient physical conditioning, it took three hours plus to reach the summit. Not everyone in our party made it to the top. Many of us—count me in this category—got so close. The mountain was fierce. There were other factors, but cold temperatures (mind over matter) were the main contributors that hindered us from achieving our goal to conquer the mountain.[71] So much raced through my mind during those brief moments, I could never explain my emotions or exactly my focus at that moment in time.

I ruminated about family members that I wished could have shared the experience with me. I wondered whether they would have appreciated the meaning of it all. I thought about my special young lady-friend who I loved dearly. Would we return one day to take it all in together? I recalled that just eighteen months earlier, I had graduated from college with an unknown future. Here I stood, 8,300 miles away from home, still with an unsettled future that would be front and center again in less than nine months. I reflected on when this journey began in June of 1966. I took my very first flight from Philadelphia, Pennsylvania, to Milwaukee, Wisconsin, for the Kenya Advanced Training Program for Agriculture at UWM-Milwaukee, UW-Madison. I considered my time at North Carolina A and T and the week we lived with the black tobacco farmers. Finally I reviewed the 1966 Tuskegee Christmas experience before we knew who the thirty-five PCVs would be. Nothing could undo the things that I had experienced during my tour of duty as a PCV, topped off by our Mount Kilimanjaro climb. Words could never express all that was going through my mind on that day. Stewart County, Georgia, was a distant memory. As I reminisced about my Kenyan PCV tour ending, I felt much removed from my early years in Georgia. My PCV thoughts were captured and mentally recorded in my time capsule but never shared with anyone until now.

I wished that those who were important to me could partake in these very special moments. I feared that I would be unable to ever explain what I had observed and learned with anyone, not even family, and especially my young lady to whom I felt so emotionally attached. I vowed to package and lock this trip and all that it offered in my mind for life. I felt as if my PCV experiences were bigger than life.

Fifty years later, the flame that ignited my emotions on that day is still burning. There I stood, looking at a mountain as a mirror image in a swimming pool. In retrospect, I concluded that my heightened feelings had nothing to do with the mountain. Rather the PCVs had melded relationships and ties. Our hearts were bound together. I had finally matured enough to recognize that people mattered. "And let us consider how to stimulate one another to love and do good deeds, not forsaking our own assembling together, as is the habit of some, but encouraging one another; and all the more as you see the day drawing near" (Hebrews 10:24–25).

Upon arriving in Kenya in August 1967, I was like most tourists, taking pictures of any and everything! After living in Kenya for a while, I took fewer pictures. All of us on the eight-day safari had cameras and took pictures. The pictures meant less to us than the shared memories frozen in our minds. Much has happened in my life and in Kenya since thirty-five optimistic young men, among whom were three blacks and thirty-two whites, met, made individual life changes, positively impacted one another, Kenya, America, and ultimately, the world, if only for a little while.

Supreme Focus

Time was flying by. I would soon be back on American soil. I was longing to see the delight of my heart, my beloved special friend from Jersey City. I was gaining confidence, and my smile grew brighter as the tone of her letters sounded more and more encouraging. I convinced myself that it was meaningful that she took the time to go to the post office and bought the aerogram and wrote letters to me in her own left-handed beautiful printing style.

Nearing the end of my Kenyan tour, I rode my motorcycle along the countryside, taking in panoramic views of the most beautifully landscaped scenic countryside and rich farmland on earth. It had been the best two years of my life. As I traveled on my bike, I recalled all the good things that happened to me since my arrival. I thought, if only my endeared special friend had been there to share those moments. Not a day went by that I did not think about her. I wrote and told her about my days. At the end of each letter, I assured her that she was in my thoughts and that she was the person I missed the most.

It was now time to plan for my return trip home. I obtained visas to travel back to America with a fellow PCV who shoveled snow his entire time in Kenya. He and two female companions were going to journey through the West African countries of Senegal, Ghana, and Liberia. I was going to join them before I boarded my flight home. Until arriving in Kenya, I thought the only snow was on Mount Kenya and Mount Kilimanjaro. The shoveled snow was a very attractive blond-hair woman from Kansas.[72] We were on the same KLM chartered flight to Nairobi two years earlier. She served at the US Embassy in Kampala, Uganda, along with a young lady from New Hampshire. They visited with us several times during my assignment in Nakuru. They took leave time, traveled east by land, from Kampala through Nakuru to Nairobi and Mombasa's beaches. I loved visitors and went all out and prepared meals for them, especially females. I prepared the meals, but all guests contributed to the cost of the food. Being able to cook food from scratch was one of the skills I learned while growing up on the farm, and it has paid off abundantly throughout my life.

After getting some very encouraging letters from my sweet friend in Jersey City, I quickly decided to leave my Texas snow-shoveling friend and his companion from Kansas and her female coworker from New Hampshire. I took a direct flight from Nairobi to New York instead of traveling with them by way of West Africa. My Texas friend later told me that the snow melted somewhere over the Atlantic and was over upon landing at JFK Airport. I guess my friend decided due to Texas heat, snow wouldn't last. So he melted the snow artificially instead of letting it melt naturally. After they arrived in New York, he said goodbye to her. He went home to Suffolk, Texas, and she went home to Kansas. She deserved better treatment. I said those exact words to him many times. She was a true friend and shared her sincere feelings while he did not.

After few years of separation, my friend from Suffolk, Texas, and I reconnected in Miami, Florida. He and his lovely bride had just moved to Miami. She was from Passaic, New Jersey, and was the daughter of a preacher. I met her previously on the Peace Corps KLM chartered flight in August 1967 to Nairobi. She only recalled the flight, not any of the thirty-five all-male PCVs bound for Kenya or the two women who served in Kampala, Uganda. She and a group of teachers transferred in Amsterdam for a flight to Cameroon and Senegal. My friend and his bride both earned doctorates at the University of Miami. He spent almost forty years at the university as vice president of human resources. His lovely bride retired from Miami Dade Community College as a professor.

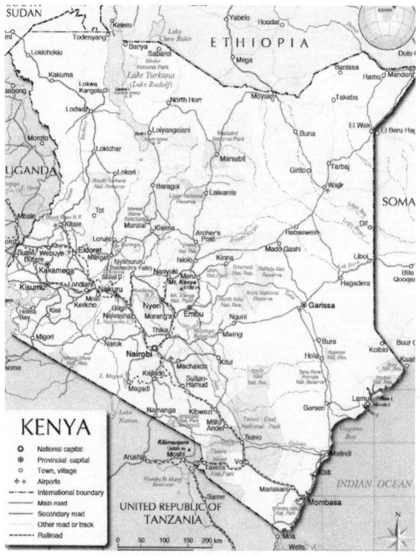

Map of Kenya, Nakuru, cities and towns I worked/
visited during the two years I lived there.

13 PCV's on top of the Menegai Carter just sightseeing the area.

Map with Kenya shown on the east coast of Africa.

PEACE CORPS

P.O. Box 30518

NAIROBI, KENYA.

TEL: 27081/2/3

DESCRIPTION OF PEACE CORPS VOLUNTEER SERVICE

Grover Jackson - Volunteer No.158237 - Kenya

On June 17, 1966, Mr. Grover Jackson entered advance training, at the University of Wisconsin-Milwaukee and on August 28,1966, completed an intensive ten week program. Included in the training curriculum was Kenya area studies, Swahili and seminars and practical work in agriculture and technical studies. Mr. Jackson, upon graduation returned to training for six more weeks, at Tuskegee Institute, Tuskegee, Alabama. The training curriculum was more intensive studies in Swahili, cultural, geographical knowledge of Kenya, as well as seminars and field work and technical studies.

As a Peace Corps Volunteer, Mr. Jackson was responsible to the Ministry of Agriculture and Animal Husbandry. His duties were to assist 75 New African farmers, consisting of more than 50,000 acres, improve their farming practices. Mr. Jackson put emphasis on calf rearing, fodder crops, as well as farm planning and establishing a system of recording. He held seminars and meetings in the native language (Swahili) and organized demonstration plots and field days on coffee, corn, wheat, vegetables, animal husbandry and machinery maintenance. During his spare time Mr. Jackson, also, assisted a government secondary school in athletics. Mr. Jackson was regarded by both Peace Corps, Kenya and the Ministry of Agriculture, as a very effective officer.

Pursuant to section 5(f) of the Peace Corps Act, 22 U.S.C. 250(f), as amended, any former Volunteer employed by the United States Government following his Peace Corps Volunteer service is entitled to have any period of satisfactory Peace Corps service credited for purposes of retirement, seniority, reduction in force, leave and other privileges based on length of Government service.

This is to certify in accordance with Executive Order No.11103 of April 10, 1963, that Mr. Grover Jackson served satisfactorily as a Peace Corps Volunteer. His service ended on August 1, 1969. His benefits under the Executive Order entitlement extend for a period of one year after termination of Volunteer service, except that the employing agency may extend the period for up to three years for a former Volunteer who enters military service or pursues studies at a recognized institution of higher learning.

July 25, 1969
(Date)

Calvin H. Raullerson

My job description as a Peace Corps Volunteer in Kenya.

Me on my motorcycle.

Menegai Crater viewed from my front yard.

My Nakuru, Kenya residence, dressed up & no place to go.

Menegai Crater and coffee farm in foreground and in my front yard.

Rolf, my German friend and housemate in front of a Kenyian hut.

The container we collected rain water for our person use.

Thomson Water Falls.

Just one of my many visitors atop of Menegai Crater.

An African fishing boat with sails at sunset in Zanzibar.

Rhion grazing in the Serengetti.

Herd of Wildebeeasts grazing in the Serengetti.

Lion and her cubs in the Serengetti.

2000 feet on the rim of Ngongono Crater that we drove down into.

The YMCA swimming pool in Moshe, Tanzania after our climb
of Mt. Kilamanjaro Africa tallest mountain 19,341 feet.

The YMCA the place we spent the night.

Mt. Kilimanjaro at 3pm about 10 mies from the last cave before our last 100 yard vertical climb at 3am to reach the top by 6am sunrise.

Kilimanjaro climb day 2.

Two Americans who often visited us in Nakuru during
weekends and we spent sightseeing near my house.

Chapter 11

Day, Time, Place—All Remembered

Suspended in Space

We have all heard the phrase "don't put all your eggs in the same basket." That may be true for eggs, but in a relationship, anything other than together is a total disaster or failure. There is another saying relating to commitment, it is an old tale about a chicken and a pig. As the legend goes, a chicken and a pig ran upon a hungry person and discussed doing something about it. The chicken offered eggs and suggested the pig supply bacon. The essential point is that the chicken was willing to contribute while the pig would be required to make a total sacrifice—his life. The same could be said about a relationship.

When I was young and enchanted by my first love, I trusted my heart to an innocent very smart lovely young lady. Then I voluntarily left the country for two years. I was misguided in my thinking. I assumed that an educated beautiful, twenty-two-year-old lady would put her life on hold and yearn for my letters every two weeks. The letters would contain assuring words from me about us. I'd tell her I missed her terribly. I would share the excitement I felt about my time in Kenya. I would speak about the people I met and the places I had seen while never once mentioning commitments concerning our next steps. The story below puts on full display what happens when true communication is stunted by naivete, immaturity, and selfish desire.

Upon returning home and clearing customs on August 1, 1969, I found the first pay phone available (cell phones had not yet been invented). I called the home of my special friend's uncle with whom she lived. People rarely changed phone numbers back then. So I dialed the same AT&T number I remembered calling many years earlier. I was excited about being home and was also quite nervous. I wanted to surprise her and hear her voice. I had been anticipating the thrill of this very scene for two years. The phone rang, and with each ring, my heart seemed to beat faster. It may have even skipped a beat or two. On the fourth ring, her Uncle Sonny answered the phone. His demeanor toward me had not changed. I could hear it in his voice. He did not trust me. I on the other hand liked both him and his wife, Estelle. I always treated them and their niece with the utmost respect. To my knowledge, I had never said or done anything to foster such a distrusting attitude. After I identified myself, I asked to speak to his niece. He said, "My niece has her own apartment."

She had not mentioned in any of her letters that she had moved or thought about moving. The very careful words he used next, and the emphasis he put on them, nearly sent me into shock and an acute cardiac arrest. My chest felt as if it was about to explode. My entire body was weakened. I lost control of clear thinking. For all practical purpose, I blacked out physically, although mentally, I remembered every syllable of every word and I understood the repercussions of them. I didn't have time to regroup and analyze the words to the song by the Shirelles, "Mama Said," that spoke to a time when there would be days like August 1, 1969. In my most memorable dream, I could have never imagined hearing such words. They were, "My niece is engaged to be married in three weeks which you already know." He was sorely mistaken; I did not know.

If I had known, I would not have flown eight thousand miles directly to New York, with my heart in my hands, to see her. He begrudgingly gave me her new telephone number. Completely disheartened, I called her and we exchanged pleasantries. Then I asked her why she did not tell me about the other guy. I inquired, "What happened?"

Her response was, "You did not make any commitments." She was totally correct, and I had not made any promises to bind our relationship. I only implied my intentions for us. I was an old-school guy. So I felt that I had to be settled with a career and able to have a reasonable lifestyle. The next jolt was that I learned that the man she was engaged to marry also had my surname, Jackson. He was not a relative. That would have been a truly cruel joke.

Heartbroken and bewildered, I searched for answers. I reviewed the timelines. Something drastic must have happened between her letters and my arrival in New York. I thought to myself, *Was she pregnant, and why now?* Based on my original travel itinerary, my scheduled arrival in the USA was two weeks later. I canceled my travel visas on July 16, after I received encouraging—even upbeat—letters from her. We communicated the entire two years, not to mention the last two letters were such that my heart was overwhelmed with joy. Rather than writing to tell her the date and time of my scheduled arrival, I decided to surprise her and took a direct flight to New York. I arrived at 11:00 a.m. on Friday, August 1, 1969.

I re-examined what I could have done differently while I was away. I communicated often with her by mail. It took seven days or more for my letters to reach her. If they were answered immediately, it took about fourteen days to get her response to me.

Calling was not practical or an affordable option. In those days, a reservation had to be made with the overseas AT&T operator. I had to provide the exact time and length of the call. When both parties were connected, the reception was poor. With the analog transmission technology used at the time, there were echoes and fading signals that interfered with our being able to hold a sustained conversation. And it was very expensive, given my one hundred dollars monthly (food and household) allotment. The money from the Peace Corps was adequate while I was on the African continent; however, it could not stretch to meet my needs beyond Kenya and to maintain telephone contact eight thousand miles away. In my two years in Kenya, I called Mom only on New Year's Day, 1969. It cost twenty-five dollars for a five-minute call. It was just long enough to say hello to the family. We had no time to provide updates about my well-being or much of anything else.

The Aftermath

I called my friend again, later that day, after I adjusted to the big earthquake, the aftershocks, and devastation that rocked my world and emotional well-being. I asked her to have lunch with me. She agreed. I settled my emotions and gave it some more thought. I called her again that same day and cancelled our lunch appointment. I have not spoken with her since Friday, August 1, 1969. I have not seen her since August 1967. I wished this had been a bad dream, and after a good night sleep, that I'd wake up. Alas, it had not been a dream. Our relationship had ended long before I knew it had.

On that day, the world around me was so empty. Yet there were people everywhere at JFK, on the subway, at the port authority bus terminal, and on the streets. However, I saw none of them clearly. My world had completely tumbled down all around me. I had fallen apart before it really hit me.

I love music, especially Motown. I listened to it during junior high, high school, college, and my Kenya tour off duty. I would just drown myself in the lyrics that expressed my feelings better than any words I could utter. After the call from my lost love, the words to many songs drifted in and out of my consciousness. The songs' lyrics made me question all that I believed, for instance, Stevie Wonder's song "Sign, Sealed, and Delivered," just a portion of the first verse, "Oh yeah baby like a fool I went and stayed too long..." played in my mind. The rest of the song was meaningless and did not matter after I wallowed in the pity of my new reality.

The bottom dropped out from under my feet. When lyrics mixed with music made sense, I listened to the songs and wished I could communicate my true feelings in words just as in the songs. I was never able to do so. Nevertheless, I internalized the lyrics as words I wanted to say. They were words that expressed my raw emotions and true feelings about my heartbreaker friend. Below are a few lyrics of songs that I remembered months after that discouraging

Friday morning at JFK International Airport. I was there physically, but emotionally, I was a mess and only time would heal my pain.

In the late '60s, the Supremes released a record entitled "Reflections." In my broken state of mind, I tried to adjust to what had happened to me. My life had been profoundly torn apart in a flash. I tried to make sense of it all. As I mulled my way through every subsequent day, I reflected on the lyrics and my old memories of our time together. I convinced myself that the lyrics from the Supremes' recording related to my predicament.

> Through the mirror of my mind, Time after time
> I see reflections of you and me, Reflections of
> The way life used to be, Reflections of
> The love you took from me, Oh, I'm all alone
>   now
> No love to shield me, Trapped in a world
> That's a distorted reality"
> Happiness you took from me and left me all
>   alone with only memories

I listened to other songs, repeatedly, and to sum up my emotions, Little Anthony's song "Goin' Out of My Head...over You" was among them, the Temptations, "Just My Imagination (Running Away with Me)" and others.

> It was just my imagination once again runnin'
>   way with me.
> Tell you it was just my imagination runnin' away
>   with me.
> No, no, I can't forget her (you)
> Just my imagination once again runnin' way with
>   me.
> Just my imagination runnin' away with me.

Time and time again, I told myself to refocus and move on, but it was not possible! What was I to do with all those memories?

Martha and the Vandellas' song "Come and Get These Memories," as suggested in the song, her letters, pictures—I wanted to keep them. After so many emotions and many agonizing moments, I burned the photos my heartbreaker friend gave me before I left for Kenya two years earlier. Keeping them would only have aggravated the situation further and certainly would not have helped me get over her. Sadly, it would not.

> Love you've gone from me, and left behind so
>   many memories
> Here's your old love letters, I can't read them
>   anymore
> Here is your old picture; I can't look at it anymore
> Come and get 'em, come and get 'em.
> Here's some old valentine cards, Give it to your
>   new sweetheart
> Here's my old favorite record, I can't stand to
>   hear it anymore
> Here's some old lingering love, it's in my heart
>   and it's tearing it apart

Pittsburgh Visit

In early 1969, my brother Billy's wife, Viola, introduced me to the daughter of one of her family's friends. Her home was Pittsburgh, although she was away attending a non-HBCU college at the time and didn't know any eligible young men. The introduction took place through the mail while I was in Kenya. The young lady sent me a picture of herself. My loyalty and heart belonged, at the time, to my special friend in Jersey City. Viola did not know about my special friend. Out of respect for Viola, I communicated with the young lady from Pittsburgh and promised to visit her upon arriving home in August.

It took a while for me to recuperate from the devastating news my dear friend's uncle gave me on August 1, 1969. By Labor Day, September, I had moderately composed myself. I pulled myself up and reached out to the young lady in Pittsburgh. I asked to visit with her over the Labor Day weekend, just before I left for graduate school in Atlanta. She agreed. She lived with her parents. I took a bus from Philadelphia to Pittsburgh, and I arrived in the early evening just before dusk. Not knowing the city, I approached two guys who provided taxi (jitney) service from the bus station to areas in and around Pittsburgh. I showed them my friend's address, and they volunteered to take me to her parents' home. First I needed a place to stay for the weekend, and they suggested a place, On the Hill. They told me the room rates. It was affordable. I agreed and they took me there. I paid for the room and left my Honeywell Pentax camera, some Kenya carvings and artifacts, and other unique memorabilia from my travels in the room that I had just rented. I planned to give my Pittsburgh friend the gifts before leaving on Sunday. After our visit, I returned to the place On the Hill and when I entered the room, all my belongings were gone. The personal stuff I bought from Kenya to give to my Pittsburgh friend was missing.

My Honeywell Pentax camera, the carvings, and a few other personal items were all gone. Only my clothes and toiletries were left. I lodged a complaint at the front desk that they allowed unauthorized persons into my room. They claimed they had no knowledge of the situation. The door was locked, and the only access had to be with my key. I discovered later that the hotel rooms were rented by the hour. I also learned cabs didn't go into certain sections of Pittsburgh and many other inner cities. Those two men were a cheap cab substitutes who volunteered to fill the void. I was so naive and dumb! I had read about riots in urban areas. It seemed that a lot of other things had happened in America in the two years I was away.

I was determined to catch the individuals who ripped me off. I was sure that the two men who took me to the hotel and on to visit with my friend had stolen my valuables. The next morning early, I went to the bus station and sought those two men. I played detective. I waited patiently and believed they would reappear, looking for another sucker like me. Later that afternoon, I saw them and ran over to a policeman and explained the situation. The officer approached the two men and asked them their purpose for being at the bus station. They told him that they operated a jitney cab service. Most cities allowed them, although they were illegal and not licensed. He asked to see their driver's licenses, and both licenses had expired. Discouraged and sickened, I knew that my belongings would not be recovered but catching the two men, one black and the other one white, who stole from me was extra special. Both men were arrested for driving without a valid driver's license, although they weren't driving when the policeman and I approached them. They were walking around in the bus station.

During my visit to Pittsburgh, my friend and I went out. I went through the motions of enjoying her company. I wished we could have met at another time and under different circumstances. Perhaps those different circumstances could have developed into a special and meaningful relationship. Upon returning to Camden and before I left for Atlanta, I wrote her a letter explaining my situation. I shared that I loved someone else and she would soon be another man's wife. I saw my Pittsburgh friend only twice—during my September 1969 visit to Pittsburgh and at Viola's, my sister-in-law, funeral in 1990. She looked taller and more attractive in her forties than she had in her early twenties. We did not get close enough to speak, although I wanted badly to do so. I regretted not doing it.

After an interim period of getting over my friend in Jersey City, I became sullen all over again. The failed relationship with my friend from Jersey City shocked and emotionally floored me again to a new low. My mind started running wild and back to some of my previous actions in relationships. Malcolm X called it a chicken coming home to roost. I even reflected on my JCSU experience when I ended my relationship with DYD, an attractive freshman, after winning her affections from my friend and fellow track teammate. I reasoned that it was payback for my actions in that relationship. I had to find a reason somewhere, and this to me, somehow, seemed logical.

My emotions were all over the place. I could make no sense of anything. I thought about my two-timing JCSU friends who were no good and mistreated young ladies who cared for them. They deserved to get hurt but not me. After all, I had been true. I had not run away. I had gone to be a PCV and sacrificed for a better world, only to come home and be ambushed by a man with the same last name as mine. I wistfully thought about the cancelled trip through West Africa. It was a once-in-a-lifetime venture with my buddy from Texas and two female friends. I chucked it aside to hurry back to the States to see my love from Jersey City. I felt sorry for myself. I believed I deserved better treatment. My reasoning was scattered, and I was unable to focus. Only random thoughts kept coming into my head. Who was responsible for my pain? I needed someone to blame. I was hurting and nothing could discharge the hopelessness I felt.

My emotions were unsettled. I felt misery, guilt, gloom, emptiness, and total loneliness. I loved her. I was in total despair. I persuaded myself that my world was empty without her and it would be for the rest of my life. The 1964 recording by Otis Redding "Pain in My Heart" kept flashing through my mind. The real pain in my heart was too much to endure. I couldn't just forget about her and move on. I kept telling myself, if only I woke up from this very horrifying dream, then things would be fine. If only the agony and reminiscences were washed away. I held onto my self-pity for almost a year as I studied toward an MBA at Atlanta University, graduate school of business. I sat in my dorm room and listened to music that made me even lonelier. I studied with tears running down my face from those old memories.

Over time, it was evident that nothing good came from me drowning in my tears so I began to share my grief with a core group of coed friends. Our frank discussions helped me to eventually release the old baggage that had burdened me since returning from my PCV duties. Time healed the pain, and my more-uplifted attitude eased the memories that almost destroyed the future that awaited me. I started to become exhilarated by my new social environment and the career prospects that graduate school presented.

At registration during my first year of graduate school, I met two women, Joann and Gerry, who were English majors and later would be graduate assistants who graded some, if not all MBA, written communication skill class assignments. Joann was from Cambridge, Maryland, and Gerry was from a suburb of Newark, New Jersey (Union). I discovered during conversations that she was the cousin of my "special" friend. From time to time, I asked her about her cousin but she never shared any details. Those were some of the darkest days of my life and only those who have gone through such days can relate with empathy. However, my future was ahead, not behind, so I got a grip of my situation and focused on my future.

My friend Joann B. Bowens earned a law degree and served as a judge and later Fulton County chief magistrate judge in Atlanta, Georgia. During my travels through Atlanta, I contacted her to see if she was available for a dinner. We were unable, at the time, to arrange our schedules for a meal, but our friendship remained intact. Geraldine "Gerry" Smith-Wright, my special friend's cousin, earned her PhD. She became a professor of English and department head at Drew University in New Jersey. I have kept in touch with both friends since our days in graduate school. Both have retired from their professional careers and live in Metro Atlanta, and we get together over lunch as our schedules allow.[73]

The Investment

Nearing the end of my first year, I developed a promising relationship. I dated a young woman from Los Angeles. I even flew from Philadelphia to Los Angeles to see her during the July 4, 1970, weekend and stayed with her parents. She was a second-year MBA student. After graduation, she accepted a job in Washington, DC. I worked that summer in Philadelphia. At the end of the summer, on my way back to Atlanta, I stopped in DC to spend a couple of days with her.

Finally I had reached the point that I was no longer broken-hearted and lonely. I was cautiously willing to invest in the relationship. Please forgive the following analogies, but I was in business school with a concentration in finance. I was seeking an equal partnership, much like a limited liability company. I no longer had a broken heart; however, my investor confidence was low. It was as if there was a bear market and I was not prepared to take huge emotional risks. I dipped my fingers in just enough to test the water. My risk tolerance was low. If I was going to get back into the market,

I expected a positive return on my emotional investment. My Los Angeles friend must have sensed my skittishness. During the stopover in Washington, all the market signals suggested that my rate of return on the investment was depreciating. It was time for me to divest, cash out, and dissolve the partnership. I had entered the arrangement hoping it would be a sure thing. It was not meant to be. Upon leaving DC for Atlanta, I never looked back. This time, I arrived in Atlanta with my emotions intact. I had a renewed focus on investing in high-yield low-risk securities. It wasn't because I was skittish. This time, I was a smarter investor.

I worked in the placement office, and I gauged that the women-to-men student ratio at Atlanta University at the time I attended was five-to-one. The numbers favored me, if the theory and ratio of five to one held true. The song said it all, I had everything to gain, "Here I am baby signed, sealed, delivered, I'm yours…you've got my future in your hand." I was available for the right high-yielding assets at the right price. My new perspective was brash. "Here I am baby."

Judge Joann Bowens, Dr. Gerry Smith-Wright and me at lunch.

Chapter 12

The Decision

The Relationships

I learned that love, like aging, just happens and there is nothing anyone can do about it. It is not just a physical characteristic of a person. It's the essence of her. I experienced the capacity of pleasantness, attractiveness, loveliness, beauty, and many more attributes. As my feelings deepened in the next relationship, the description of her went from nouns to adjectives. Words like *pleasant, attractive, amiable, genial, comfortable, lovely, charming,* and endless others began to touch my very core.

I made a transition. The more I got to know her, the words I used described my feelings. I became delighted, stimulated, captivated, excited, and other heart-filled words. I was ready to fully invest again. This time, my sentiments were not the expressions of a young and innocent man. My eyes were wide open, and I was ready to commit to a long-term relationship.

Wall Street Experience

The college placement center was a great place to work as a graduate student. I earned spending money and made some key contacts. Companies sent employees to interview and to recruit candidates from Atlanta University. AU was a graduate-school-only at that time. Now it is Clark Atlanta University, resulting from a merger between Atlanta University and Clark College (which offered only a four-year college program) on July 1, 1988. Some companies didn't just send recruiters, they sent high-ranking executives, presidents, vice presidents, and other high-ranking corporate officials. I spoke with all the recruiters, even if I didn't sign up for an interview (due to class or other conflicts).

It was a new day in America! Companies were mindful that hiring blacks, especially MBA graduates, was a good investment and part of their social responsibility and consciousness. The Fortune 500 companies and others recruited and hired Atlanta University's MBA graduates for employment. In addition to the graduate school, they recruited undergraduates from Spelman, Morehouse, Clark, and Morris Brown. During a single trip to Atlanta, a company could recruit and interview the best students from five independent institutions of higher education. They knew that most of the candidates were blacks, Asians, or Asian Indians. Black men and women could now look to pursue careers in professions other than education and government.

The buzz term during 1970s was *affirmative action*. I am not sure if corporate management really understood the meaning of the term. Corporations did whatever was necessary to increase their bottom line. If they followed the law when they hired a few minorities, satisfied government statistics, and the liberals in congress, all the while increasing profits, so much the better. Some corporations recruited individuals with no intention of providing real opportunities to advance or even to promise meaningful assignments for individual growth. However, there were other firms that saw real benefits in hiring male and female minorities. They made a genuine effort, then they held all levels of management accountable for their development. While I have no statistical proof, the telecommunication industry appeared to have had the best track record of hiring and promoting minorities.

As I visited companies across America, I knew some were serious and really wanted to hire and promote minorities. Others made excuses, saying that they could not find qualified candidates. The more progressive companies, however, used the trial approach. They hired candidates for summer internships a year before they graduated. Such an approach told a lot about the company. Major urban companies usually preferred such an approach. It provided a smooth transition for both the firm and potential new hires.

Atlanta University was the recruitment hot spot for black MBA graduates. It was the only HBCU with an MBA program at that time. The graduate school dean was a Harvard University graduate. Professors were graduates from Ivy League universities and other renowned schools. AU's curriculum was on par with other well-known US MBA programs. The MBA program and many of its students were recognized and hired for positions previously not opened to blacks. Many recruiters were senior-level decision makers (executives) who interviewed during a site visit. I assumed the purpose was to make sure the student prospects measured up to their standards. Many of the student candidates worked before they enrolled in the MBA program and knew a little about corporate America. However, the actual positions they interviewed for were new to them.

When it came to interview for a job, I had two advantages over most: (1) I worked in the college placement center. So I knew before any other students the dates the companies were sending recruiters. (2) I had just recently returned from a two-year assignment as a Peace Corps volunteer in Kenya, East Africa. Many of the recruiters were clueless about people of color or diverse cultures. They wanted to understand what motivated me to join the Peace Corps, my assignment, living conditions, the people, etc. They were curious about the African jungles and the natives in Kenya. I patiently explained that Kenya has forests like those in America; however, there were big cities, suburban areas, and marvelous vistas in the countryside as well as challenges much like those in rural America. The natives were everyday people who wanted the same things Americans wanted such as food, clothes, shelter, education, and, if possible, funds for a rainy day. I gave them insights into what we did as PCVs and shared that we socialized with the Kenyans who were our neighbors. Based on my personal struggles with both the sociology professor and the subject he taught at JCSU, someone else should have shared this lesson; so I valued my experience in Kenya and as a black man in America.

So I bestowed my wisdom on them and they were impressed. I was a very rare breed and I knew it. During the interview, rather than come across as an egotist, I included my siblings and their pursuits. I explained that I was one of fourteen. I was the first to acquire a college degree, and in like manner, many of my siblings were seeking one as well. Interviewing was an acquired gift. Some students handled the interviews well. Others just crashed and did not survive. I had confidence, skills, and the ability to communicate.

Over 80 percent of the companies with whom I interviewed invited me to visit their corporate headquarters for possible employment. I took advantage of the situation. I went on as many corporate trips as I could afford to without forsaking my classroom duties. I used the interviews for some of the companies to sharpen my interviewing skills. I never seriously considered working for them. I learned early that some companies looked to fill a quota. Others were simply out of touch. Still others tried despite having no clear path for me to develop and advance in their corporate hierarchy. Several were so eager to hire me. They tried to talk me into leaving after my first year of business school with the promise of qualifying for their management development program. There were others that I liked, but they were in the wrong geographic location. I always interviewed with a purpose. I asked challenging and thought-provoking questions. I made a positive impression for myself and AU and left the doors of opportunity opened for others at the business school. The process allowed me to eliminate companies and to verify information that I had either acquired personally through research or hearsay.

The Recruitment Trips

There were games played by many students from colleges across America, including by me. I will share one key example. Be aware, since my time in school, airline practices and policies have changed substantially. During the late 1960s and early 1970s, airlines were more consumer friendly. They competed very aggressively for passengers. They booked flights and mailed tickets prior to payment. However, the tickets had to be paid in full prior to traveling.

As I noted earlier, many corporate recruiters visited the campus looking to hire qualified candidates. I was extended invitations to visit some corporate headquarters (HQ) for a job interview. To minimize travel time and maximize profit, I scheduled as many site visits to the same airport city as possible. I was invited by more than a dozen companies to visit their HQ for job interviews in metropolitan NYC. I scheduled up to five visits per week. I made reservations for each of the five days and copied the tickets and returned them to the airline unpaid. Since I had to present an airline ticket for that day as proof of purchase to the corporate recruiter, I submitted a copy of the tickets as the receipt. I purchased round-trip airline tickets that left Atlanta on Sunday evening and returned on Friday evening, then I would present each company visited a copy of a round-trip ticket on the day of the interview and was reimbursed by each company visited.

Each company paid only the amount it was obligated to pay: airline ticket, hotel room, taxicab fare, and meals. Mostly I ate at friends and/or relatives' homes. So I saved the companies' meal expenses. They paid for only the expenses for which I had submitted a receipt. Bottom line, those airline trips that never took place and for which I was reimbursed generated enough cash to allow me to purchase a new 1971 Bug Volkswagen. It was baby blue with an eight-track stereo tape player. It was my very first car, and after I outgrew it, I gave it to my sister Mary. She later relocated to Boston from Jersey and she passed it on to my niece Sharon, a student at Temple University. Sharon drove the VW to and from her home in Jersey City to Temple in Philadelphia until the car no longer worked.

Let me be perfectly clear, some may perceive what I did as ethically wrong; nevertheless, it was not illegal. It was very creative to schedule my airline trips to maximize my job visits. In class, we were taught to be innovative in our problem-solving approaches. I just used my classroom lessons in practical personally rewarding applications. Later in my career, this experience taught me how to apply the concept more broadly. I was better prepared to examine projects objectively. When adjustments had to be made to cut costs, I looked for line items that could be reduced or eliminated and still generate profits.

The Capture

During my second year of the Atlanta University MBA program, I was sitting in the women's dorm lounge, socializing with friends who also had already completed the first year of their program. New students were arriving to enroll. A taxi drove up and a young woman got out, looking very irritated. As she paid the taxi, I offered to assist her with her luggage since the taxi driver showed zero interest in doing so. I noticed right away that she was a woman with an attitude. As she paid the taxi driver, I took a sneak peek at her luggage nametag to get her name and where she lived. She caught me looking and appeared to be even more annoyed.

Now it was on. I could let it go and pretend I never noticed her air, or I could be cocky and embarrass her. I took the high road and treated her with respect. Her assigned room was on the third floor of the women's side of the old dormitory. The dormitory was three stories high and had no elevator. It was divided into two sides with a dining hall in the middle. One side of the residence housed women, and the other side was coed with men on the first and second floors with women occupying the third floor. Upon realizing that her options were few and that she could benefit tremendously from my help and kindness, she calmed down. Then I took her luggage and followed her to her room. Thereafter, she was a lot more sociable.

The young lady was from Houston, Texas, and was a graduate of the University of Oklahoma. After graduating, she worked as an accountant for an oil company for a year before deciding to enter graduate school. After learning that her intended area of study was business, I offered to show her around campus and the B-school. I even suggested classes she should take based on the MBA classes I had taken during my first year. She was cute with an edge, reserved, and a bit stuck up. No, she was a lot stuck up! Being a nice person, by my own evaluation, I kept my promise and showed her around. I made suggestions and warned her that the registration process was very painful.

I mentioned, as we talked, that I was from Camden, New Jersey. For some unknown reason, she seemed to show genuine interest in me. What I didn't know at the time was that she just tolerated me. Her sister and brother-in-law had relocated to South Jersey. So she was familiar with the area. She later confided to me that the first impression of the vintage dorm had upset her. The living quarters were disappointing. The second impression didn't get any better. The old dorm had no air conditioning, and the bathroom facilities did not meet her specifications. Within a short time after her arrival, she called her sister in New Jersey, voiced her frustration, and told her that she was considering relocating to Philadelphia to pursue her MBA studies. After she settled down, she seemed okay. From time to time, I called her to see if I could assist her in any way.

Living on campus without transportation was an inconvenience. I was one of a few single students living on campus with a car. I understood what it was like to be dependent, not having a vehicle, so I shared freely with all who needed transportation, especially the women. The food served in the dining hall was just passable. So I went out to eat often, and I invited my Houston friend to join me. By now, I was growing on her and she was happy to accompany me. Other times, we went for scenic rides, to the movies, or just got away from the dormitory and the campus. Life was good! Occasionally though, she would get a tinge bit jealous when other young women asked me to do favors for them. Her attitude surprised me. I did not understand the possessiveness. After all, I thought we were just casual friends. I didn't make a big deal over it. Remember, a year earlier my world turned upside down when I was shocked and dumped without warning. I did not need any more turmoil in my life. So I let it go. I filed it away and made a mental note for future reference.

My friend needed a part-time job to help with expenses. Since I worked in the placement center, I knew the office needed another employee. I spoke with the director, and he agreed to interview my friend. The director's last name was—you guessed it—Jackson. He was not related. Was this a coincidence or what? Mr. Jackson loved flirting with attractive young women. I knew that she would make a good impression during the interview and that he would hire her. She got the job. I was now the only male working in the graduate placement office. I was happy to be accompanied by three very attractive single females. They were Bertha, a French major, Millette, and Gloria. Both Millette and Gloria were in the MBA program. I was thrilled to share their company. I worked and took classes with two of them as well as partied with them on weekends. Both remain my very dear friends today. The one with the attitude, Millette, is my beloved wife of forty-six years. The instances of jealousy that she displayed early in our friendship were signs that she sensed the amorous connection between us long before I did. Gloria, a close friend, is now Dr. Gloria K. Clark, an accounting professor at Winston-Salem State University in Winston-Salem, North Carolina. Both she and the Honorable JoAnn B. Bowens attended our wedding in Houston on August 5, 1972.[74]

Judge Joann Bowens and Dr. Gloria King Clark.

Chapter 13

People Forks in the Road

The Past Reveals Itself

U pon enrolling in business school, I met a very stunning charming and very attractive young lady. She told me her name, and I commenced to laugh. She thought I was laughing at her name. I was not. Her introduction had brought back so many treasured memories. I shared things with her about her past that I knew personally or her family had shared with me. As starters, I provided the names of her parents, where they lived, and their occupations. I shared insights about her sibling and many other personal details. She was mystified! She wanted to know how I knew so much about her and she didn't even know me. After keeping her in suspense a while, I confided that her father, Professor Martin, was my teacher in the mid-1950s. He talked about his daughter, and eleven years later, I still remembered what he shared.

She had an uncommon first name—Venzula. I was then and I am still a master at mind games. I used them with young ladies just to prolong the conversation and to have some good laughs during the process. Even if Venzula wanted to walk away, she couldn't. I had captured her attention by sharing so much about her and her family. She was about seven or eight years old when the Jacksons left Georgia. Professor Martin and his family lived in Lumpkin, some twenty miles from Omaha. So Venzula never knew the Jackson family. By the time she was of age, we had moved to New Jersey. After we both earned our master's degrees, I lost track of Venzula; so I received updates of her status from her father.

During my second year of graduate school, one of my childhood friends from Stewart County was killed in Vietnam. I drove to Omaha for the funeral services. On our way there, a police trap had been set up. After going through a posted reduced speed limit, there was a state of Georgia sign to resume speed at forty-five mph. About one hundred yards from that state of Georgia sign, there was a local sign that posted a twenty-five-mph speed limit. It was designed to trap drivers. It was a no-win situation. There was a local policeman waiting to pull us over as soon as we reached the forty-five mph speed. It appeared they pulled over cars with out-of-state tags and military personnel assigned to Fort Benning. I was driving Millette's vehicle. It had a state of Texas issued tag.

In those days, they didn't issue tickets in the rural areas. They took you to see a clerk of the courts who accepted cash only. If you had the cash, you were relieved of your punishment for the traffic transgression. Between the two of us, Millette and I scrounged up twenty-five dollars and paid the fine. After that delay, we continued to the funeral services. Eleven years had passed since we left Georgia, moved to New Jersey, and it was my first visit back to Stewart County. I got to see family and friends who still lived there. Not much had changed since we migrated to Camden. However, the distance between places we used to walk seemed much shorter than they appeared to me as a child. I reconnected with a former teacher we called Professor Martin at the services. I updated him about my family. I had so much respect for him. It felt odd that the conversation was not teacher to student, rather it was adult to adult.

Professor Martin's most salient comment was that moving away was the best thing that could have happened for our family. He was a man of wisdom, and I agreed with his assessment. I was in graduate school at that point, and my younger siblings were enrolled in college and were on track to graduate in the near term: Mary Lou, sibling 12 (graduated in 1971); Otis, 11 ('72); Annie, 13 ('73); George, 10 ('73); and Christine (Chris), 14 ('76). Professor Martin was the teacher who created the spark that glowed in the distance for me.

He inspired me to learn as much as I could and to not be limited by another person's expectation of me. Others along the way helped to ignite the flame. First among them was my mom. Her consistency, work ethics, and encouragement fanned the spark that grew into a flame. Years have passed, yet each day, I still marvel at the fact that my mom's physical body is no more but her love and spirit lives on forever with each of her children. Life is a journey. It is not determined by one step or a misstep. If we keep focused on loving one another and maintaining our faith in God, the strength of the Holy Spirit will guide us so that God's will, will be done. Mom's very essence was based on faith and the Word of God. Romans chapter 12 comes to mind, "It wasn't so much as our trust was in mankind, rather in God who created and controlled and still controls the actions of men and women."

Career Opportunities

For several months, March and April, I was on the road visiting corporate headquarters of potential employers, primarily in Metro NYC, White Plains, Connecticut, Chicago, Philadelphia, and Boston. Truthfully, with only one exception, I never considered working for any company located outside of New York City (NYC). Strangely at that time, one of my key selection criteria was to be in a city with four professional sports teams. I prescreened for financial and nonfinancial companies with corporate HQs in New York City. They all qualified.

In the early spring of 1971, I received an offer letter from the US State Department Agency for International Development (USAID) for assignments in Tanzania. My assignment would be in the field of agriculture economics. After I shared the news with my forever love, she too was excited but for a different reason. She had marriage on her mind and going to East Africa as a couple. Oops! There was conflict, and we were not even engaged. She was in her first year of a two-year MBA program. I was in my last few months. My thought was to leave without her then get married after she finished. After a quick flashback, I remembered my August 1, 1969, experience. That was not a viable option. So I turned down the once-in-a-lifetime US State Department job opportunity. It was my one exception to the New York City selection criterion. I would have worked and lived in East Africa. It was the same geographic area where I served as a Peace Corps volunteer. I would have loved to return there as a US diplomat in a new country and different capacity.

I was thrilled and excited! In retrospect, I gave little consideration of government service as a career choice. I determined that any position I accepted must be situated in a large city with four professional sports teams. Certainly this limited my opportunities to just a few companies, primarily banks. Why did I limit myself to such strict criteria? What was the purpose?

After declining the US Department of State's job offer, I accepted a site visit with a firm located in New York City.[75] The interview was insightful. The firm offered an attractive career path, and it was financially sound; however, living in Syracuse during the winter was a nagging concern. I received an offer to work for the technology company. I would initially be situated in Atlanta. I would have a tour of duty in a company plant located in Rochester, Minnesota. I kept thinking it would be cold. I can't do this. So for weather-related reasons, the Upstate New York based company with a Rochester plant location option was off the table. I grew up in South Jersey; while it was frequently cold, it was nothing like I imagined it would be in Upstate New York or Rochester, Minnesota. For four years, during my junior high and high school years, I walked to school. When I arrived, many days, my hands were so cold I was unable to write. Therefore, I opted to avoid such situations, even if the assignment was temporary. The firm would have been a great place to work. Its reputation was stellar. It touted a positive employee culture and opportunities to advance.

As the temperatures got warmer, I scheduled site visits to Chicago, just to visit the city and see some former classmates from undergraduate and graduate school. To be honest, I had zero interest in working in Chicago or any other Midwest city. I accepted a site visit to a Midwest company that came across as honest and genuine. They answered all my questions and expressed a sincere interest in me joining their team. For many reasons, at that time, it was the right company in the wrong city for me. It was the only company where the job details were discussed in any real detail. The company addressed its approach to how projects are justified and funded and how I would fit in based on my interests and areas of study. The management team seemed seriously interested in the contributions I could make. There was one key problem: location, location, and location. In the 1970s, the Midwest lacked an additional adder to appeal to me. I was a single black young man, born in the South on a farm. After age fourteen, I grew up in a highly diverse urban area. I did not perceive this Midwest community to offer warmth during the winter, cultural diversity, or, in other than Chicago located some miles away, to be urban.

Clearly my decision-making lacked maturity or God had another plan for me. I turned down the employment offer from a well-respected growth-oriented culturally diverse firm for weather-related reasons. I did that knowing that my initial assignment would have been in Atlanta, Georgia. It was clear that tours of duty at either Upstate New York, Rochester, Minnesota, or both would have been temporary, perhaps less than three years at either location. The technology company had locations in major cities throughout the US. Future assignments to more desirable cities were certainly possible. And I dismissed a Midwest company that seemed a terrific fit that offered me a management opportunity with real growth potential.

The MBA

I returned to Atlanta University. I completed my MBA and reviewed other offers, including a position with a Wall Street bank. The bank did not try to sell me or parade executives in front of me. It was a low-keyed approach. I met others who were recently hired from major MBA programs—Stanford, Harvard, Penn, Columbia, University of Virginia, London School of Economics, University of Chicago, Notre Dame, and many others. The highest-ranking executive who spoke with me was a second vice president. He explained the program, the progression, the promotion, and the expectation, and then returned me to my personnel host who asked me if I wanted to work for the bank based on the things that had been discussed. The personnel executive had a copy of my transcripts (undergraduate and graduate school), recommendations from those who interviewed me, and had the authority to make an offer, even if some whom I talked with didn't recommend me for employment. He had the final say based on his assessment of me. The bank offered a two-year management program, ranging from analyzing financial statements to time spent assisting loan officers with assigned accounts.

I had received seven job offers worthy of legitimate consideration. Any one of the seven was very tempting, and I wished I could take a portion of each and design my own job. Finally I had to decide; but before doing so, I called my contact for one last conversation. He laid it on the line. The net of the conversation was, "Here's who we are, here's what we do, and these are some of the things you will learn and must do. Are you interested?" I answered affirmative!

The Dream Job

Finally, I accepted a position with a Wall Street bank with a management training program. I was in the class that started in September 1971. Many of the new hires spent the summer in an accounting class sponsored by the bank and taught by either a college professor or an employee of the bank. I was exempted as an MBA new hire. I started my career along with many other recent college hires in the program in September 1971. I worked from June 1971, to September, at the National Urban League sponsored by the Wall Street bank. As I anticipated, I met and worked with some very smart men and women. I felt as if I was on the top of the world. I got to compete, firsthand, with men and women from colleges and universities from across the world. Our everyday interactions bridged the gap between the classroom and the real world.

In retrospect, the bank provided me a foundation for my future development. It presented real world applications using my academic knowledge. My business school insight was superb. I earned As and a spot of Bs in my classroom work. However, Atlanta University had not prepared me for the bank's day-to-day cultural nuances about which I was not savvy. I was vinegar mixed with oil. I was out of touch.

I worked for a bank with steep historical roots. Its traditions were conservative. There was a general conformity in the way that people dressed and, to some degree, in their beliefs. I wore sports jackets to work and everybody else wore dark suits. I supported McGovern for president with pride. I wore a "George McGovern for President" button on my lapel. I greeted David Rockefeller, chairman and CEO of the bank, and other bank executives in the elevators with a smile, wearing my liberalism on my chest. Nobody ever said a word to me about my dress or my political choice. I was not in tune with the political or dress traditions. In the early stages, I was not even sensitive to it. The senior executive managers were probably shaking their heads in dismay. Either that or when they opened the door for diverse candidates, they had prepared themselves for all that it entailed. Nevertheless, life was good. I absorbed a huge amount of information. The experience was the basis on which my career was built and maintained for the next forty years.

The Dream Apartment[76]

Instead of living in New York City, I rented an apartment in Troy Towers, 380 Mountain Road, Union City, New Jersey, on the thirteenth floor of a twenty-two-story building. The Towers sat atop a cliff overlooking Hoboken, New Jersey, and the Hudson River was in the foreground beyond the landscape. The Midtown Manhattan skyline was in the background, across the Hudson River. I had a spectacular panoramic view of Midtown Manhattan, ships on the Hudson, the World Trade Twin Towers, and so much more. The building and every apartment in the high-rise faced New York City. Every room, my bedroom, living room, and the balcony had access to the priceless city skyline. I paid for that luxury. My monthly rent payments amounted to 30 percent of my salary with an add-on 6 percent fee to park my new Beetle in the garage. I commuted to New York City's Forty-Third Street bus terminal by bus. Then I took a train down to Wall Street. I used the car only on weekends. My starting salary was very competitive with other salaries offered to MBA graduates. In those days, a starting salary was just an entry number.

The expectation was that salaries increased quickly. It increased based on individual and corporate performance. There was competition among companies. Every company was keenly aware that other companies recruited and paid for trained MBA talent. To keep talent, salaries increased annually. Still I had some more maturing to do. I now had more money, therefore, I had to more astutely learn to match my expenses with my income and budget. I had stretched my Peace Corps volunteer allotment to cover all my needs, and I still had funds leftover for discretionary spending. The New York City area was very different from Kenya. Money did not go as far.

Iran-Kenya Connection

Mary Lou, sibling 12, was in the sixth grade when I graduated from high school and was a student at Rider College during the years I served in Kenya as a Peace Corps volunteer. She earned her BA from Rider in 1971, the same year I earned my MBA degree from Atlanta University.

I accepted the bank job on Wall Street. She accepted a teaching position in Jersey City, New Jersey. Being straight out of college and broke, she needed a place to stay; so we shared my Troy Towers apartment in Union City, New Jersey. She used my Volkswagen for transportation. This was the very same VW purchased with the reimbursement money from those recruitment visits. It worked out great since the car was parked in the garage and Mary Lou needed to get back-and-forth to school. She taught business education at a Jersey City High School.

Rose, who was active in politics and politically connected, used her influence to help Mary Lou get a teacher assignment at a new school. A year later, we both moved on. Mary moved to Boston and entered the University of Massachusetts graduate school and taught as she completed her master's. I left Wall Street for Houston, Texas, and got married. Mary Lou earned her master's degree, moved to

Cleveland, got married to a Ghanaian, and divorced after five years. Several years thereafter, she accepted a two-year assignment in Iran, teaching business education for the Iranian monarchy while the Shah of Iran was still in power.

Mary Lou was very smart and was well-versed on many topics. I often wondered how she knew the issues and subjects so well. After conversing with her over the years, I accepted it as a fact that she was much smarter than me. I was considered the family financial subject matter expert. Siblings consulted me when it came to financial matters. She handled her own financial matters and did quite well.

Mary always wanted to travel internationally. She was a vivacious reader. When she was very young, she read about different places and people having exciting adventures. Then in detail, she would recount their experiences with us as if they were hers. If she had gone to bed reading a novel, she would wake up and tell us that overnight, she had been to Germany, France, and other exotic sites mentioned in the book. She was attracted to and curious about diverse cultures and societies. She was inquisitive. She had an unquenchable desire to learn about all things spiritually uplifting or otherworldly. She loved to explore. If it meant that she had to do it alone, she was fine with that. Mary was equally comfortable being alone or being with family and friends.

Mary was a calculated risk-taker. She was adventurous, and she welcomed new and challenging opportunities. Admittedly I don't think even she could have predicted the student unrest that led to the turmoil in Iran. The tensions seemed to develop quickly. There were riots and police disturbances being steadily broadcasted on the three evening news channels. This was before cable. The news channels were only ABC, CBS, and NBC at the time. There were reports of Iranians taking control of the American Embassy and hostages being taken. We did not hear from Mary during the hostile disturbances and nothing was publicized. Our focus was glued to our televisions and everyone worried that she would become a hostage.

When Mary returned to the states, she established residency in the metro Washington, DC area. She transitioned from classroom teaching to recruiting and training Job Corps students for employment. Several years later, she relocated to Atlanta to run the program in Metropolitan Atlanta. She lived with my family and me until she secured her own apartment. She ran the program in Georgia for about five years. Mary relocated again to Washington when funding for the Job Corps program was severely cut. The move back to the DC area allowed her to be close with her network of friends, many of whom were in the US State Department Diplomatic Corps. She remained in the Metropolitan DC area until she passed away from a cancer diagnosis on March 16, 2010. Mary, George, and I are the only siblings, out of the fourteen siblings, who once worked and lived outside of the United States.

The Move, the Marriage, and the Moron—I'm Moved

I asked Millette to marry me and gave her an engagement ring in October 1971, her second year of graduate school. We agreed to marry the following year on an August 5. It was the date her mother and father married.

Our next step was to decide where to live. She pursued employment in both New York City and Houston where her parents still lived. I looked for employment in Houston. If offered a position in Houston, I needed a job reference from my current employer. I explained my situation to my manager. He agreed to provide a reference if I was offered a position in Houston. This was new territory for me and very tricky. However, I got a job reference from David, my manager. He was a Californian, a graduate of the University of California at Los Angeles (UCLA), and was a very serious-minded individual. We stayed in touch for years thereafter. He left the Wall Street bank and moved back to Los Angeles. After six jobs for me and ten years later, I was in Los Angeles on business and visited him at his office. He was on just his second job but had time to catch up with me.

During the early 1970s, both companies and headhunters avidly recruited minority candidates nationwide. If a minority MBA graduate failed to gain employment, it was probably because they never interviewed or had expressed a desire to not work. I turned down plenty of job offers, and companies continued to call and made unsolicited offers. Therefore, I was sure my fiancée would be offered a position in Houston. She was a National Merit Scholar and salutatorian at her Houston, Texas, Wheatley's High School class.[77] She attended the University of Oklahoma (OU) on scholarship and graduated with a bachelor's degree in business of administration. After she graduated from OU, she worked at Shell Oil in Houston. We were confident she would find a position there after graduating with an MBA. Houston was a major city with a growing job market. New York City provided great career opportunities as well, so we agreed to relocate based on which one of us landed a job first.

I sent my resume to banks and oil companies in Houston and received inquiries. I interviewed with two banks and two oil companies. I accepted an offer as a treasury analyst with an oil company that involved analyzing non-gas and oil investments.[78] I relocated to Houston in June, at the expiration of my Troy Tower apartment lease in Union City, New Jersey. We found an apartment on Brompton Court, not far from the Astro Dome. I moved in alone until our wedding on August 5.

As we were growing up, my mother taught us how to cook, wash, iron, clean house, and many other things. She never taught me anything about marriage. Of course, I left home for college in the summer of '62 and didn't spend much time there after I left for college. Ten years later, I missed some very wise motherly advice that would have been priceless. By the time I got married, seven siblings had gotten married, including my two older brothers; however, until I attended George's wedding, I had not attended any of my siblings' weddings. They had not shared any advice about the etiquette of asking the father of the bride's permission to marry his daughter. I never had any father-and-son discussions with my dad. I'm not sure he was ever aware of the custom, or if he was aware, would he have shared that knowledge with me? I really did not know. The absence of that very insight almost cost me my beloved bride, my partner of forty-five years.

The evening before the wedding, my father-in-law, a godly quiet and low-key man, said to me, away from the family, "Grover, you want to marry my daughter, but you never gave me the respect of asking me."[79]

Instead of being humble, I was arrogant and I brashly said, "Your daughter and your wife made all the arrangements and did all the planning." I acted as if they had forced me to marry her. I do not recall the rest of the conversation, but I do know he never raised his voice. Upon reflection, I'm sure he was saying silent prayers for God's protection of his daughter and for God's salvation and the delivery of my soul.

I even showed out with the preacher as he counseled us.[80] I challenged him on his belief of the biblical Scripture. I asked the preacher, "Do you really believe Moses really parted the Red Sea and that the Israelites crossed on dry land?" Why didn't I keep my mouth shut? Why had I been so cocky? I honestly do not know. Now I believe that during these premarriage encounters, God planted seeds that He cultivated and used later to yield fruit. Her father allowed the wedding to take place. As I evolved and grew to know my father-in-law better, I regretted my disrespectful manner. We became very close. I ended up loving and respecting him enormously.

We did not have any evening activities since our wedding was an afternoon affair. I purchased alcohol for those who drank. My in-laws were nondrinking Christians. I am not sure if they even approved of having alcohol at the event. I never asked. I just bought it and set it out. My brother Charles drank more than his fair share of it. In fact, Saturday evening, he got sloppy drunk. He had an early Sunday morning flight back to Newark, but he was out cold when it was time to leave for the airport. Unable to stir him, my bride and I got help and threw him in the back of our Volkswagen and took off for the airport. After we arrived, he was still drunk and we were unable to find his Eastern Airlines plane ticket. In those days, non-passengers could freely accompany passengers to the gate. The Eastern Airlines attendant told us he could not fly inebriated. We were disgusted and left him there. We never checked to see if he found his ticket or was able to board the plane. We learned later that he talked his way onto the plane without a ticket. Apparently his blood alcohol level decreased to an acceptable level. So he boarded the plane and flew home. We assumed his reservations and Eastern proof of purchase was proof enough. Regarding his ticket, I found it about twenty years later when I took the drawers out of the chest frame. It had fallen behind a drawer in the chest of drawers in my apartment bedroom where he had spent the weekend.

After we dropped Charles off at the airport, we attended Sunday services at Good Hope Baptist Church. Rev. Kimball, the pastor, preached to me, but he did not call my name.[81] Only three of us knew to whom he spoke. He said, "There is someone here who needs to be saved, I pray that God convict and save him." I sat and listened. I told no one that the message was targeted at me. Only Rev. Kimball, my wife, and I knew. After the services, we were off on our honeymoon. We stayed in Houston five months. Neither my wife nor I attended Good Hope Baptist Church or any church on a regular basis during our residency there.

For our honeymoon, we visited my spouse's paternal granddad in Fort Worth, Texas. This was the first and last time I saw him. Her family, unlike mine, was quiet, reserved, and never discussed family members. My wife's mother had one living sister who was childless and lived in the same Houston neighborhood of Pleasantville.[82] Her father had several living brothers and sisters. However, I never met any of them. Her uncles and father invested in land in West Texas and leased it and collected royalty on the natural gas pumped from it. Since my wife and her sisters inherited the properties, I have spoken with her uncles, who lived in Las Vegas and California, by telephone, but Millette knows little about any of her relatives.

Over the years, I urged my bride to do a celebration and appreciation banquet for her parents while they were alive and of sound mind. Both young and old loved Mrs. Waters for who she was and the service she performed for her community, church, and for her beloved city of Houston.[83] Her mother would have objected but would have enjoyed seeing so many beloved friends of all ethnicities at such a gathering. She knew people and loved Houston. My wife insisted that her mother did not want it. I knew her mother well enough to know she would have enjoyed having friends to fellowship with and to celebrate her years of service. It did not happen. Years later, after Millette and I moved away, each time her mother and I talked, she continued to promote Houston's high points and offered to talk to people in position of power to land me a job in Houston. She even persuaded me to consider returning; and I interviewed and was offered a position[84] at a bank in Houston. I seriously considered it so the kids could spend more time with their grandparents.

My wife is the youngest of three sisters. I will use initials for each of her siblings and others. LWD is the oldest and was quite rebellious growing up. LWD rejected her parents' advice to get an education. She joined the navy, botched it, and was discharged from the service. LWK earned a college degree from Dillard University, then joined the army and served in Germany. She earned the rank of captain, met BK, her husband, in Germany where they both served. JWK was the first of the three girls to get married. They had two sons, SK and DK. Both SK and DK followed their dad's career path and are attorneys. BK worked many years as a litigating US attorney in the state of New Jersey and at the US Justice Department. In addition, he still found time for a career in private practice. LWD married shortly after me and Millette. Her parents didn't embrace her marriage. However, they did not outwardly object to her spousal choice. They treated him very respectfully. He passed away after some twenty years of marriage.

Millette and I moved to Miami, Florida, after only five months of marriage. It was just six months after I relocated to Houston from New York. There was nothing wrong with the oil company, the job, or Houston, and I had no good reason to move. I just got restless, dissatisfied with the job and the city. And I wanted a change. Perhaps it was divine intervention. I accepted a job with a bank in Miami. I had only one visit to Miami to interview for the job, and I accepted the job on the spot.

Our Sundays in Miami consisted of sleeping in or going on long drives to the Florida Keys. During the spring of 1973, the Sunday routine got old and stale. Millette had gone to Houston to visit her parents. Out of the blue, one Saturday afternoon, while visiting my first cousin and his family, I asked my cousin for a recommendation for a local church to attend. He told me about one; he called it a sophisticated church. The Lord honored Rev. Kimball's, the Good Hope Church pastor, request! The church must have prayed for me. The seeds were taking root. I was about to be saved.

I had no idea what my cousin meant about a sophisticated church, but I checked it out. Despite my spiritual upbringing and my mother's teaching, I had become weary of black churches. My image was that black preachers rode in big cars and smoked cigars. I would soon discover that I needed a head makeover and a heart transplant. I visited the sophisticated church, Glendale Baptist, that my first cousin[85] told me about. I was wrong about God's servant, the minister, Rev. Joseph C. Coats. God displayed before me, in living color, His love and fellowship through the pastor. There were about six hundred people in attendance that Sunday. Most were young families with children. The pastor and his wife had eight young children. As in many black churches, during the service, the pastor invited all visitors to stand and be recognized. I did not do so. I wanted to blend in, and I hoped to exit without being noticed. Being there was God-ordained and was a divine appointment. Like Jonah, I was running away from God's intention. Looking back, I truly believe the Lord led me to Miami.

At the close of services, the pastor stood at the door. He greeted and shook hands with all the parishioners as they left the church. It was clear that he knew all the members since he addressed them each by name. He showed an eagerness to greet and meet all the attendees, especially the visitors. I thought I could slip away through the crowd unnoticed; unfortunately, I failed. Rev. Coats spotted me like a huge stain on a white shirt. He asked me if I had a few minutes to talk after he finished greeting the attendees. I agreed. We went to his office and he warmly welcomed me. He asked if I had just moved to Miami or if I was just visiting. He made me feel very comfortable and relaxed. He spoke with me and didn't rush, even though his family waited in the station wagon. Without pressuring me, he stated, if I didn't have a church home, I should consider becoming a member of Glendale Baptist. I advised him that I would have to wait until my wife returned from Houston and both of us would attend and decide.

Upon her return from Houston, we attended as I promised. We received the same genuine friendly welcome that I had experienced earlier. He met with us and explained his understanding of being a Christian. He noted that Christ taught His disciples. Therefore, a new Christian must be taught and instructed according to the biblical Scriptures. Once learned, a follower of Jesus must obey His teachings, just as His (Christ) disciples did. We felt so spirit-filled, we joined Glendale Baptist the next Sunday. Rev. Coats invited us to return to church that evening to begin our (Southern Baptist) orientation studies which is called Training Union. Then he added, "The devil will throw everything in his bag of tricks to keep you from returning this afternoon to start your learning."

After attending the morning worship services, Millette and I returned to our apartment. I then drove to South Miami. I don't recall the exact reason we went there, but on the way back to our apartment, a Dade County Police Officer put on his siren and motioned for me to stop. There was no convenient place for me to pull over, so I neared the apartment entrance and stopped. Feeling that I had not been responsive to his signal to stop, the policeman arrested me and took me to jail from Dadeland, South Dade County, to downtown Miami, about twenty miles away. Several hours later, it was not clear why he flashed his lights, turned on the siren, and stopped me. I was released from jail using my Florida voter's registration card, and no charges were filed. We missed the Sunday evening orientation class. It seemed that the pastor's words about Satan had come true. Being detained had prevented us from attending the evening service. Our will was being tested; nevertheless, we made it to the next scheduled session. The subsequent conversations we had with the pastor about God's Word contributed to our spiritual growth and wisdom about the Scripture.

For our training, we were steeped into a Southern Baptist Bible study curriculum. The classes extended from a basic orientation to advanced courses. Among other things, we were challenged to memorize the books of the Old and New Testaments. Our charge was to know who wrote each book and when it was written. We were schooled on how the books were chosen for the Bible. As part of the educational process, we had to recount the theme of each book in the Bible. During these sessions, as new Christians, we learned what the Bible tells us about God and our responsibilities as believers. It was a very powerful orientation. The delivery was unabridged. Once learned, we felt armed to handle any situation, particularly if someone tried to lead us astray with false teachings or misinterpretations of Scripture.

Reverend Joseph C. Coats didn't smoke nor did he drink anything stronger than coffee; so much for my cynical premise that black preachers drove big cars and smoked cigars. He was a genuine servant of the God, Lord, and Savior. He took a personal interest in us. He taught and nurtured us in God's ways. As an obedient servant, God used me to be a part of what He was doing in Miami's Richmond Height's community. While we were in Miami, God refined my talents and used my skills for His purpose. As a banker, He used my influence and connections to acquire land to further develop the community. He used my sphere of influence to get financing to construct some needed educational space in Glendale's expanded church facilities.

I left my first Miami job at Florida's largest bank for a position as cash controller at a truck leasing company. The CEO, a client at the bank, recruited a team to assist him through a financial crisis. His company was embroiled in it due to an economic downturn in a credit crunch. Short-term interest rates were high, at 20 percent, and this created a soft-lease market. The company was unable to service its debt due to the high prime interest rates. Early on, when interest rates were low, management tried to minimize its long-term debt by using short-term lines of credit. No company could survive paying such high rates on huge outstanding loans.

After six months of employment, there was no cash to track. So there was no need for a cash controller. The financial markets had dried up for borrowing short-term. The company was close to defaulting on long-term debt loan covenants. Although I reported to the controller, my job functions and activities were more treasury oriented. The treasurer and controller, both British, had personal conflicts, and I was caught in the middle.

It was obvious that the company could not continue to operate normally. In early January, the dominos fell. I reported to work, knowing my firing was imminent due to the company's debt crisis. The company had cash-flow problems. As I sat in my office, a vice president got up, picked up his jacket, briefcase, and walked out and never returned. I surmised he had been fired. I wondered who would be next. Later in the day, another vice president and regional manager left and didn't return. This daily exit went on for about two weeks. I knew it was just a matter of time before I would also be released. The day and time finally came. I was called to report to human resources. Nobody had to explain it to me, I knew why I was there. News about the company's financial crises had made front-page headlines in the newspapers for weeks.

My next job was with a federal savings and loans bank that decided to grow by expansion and planned to open new branches. It looked for and hired experienced, qualified candidates with MBAs to run them. After I was trained at different branches for six months, the bank senior team decided not to expand. I was unemployed again for more than six months. We were expecting our first child. Millette was working long hours, and she was our sole income provider.

During my unemployment, I chased every lead, whether cold, warm, or hot. After six months, I received a call from the executive vice president of human resources (HR) of a Miami bank. He had been my previous employer at the bank that recruited and relocated me from Houston to Miami. He asked me to join his staff and become the HR manager for the bank's data processing division. The division employed nearly ninety people, including the Data Processing Division (DPD) executives and the president. Because of my position, I had access to the DPD employee records salaries and appraisals. I had responsibility to identify potential new hires. I screened them and presented qualified candidates to senior management for hiring consideration. All personnel matters for DPD came through me. As part of my duties, I pointed out inequities with position pay and promotions.

I reported to a VP with a dotted line to the senior executive vice president of human resources (the person who had recruited me).

He, along with other key executives, established some of the bank's key policies. The senior executive vice president of human resources, who had a PhD in economics, really liked me. He recommended me to teach at Florida International University.[86] I taught a finance class there as an adjunct professor, part-time, while working at the bank. He pushed me up the organization's ladder, opened doors, and was instrumental in getting me involved in Miami's business community. He was recruited from a large North Carolina bank with a mandate to change the culture of the bank. In the early 1970s, many of the executives at the banks were not particularly champions for blacks and other minorities' advancement. It was unthinkable that I was being accepted as a peer as a black man. My boss, who was also my friend, was a liberal, and together, we tried to affect change. Everything we did was very professional and consistent with the bank's stated mission, yet some did not share our commitment to promote the bank's goals. They tried to avert my authority but to no avail. We anticipated that they would maneuver around me, if given the chance. When they made their move, their intent was obvious. We gained advantage, cornered and checkmated them. I learned a lot about office politics in this job.

In addition to the responsibilities mentioned, I had the responsibility as the holding company's affirmative action program manager for all the bank's operating entities. The entities consisted of twenty individual banks owned by the holding company. Florida banking laws, at the time, limited a bank to a single location with no branches. That means there was only a street address and building.

They sidestepped the law by creating a shell organization called a holding company. I worked for the holding company that owned the individual banks and had the authority to see the personnel records and salary of each employee, from the CEO down to unskilled laborers. I was an officer and the highest-ranking black who worked for the company. During the early 1970s, there were not many blacks in management positions at banks in the South, especially in Miami. Many at the bank did not like me. The executives I worked for previously, as a loan officer, did not care for me knowing their salaries and every detail of their employment history, like the date of their last raise, amount of the raise, or their next scheduled raise. They tried to deny my access to such detail. Again my boss and friend didn't go for such tactics. I was given all that I needed to be successful in my role at the bank.

I had the support and respect of the senior executive vice president of human resources, and we were making incremental progress at the bank. I learned a great deal in the HR assignment. Under my boss's mentoring, I became more aware and savvy about office politics. I had made meaningful contacts via the firm, within the industry, and in the community. I had significantly improved my real world business acumen. There was career and salary growth potential at the bank. I had developed professionally and personally. Still I was perhaps the most miserable person in Miami. I had a working wife and a three-month old son, and I was ready for another job change.

The Friend, Coworker, and Church Family

The bank employed another black, a Clemson graduate, with a master's in business administration from the U, University of Miami.[87] During my few years as the bank's employee, only two other black professionals were employed: one in check processing and the other one with the bank credit cards division. The credit card professional was the U MBA graduate. He and I discussed the cultural challenges at the bank, namely a lack of diversity and equity. He was smart and one of the first blacks to enroll at Clemson University in the late '60s. He knew firsthand about discrimination from growing up in Columbia, South Carolina, and had experienced it firsthand as a student at Clemson University. We discussed leaving the bank and working for a different company. There was a slight problem. The economy was in a tailspin. Bank loan short-term interest rates were still at 20 percent, and jobs were hard to find. Some said timing is everything, but I said God is in control of time. My coworker got a lead from a friend in Columbia that a technology company was looking to hire sales representatives for the Fort Lauderdale office.

My Clemson friend called the Fort Lauderdale office for an appointment. He was told the company had positions available in the Miami office as well. He contacted the Miami office for an interview. I requested that he refer me, if there was another opening available. He interviewed and was offered a sales position, and he accepted the position in the Miami location. The company was the very same one that offered me a position out of business school eight years earlier. I still had a very favorable opinion of the firm. Then, I was unwilling to relocate to Rochester, Minnesota, even for a short period of time and deal with the frigid winter temperatures. Eight years removed, I looked for another opportunity to work for the company. This time, the location was perfect but I had no experience in sales.

Unlike the biblical characters, the baker and cupbearer who were released from prison and forgot about Joseph (Genesis 40:1–23), my friend didn't leave me behind. He asked the manager about other sales positions in the Miami office and referred me. I submitted my resume and interviewed for a sales position. I told my boss, senior executive vice president of human resources, my friend and mentor, I had interviewed at a technology company and if I was offered a sales position, I would accept it. We had discussed my preferences before he hired me. He knew that human resources was not my comfort zone. He understood my decision, and we maintained our friendship until he passed away years later.

In 1982, God picked up the mantel and moved me out of Miami to Atlanta, Georgia. It was about four years after I started my work in sales. I had completed my religious conversion and the job that He had assigned to me. We had lived in Miami for ten years. I learned and shared my talents with others as we grew spiritually. We became members of the Glendale Baptist spiritual family. We built relationships that remain closer than some blood relatives. Two of my three sons were born in Miami and their godparents are there. The daughter of my son's godparents lived with us several years while attending college in Atlanta.

About a year before we transferred to Atlanta, we built a house with a pool and always had lots of company. Although most of our free time involved church activities, we never concerned ourselves about our sons. The godparents' family and other youth from church were always eager to care for them. We were a big loving church family. In the ten years we lived in Miami, we saw the Glendale Baptist Church grow from six hundred members to nearly five thousand. Pastor Coats led by example. He was God's instrument. He taught us God's Word and sent us out as Christians to apply our talents to service in God's other ministries.

The Money Revealed

I had never seriously considered a sales career, but it turned out to be a perfectly natural fit. I accepted jobs in finance, and I expected to spend a career in my chosen discipline. Yet I walked away each time. For a short time, I transitioned to a career in personnel and human resources. I had very little interest in that field. Looking back, that was not a misstep. The human resources job fine-tuned my people, presentation, and negotiation skills. It taught me the ins and outs of office politics. Each job enhanced my networking and management skills. I didn't realize it as I lived through the successes and failures, but each employment experience prepared me well for the job that I loved at the technology company and thereafter.

My new sales career started with eight weeks of formal basic sales training in Dallas, Texas. After I completed the training, I was assigned the least attractive sales territory in Miami. It did not bother me. It is not customary to give a new employee an exceptional territory. I was excited about my new career opportunities, and while it was a struggle, I succeeded. I made my annual objectives on December 27. Management gave me a new territory the following year. I made my annual quota in October. As I gained experience, I developed my sales techniques. I learned the art of selling and how to maximize each potential. The company's market areas were assigned by street and address. The next year, I started out with more buildings to survey and more potential client leads to pursue.

Like everything in life, sales opportunities change. They occur unexpectedly. An example of that happened with me as the beneficiary. The sales representative assigned to the nation's fifth largest public-school district, at that time, told an executive that he took money out of her pocket when he purchased competitive products. The executive was not pleased with her remarks and began to allocate even more budget dollars to other manufacturer's products. He purchased from her only when he had no other options. Either she quit or was removed from the account. I benefited. My first two years were great experience and training. My third year as a professional sales representative, I was assigned the public-sector territory. I had state and local government and public education accounts. Those accounts were in territories that had underperformed. The accounts had not been buyers either because of the sales representative or the products. Both factors began to change, and I was the primary benefactor.

As users requested information, I always exceeded their expectations. My customer service led to a lot of demonstrations and equipment trials. The equipment stayed with the user for up to two weeks with the understanding that if they liked it and it made them more productive, they would buy it. It worked. The users wanted to keep the demonstration equipment. That was not allowed. I would write up an order and expedite it. My third year in sales, I sold more of my company's products than any other individual in the state of Florida.

My success resulted from treating every person, regardless of title, with respect. They appreciated it. I treated each new purchaser with kindness, and in turn, they called another school or principal beaming praise about the service they received. Those references generated more new orders just for doing my job and treating people deferentially.

I volunteered and taught a keyboarding class from time to time, just to give the teacher some relief. I learned keyboarding skills in high school on a manual typewriter. I was one of the few male students to do so. Now my noncollege preparation course and skill were paying off. As new portable technology was announced, I took it with me on customer visits. I did demonstrations and showed off my keyboarding skills and showed off other new portable technology. Additionally I showed off the productivity of the products.

I was in demand and loved every moment of the time I spent as a salesman in a customer-facing scenario. Some of the products could talk and read. Many unique and very new computer features were being rolled out to the industry at that time. The company's research and development division were ahead of its time—in the 1970s–1980s.

The bottom line, I accomplished my annual company objectives in April. Soon every account executive in the Miami office wanted me to make sales calls with them, and I did. My success changed their perception of me. The prior two years, they taught me the art of selling, now the role was reversed. As I made calls with them, I understood why I was successful. It boiled down to being natural. I communicated with confidence. My attitude, my actions, my conversations were positive. I never acted or displayed negative or nervous tendencies. I finished my fourth year 211 percent over my sales quota. The next year, management promoted me to staff in Atlanta. Eventually I matriculated from regional staff to area staff and on to headquarters. I won several area manager's awards. As the area manager presented the awards, he commented that whenever he felt down and needed a lift, he would walk around and stop at my desk and leave energized.

Job Training from Bottom Up

Four years after I joined the company, I was promoted to the Atlanta regional sales area office. I still lived in Miami. A year later, we moved to Atlanta as the company reorganized its sales divisions. I worked out of various headquartered locations and received many job assignments, promotions, and recognitions. I am most proud of being chosen to be one of the original employees of the financing unit. Thirteen senior-level sales professionals and I grew the revenue base and sold financing to our clients. We financed products and services that companies needed to operate a business. One of my clients purchased $48 million of equipment, the largest single-financed transaction at that time.

Over the course of my professional career, I came face-to-face with some very smart individuals. I worked for seven employers. As I reflect on my career decisions, I sometimes mixed up my ability with my desire. I spent time performing jobs that I did well. They may not have played to my strength, but be that as it may, along the way, I enhanced my value and picked up useful skills that I applied in sales. While I did not ultimately work day-to-day in finance firms, my business school and work lessons learned in banking added to my success in sales. The cash-management role I played for the truck leasing company prepared me for the role I was about to play in the financing arm of the technology company. While I did not enjoy the human resources, headquarters administrative staff jobs, those assignments taught me lessons that came in handy. I had gotten tremendously better at office politics. I learned to avoid the landmines and became astute at properly networking and nurturing friendships at this point in my career.

During my time on staff, I coordinated and rolled out many marketing programs to support the territory sales teams. One of the programs promoted the use of the company airplanes assigned to take clients for sales briefings at plants and product development labs. The company divided the sales organizations into geographical sales areas and assigned each area six weeks' use of the company owned jets. Instead of waiting for the territory executives to call requesting the airplanes, I called them. I offered them the opportunity to schedule the airplane for team or client trips. I went along on some of the trips based on seating availability. I learned things at the briefings that benefited me later in my career. My proactive approach got more use of the airplanes than any other sales region. I called the flight department and asked them to give me first right of refusal when the airplanes were being underutilized. Then I proactively reached out to the client teams to get their wish list of clients to take to technology briefings. I made it happen. I was assigned and used the company's jets more than any other area during my time on area staff.

I was an area staff program manager. We had the responsibility to prepare the annual performance sales review that area management presented to corporate executives. I created marketing programs to execute selling. It took up to two weeks to finalize the presentations due to revisions. The team worked feverishly to add the finished touches and scripting. To show appreciation and to team build, area management went out with the staff for happy hour from time to time. I went along and heard the rumors that came out of headquarters. I also witnessed the loose tongues and changed personalities, after a few drinks, in some of the teammates. A dear friend and teammate asked the director of marketing, after a few drinks, why he always assigned me to do his confidential presentations. He went on and implied that, "We are all professionals and are just as capable."

The director responded, "I ask Grover because I trust him. I know he will not discuss it with anyone. If I asked you, you would tell the world and I would have to fire your ass." Then he laughed. The director of marketing went on to become the company's chairman and CEO, and we communicated casually until both of us retired.

DEPARTMENT OF STATE
AGENCY FOR INTERNATIONAL DEVELOPMENT
WASHINGTON, D.C. 20523

March 31, 1971.

Mr. Grover Jackson
Atlanta University
P. O. Box 124
Atlanta, Georgia 30314

Dear Mr. Jackson:

Reference is made to our recent conversation in which I advised you
that you are under active consideration for appointment to the Agency
for International Development as an International Development Intern in
the field of agriculture economics. Your salary rate will be FSRL-7,
$15,350 per annum. You have been selected for assignment to USAID/Tanzania
for the IDI class beginning July 1971. Please confirm your acceptance of
this position as soon as possible to enable us to process an alternate
candidate if you are not interested. Attached is medical and passport
authorization. Please complete the medical examination as soon as possible.
In addition, please complete and return the attached forms as soon as
possible in the enclosed self-addressed envelope:

    SF-86 Please update. Where there has been no change in
        the information which was submitted on your previous
        forms, please so indicate.
    SF-87 Fingerprint Chart. Complete and return
    AID 6-85 Please update and return
    AID 4-42 Complete and return 2 copies
    AID 4-150 Complete and return 2 copies
    AID 6-28 Sign and return
    SF-144 Complete and return

Your proposed appointment is subject to certain clearances which are now
in process. Therefore, under no circumstances should you construe this
letter as a firm offer of employment, make plans to terminate your present
position or in any other way change your present status in preparation
for this assignment. If you have any questions, please do not hesitate
to contact me at AC 703-357-5365.

        Sincerely yours,

        Janet C. Rourke
        Personnel Staffing Specialist
        Program Management Staffing Branch

U.S. Department offered me a position to
return to East Africa (Tanzania).

My first apartment out of gratulate school and view of Hoboken, NJ, NY, the Hudson River, Midtown Manhattan, NY from my apartment.

Information was shared by her best friend Charlyn during a visit to Houston in 2015.

Gulf Oil Company - U.S.

TREASURY DEPARTMENT

Michael E. Shannon
Treasurer

P.O. Box 2100
Houston, Texas 77001

April 24, 1972

Mr. Grover Jackson
Troy Towers, Apt. 1306
Union City, New Jersey 07087

Dear Mr. Jackson:

Confirming my telephone conversation with you on Friday, I am pleased to offer you a position as Junior Analyst in the Gulf Oil Company - U.S. Treasury Department here in Houston. The annual salary will be $18,000. This offer is contingent upon your passing a physical examination administered by our Medical Department. If you are at all concerned about the outcome of this exam, we will make arrangements for you to take it on the East Coast before you make your decision on Gulf.

If you accept, Gulf will pay for moving your household goods and personal belongings to Houston and also your transportation costs. Should you drive your own car, we will reimburse you at 10¢ per mile from your current residence to Houston. In addition, Gulf will reimburse you for meals and lodging en route and during a period not exceeding seven days after arrival.

We would like to have your answer as soon as possible, but in any event by May 12. Should you decide to accept our offer, please complete the lower portion of the attached copy and return it in the enclosed envelope. Meanwhile, let me know if you have any further questions.

Sincerely,

MICHAEL E. SHANNON

MES:pw
Enclosures

Job offer from Gulf Oil Company later was purchased by Chevron

My lovely bride

Rev. Crawford W. Kimble, Sr, Charles, my best man and me

My bride, her father, & mother, and my mother

My lovely bride and Mrs. Lucille Vinable, her mother's sister & aunt

Mrs. Hattie B. Waters and daughter, at our wedding August 5, 1972

Houston National Bank

May 20, 1974

Grover Jackson
7765 S. W. 86th Street
Apartment F2-101
Miami, Florida 33143

Dear Grover,

This will confirm our telephone conversation of May 14, 1974, offering you employment as a Loan Officer in our Commerical Banking Department. The beginning annual salary, if you accept this job, will be $15,000 per year.

I am sorry for the delay in confirming this offer but it had slipped my mind. Thank you for calling me this morning and reminding me of this. We look forward to a favorable response from you.

Sincerely,

Positioned offered from a Houston bank to return to Houston

Roosevelt Cox with his wife and two of his three daughters

FIU adjunct professor performance

A friend since 1972, worked at two different companies
together and retired from the last one we joined in 1977

Chapter 14

The Funeral's Visitor

Mom's Funeral

M y youngest son, Gustin, was less than a month old when Mom passed. My wife and I were scheduled to fly to Phoenix to be with my finance sales team, our band of fourteen, to celebrate our overwhelming first-year success. My mom had agreed to care for my three sons while we were away. She loved visiting us, especially to see her grandsons. So I mailed her a round-trip airline ticket. She was ready and packed for her trip to Georgia, although the visit was more than a week away. She didn't wait until the last minute, instead she always packed many days, if not weeks, ahead of time. Waiting until the last minute was not her style. She passed away in her sleep a week before the trip on January 22, 1984.

It was the company's procedure, upon the death of an employee's immediate family member such as spouse, mother, father, or child, to have a company executive communicate directly with the employee to express condolences. In most cases, if the employee gave consent, the employee's manager offered to attend the services or send something appropriate representing both the employee's management team and the company. If the employee's manager was remote, the manager usually contacted a local executive to represent the company. Out of respect, the manager conveyed to the employee that a company's representative would attend the services with the employee's approval. My manager traveled from Pittsburgh to

Camden to attend my mother's funeral, and I thought it was odd.[88] He just showed up at Mom's funeral without communicating with me. He did not know me personally and I had reported to him for less than three weeks. He was not new to the company, just new to my group and team. He should have known the protocol; he knew nothing about me other than my name, address, degrees, years of service, and my performance ratings over the years. He knew nothing about the black church, its culture, my family, and I doubted if he had ever gone to a black funeral before. Most managers would have called and requested information to determine if it was appropriate to attend or if the funeral was public or private. It was not customary for an executive to invade a family's privacy without the employee's concurrence.

My parent's neighborhood wasn't the blue-collar Irish, Polish, and Jewish one we had moved into many years earlier. It had transitioned, and other income brackets and ethnicities now occupied the homes once lived in by nonblack middle-class families. The funeral was held at Harris Temple AME Church, just several blocks from my parents' Florence Street home. It is now the site of a new expanded H. B. Wilson Elementary School. I remember that home very fondly. During my mom's service, we sang, rejoiced, and laughed. It was truly a home-going celebration. We knew Mom wasn't there, just the shell of where she once lived. We knew that she was in the arms of Jesus, so we celebrated it. It was a long service and eulogy, and every seat in the church was filled. Many other attendees were standing. Mom was well-known in the community, and she had become an active elder in the Harris Temple Church family.

When I saw my new manager, he appeared very uncomfortable. There was no reason to be uneasy. We were in church. Even if he had been outside, no one from the community would have harmed him. Although the community had gradually changed, no crimes were being committed. Everyone knew the Jacksons, especially my mother. My manager was not the only white person in attendance. My brother-in-law and other white friends of the family attended the service. If he was uncomfortable, and I believe he was, he put himself in the position and had only himself to blame. He invited himself. The funeral was probably none like any he had ever witnessed.

In the weeks that followed, I noticed that his dealings and conversations with me were a bit strained. Keep in mind that he was new to the team. I worked out of Atlanta, and he worked out of Pittsburgh. He never explained his presence at my mother's funeral. Based on the things he tried later, he had come to the services to gather insights about me. He had determined, given his findings based solely on his experience at the funeral and his assessment of my community background, that I was unworthy of my position. Let me explain. In the early '80s, few blacks served in financial positions for my employer or very few other companies. They just weren't placed in financial positions. I had earned the positions and was well-thought-of by the management who promoted me to that position. He set out to eliminate me. He failed to understand that I had earned my position. He also did not realize that I had a network of corporate sponsors, even though I was the lone black on our finance management team of fourteen.

The Company's Climate

The technology company had, as a core value, respect for the individual. This was practiced and honored by employees at all levels; and it was enforced. The core value separated my employer from all the rest in the industry, and it was, at the time, the culture that corporate America envied. It was a family culture, and all appreciated and respected the relationship. Every employee mattered and was treated with respect across the entire corporation. Every employee was called by his/her first name, from the CEO down to the mailroom employee.

In the early 1980s, many companies changed their method of acquisition from outright purchase to leasing. I was one of fourteen handpicked sales professional, also called financial advisers, to implement the company's leasing sales strategy. My territory covered the entire Southeastern states: Florida, Georgia, Tennessee, South Carolina, Alabama, Mississippi, and Louisiana. I was an experienced senior sales professional. I was excited to report directly to an executive and having a direct line of communication to the president as required on big deals. We negotiated directly with client senior level executives and enjoyed every moment of the job. The company grew very fast. The demands for leasing products grew much faster and beyond the parent company's expectations.

To our detriment, layers of management were added due to our entity's growth. About six months after we were appointed to run the lease division, the company assigned a regional manager to supervise us. Previously we reported directly to a director. It was a client executive's dream to have as his first line manager a senior level executive. Now we reported to someone we did not even know. After some investigation, we learned that our new manager was removed from his previous position due to a bad employee opinion survey. That was not good news. We hoped that he would try to redeem his career by allowing us to do our job—sell and generate profits. Having met him only once, at my mom's funeral, I really didn't have a positive opinion of him; however, I was willing to give him the benefit of the doubt.

Immediately after Mom's funeral, he started making demands of me. Instead of asking, he told me the date he would visit with me in the territory to call on clients. The standard protocol was to ask to accompany me on a visit and to request a convenient time to visit. As a financial adviser, I did not have direct access to clients. The assigned client executive controlled the access to the clients. The normal protocol to a client was through the territory client executive. It was not proper protocol to go directly to the client without permission nor would I ever attempt to do that. Anyway my manager insisted he was coming and he did not allow time for the client teams to arrange appointments. He ignored my common sense approach and said he was coming anyway.

I figured two could play games. I called a client executive in Birmingham, Alabama, told him the entire story, and asked him to set up appointments at some competitive accounts. He did; we spent an entire day calling on very low-prospect clients. I'm unaware if the client executive told his prospects the story of my new manager. It turned out better than any script I could have written. We visited prospects, talked about their installed products and their satisfaction with them. They piled on thick accolades about their installed products. I rejoiced inwardly at the support and teamwork provided by my friends whom I had known for many years before my current assignment.

Upon returning to Atlanta, I dropped my new manager off at his hotel; he asked me to come in for a minute. I did without any idea of his intentions. He started the conversation with, "You wasted my day." He said it as if I was supposed to do something extraordinary for him. I did make sure we didn't call on any of the company's installed accounts.

About two hours later, I got up and excused myself, then said, "I am going home, get into my bed, and have a good night's sleep. I hope you will do likewise." Then I left.

He tried his best to remove me from the position, but I had too much history and too much political capital invested with headquarters, management, and local and territory management. For reasons unknown to me, he was employed less than a month after our encounter. I continued in the same position as financial adviser. I was always a team player and treated everyone exactly as I wanted to be treated. I also knew the corporate culture—if I crossed you today, you could be my manager tomorrow. I went out of my way to be nice, always helped others, even when it impacted me personally. My entire professional career and life, I helped others and many have helped me.

Dad's Funeral with a Twist

Unlike my mother, Dad was a loner and did not like to leave home. When my family and I lived in Miami, I was able to get him to visit us only once during the entire ten years we lived there. My sole desire for Dad to visit was to see his brother, Grover. He had not seen him for many decades; certainly not since we had moved north in 1958. He reluctantly visited and brought some of his old habits, like smoking and drinking, with him. I had a rule for my home. No smoking or drinking inside my house. I never appreciated his smoking and drinking outside either. The smoke permeated his clothing and his skin. That prominent cigarette smell seeped into my home. Dad's clothes smelled of smoke and being around him for any length of time caused me to get sick. I had allergies, and the smell penetrated my senses. During his stay, I found a liquor bottle in his room and poured it out. Of course, my actions did not stop him and I knew it would not; but I had young boys and I did not want them exposed to such bad habits, especially coming from their grandfather.

During one of Mom's visits to Atlanta, she went to First Baptist Atlanta Church services with us. Thereafter, she never stopped talking about the services, both worship and Sunday school Bible class. After she returned home, she watched the *In Touch* television ministry program and listened to the daily radio broadcasts. Apparently she got Daddy hooked on listening to Dr. Charles Stanley as well.

During the time I served in the financial adviser position, I traveled to the headquarters from time to time. During my travels, I stopped in South Jersey to visit my dad. After Mom died, the house was in foreclosure. Dad had not paid the real estate taxes. My sisters moved him out of the house into an apartment in Lawnside, New Jersey. I paid the real estate taxes, and my brother Otis sold the house. He had lived in the house since 1958, a total of twenty-four years. While I visited with him, his entire conversation focused on my mom and my pastor, Dr. Charles Stanley, the pastor of First Baptist Church Atlanta. His radio was tuned to the local Christian station that broadcasted Dr. Stanley's, *In Touch*, daily radio program. My pastor was mostly what Dad talked about. He would also say, "I miss your ma." While death is a heart-wrenching experience, we will all die. If Christ returns during our lifetime, "But we shall all be changed—in a moment, in the twinkling of an eye, at the last trumpet" (1 Corinthians 15:50–53), according to the Bible, "And just as it is appointed for man to die once, and after that comes judgment" (Hebrews 9:27, ESV).

I saw Dad alive for the last time on my trip to the company's New York headquarters in November 1985. He was hospitalized; I believe based on his condition, death was only a matter of days, if not hours away. The next week, Mamie, sibling 6, called and said he had passed. I was prepared, not surprised or saddened. I had made my peace with him years ago. I simply said goodbye. After more than fifty-five years of marriage to Mom, I understand the loneliness he felt after her death. I realized he loved her. He did not know how to express, in words, his emotions for her during her lifetime. He loved all of us, his wife and children.

Solomon, the wisest man to ever live, according to the Bible, sums up life as "'Everything is meaningless,' says the Teacher, 'completely meaningless!'" (Ecclesiastes 1:2, New Living Bible Translation.) Ends with, "Here is my conclusion: fear God and obey His commandments, for this is the entire duty of man" (Ecclesiastes 12:13).

Rev. Robert C. Venable, Mom's pastor and a member of Camden Public School Board of Education, officiated at my father's funeral and delivered the eulogy. He was the pastor of Harris Temple AME Church, the same church Mom was a member and attended. Although the church was just several blocks away from my parents' home, my father did not attend it. He was a deacon at Saint Elmo Baptist Church in Omaha; after relocating to Camden, he joined Nazarene Baptist Church. He attended the church for only a short time after we migrated from Georgia to Camden.

At the request of the family, Pastor Venable officiated my dad's funeral. I'm sure it was also out of respect for Mom, who was a faithful elder and supporter of Harris Temple, that he delivered the eulogy. Mom had passed twenty-two months earlier. Although Rev. Venable knew Mom well, he had not spent any significant time with Dad. I am sure that each of my siblings sat during the going-home service recalling their various interactions with Dad. Some thoughts were more positive than others. Hopefully all were in a forgiving mindset. During the eulogy, Rev. Venable lost his train of thought. It was either a slip of the tongue or he forgot the name of the person he was eulogizing. Instead of saying Frank, my father's name, he said George, my brother's name. The slipup jolted us out of our private thoughts. Most of the family laughed, not being disrespectful. It was unexpected and broke up the solemnity of the moment. The slip of the tongue, although unintentional and perhaps embarrassing, served a real purpose. It took our minds off the death of our father for a moment. We all peered at each other. We thought, *He doesn't know it was Frank's funeral, not his son George.*[89] George had a smirk on his face. In error or not, I don't think he appreciated being eulogized at that stage in his life

The Expedition: Family and Journey

I hesitated to share this story. Then I decided it was relevant to the collective innocence and purity of our 1958 relocation experience when juxtaposed against today's downtrodden reality of life.

Several years ago, I had an encounter with a family acquaintance who is now homeless. The meeting sent me back in time to our family's trip from Omaha, Georgia, via bus to Philadelphia, Pennsylvania, almost sixty years ago. My acquaintance had traveled sixteen hours by Greyhound bus to come to Atlanta. She wasn't coming from a dirt-poor rural area to seek a better life in the big city. She did not have nine kids in tow who had never been more than fifty miles away from their birthplace before they took their eye-opening thirty-two-hour trip north in the back of the bus. She was coming from a city whose population is five times that of Atlanta.

There were similarities though. She was loaded down with more than nine bags. They were cheap dilapidated tote bags. Their contents were in disarray, hanging out and exposed. Our belongings were packed in pillowcases, cardboard boxes, and sheets creating a visual much like her tote bags. We were hopeful, making the northern trek to escape the poverty we had been born into. She had made life choices that rendered her in a situation of homelessness and hopelessness; so in reality, she was hopeful that someone would give her a brief reprieve from her current situation.

I remember our one-way trip to Philadelphia as if it had happened yesterday. I was very young and excited. I was anticipating a new beginning. She had made the bus excursion to seek out my wife and me. Her trip was only a temporary escape. She had gotten into a bind. Her meager cash flow had dried up, and money was very tight. Though she had no actionable plan, she was hoping to rebound soon. She didn't mind her many bags. She had gathered them over the years that she had fallen into homelessness. They traveled easily with her, like my mom's nine children with her in 1958. I had been totally embarrassed carrying the sheets that wrapped up our paltry belongings.

I compared her life's experience to mine. It struck me that we both had a bus ride; after that, our paths diverged. We had nothing in Omaha. Our trip had been planned to come north to be with loving family members who had sacrificed financially and, in many other ways, to help us start a new beginning. Our homeless friend had ignored her family who had, for many years, provided support and a loving home. They nurtured her as a loving daughter, gave her solid advice and counsel, and provided her opportunities to have a bright future, consequently like the prodigal son (Luke 15:11–32). She rejected those teachings and squandered the financial resources given to her. Unlike the prodigal son, her parents could not welcome her back home. They had long passed by now.

There are no more comparisons I can make between our family's trip to Philadelphia and our homeless friend's trip to Atlanta. The gist of the story is that, after not seeing or hearing from her in nearly fifteen years, she invited herself to our home. She gave my wife less than a day's notice that she was on her way. Because of some history, Millette suggested that she not come! She had much to do at work and she still had to prepare our home for our son and his family to visit in a month. Millette called her sister in Burbank, California, and related the call. They both concluded that our homeless friend was testing the waters and would not come for a visit unless she was invited. Wrong! Upon arriving from church the next day, I received a text message that stated, "I am at the bus station now, what do I do?"

After my wife composed herself, we went to the bus station, some twenty miles away, with the plan to buy a bus ticket and send our visitor back to her point of origin. I sat in the car while Millette went inside to talk with our uninvited and unwanted guest. About twenty minutes later, she called, asking me to come inside the bus station. I went inside and listened to the conversation between Millette and the homeless uninvited guest. Finally Millette made the decision to buy a return bus ticket to the visitor's city of origin. The bus was scheduled to depart later that Sunday evening. Our uninvited guest said, "I'm not going back today, I've been riding sixteen hours and I'm tired." We tried to be loving and as kind as possible, but we were determined not to allow our uninvited guest to dictate the terms of her uninvited intrusion. We compromised and agreed that we would buy a one-way return bus ticket and pay for a motel room overnight on the basis that she would return the next day to her city of origin.

I know, at this point of this story, you are probably saying, Grover, what about:

- Extending the courtesies to your friend that were given to your family by your farm neighbors in the 1940s–1950s?
- When you went to Kenya, you spoke about the hospitality that you extended to visitors and they shared when they received you. Where is it in this case?
- "Do not judge, or you too will be judged. For in the same way you judge others, you will be judged, and with the measure you use, it will be measured to you" (Matthew 7:1–2).
- "The King will reply, truly I tell you, whatever you did for one of the least of these brothers or sisters of mine, you did it for me" (Matthew 25:40).
- And so on.

Hold on, I am not finished.

I bought a one-way bus ticket for her to depart on Monday at 1:30 p.m., at a cost of $120. Then drove to a motel nearby. I parked the vehicle, asked my wife and guest to sit while I went in and inquired about a room and price. I explained a bit of my situation with the hotel clerk. I asked about the room rates and whether there was transportation from the motel to the bus station. The motel room was $118 per night.[90] It included breakfast and transportation to both the bus and train stations. Satisfied with the answers provided, I registered our guest and paid for one night only. I told the clerk not to give our guest anything related to the price of the room with my name on it. Our guest had not eaten for sixteen hours, so we drove around and found an establishment nearby that served dinner.

Before dropping her off and her many bags, she wanted a Subway sandwich for an evening snack. So we stopped and got that. We made one more stop and returned to the motel. The room was located on the ninth floor. Our guest didn't appreciate that room. She did not feel comfortable and did not want to be on the ninth floor. At that point, I was totally exhausted and it showed. I refused to request a room change to a lower level; Millette returned to the front desk and requested to be reassigned on a lower level. Early on, I thought her bags seemed unmanageable so the other stop was to purchase three suitable pieces of luggage for her. I consolidated all her items into the new luggage (to be candid, I am not sure whether the new baggage was intended to improve her status, i.e., offer her a glimmer of hope, improve her self-esteem, or was it to address my personal flashbacks from June 10, 1958).

Upon leaving the motel, I reminded the clerk, "Please do not give our guest anything related to the room cost with my name on it." I also requested that she put in a wake-up call for our guest and to remind her to be downstairs in the lobby by noon to get on the shuttle bound for the bus station. Millette and I finally returned home after a very long and somewhat-stressful day.

Late Monday night, my wife and I were curious and opined that our guest must be on her way to the city of her origin. We didn't dare call. Late Tuesday afternoon, my curiosity got the best of me. I called and asked her, "Are you back home yet?" She had not left Atlanta. On Thursday morning, I was reviewing my bank account online and noticed a large sum had been withdrawn by the motel where I had registered our friend on Sunday evening. Shocked, I drove to the motel and asked to speak to a manager. I explained that the motel had taken unauthorized funds from my bank account in the amount of $964. I went on to say that I had authorized and paid $118 for Sunday evening only. I didn't ask why the overage had occurred. I just wanted my funds back in my bank account.

Our friend never had any intentions of boarding the bus at 1:30 p.m., Monday, and never checked out of the motel. The manager argued that she would fight me regarding the charge. She said that I bought and left a homeless person at the motel. I did not argue, just walked out and called my bank and explained what occurred and that the charges were unauthorized. While I was there, the manager called my friend's room because she didn't know that she was still there until a clerk told her and described my friend's physical features. She demanded immediate payment from my friend and asked her for a credit/debit card to pay for her stay. My friend gave the motel manager a Chase debit card, and the motel took the money that she had deposited in Chase Bank earlier. The motel didn't refund my money. My bank reversed the motel charge and refunded me. My friend called Chase and told them the motel had not been authorized to take funds from her account and Chase refunded her money as well. The motel was left empty of payments.

Let's review just the finances from Sunday through Thursday: I authorized and paid for a bus ticket $120, meals $35 because I ate as well, one-night motel stay $118, and some incremental like parking, for a total of $348. The $964 unauthorized withdrawal was refunded, but there was an aggravation fee associated with it (the bus ticket expired since it was purchased for a specific date and time). I received a phone message on Friday asking me to take her Social Security check that was forwarded to our home address to the branch manager at Chase Bank's downtown Atlanta branch and deposit it. My initial reply was no, however, after thinking it over, I complied and drove some twenty-plus miles, one-way, to the branch and deposited the check.

On Friday afternoon, I received a call from our youngest son who was home alone. He responded to a knock at the door and answered it. It was our friend who had talked a total stranger into driving her to our home, some twenty miles from downtown Atlanta where she had stayed. I called my wife at work and told her our guest was at our house. Our son had my wife's SUV, so I picked her up from work. After we arrived home, I said hello to our friend and made a beeline to our bedroom and left my wife and our guest to settle matters. Our friend had accomplished her mission. She had come to Atlanta and spent a week until the issuance of another government Social Security and veteran's check. After not having any contact with her for fifteen years, we rejected her idea to come to Atlanta to spend a week with us. So she devised a plan and succeeded in staying at our home anyway, if only for one night.

Early Saturday morning, around ten o'clock, we set out to put her on the 1:30 p.m. bus back to her city of origin. I stopped at Publix's Grocery Store to cash a government-issued check in the amount of $529. We were unsuccessful. It was more than the supermarket's $500-limit. Next stop, Walmart; its check-cashing limit was $3,000. Just Millette and our guest went in to cash the check. I monitored the time that they were spending in Walmart, and after more than an hour, I went in to look for them. I found them at the Subway shop getting a sandwich and chips. Time was of essence if we were going to put her on the 1:30 p.m. bus.

By the time we all returned to the vehicle, it was well past 1:00 p.m. I was a bit upset when I realized that I was suffering while my guest was calm as if not a care in this world. I accepted the fact that it would be 9:00 p.m. before the next bus would be leaving for her city of origin. This time, we had not bought the ticket in advance. So we didn't lose another $120 because of our delay. We bought the ticket upon our arrival. We sat in the bus station from about 2:30 p.m. until 9:00 p.m. and personally saw her board the bus with a Subway sandwich and a drink in hand.

A year later, during the week of Easter, we visited another friend in our uninvited friend's city of origin. While there, we tried to locate her but were initially unable to do so and we did not have an in-service (mobile) contact. She was a longtime family friend. So when we did find her, we added a mobile phone to our monthly service to make sure we always had a way to contact her or vice versa in an emergency. I ordered her a smartphone and had her pick it up at the local AT&T store. She decided she didn't want that phone and downgraded it to a flip phone. Every week, for about the next ten weeks, she called, expressing her appreciation for what we did, then she said, "Can you spare thirty dollars?" And I would go and deposit one hundred dollars into her Chase account.

Thereafter, several times, she would have the management of the extended-stay motel call and inform me that her bill was more than $400 in arrears. The second time I received a call, I realized that she couldn't afford the motel if she were also going to eat. The cost was more than she received monthly. I suggested that she look for a more economical place. After I spent more than $1,500 over a two-month period, I stopped in my tracks. I explained to her that I could not afford another dependent or a mortgage. I strongly suggested that she contact her city's Section 8 housing department for assistance. A year later, she hadn't completed the application for housing. I told her not to call me again until she had done so. Eventually I stopped taking her calls. Recently I got a call from her apartment complex manager who said she evicted my friend for nonpayment of rent, and she was $1,400 in arrears. I told the landlord that my friend is an adult and that any conversation was between the two of them.

This is the end of my chapters in our book. I hesitated to add this experience with my friend, the uninvited visitor to Atlanta. I did so because we are sent here to serve one another. Throughout my life, I received help from others. Without the help of my siblings, Mom, friends, mentors, workmates, and many others, I would not be the person I am today. "As each has received a gift, use it to serve one another as good stewards of God's varied grace" (1 Peter 4:10). Mom drummed these morals into our souls. In the instance of our uninvited friend, I tried hard to share my blessings. I turned the other cheek as often as I could. Alas, it was not seventy times seven. I believe at some point, we must journey toward self-sufficiency regardless of our status in life. We are to extend a hand to one another. As that hand moves to pull you forward, your body must also go into motion. Our friend did not have the determination to move forward. She was not able or willing to partner in the journey for independence and self-reliance. We still care about her. Perhaps when our paths cross again, we will be better able to help one another.

In Loving Memory

of

Rosie Lee Jackson
1910 -- 1984

Thursday, January 26, 1984

Harris Temple A. M. E. Church
926 Florence Street
Camden, New Jersey

Rev. Robert C. Venable, Pastor

Mom's Funeral Program

Home Going Service

for

Mr. Frank Leonard Jackson

Thursday, November 21, 1985
11:00 o'clock a.m.   Viewing 10:00 to 11:00

Harris Temple A. M. E. Church
Tenth and Florence Streets
Camden, New Jersey

Reverend Robert C. Venable, Pastor

Dad's Funeral Program

315

Ramada Plaza by Wyndham Atlanta Downtown Capital Park

Chapter 15

Sibling 10
The Journey and Endeavors

The Early Years

I hate farming. I hate mules, yard birds, chickens, hogs, cows, peanuts, plowing, and most of all, everything about cotton. My very first memory of life was looking up the rear end of an old black mule.

For the first twelve years of my life, my father had two objectives for my siblings and me. The first was to meet the mule on Monday morning and the second was to stay in school as much as possible. Perhaps my hatred for farming

comes from my name. My name is George, and I was born in 1946. I am from a small town in Omaha, Georgia. Between 1950 and 1958, Omaha's population was reported to be 103 residents. You could ride through Omaha in five minutes or less. As I recall, it had one traffic light in the center of town and just a few stores.

Most of Omaha's residents were black and related in one way or another. Omaha was a farming community. There were a few black families who owned their own land. For the most part, blacks worked as laborers or sharecroppers for white landowners. A few others rented land and farmed it independently as we did, except for 1951.

There were fourteen siblings in my family, eight girls and six boys. Of the fourteen, I am the tenth born and the fifth male. Most black people in the community had large families. Large families were needed to harvest the crops. Farming was tough, but it was our only means of survival. When I was younger, I hated my name; even so, I never knew why. As I grew older, I took the liberty to look up its meaning. It derives from Greek and means "tiller of the soil or farmer." Perhaps now, you get my drift of my hatred for farming. It was an intuitive reaction to protest a predestination that I was unwilling to accept.

Although there were fourteen Jackson brothers and sisters, only ten ever lived in any of the places we moved at the same time. When I was very young and before my younger siblings came along, some of my oldest siblings left and went north to New Jersey. That left room for our family to continue to grow and eventually leave ten of us on the farm with Mom and Daddy.

By the time I was ten years old, my family had moved three times. It seemed like each move was a step down. I was very young when we moved over the creek, but it was by far the best place we ever lived while in Omaha. I only recall living there about three months. That farm was the only one where we had a horse and a mule. I am not quite sure why we had to move but using vintage TV references from the 1960s and 1970s that I later began to appreciate, we imitated Jed Clampett of *The Beverly Hillbillies* and "moved away from there. The difference is that Jed was white. He moved his family to Beverly Hills, California, from their home in the backwoods of Arkansas in the Appalachian Mountain region, after he struck oil on his property. Keep in mind, we were not moving on up like George Jefferson of *The Jeffersons*, also a vintage TV reference from that same period. George Jefferson, by contrast, was black. He had worked for many years and became the proud owner/operator of a chain of dry cleaners in New York City. He and his family moved from a New York City row house to a penthouse in a high-rise building in the city to celebrate his success.

The Jacksons were constantly going backward. When I was a kid in Georgia, we lived in the quarters on various old plantations. Most of the houses were not a step up or anything to brag about.

The quarters were a generic name for a bunch of shacks all in a row on various plantations. There were several quarters in and around Omaha. Quarters were living areas on a plantation farm where the workers lived, whether they were field hands or sharecroppers. *Dirt farming* (term associated with farming without hired help) with an animal was hard work. Sharecropping, sometimes more mechanized, was no joke either, even if one had a decent landowner. There was a lot of manual labor associated with raising cotton. By comparison, it was easier to grow and pick peanuts and corn. You had to allow spacing between the cotton plants. Cotton plants and weeds competed for the fertilizer used to support cotton growth. The weeds grew in between the plants and cultivation. The soil didn't stop the spread of the weeds; therefore, manual cultivation was required. The manual cultivation was called chopping cotton, although one never touched the cotton plant, just the weeds. A better definition would be chopping weeds where the laborer used a hoe to remove the weeds from between the cotton plants in the row. Upon fertilizing the cotton plant, it would absorb the nutrients, causing it to grow and yield more cotton.

The main purpose of sharecropping is to keep a person in the landowner's debt forever. It is very hard to get out of debt, especially if you have a dishonest landowner; and on a scale of one to ten, you wouldn't find many honest ones during that era.

In our section, the quarters consisted of three houses. They were all built from wood frames and had tin roofs. Since they were old by this time, the roofs were brown and rusted. All the houses set upon either brick blocks or wooden stumps. There was no such thing as a loft. Therefore, when it rained at our residence, we could hear it cling against the roof as if we were standing in the rain outside. Since the roof leaked, many times, we could feel it as though we were outside as well.

The landscape of the quarters included a well from which quarter residents drew water. Since there were many snakes crawling around, everyone drew water during the daylight hours. There was a main dirt path and trail leading to the well. Extending beyond the path in the distance was a main road or highway for cars and wagons further back into the woods. On this road, one could see my aunts, mother, sisters, and brothers carrying buckets of water for both family and animals. From time to time, my mom and aunts would simultaneously carry water on their heads and in their hands, just like it appeared in textbooks during slavery.

At one point, everyone who lived in our quarters' section was a relative. My grandfather and one of my aunts lived in the first house. Another aunt and uncle lived with six children in the second home. My family lived in the last one. It was around the bend in the corner of the woods.

None of the houses had more than three rooms and a kitchen. The kitchen to our place connected to the main bedroom. This room also did double duty as an all-purpose room.

The number of individuals sleeping in this room included my mom and dad in one bed, three brothers and me in a second bed, and my two younger sisters slept in the corner in a third bed. Although there was no privacy, this room did have a luxury in the form of a fireplace. An opening separated the third room of the house from the other rooms. This is where my older four sisters slept. As I recall, it served as the living room as well.

Located outside, across from the kitchen, was a smokehouse. Most all the houses had smokehouses that stored canned goods and cured pork hams and shoulders for later consumption. The name says it all; a smokehouse was where meat was smoked, cured, and preserved and kept for a very long time without spoilage. Refrigeration was not available for ordinary farmers. The only time fresh meat was available was immediately after being slaughtered. Otherwise the meat was cooked, canned, cured, or preserved with salt. Salt was used to preserve both pork and fish but never beef. After a calf was slaughtered, the meat was canned for future use.

During my boyhood, all of the houses on Child's Quarters must have been at least one hundred years old or older. They all had dirt yards and were surrounded by woods. Around our house was a pasture that was enclosed with a wire fence stretching across the property. We kept the animals in the pasture. Our animals consisted of a milk cow, one mule, chickens, and a few hogs. All the animals were somewhat protected from the weather, meaning that our mule had a stall with a cover on top. The mule was housed in a stall with a tin roof, just like our house. The stall had hay on the floor to cushion the ground in case she wanted to lie down. The pasture also included the family outhouse which was situated in the middle of the pasture. The side of the pasture by the road was a wider area and was used for play. When nearby neighbors would come over, especially on Sundays, we would play baseball in the pasture. We called it baseball, but it really was stickball. I didn't realize it was stickball until we moved to New Jersey and played with the same type of rubber balls and a stick in the schoolyard.

Located outside of the pasture near the house was our chicken coup. Chickens were the only fowl we always had in ample supply. This is due to the fact they laid eggs and hatched them frequently which produced many more chickens. Located beside the chicken coup was the woodpile, and alongside the woodpile was a large black pot which was used for boiling or washing clothes.

The interesting thing about the quarters was the name. It wasn't until I was in college and writing a research paper on black history that I discovered why our place was called the quarters. While in the library, I checked out a book; while looking through it, I noticed some old tin houses which reminded me of where we used to live. I started to read and discovered that these houses were called slave quarters. The houses in the book looked exactly like ours. It was then clear to me that we lived in old slave quarters.

As a child, going to church on Sunday was mandatory. To prepare for church, we would gather water from the well early on Saturday evening to take baths.

All bathing took place on Saturday nights behind the stove in the kitchen. As I recall, all my brothers took their baths first, one at a time, in a tin tub. The tub was about three to four feet in diameter and no more than twenty inches in height. Once we were finished it was time for my two younger sisters to take theirs. My three older sisters would take theirs across the hall in a separate room.

Whenever it rained, one could be assured that it was going to be muddy in the dirt yard and up and down the dirt road. Regardless of what was happening, come Sunday mornings, rain or sunshine, we were off to Sunday school or, once a month, to worship service. The churchyard was, and remains, unpaved. The road that led to the church was, and still is, one way in and one way out. Located further into the woods was a baptism pool, and on any given day, you could see snakes near or in it. Our primary method of getting to church was to walk. However, there were a few people who drove their trucks, and if we were nearby or on the road when they came past, we would be given a ride. I remember that all my brothers and I wore short pants and short-sleeve shirts to church and Sunday school all summer long. I hated the way we dressed more than farming. The church was and remains a small Baptist Church, located way back in the woods with trees on all sides. Members who didn't have automobiles drove their wagons or rode their mules to church. The mules were usually all black. They would tie them to the trees until service was over. I don't remember anyone ever having a horse to ride. Today the church remains an active small country church. At last count, two years ago, there were approximately thirty members.

I will never forget our mule's name and that's because it was a female. Her name was Cora. I felt terrible about having to work her in the fields and in other capacities because she was a female. She was used for pulling the wagon, plowing, and planting. We planted corn, peanuts, cotton, various vegetables, and watermelons. For years, Cora was our primary means of transportation for wherever we needed to go.

Farming required a lot of work and the work started early in the morning. The rooster served as our alarm clock. The rooster did not require a battery, just some corn, and he would ensure that we met the mule and plow on time every time before the sun rose. Things we had to do before preparing for the fields were: milk the one cow, feed the chickens and gather the eggs, slop the hogs, eat breakfast and hitch up Cora to our one-horse wagon.

The fields were quite a distance, perhaps up to two miles from the quarters. My father would take me, my brothers, or whomever he needed for that day's work and off we were to the fields in our one-horse wagon. The trip consisted of going through some woods and water from springs running across the dirt path or road. On the way, we were almost sure to see several snakes before reaching our destination. There were many types of snakes waving at us as we traveled to the field. The most frequent types of snakes seen were rattlesnakes and black snakes. Of course, the only good snake back then was a dead snake. If we were bitten, the venom could cause certain death. There was no means to get treatment in an emergency.

When we reached the fields, our charge was to accomplish our primary objective—to farm. In the early spring, we would plant corn, peanuts, and cotton. Later we planted vegetables and harvested them in the early summer, long before cotton, peanuts, and corn became ready to be harvested. Most of the vegetables ripened in less than three months. We had okra, string beans, butter beans, tomatoes, beets, cucumbers, squash, turnips, and watermelons, just to name a few. Sweet potatoes, which grew in the soil as a root, took the entire growing season from late spring to early summer, before the first frost, to be harvested. For vegetables, the rows were not very long. However, for corn, peanuts, and cotton, it seemed that each row was at least one-half mile or more. All the planting was done with Cora, the black mule. Unless one is familiar with plowing a mule, it would not be known that mules understand signals. If an experienced mule is told to "gee," that means the mule will automatically sway to the right and if "ha" is said, the mule will likewise sway to the left. I now suspect it is not because the mule was so smart but because it had been hit in the head many times in attempting to learn the language.

Although planting was relatively simple, gathering the crop was brutal. Picking cotton by hand should have been a crime. I hated picking cotton more than anything; although at my age, I picked very little. Once cotton was ready for picking, everyone in the family who was able had to stop whatever they were doing or thought about doing and go to the fields. If school was in session or someone was building a space capsule or making a hit record, it all stopped and cotton picking became everyone's priority. Are you starting to appreciate my feelings for Cora now and understand my hatred for farming?

Perhaps the most expedient method used was to work the picking in concert. That means the Jackson family would help the Green family pick their field and when finished, the Green family would help us pick our field. The same concept worked for shaking peanuts and pulling corn. Once a family had finished picking their fields, then we were all hired out to pick the white man's fields. Picking cotton only paid us three cents per pound.

Although my father's primary objective for his children during harvesting season was for us to meet the mule from Monday through Friday, my dad believed in sending us to school. He believed in education, but he would always say that he only went to school two days. The first day, the teacher didn't show up, and the second day, school was closed.

The first school I attended was a one-room schoolhouse. Each time I watch the vintage TV show *Bonanza*, I am reminded of that little red schoolhouse. It was located way back into the woods. It was located in the church and was within walking distance. My cousin was the teacher. She had a college degree which was rare for blacks during that time (for black schools, in many cases, a person could teach school with only a high school education). I attended that school from first grade through second grade. I don't remember any schools during that time having a kindergarten class.

My cousin was an excellent teacher. She would put fear into us and would make us learn. The fear was the belt, paddle, or switch. To this day, I cannot understand how beating someone could result in learning, but it did. She beat us from Monday through Friday in school, but we were invited to her house after church on many Sundays to fellowship and have fun.

Anyway after my second year, the one-room schoolhouse was closed. For third grade, I attended the school in downtown Omaha. It was sort of rundown and in need of lots of repair work. However, that school covered classes from third to eleventh grade. After attending that school for third grade, the county built a larger all-black school which was located quite a distance away from the quarters. Although segregated, we were provided free bus transportation and lunch. I remember many days, on the hour trip home, the students were taken through hills, woods, valleys, and many dirt roads. On rainy days, we were always afraid of running into a ditch. The quarters happened to be the last stop on the school's route.

I attended the new all-black school from the third until sixth grade. After the sixth grade, my family relocated to New Jersey. My last memory of the sixth grade was getting a whipping by the teacher. I am not sure what the whipping was about but during that time in schools, teachers could discipline students by whipping or spanking them. Being whipped was not the embarrassing issue, for me. Getting the whipping in front of my girlfriend was the real issue. The offending student had to lie down on a chair, in front of the entire class. Then the discipline was administered. Most often you shared classes with all of your friends. If you had a girlfriend she was likely in the same class.

Reminiscing

I used to sit and imagine that my family and I had moved away from the farm; the unrelenting heat, the snakes, and white hatred. One day, that time arrived. In 1958, my family left Omaha, boarded a Greyhound bus in Columbus, Georgia, and headed for Camden, New Jersey, by way of Philadelphia, Pennsylvania. I remember our leaving as clearly today. We left Georgia on June 10, 1958. Mom and nine of her children—my four brothers and five sisters—boarded that bus. Because we were black, we were ordered to the back of the bus.

We packed food for our journey in brown paper bags and in shoeboxes. The trip took a day and a half to arrive in Philadelphia. I think we pulled into the bus terminal around 3:00 p.m. or 4:00 p.m.

The most exciting change that had ever occurred in my life was when we arrived in Philadelphia, Pennsylvania. Prior to my arrival in Philadelphia, I drove an old black female mule through a one horse town with a few rundown stores with old white men chewing tobacco and either spitting it at or near me. Philadelphia was like Dorothy in the movie *Wizard of Oz*, on the yellow brick road. In Omaha, the biggest and tallest building was the big house, a two-story structure, the landlord's residence. In Philadelphia, I saw tall skyscraper buildings, lots of people, cars, stores, shops of all kinds, and loud music playing everywhere. Looking back today, it reminded me of Stevie Wonder's hit song "Living for the City." It was both scary and exciting at the same time. I believe that if I had been approached as the character in Stevie's Song had been, I would have been just as naive and reacted the same as he did.

From the bus station, my older brother, who had left Georgia eight years earlier, picked us up. I had only seen him once in eight years. We ventured from the bus station to our new home, located in Camden, New Jersey. Recall how I described Philadelphia when we first arrived. Well, Camden was also different for this country boy. At the time, Camden was a very nice though congested city. In 1958, Camden was likeable. There were stores on almost every corner in all the neighborhoods. They were supported and provided for most of the neighborhood's needs.

The neighborhood that we initially moved into was not one of the most desirable ones. The street consisted of row homes and lots of people. It was located not too far from Broadway or downtown where there were many stores for shopping. There were three bars on the street we lived on. Each was situated on a corner, located within thirty seconds of our house. Bright lights and noise occurred all nights, including Sunday. Many of the young men between the ages of twelve and eighteen who lived in this section of Camden had been to reform school or headed there. It seemed like all the young guys wanted to fight all the time. Alternatively, like on many inter-city streets, one could see young girls jumping rope or playing jacks.

It was very hard then, living on our city block, adapting from country life to city life. Children talked and laughed at the way I talked or dressed. They would ask me, "Man, where are you from, talking like that?" I was so ignorant of many things. For example, my older sister sent me to the store to purchase a soda (meaning a refreshment drink). I came back with a box of baking soda. I would hear loud noises all night long. The noises came from men cursing, fighting, and drinking; nevertheless, for all the unpleasant things about the street we lived on, there were some things I really appreciated. There were lots of girls. The neighborhood residents consisted mostly of blacks and Puerto Ricans. I had never met someone who spoke a different language before moving to Camden.

I started school in Camden in seventh grade. I remember having to stay after school many days because I didn't participate in class. When asked a question by the teacher, I would keep quiet, even though I knew many of the answers. By my nonresponse, many students thought that I was dumb or stupid. I was neither but afraid that they would laugh at the way that I spoke. I survived on that street at that school from September through November, then we moved to another neighborhood.

Our next move was across town. It was across the tracks in a predominantly-white neighborhood. There were only five black families living in this large section of town. I had never lived in a predominately-white neighborhood before now, but we never encountered any racial problems. I had friends on both sides of the tracks.

This was a quieter neighborhood with much more to do. I was in the eighth grade, and my school was less than a minute from my house. I was the only black male in the eighth grade, and there was one black female.

Perhaps the most memorable event occurred in this school when the teacher, who I liked a lot, asked each person in the class to stand and tell the class about their ethnicity or nationality. She started with the first row and continued around the room. I was sitting in the third row; when it became my turn, she asked me not to stand because everyone knew where I was from. The whole class laughed, and she never apologized nor commented on the matter.

This neighborhood had everything the former one did not have. One of the things which it had, which I benefited from, was a great Little League organization. I am quite sure that I was either the first or the second black to ever play in that organization. I was both a pitcher and a third baseman. I only played one year. However, I was selected and started at third base in an all-star game.

One of my newly made friend's father was the manager of my team. We were the Blue Socks. Before each game, I would meet at the manager's house and ride to the game with the family. The family had a dog, and each time I would arrive at their house, the dog would play with me and there were no problems. Until one day, I arrived when the family was about to eat supper. As I was sitting on the couch, waiting for them to finish eating, the dog began to stare directly at me. I became a bit nervous and started to move on the other side of the couch. Every time I would inch over a bit, the dog moved toward me. I got nervous and started to stand up, and when I stood up, the dog jumped toward me and started chasing me. I ran from the living room, from where I was sitting, into the kitchen where the family was eating. I circled the table a couple of times before the manager caught the dog. When the family finished eating, the calamity I created was forgotten. We all got into their car and drove to the game.

Living in this neighborhood gave me many options related to sports. I would go across the tracks to play basketball with my black friends often. However, during the summer recreation playground leagues, I would play with my white friends. We would win against my black friends. The key to winning was, I knew my black friend's moves. They had fancy moves. They would dribble through their legs, even though they played no defense. I would tell the white boys just how to play each one of them. When I went back across the tracks, my black friends would be a little mad at me, especially if they lost badly. The ninth grade was, by far, the quickest school year that I can recall. It was fun because I would meet friends at certain neighborhood gathering spots. We would then walk together, and we would all arrive at school in groups. We would pal around and have a great time. When school ended, we would all meet and walk back home together.

Regarding sports during the ninth grade, I spent most of my time playing basketball, stickball, and baseball in the schoolyard. It was only minutes away from our house. I also had begun to investigate the more established recreational basketball leagues around the city, in addition to organized church leagues.

From the ninth grade forward, I really developed the love for basketball and baseball. My friends and I would play basketball in the snow, rain, or any type of weather. I was always a good athlete and sports came naturally to me. Even though I could play football, I hated being tackled.

If you were a male living in Camden during that era, you had to participate in a sport. It did not matter what side of the tracks you were from. When it came to basketball, during the summers, men and boys came from across the city to the projects. That's where everyone gathered in the evenings to play basketball. It was the event. There were three courts: one for beginners, one for teenagers, and the main court. There were lights, and the crowds were always large. There would be college players, and great high school players. And there would be many beautiful women dressed in fine summer outfits to cheer them on.

High School

After completing ninth grade in middle school, my real big challenge was entering high school. During that time, my high school started at the tenth grade. Perhaps the thing that I remember most is that I did not have many clothes. My older brother Grover was a senior as I entered my freshman year. Because we had a limited supply of clothing, we had to alternate wearing the same pair of pants.

Initially I didn't have a lot of confidence. I felt very inferior. This was, in part, due to the teasing I received from my first neighborhood and my seventh-grade class. And I was the second smallest guy in my class. However, by the time I graduated, I had grown substantially in size and assurance.

Although apprehensive at first, my high school years were very productive. Looking back, the one thing that I learned regarding high school was you cannot get away with taking the easy way out. I did well in high school, although my counselors guided me to a curriculum that was not very challenging. I chose general education and graduated 215 out of a class of 400. The curriculum was not intended to prepare me for college. Without any follow-up specialty training, it was assumed that I would become an unskilled laborer. I was not dumb or stupid. My high school was ranked as one of the best high schools in the country during my three years. Our principal had a doctor's degree. However, with all those credentials, if not properly guided, students did get lost in the system. We had two counselors, a white female and a black male. Many times, when advising black students, the white counselor would recommend easier classes, even if they were planning to attend college. The black counselor would do the same. White students, for the most part, would be advised and get help to enter the colleges of their choice. If they were college-bound at all, the black students were recommended to attend historical black colleges and universities. The most recommended career for black students was teaching.

I was always a good athlete. In middle school, I played Little League baseball and recreational league basketball. In high school, I played baseball and ran cross-country. I even thought that there was potential for me to play baseball at a higher level. However, a rotator cuff injury in high school changed that possibility.

Although my high school years proved to be some of the best days of my life, I was not necessarily popular. I was not unpopular either. I knew of the popular young ladies, and they knew me. However, the ones I liked did not necessarily like me. I had no problems finding dates for proms. As a matter of fact, I went to four proms, two juniors and two seniors. I went to the second senior and junior prom two years after I graduated. It may have been because I had my own car at that time.

The Military Calls

After graduation, a friend and I had volunteered to enlist in the US Marines. I performed poorly on the entrance examination. After the Marines idea didn't pan out, I got a job directly across the street from where I lived. It was a uniform supplier and cleaning service for small businesses. I worked there for two years, then I was drafted into the United States Army.

It was during the hot part of the Vietnam War. Young men from our area were being drafted daily by the dozens. Many of my high school friends were drafted at the same time as me, and we all served in basic training together at Fort Dix, New Jersey. One of the first troops to die in the war from New Jersey had been in my high school homeroom class.

Basic training was fun to me. I will never forget the very first day we met our drill sergeant. He was one of the biggest and toughest-looking black man I had ever seen. He was about six feet and two inches tall. He weighed about 250 pounds and was all muscles. He stood there and called us every unpleasant name in his vocabulary. He called us, among other things, a bunch of punks, homosexuals, and weaklings; but above all the things he said that stuck out most to me was that there would be trophies for the best performance by a trainee at the end of the two-month training period. I responded back to him that the trophy would be mine. After the first full day of training, I was made a squad leader, responsible for ten other trainees. I was responsible for them getting up on time, making their beds, exercising, and falling into formation and going to breakfast. Recall, I was always a good athlete, so none of the physical training was hard for me. I could do as many or more push-ups as the drill sergeant.

Throughout the two months' training period, I kept improving on the exercises required for completing basic training. I had gotten so good. I welcomed anyone to challenge me in anything. The last requirement was the physical test and we had to pass it or repeat basic training. All the trainees had to compete on the same day. There were approximately two thousand trainees. The test included the low crawl, push-ups, sit-ups, infiltration course, monkey bars, squats, and more. After we completed our exercises, each trainee had to run a mile within a set time. When the day was completed and all scores totaled, I had the highest total of all the trainees. As predicted, I received the trophy for the physical (PT) training course at Fort Dix, New Jersey, in the summer of 1968.

From basic training, I was off to Fort Lee, Virginia, for Quartermaster School which lasted three months. I was made squad leader for a much larger group of soldiers who were training in other areas. Once training was completed for whatever your military occupational skill was, that individual or group was sent to their permanent unit. It was the heart of the Vietnam War, but I could have been sent anywhere in the world.

As squad leader, I had many night duties which meant that I oversaw receiving incoming orders and placing them into the proper files for the sergeant to issue to troops on the following day. These orders designated assignments to Germany, Korea, Vietnam, Japan, or Stateside.

It might seem incredulous, but many troops were requesting to switch orders from other assignments to go to Vietnam. Many felt a duty to America, and some felt that the pay would be better than remain Stateside or get other assignments. Since I served night duties in headquarters, I knew where some of my friends were going to be assigned, and sometimes, I would tell them. In some cases, telling them would help them make an informed decision of whether they wanted to request a switch or keep the orders that they were assigned.

Upon graduating from the US Army Quartermaster School, I was assigned and shipped to Germany. It was my first time ever on an airplane. It was one of those cargo planes and all the seats were facing backward from the pilots. I am not sure how many hours the flight took, but I do know that it was not quick. The plane landed in Frankfurt, Germany.

Once departing from the plane, I was off to my duty station which was in Erlangen, Germany, which was hours from Frankfurt. My orders stated that I had to take a train to Erlangen, Germany. I had never been on an airplane before nor had I ever been on a train, and now I am about to take a train—alone in a foreign country. With my backpack and American uniform on, I was directed to the correct train. Thankfully Frankfurt is one of the largest cities in Germany with many people who spoke English. Two things happened in my favor: the first is that many of the train conductors spoke English, and secondly, a troop assigned to my unit was on his way back to the unit from vacation. He sat beside me. I was home free from there, in relationship to finding my way to my new assignment. Neither he nor I knew at the time, but I had been assigned as one the roommates of the soldier I sat beside on the train. As I got to know him, I learned that he was from South America. He joined the US Army to become a citizen of the United States.

The very next morning after arrival, as my unit fell out for revelry, the first sergeant handed me the flag for company A. There were four companies within my barracks. They were companies A, B, C, and D. From that morning on, for the next eighteen months until my discharge, I was the flag bearer for company A. My duties included lining up in front of company A each morning for revelry and participating in parades and special military ceremonies at select US bases throughout Germany.

The flag-bearer participated in ceremonies that involved a US General. If someone was being honored or promoted or a special unit was celebrated for a specific accomplishment, a flag-bearer was required. Sometimes these ceremonies occurred in the most inclement weather.

Although I liked my unit and where I was stationed, initially I felt that I would not have voluntarily joined the army. Post-service experience, I believe the US Army is a place where all able bodied young men and women can learn a great deal about life and responsibility. For me, it was a place to grow and be exposed to how the other side of the world lived. There were many experiences that helped me grow. I was what you might call a strike trooper—in other words, a very efficient soldier. Because of my efficiency, I avoided many duties that other troops had to endure. For example, due to my clean and professional dress and knowledge of the US Uniform Code of Justice, I did not have to serve too many nights on guard duty, kitchen patrol, or night desk duty.

Because of my professionalism, I was sent to the US Noncommissioned Officer Academy. The academy is comparable to West Point Academy for noncommissioned soldiers. The academy training lasted six weeks. I was taught all aspects of leadership skills from a noncommissioned officer. Before entering the academy, I carried the rank of an E-3 soldier. Upon completion, I was promoted to E-4. The promotion meant no more restrictions. I could leave on weekends and return any time before revelry on Monday mornings. I did not have to serve, even the occasional kitchen patrol or guard duty.

My unit provided me the opportunities to play basketball and softball. I played guard on a good basketball team and second base on a very good softball team. Both teams started out as just pick-up teams, then they developed into competitive teams. The basketball evolved from basically a recreational team with some good players. We ended up competing with some good teams from other bases.

We recognized that if we had a coach, we would be able to compete. We asked the sergeant who ran the gymnasium to be our coach, and he agreed.

Our softball team started out playing recreationally. Just like our basketball team. The four companies A, B, C, and D played against each other each evening. Our company commander noticed the talent and decided to form an official team with a coach. This was a fast-pitch softball league with some great ball players. We were fortunate enough to have two pitchers who had signed contracts with semipro teams.

When I was in high school, I played third base and injured my arm. I needed to shorten my throw. So for this team, I played second base. By the time the team had developed, I was known as a long-ball hitter. Just about the time the team was beginning to play other army bases, I was chosen for the academy or noncommissioned officer school. While there, the team started to travel to many bases across Germany. The team's winnings kept increasing. While at the academy, one of my best friends started playing second base in my absence. After my six weeks at the academy, the team was tied for first place in our division. On the same day of my graduation from the academy, the team was packed and ready for travel to Berchtesgaden, Germany, for the US Softball Championship in Europe. The team wanted me to rejoin them, so they waited for me. After my graduation, we were off to Berchtesgaden for the championship. It was a seven-hour trip. Berchtesgaden is located right on the Austrian border.

Upon arrival, we settled in and prepared for an arranged trip to Austria the following morning. After spending a day in Austria, we returned and prepared for practice the next day. Our practice took place in a real stadium. I was shocked at how all the players had improved. Before I went to the academy, I felt that I was the main man. Now after seeing the practice, I was not sure that my talent would be necessary.

It was a most beautiful day for any type of sport, especially for softball. There was a great crowd, with US Army personnel from all over Germany. Some high-level officers flew in on helicopters while others had special drivers. I had never seen that many people at a sporting event, except on television.

Due to our winning record, the championship had two possibilities; if we win the first game, we would win the championship outright. If our opponents won, then there would be a second game tiebreaker. The situation for me was this: if we won the first game, I would not get an opportunity to play. Fortunately for me, we lost the first game due to an error by my replacement while playing second base. This meant that I would possibly start the next game—which I did.

My first time at bat was a fielder's choice. My second time at bat, I hit a single but did not score. I was up for the last inning and the score was tied. I hit a triple and drove in the winning run that made us the softball champions in Europe in 1968.

A major heartbreaker occurred during my military service. My brother Robert passed away. He was a year older than me. He was frail and suffered from asthma for most of his life. At about midnight (the weekday escapes me), I was called downstairs to the duty sergeant's desk. Upon arriving, he looked sadly into my eyes and informed me of my brother's passing. Out of the fourteen brothers and sisters, he was the first to be deceased.

The College Years

I am from a large family so I never envisioned attending college. However, Grover had attended and graduated from college and afterward joined the US Peace Corps. He convinced me that I should apply. I was honorably discharged from the US Army. I worked for an automotive parts distributor as a truck driver for one year. While working, I applied to various schools. I was accepted at Hampton Institute in Hampton, Virginia, in the fall of 1969.

It was one of the best decisions I have made in my life. If my brother had not encouraged me, I probably would not have applied. I did not think that I could perform at the college level. I had never seen Hampton before applying. However, I did have friends who had or were attending at the time of my acceptance. I also had gotten an acceptance letter from a two-year business college in Philadelphia, Pennsylvania, which now is a well-recognized four-year college.

One of my primary reasons for choosing Hampton was, it is a historically black college and university. Hampton also catered to American veterans. There were many officers and enlisted veterans applying to Hampton due to the GI bill.

My first year was a good one. My grades were good, and college life was great. I was the first freshman allowed to have a car on campus. The fact that I was older than my incoming classmates put me at somewhat of an advantage regarding maturity. I chose business management for my major and did well.

I was a veteran and an older student. I was expected to participate in various activities. I served as the veteran's president for three years and as the intramural sports coordinator. I was asked to serve as Hampton's assistant basketball coach. However, I turned down the opportunity in favor of devoting more time to my studies. I served as big brother with the local Big Brother Program of America. I gave my little brother his first basketball. He was twelve years old and nearly 5'8" tall. He grew to be 6'7". From his high school playing experience, he received two full college basketball scholarships and could not attend due to an illness. He now has three children and several grandchildren. During my junior year, I met and fell in love with Linda Watson who was a sophomore at Hampton. She later became my wife. Linda majored in speech pathology and later worked for two technology companies and the US Department of Defense.

The Working and Marriage Years

My time at Hampton Institute was well-spent. To cap it off, during my last semester, I made the dean's list. I graduated from Hampton Institute in May 1973 with a degree in business management. Before graduation, I had secured a position with a major technology company in Upstate New York. My start date was June 1973. My very first meeting with the company occurred on the island of Bermuda.

In August of 1974, Linda and I married. We have one daughter, Erin. Erin graduated from Howard University with a degree in mass communication. Currently Linda works for the Department of Defense and is considering retirement. Erin is a stand-up comedian with some great accomplishments. She has appeared on *The Last Comic Standing* twice, opened for Bill Maher, guested on the talk shows for both the Ellen DeGeneres and Conan O'Brien, travels internationally, and continues to perform at colleges, universities, and lots of stand-up comedy venues in New York City.

During my tenure at Hampton Institute, there were many major companies visiting and recruiting graduates for jobs. I researched and personally interviewed with about forty of them. After many interviews and site visits, I chose an Upstate New York corporation. It is a major technology firm with major emphasis on consumer housewares. Most consumers will only recognize it by its consumer product's name.

At the time, the company did not have much experience in hiring African Americans. As a matter of fact, I was only the third black employee hired at its consumer sales division. It was a very good company. At the time, it just had never made a specific effort to hire African Americans or Jews. I was hired as a sales representative calling on distributors and retail sales. From the very first day of employment, I received an expense account and a company car. My first territory was in the New Jersey and New York Metro market, catering to such retailers as Macy's, other major department stores, and mass merchant retailers within the trading area.

There was a big emphasis on the distribution network. Most manufacturers sold through a two-step distribution system. We sold to distributors, and, in turn, they sold to retailers. My responsibility entailed selling products to distributors, and they provided sales and service of my products to retailers, big and small. Getting the product from my distribution location to customers included shows, special promotions, or other means. My company's products were widely traded which meant that wherever the products were sold in America, the manufacturer's retail selling price remained the same. Getting products from my wholesale customers to retailers required working distributors, making presentations to retailers, offering special promotions, and other selling tools. Metro New York and the New Jersey market still is one of the toughest to work in the country due to its vast competitive base.

After three years, I was promoted to Pittsburgh, Pennsylvania, which was a larger territory. I lived and worked that market from 1976 to 1979. The market covered Western Pennsylvania. This was the Cleveland region. It spanned from Harrisburg, all of Pittsburgh, and into the Ohio border. The region also covered the West Virginia market. In 1979, I earned salesman of the year. I spent three years covering Western Pennsylvania, then I was promoted again to a class 1 region in the New England market. Class 1 market was the largest market a field sales manager could manage. The distribution network, along with multiple retailers, increased the dollar volume by millions. I lived in Milford, Massachusetts.

In my class 1 market, I was bombarded with visitors from headquarters. This included president of the consumer division, national sales and marketing managers, along with other marketing people.

Most headquarter personnel liked the New England market because of its seafood and the Boston nightlife. The market area included the state of Massachusetts, Connecticut, Maine, Rhode Island, and Vermont.

New England was a sales manager's dream. It had a vast supply of retailers and wholesalers. There were likely more wholesalers and retailers in this market than in any other part of the country. Retailers included mass merchants, department store, drugstore, and supermarket chains. My primary distributor ranked among one of the largest in the country.

In 1982, a consumer sales manager from the West Coast suggested that my company begin making sunglasses. We were already making lenses for major optical companies. The idea was to capitalize on the total glass market. It was a start-up of a completely new division. I was convinced that it would be good for my career, so I signed on with the start-up division. This sunglass division, for the first time, hired people from other companies. This was something my company had never done before. All employees prior to that point had been homegrown. I decided to take the opportunity. It would get me back to New Jersey and closer to my family. The headquarters for this new division was located on Fifth Avenue and Forty Second Street in New York City.

After three years of dissecting the market, the sales team and senior management decided that the market opportunity would not produce the profits we needed to be successful. So we exited the business.

After the demise of the sunglass business, I was offered another job by the vice president of the consumer division who later became CEO of the total company. The job offer was supermarket manager. This was again a new start-up business. He noticed that I had concentrated on some supermarket chains while managing the New England market. With this new assignment, I had free reign to develop the business any way I saw fit.

It took me three months to render an analysis on the entire trading area. My market area entailed the entire East Coast to include all major food chains from Maine to Florida and as far west as Pittsburgh, Pennsylvania.

That same year, I was given additional responsibility to pick up the remaining wholesalers left on the East Coast. I earned the best salesmen of the year award. My numbers resulted in 114 percent of my sales goal for that year. To obtain that volume, my manager and I convinced one major wholesaler to purchase products for the future. Although there were special discounts for the purchase, the purchase order totaled four million dollars.

After a successful year, being back close to family, relatives, and friends, I decided that possibly relocating to other markets was not in my best interest. So I remained in the New York-Metro New Jersey market. I also decided that I needed to be in a place where I could work and give back to the community. So that is what I did. I found a local church, joined, and became active. My involvement included working with my church's Sunday school program, Young Christian Men's Organization, Boy Scouts, and other community events.

My minister and the church elders recognized that our neighborhood and church programs were offering value to the recipients. I was asked to join the deacon ministry. After accepting the deacon ministry, I was asked to become superintendent of Sunday school. My spiritual life, along with my career, started to thrive and make sense.

The following year, the company decided, as its goal, to extend its market share by purchasing other consumer housewares companies. The company purchased a major competitor that increased its market share and changed the way sales managers were to manage the business.

Due to the new business volume, more sales managers were added. Each manager was given more account responsibility. All new and old managers' job titles were changed to food broker managers. A food brokers is a local area or regional sales force hired by manufacturers to sell their products to local retailers and wholesalers for a commission.

For the last fifteen years of my corporate life, I worked the northeast market as a sales manager, managing food brokers within the Metro New York, New Jersey, New England, Harrisburg, Pennsylvania, Maryland, and Virginia markets. Perhaps the greatest confidence-builder gained from my career was the fact that my company's product remains a most-wanted consumer product. One thing that continues to make me smile, long after I have retired, is that I was in an industry that did not employ many African Americans. Many of my customers (buyers) had not interfaced with many blacks in my position. Some of them disliked me because of my skin color.

However, they were buyers and knew full well our products were in high demand. So they had to purchase them through me.

Retirement and Relocation

After thirty years in sales with one company, in 2003, I retired. During those thirty years, I gained a great deal of confidence, tremendous managerial and marketing experience, improved my negotiating techniques, traveled extensively, and earned a decent salary.

Upon my retirement, my wife and I decided to move to Hampton, Virginia. We built a sizeable house in a middle upper-class neighborhood. Our house was the fourth one built in a complex that now has fifty.

Since we were among the original dwellers, I became actively involved in the neighborhood. Initially I was convinced to become a block captain for the homeowners' association. After accepting the block captain's position, next I was asked to become the neighborhood watch coordinator. After accepting the neighborhood watch coordinator position, I was asked to become a board member of the neighborhood civic association to which I complied. All my nonpaying duties kept me rather busy.

While performing my neighborhood and community roles, I was asked by my new church to become a member of its prison ministry. That membership included teaching the Bible at the local prison each Wednesday evening. In addition to Bible study, the ministry presents an annual workshop for ex-offenders and their families.

Along with the neighborhood responsibilities and prison ministry, I was asked and accepted a position as a Sunday school teacher. After teaching prison ministry and Sunday school for nearly ten years in Hampton, I decided to take on another assignment. That assignment was substitute teaching at all the high schools in Newport News, Hampton, and Isle of Wright County, Virginia. I chose to do this due to my experience with teaching Bible study at the prison. As I listened to the personal stories of some of the prisoners, I thought, maybe I could have a positive influence on some of the young men still in high school in black urban areas. I thought if I could give them the benefit of my experience, perhaps I could point them away from the life choices that might lead them to prison time. Today full-time teachers are instructors, counselors, mentors, and disciplinarians without the authority to discipline. I have discovered that regular substitute teachers simply do not have sustained exposure with students to build the kind of rapport students often have with their teachers. After five years of subbing, I have determined the best time to even start trying to get young people on the right track is prekindergarten when they are very young at home with their parents. Kids learn respect for others and right from wrong when they are very young. Mostly they learn from those closest to them from infancy. Because of the people I encounter at my prison ministry, I won't give up on my effort to make a difference. I will continue to influence those students who will listen to me.

Two years ago, my wife and I decided to sell our house in what I had always considered to be one of the best communities in Hampton Virginia. We downsized to a condominium in the nearby community of Carrollton. I am still a high school substitute teacher, teaching two to three days a week, a Sunday school teacher, and remain a member of my church's prison ministry. I am also a loyal Hampton University booster, attending both football and basketball games.

Chapter 16

Sibling 11
Unchartered Territory

Fitting In

No matter the season, poverty was the life I was born into and lived. I'm Otis, the youngest of six sons and the eleventh child, born to Frank and Rosie. Farm life in Georgia was the only life I knew from birth until age ten. It was not until the family left Georgia that I realized we were even poor because I never had anything else  with which to compare my living conditions. Living in an environment where everyone is the same around you can cause a reverse bias that does not manifest until you are removed from it. When contrasted with life today, it was better from a cultural standpoint. We did not have crime, teen pregnancy was not a problem, and illegal drugs were unheard of. Despite all of that, it was a life with no future, no goals, and no hope of anything but poverty. Had it not been for a revelation given to my parents, we would still be there, doing life with no chance of freedom. When I learned that we were going to move north, my imagination began to take extraordinary liberties.

During my entire lifetime in Georgia, I never remember traveling more than twenty miles away from my house. I had never socialized with any whites, whether adult or child. I had never attended school, church, nor played with a white person. It was a time of segregation in the Deep South. I was a nine-year-old living in the only world I knew with nothing to compare it to. Every other place was foreign to me. I did not know that many of the places that I would soon be exposed to even existed. Places and locations other than my hometown and immediate community existed in books and through the experience and imaginations from others.

Camden, New Jersey

When I first heard that we were going to move to the city, I imagined a life of wealth and luxury and never being broke again in life. That was the only picture I had of the big city. I remember having an image in my mind of a wallet always full of cash to spend as I wished and when I wished. The city was located an entire universe from where I lived; but dreams are meant to give hope, even when they seem hopeless. I started to imagine life without my friends that really made me sad. When we finally did leave, it was like getting a final image of the place and people, some of whom I have never seen again. All that remains now are memories. Even the place we stayed no longer exists, and most of the people have relocated or died.

My family's arrival in Camden, New Jersey, in 1958 was a big disappointment as it destroyed all the dreams and imagination that I had developed. Just seven days after my tenth birthday, on a hot summer day, on June 10, my whole world changed in an instant. The big city was nothing like I had imagined it would be. It was very congested with people everywhere and houses attached to one another. There were smells that were new to me. Since we were located in downtown Camden, I could smell the Campbell Soup Company factory located less than a mile from my new house. Next-door to my house was a bar that played music through the night. Located down the street was a bakery that smelled of fresh-baked bread. A few blocks on the opposite end was a railroad freight yard and on the other side of it was the Delaware River, all located within my immediate community. From the steps of my house, the skyline of Philadelphia, Pennsylvania, was quite clear. There were ethnic groups I had never heard of or seen before such as Chinese, Puerto Ricans and others. My immediate thoughts were, I did not like my new home, but there was no turning back.

Since we lived downtown, there were transit buses and taxi cabs, both of which I had never seen before, along with streetlights at night. Next-door to us was a building that had three floors. It was a house where people lived. That was also new to me. All the houses in my old neighborhood were single stories.

Junior High School

One of the greatest times of my life was at Hatch Junior High School. It was probably where I started to mature. They had an elective position called mayor which is like president of the student government. It was a highly respected position that met frequently with the principal who, at that time, was Walter Gordon. Mr. Gordon really took me under his wing and taught me a lot about life because he sensed I was mature enough to handle it. He taught me that leaders should be an example to others and that being a leader was a sacrifice. There were several teachers who took an interest in me as well. They made me realize, as a junior high school student, that I would have very few friends in life if I became a leader. It was a transitional time in my life when most children were children. Yet I was being trained as a responsible adult. When I got to high school, I no longer wanted to be a leader, but the damage had been done. I sought no elective office while I attended high school. I no longer wanted to be an example to other students. Instead I chose to head the yearbook design committee where we produced two high school covers.

Mr. Gordon was the father of both Donna, who graduated with Grover, and Bruce who graduated with my brother George from Camden High. Bruce, after graduation from college, accepted a position with a telecom company and rose through the ranks of corporate management and became head of retail marketing. During his time in management, at a local telecom, he recruited my youngest sister, Christine, who worked her way through the ranks and became the first black female director of the New Jersey telecom unit.

School Adjustment

My new school was located several blocks away from our new home in Camden City. When I went to see it, I learned it was three stories high. The school I attended in the South was one level and it was all-black. Broadway school where I was to attend was multiethnic and every race was enrolled. The teachers were even white which had never occurred to me before, and the building was located on a busy street. City public transportation was located a very short distance from our house. Life as I knew it had changed completely. It was a new world, and it was scary. I would have to make all-new friends in a new world. On some days, I was disappointed and wanted to return to the only world I knew. On other days, I accepted my new home and tried to make the best of it. In many ways, I expected to find a pot of gold in my home; but since I did not know what to expect, every new experience was a plus.

I never got use to the new school. I simply could not adjust to all the new and sudden events. I was emotionally unprepared. In fact, I remember very little about the school, except that my classroom was located on the second floor of the building.

Camden was a place of many things that I had never seen before. I distinctly remember a truck used to come around near the weekend to sell clams that was another new event. They were eaten by prying open the shell and pouring hot sauce on them and swallowing them raw. I found this disgusting and still do until this day; however, it was a new tradition that was part of my new home. A short time later, we moved into another house in South Camden next to a grocery store. Here, I found a new form of segregation. The blacks lived on the other side of the tracks, and we lived in the white section in a very old house. We only lived there a very short time before moving up to Florence Street, next to HB Wilson School.

It was a good school where I met the first and only two bullies of my life. They were two white boys who were bigger than me, but I had a dilemma. They wanted to fight me. My father's advice was, you do not let anyone beat you up. My choice was either fight and beat the two guys or risk getting a beating from my dad. The first guy and I met on the lot next to the school, after school hours, for two consecutive days and fought, and I prevailed in both. The next guy and I fought afterward, and I beat him as well. From that moment onward, I never had another fight in school.

During my high school years, I almost got into my third fight. One day one of the most violent guys in high school sent word that he wanted to fight me after school. I was scared and for a good reason. This guy and his friend had terrorized people in Camden with guns and by other means. Later he shot a person who was on a front porch. He always seemed to get out of trouble because of his aunt's help. The day he threatened me, I had a friend from my community, who was also a thug, who I walked to school with. Not only was my friend a thug, he was an excellent boxer and had a reputation of going for bad. After he heard about the threat to me, my friend told me he had my back and they never bothered me again.

Summer Remembered

During the summer of 1967, while a junior in high school, I applied for and received a very interesting summer job selling magazines door-to-door. The job was designed to take me across the country. It started in Queens, New York, where the employees stayed in a motel. We started in Long Island by working towns and incorporated villages. We would be driven to a town and dropped off where we would sell by knocking on doors. We had a script that we learned which surprisingly worked well. The only problem was that we were supposed to get a permit from the town we entered, and that was seldom done. As a result, often the police would come and escort us out of the town after someone complained. I cannot remember how many towns I was escorted out of trying to sell magazines. After so many hours, we would be picked up and taken to a new location. We did everything together. We ate together and we met every morning before we went out to sell. Despite all the positive things that occurred, there were also a lot of negative things that also happened. We traveled with a group thirty to fifty people, each having a manager. One of the managers, after drinking, would beat up his wife and she would appear the next day with sunglasses to hide her bruises. Every Friday night, before leaving whatever city, management encouraged us to go out and have a good time.

The routine remained the same, no matter what city or town we were located. Eventually we arrived in Upstate New York, in Albany and Schenectady. One night, we were working a small town in Upstate New York and arrived to eat at a restaurant. One of the people in our group was a young lady from Newark, New Jersey who was very attractive. When we got to the restaurant, there were some black guys standing outside, and she began to exchange words with them. Evidently she said some things they did not like. In the meanwhile, the guys were looking at the men in our group that numbered less than their group. They stopped looking at her and began looking at our guys, saying we will see you when you come out.

I was scared. I was a long way from home in a town that I knew nothing about, preparing for a do-or-die situation that I had nothing to do with. Finally we went in to eat and all I could think about was the men waiting for us outside and what I would do if a fight broke out. After what seemed like a lifetime of waiting, when we came out, the homeboys were gone and nowhere to be seen. Until this day, I believe my mom was praying for me and, boy, did I need it.

Eventually I stopped selling magazines because they wanted me to quit high school and work for them that I was unwilling to do. When we worked our way back to New York, I left the group and went to Jersey City to stay with my sister Rose and worked there for the rest of the summer.

By the time I quit the program, I had become a smoker and had a young lady in the group that wanted to marry me. I had also witnessed one of the workers suffer serious epileptic seizures all in one summer's time span.

A few times since then, I have had people come to my door selling magazines. In over fifty years, the script has not changed. In fact, I simply would tell them I used to sell magazines and knew the script and did not want to waste their time at my door. There was not going to be a sale.

A Sibling Leaves Us

In the fall of 1967, my brother Bob died. While on my way home from school, I was met by one of my sisters about four blocks from our home. She simply told me that the hospital called and said my brother had been there and that someone needed to contact them. When I arrived at home, I called and the hospital told me that I needed to go there and no other information was given over the phone. I took a bus to the hospital and saw my mother on another bus going home. When I arrived at the hospital, I requested an update of my brother's condition. The doctor told me that they had done everything they could to save him. He was dead. I could not believe what I was hearing. That was all that I remember. I was caught completely by surprise because I thought I was going to check on him, only to discover he was dead.

It was a very difficult time for my family as it was the first death of a sibling. All I can remember was the sadness had totally engulfed my home. It was an experience I will always remember. Most of the time, I was numb. I could hear the cries of my mother in the night, not being able to eat, and the constant flow of people to our house.

After my brother was buried, all I wanted to do was get away from the sadness. I was jealous that two of my brothers, Grover and George, could get away from it by returning to Peace Corps duty in Kenya, East Africa, and to the military in Germany. I felt stuck to hear the crying and sadness that had overtaken my home.

The following year, I finished my senior year in high school, graduated, and entered Shaw University in the fall of 1968. The day before our Thanksgiving recess, my dormitory caught fire and was destroyed. Since we were scheduled to go home the next day, we had to spend the entire night at the Raleigh-Durham Airport until my scheduled flight home the next day.

While at home, all the residents of the dormitory awaited word from Shaw about what they were going to do about housing for us. This was a time during the draft and not enrolled in college full-time meant being drafted into the military. When I could wait no longer, I enrolled in Glassboro State College full-time, at night, to avoid being drafted. That meant I had to catch a bus from Camden to Glassboro and take all twelve credits at night. At one time, the military sent me induction papers to report for military service. The only thing that prevented me from induction was the fact that I was registered at Glassboro, taking twelve credits which I had to show written proof.

This was a rough period during my life. Usually I did not get home until ten o'clock or later after working an eight-hour job. I also had classes on Saturdays. This continued for one year until I was admitted to day classes at Glassboro State.

In 1971, a new federal program was introduced called Volunteers In-Service to America (VISTA) which was a volunteer service program, and it paid a stipend of one hundred dollars per week. It allowed college students to do community service while also completing their education. It was administered by the same agency that the Peace Corps is under. The opportunity was such a help. I could quit my full-time job and live off the stipend alone until I graduated from college. It later led to a job working with BPUM Impact Corporation in Camden City which was the same organization VISTA assigned me. It was an economic development organization that developed fully owned businesses and assisted minorities to start businesses or to capitalize existing ones.

Working there led to my meeting some very famous people through conferences and conventions. I met Byard Rustin who organized the March on Washington several times. I also was able to meet A. Phillip Randolph on three occasions, along with Fannie Lou Hamer, the civil rights activist, who was able to unseat the Mississippi delegation to the 1964 Democratic Convention in Atlantic City, New

Jersey. Some colleagues and I met Joe Biden several times on the train while he was in the senate, long before he became vice president.

Perhaps one of the greatest honors ever placed on me was that I was considered as a candidate to be the first black mayor of Camden City, New Jersey. The choice was between another person and me, with whom I worked with at BPUM Impact Corporation. The person who made the selection was the current mayor and city political boss at that time. My colleague won out because his family's name was better-known in the city. I often think about how different my life would be had I been selected instead of him.

Mom Leaves a Void

It was a normal Sunday. My wife, the children, and I attended church as usual in Glassboro, New Jersey. When we got home, we received a telephone message from my sister. My wife answered the telephone, and afterward, she had a look on her face that indicated something was very wrong. After hanging up the telephone, she simply said, "Your mom has died." My sister said the family had been trying to reach me all day to tell me that my mother had died. I can still remember the dining room chair I was sitting on when I received the sad news. As it turned out, I was the last one in the family to be notified of her death. By contrast, I was the first to learn of my brother's death and the last to learn of my mother's passing.

The sadness in the family's home had returned once again. Life teaches much but rarely teaches one how to mourn and let go of a mother like mine. She was the undisputed matriarch of the family, and her reign was over and no successor could be named in her place. When a mother dies, the tradition of the family is over. It is an unofficial signal for the family members to start their own traditions. There would be no more Thanksgiving dinners, Christmas, or conversations to look forward to as it had all ended. All that was left were memories of her life to be carried out by each sibling in their own way.

There are lots of Scriptures in the Bible about death, and many of them are very encouraging. While death is part of God's order, the funeral experience is a cruel event. You have hundreds of people who come and ask the same question, "What's happened?" You must repeat it for each one of them. Then people expect you to have food prepared for them to eat, even if they only live next-door. Many come to the home to just eat at your expense. Afterward you are escorted to the funeral home at your most vulnerable time to select expensive burial material and to sign an expensive financial obligation. You are also expected to clothe the dead person in the casket while still emotionally charged. After the funeral service, you are expected to feed hundreds of people while still mourning. Some of these people live right next-door where they can go and get a meal on their own. After everything is over, the crowd leaves you alone to cope with the loss of your loved one and the expense of having done all these things expected of you.

Funerals are cruel to the survivors. My mother's death really touched me because I was left with the task of clearing the house to make it ready to be sold. Each day at the house was especially difficult because every area of the house was a memory. The children were encouraged to take the things they wanted, and I was left with the task of getting rid of what was left over. It was a difficult time period. Memories of my brother Bob's death came back, and I felt all alone again and, on some days, wanting to be far away from the responsibility and task before me.

Nevertheless, I aspired to complete the task at hand as there was no choice. The house had to be sold. It was hard to realize that we would no longer have the family home as a gathering place.

After the home was sold, I would pass by the house often to stir up memories. Now that a school has been built on the property, I can still tell where the house was located. I go there when I am in the area.

Chapter 17

Sibling 14
Chris's Story

My Family

I'm Evelyn Christine, and I am the fourteenth child of Rosie and Frank Jackson. My mother was forty-four years old when I was born.

Our northern migration landed us in Camden, New Jersey. We lived in three houses after we came north. Most of my memories are from the last house we moved to, at 812 Florence Street, and the only real property my parents ever owned. I do not recall more than six other kids (Grover, Bob, George, Otis, Mary, and Annie) living for any substantial period with me in that house while growing up. Billy, Mamie, and Geneva lived there for a short time and thereafter married and moved out. Even after moving out, they were always close by. My brother Charles and sisters Leola, Rose, and Josephine and their families lived in Jersey City, New Jersey, and came to visit on holidays. At some point, when I was in my teens, Josephine, her husband, Gil, and her nine kids moved to Camden and lived on Lake Shore Drive. They stayed for several years and then resettled in Baltimore, Maryland, until she passed away, many decades later.

Rose and Leola's children came to stay in Camden during the summers. Their children were about the same age as me. So we were good playmates. We enrolled in the summer programs at HB Wilson Elementary School to stay out of trouble. Under the supervision of counselors, we took field trips and played organized games in the schoolyard like stickball, baseball, yard racing, and basketball. We played other games like Chinese jump rope, double Dutch, and we hung from the monkey bars. During the early to mid-1960s, children played outdoors frequently.

Like all families, the siblings who shared our 812 Florence Street residence had disagreements with one another. Using our family's favorite TV character, Perry Mason, as our model, we resolved our arguments by way of a judicial system. Someone would be the judge. The accused child would have an attorney to represent him/her, and the others would be the jury. It was not that way all the time. Sometimes we could be paid off. I recall, for instance, that George paid me fifty cents to wash dishes for him for the rest of his life at our house on Florence Street. I do not know how old I was, but clearly, I was pretty "green."

My parents generally resolved their dissatisfactions with us in an altogether different way. They believed firmly in disciplining by using a man's leather belt or switch—whichever was readily available. My mother told the offending party that she was going to beat or whip them. She then went about her business throughout the day. She made the offender wait all day. At some point during the day, that person might falsely imagine that she had forgotten or changed her mind. Then she came with her strap, and the beating would begin. Not only did she beat the child, she created a singsong rhythm of beating while telling the child why she was beating him/her. My father also believed in beatings. He had a razor strap across the closet door in his bedroom. He used it or a freshly torn-off switch from any accessible tree. My sister Mary, upon being beaten, refused to cry. This only made our father try to beat longer and harder to cause her to do so. That combination was a test of wills. Mary was equally stubborn and determined not to give in. I recall only getting beaten once by my father. It angered me so that I called him by his derivative first name—Frankie—thereafter for the rest of his life.

My Background

The 812 Florence Street address in Camden was a two-story row house connected on one side to a neighbor. Today it would be called a twin. There were windows in the front of the house. There was an upstairs and downstairs view at the rear of the house overlooking the backyard. We could also see into the alley between our home and that of our next-door neighbor to the right. Our house had a screened-in porch where we sat on lawn chairs. The chairs were the kind that could be restrung if the matting got stringy or worn away from too much use. They were strung in an over-and-under fashion like the potholders we made during our summer program activities. We sat on the porch a lot, talking to our neighbors and playing with our friends. We played jacks on the steps. In the front of the house, we used old clotheslines (that were previously used to hang our clothes out to sun-dry) to jump rope, rubber bands connected to play Chinese jump rope, and we had chalk and a rock to play hopscotch.

The house had an old-time basement that one could also enter from the outside. The door latched on the inside. This was reminiscent of storm shutters. The basement was concrete and not well-lit. Its main function was storage. The fuse box for our electricity was in the backroom of the basement. The tank for oil used to heat our home was in the front of the basement, under the kitchen and dining room. My detailed memory of this is faint, but at some point, Frankie got some chickens and they were kept in the basement and backyard. It was during this period that I learned that chickens can still run and flutter or fly after their necks are wrung off. Witnessing this used to frighten me, Mary, and Annie.

The kitchen provided indoor access to the basement. White metal cabinets were hung on two of the kitchen walls. We ate at a 1950s-style metal table with matching metal chairs that had thick plastic backrest and seating, just like the ones seen on the TV show

Happy Days. The kitchen appliances included an electric mangle/wringer washing machine, situated next to the sink, a gas stove, and a refrigerator with a freezer compartment. The washer was close to the sink to enable us to manually run the water to the washer tub by using a hose connected to the sink. This machine was pre-automatic laundering. There was no spin cycle to wring the water from the clothes. Instead there were electric powered upper and lower rollers on the washer connected above the washer tub. They rolled when the machine was on. Before putting the clothes through the mangle/wringer component, you had to hand-squeeze the clothes with much strength and might. Thereafter, you put the clothes close to the rollers so they rolled between the top and bottom rollers to squeeze the water out. As I reflect on that process, the machine was appropriately named a mangle/wringer. I could never make the proper adjustment to get the clothes through without also getting my fingers stuck between the rollers. It was an often and painful occurrence to get my fingers mashed between the rollers of that wringer washer. We did not have a dryer. Clothes were either hung in the basement during inclement weather or outside to be line-dried by the sun.

We used every living space in the house. In the living room, we had a black-and-white television, the only one in the house, sofa, love seat, a chair, and several tables. The seating furniture was covered with a green upholstery that had a darker green design embedded in it. To protect it from its constant use, it was covered with thick plastic seat covers. The tables were filled with framed black-and-white pictures of family members. A long table positioned in front of the sofa had the family Bible on it. The Bible was white, leather-bound, and took nearly one-fourth of the table surface. The Bible was filled with colorful religious pictures and Scripture was printed in red and black. The pages of that Bible were delicate, lightweight, and were well-worn. My mother read it regularly. She handwrote important dates in it too. Such documentation included birthdays, baptisms, and dates that family members married and died. She also had a personal Bible that she read regularly in her bedroom.

In addition to white paneling, the living room walls were covered with pictures and various certificates of achievement, college degrees, army certificates earned by George, and honor roll certificates earned by me. Once something was put on the wall, it was never taken down. The white-wood grained paneling also filled the dining room and stair wall. The other side of the stairs was dark wood railing with wooden spokes with a banister at the base of the stairs. The dining room had a heavy wooden table with six chairs, a sturdy china closet against the wall that we shared with our neighbor, and a chest of drawers under the windows on the wall next to the alley. There was a white tile-dropped ceiling throughout the house.

The house had four bedrooms, one upstairs' bathroom, a living room, dining room, kitchen, and—using today's description—a mudroom in the back which was not that glorious. The boys shared the two middle rooms, and the girls had the room in the front of the house that overlooked the street. Frankie and Mom had the room overlooking the backyard.

My Mom

My mother was a regular churchgoer. During the 1960s, she attended Nazarene Baptist Church on Eighth Street in Camden, New Jersey. Sunday services were an all-day affair. It was required that we attend. It was also a requirement that we dress up to attend church services. On Sundays, when Mom was not an usher or on missionary Sundays, Mom wore dresses accessorized with beautifully crafted colored hats created by the neighborhood millinery, veils, and gloves. One day a month, she wore only white to church, from her head to her toes. She wore a white dress, gloves, stockings, because at this time, they did not have pantyhose, and white shoes. The white shoes were like those hospital nurses wore in the 1960s.

In reverence to the Ten Commandments, the seventh day was for rest; Mom made Sunday dinner on Saturday. She completed all her Sunday meals, including dessert, on Saturday. My favorite was her tea biscuits. She didn't cook anything on Sundays. I think white rice was served every Sunday. She often made cabbage, collards, turnips, or some other kind of greens. Corn bread was a constant menu item. When Mom sat down to eat her greens, she mixed vinegar into them, mashed them up with the corn bread, and ate the greens and corn bread with her fingers. She said the greens tasted better that way. The girls were often called upon and took turns cooking during the week. I did not look forward to cooking. We had a variety of meat to eat like pork chops, meat loaf, and ham. When it was my time to cook, it appeared that only chicken was on-hand. In those days, you could not buy chicken parts. Only whole chickens were sold. I was unable, seemingly, to cut the chicken without also slicing into my fingers or hand. So we always had a full supply of large Band-Aids on standby when I cooked.

During the week, after putting in a full day as a domestic, cleaning homes in Haddonfield and Cherry Hill, New Jersey, my mother went to church in the evenings to attend committee meetings. She was also a member of the Eastern Star, the female component for the Masons. When she was not at church, she spent a great deal of her time at the Masonic Hall on Kaighn Avenue in Camden. She was always secretive about what she did as an Eastern Star.

Mom never learned to drive. She walked to the bus stop, waited for it to come, and took two buses to get to the homes she cleaned. Other than that, she depended on church friends and her children to take her where she needed to go. It was not until she was in her late sixties that she even expressed a desire to drive. By that time, we discounted it and told her she was too old to do so. I had graduated from college and was working for a large telecommunication's company in Philadelphia and was still living at home.

Mom made the most out of the resources she had available to her. Often when she went to the supermarket to buy food for us, she did not have enough money to pay for it. I recall many times, getting to the register and having to put things back because she did not have the funds to pay for them. I was embarrassed. She was not. As I grew older and drove her to the store, I remember fussing at her for doing that. Later still, after I got jobs, summer, and career, I gave her money to cover the expenses. She bought clothes and Christmas toys for us on layaway. Layaway, in those days, was not limited to the last three months of the year. You could layaway clothes, toys, or almost anything, except food, all year long, for as long as you needed to. As often as she could, Mom put money on the layaway so the stores would hold the product until it was paid in full. To stretch her money, Mom bought things for us to share. So we mostly got board games. One year though, I remember getting my first watch. It was a Cinderella watch. It came with a Cinderella figurine. She had blond hair and was dressed in a blue-and-white gown. Annie got one with a Snow White figurine.

Mom used to sew by hand. She made quilts, sewed hems on our pants and dresses, mended socks, and made repairs as needed. She asked Annie, Mary, and me if we wanted to learn to sew. Mary and I said no definitively. Annie was the only one to say yes. Perhaps hopeful that Mary and I would change our minds, one year, Mom bought a sewing machine for Christmas. Annie took lessons. To this day, I cannot sew. Replacing missing buttons on clothes remains a challenge. The next best invention for me came about ten years later. It was called the Buttoneer. It had two components: a little handheld plastic tool, about the size of a nonelectric razor, and a small piece of plastic each end, shaped like a T. Using the small tool and a button, you could reattach buttons with a simple pinch maneuver. To this day, I still cannot sew a thing. It is not one of my biggest regrets, although I appreciate the skill when others have it. I still have one of the hand-sewn quilts Mom made. Ironically I also have the blue sewing kit filled with multicolored threads, thimbles, and scissors that she kept.

When I was about eleven or twelve years old, Mom got a job in the kitchen of Morgan Village Middle School. My brother Otis had some political connections and helped her to get the job. She used to bring home leftover chocolate and white milk, juices, luncheon meat sandwiches on white bread, and snacks. We ate well during those times.

I was the youngest child, and while young, I had many aches and pains. I was diagnosed with osteoarthritis at age thirteen. I blamed this on Mom. She had me when she was forty-four. I told her she handed down old people ailments by having me so late in life. Age thirteen was a memorable year for me. It was the first time I went into the hospital for an overnight stay. I had bunions removed from both of my feet at the same time. It was the first time I had ever used crutches. Prior to the operation, I was in terrible pain all the time. I cried incessantly. To make the pain stop, I used to bang on my feet with a hammer. I know now that made no sense, yet it was my irrational response to the pain. Now I also know, all I needed were good pairs of shoes. The trips to the second-hand shoe store with Frankie had caught up to me.

When I was thirteen, my sister Annie and I converted to Catholicism. We joined St. George's Roman Catholic Church on Ninth Street in Camden, around the corner from our house. I grew to like the Catholic religion. We were exposed to Catholicism for the first time when we visited my sister Rose in Jersey City. She and her family were Catholics at the time. My first impression was that Catholics kneeled too much. I had arthritis so kneeling caused me discomfort. After a few visits, I got used to kneeling. I appreciated that Catholics did not stay in church all day. I did not have to dress up to attend mass, and most importantly, the masses seemed calm. Priests delivered their sermons in a regular conversational voice. They were not theatrical. The service had lots of rituals and parishioners had to stand up, sit down, and kneel a lot. At this same occasion, females had to wear a veil or some head covering. But, no one ever got happy during the services, spoke in tongues, flailed uncontrollably, or passed out, resulting in ushers rushing to provide them special care. I had witnessed all those things over the years at Baptist Churches, and it made me uncomfortable. Mom used to say she did not care what religion we were if we believed in God and went to church. So we converted. Annie later joined a United Methodist Church and remained a member until she passed away.

Sadly I was thirteen when I came home from school and picked up an ominous telephone call. It was a nurse from Cooper Hospital. She did not tell me that my brother Bob had died. She calmly said that he was in the hospital and someone needed to come to the hospital to see about him. Bob had been born with a hole in his heart. He had been in and out of hospitals much of my young life. He had some learning disabilities that did not keep him from possessing a wry sense of humor and an engaging personality. He had recently begun working for Goodwill. He had his own source of money and had gained some independence. He must have been feeling good about himself because we later learned that he had bought an engagement ring and was going to propose marriage to a girl he met at the job.

Bob was the first person I had ever known to die. There was a void in our house for me after he left us. I do not recall Mom, Frankie, or anyone in the household talking much about Bob after his funeral. His was the first funeral I had ever attended. His funeral service stayed with me throughout my entire adult life. I found the whole experience frightening. I could not go to another funeral for years thereafter. I still find viewings, closing the casket, and lowering the casket into the ground to be emotionally stressful. Thanks to some long sessions with a psychological therapist, years after my mother passed away in 1984, I handle funerals better. I have, however, informed the family that for me, there is to be no viewing, a memorial service is acceptable, and cremation is the only approved disposition for my body.

Mom did not have the education to help us with school assignments, but she preached to us about the importance of having a good education. She witnessed many of us achieve that goal. Had she lived, the paneled living room picture wall at 812 Florence Street would have had no empty space. Over the years, ten of us completed college and received undergraduate degrees. Five of us earned advanced degrees in our academic fields.

My Father

Unlike Mom, Frankie did not go to church regularly. He was a bit of a loner but made friends easily. He knew people in the neighborhood. He borrowed money from them frequently. Since none seemed to be angry with him, I imagine he always paid them back.

He used to walk every place he went. Perhaps it was befitting since he had a job as a trash man, and he walked behind the trash truck emptying rubbish put in trash cans by residents throughout the city. He walked me to school when I was in preschool and kindergarten. I remember holding his hand as we walked. He walked us to buy used shoes at a second-hand store on Ferry Avenue. He walked me to buy the first pair of new black-and-white oxford shoes I ever had. They were steel-plated. I needed them to correct some childhood foot ailments.

Frankie did many things that annoyed and unnerved me. He liked to be served. Just as we began to play or sit down to watch television, he would call to tell us to bring him something or to make him something to eat. He only called the girls to make his comfort foods like grits, oatmeal, bacon, and cream of wheat. At that time, there were no microwave ovens or out-of-the-box two-minute meal preparations. For some inexplicable reason, watching the bubbles from the boiling grits and oatmeal caused me to get a creepy itchy feeling. I would often break down and cry. Those cooking experiences had a profoundly negative impact on me. It was not an intended affect. My sister Mary Lou got tired of my father calling her to cook for him. So she intentionally oversalted the food to avoid him asking her to ever cook again. I was not trying to rebel. My body and mind just became fragile when I was preparing Frankie's food.

My father often fished off the Fairview Bridge and only caught catfish. They were large black slimy fish with whiskers. Rather than clean them, Frankie would bring them home and put them directly into the freezer. Then he would instruct one of the children to clean them. The freezer was not a separate appliance. It was the top component of the refrigerator. To get to it, you opened the refrigerator's door and then a hard white plastic door at the top of the refrigerator unit. It held ice trays and other meats that needed freezing before cooking. Unexpectedly one day, I opened the freezer door. I immediately jumped back from a scare. Seemingly, looking directly at me was an enormous catfish head and all, waiting to be cleaned.

At some point in their relationship, Frankie and Mom moved into separate bedrooms. Since Florence Street was only a four-bedroom house, it was likely after George had gone into the army, Grover was off to college, and Mamie and Geneva had married. Mom took over what had been Bob's room.

Frankie did not believe in changing into fresh clothes daily. He bathed weekly, and he changed his long johns as frequently. He patrolled the house with them on. In the evening, he seemed to have an unquenchable thirst for water. When he did not call us to bring it to him, he went to get it himself. At bedtime, when he came to get water, Frankie would use one hand to hold together the flap in the back of his long johns to avoid exposing his behind. When he was on an alcohol binge, the front of Frankie's johns stained and smelled like urine. The stench was unbearable. Frankie's house patrol seemed to increase in frequency when the girls brought a date over to watch television with the family. To minimize the embarrassment, Mamie, Geneva, Annie, and I explained to our dates beforehand what to expect when they came to visit. Mary dated and married a Ghanaian but later divorced him. He lived in Boston, Massachusetts and did not visit much. Therefore, *Mary* did not have to deal with the exposure or the embarrassed explanations. Aside from Billy, his wife, Viola, and Otis, with his wife Mary, I do not recall the boys bringing dates to the house in the evening. I do not know if that was by design or coincidental.

The Florence Street house had an alley between it and the house next-door. The alley led to our backyard. When he began to drink more frequently, rather than go to the bathroom in the house, Frankie urinated against the neighbor's house in that alley. There were no windows on the alley side of our neighbor's home. He did not try to hide it. When we witnessed that act, our distress was palpable.

Frankie was not at all handy around the house. When he had a little money, he hired a handyman to do repairs. Unfortunately the repair people had only minimal skills to do home improvements. So many things around the house stayed in disrepair. It would be an overstatement to say that the jobs that were attempted were half-done.

Unlike Mom, Frankie was not much involved in the children's lives. Therefore, it surprised us when he bought a car for Otis, Annie, and me to share. It was an old blue manual-shift Chevy. Without power steering, it took lots of strength to turn and maneuver. It felt like I was driving a military tank. In the early stages of our co-ownership, I recall running into the steel trashcans we had at the curb after trash pickup day. It did not put a dent in the car. Nevertheless, the metal trashcans were forever misshaped. That car lasted a long time. Annie used it to pick me up from school when she was at Rider College and I had just started Douglas College in 1972. The two schools were no more than forty-five minutes from one another.

My Youth

As a child, I had been called Chris or Christine for as long as I can remember. I did not realize that I had any other name, let alone a first name of Evelyn until I started school at six years old. Even after age six, I barely realized that I had another name. It was not used by anyone to call me, so it had little impact on my life. I went to a Catholic high school, full of old-timey nuns in attitude, behavior, and dress. They insisted that I use my first name because it was my proper name. I developed a great dislike for the name Evelyn thereafter. Not just because I had never gotten comfortable with being addressed that way, but people began to take liberties with the name. Acquaintances, who I clearly did not know, started using abbreviations of Evelyn like Ev and Evvy. Over time, to conform, I accepted that I had Evelyn as my name, and the nuns and I compromised. E. Christine evolved as my preferred nomenclature.

As mentioned earlier, I had several health problems that extended into my adult life. One of the problems was bad feet. This triggered getting a pair of brand-new steel-toed black-and-white oxford shoes. Aside from correcting a foot problem, those shoes came in handy. I sucked my thumb when I was a child. This caused me to be mercilessly picked on by my siblings. They tried everything to break me of the habit. They got annoyed when I sipped the spit too loudly. So they yanked my thumb out of my mouth. They employed many cruel tactics to get me to stop sucking my thumb, including spitting on my thumb, wrapping it with gauze and bandages, and putting hot sauce on it. I soon learned to use my steel-toed shoes to defend myself. I fought back when they pulled my thumb out of my mouth or tried to otherwise modify my thumb-sucking. Upon their approach, I hauled back and kicked them with all my might. I must have kicked with those shoes for other reasons as well. Mary told me that I once laid into her shin with them. As a result, as an adult many years later, she felt the pang and pain in that same spot whenever it rained.

When I was nine years old, while visiting my sister Rose during the summer, I had my first period. I thought I was dying. I had blood everywhere. I guess Mom thought my sisters had told me about the body changes to expect. They had not, so Rose explained the facts of life to me. I may not have been dying then, but thereafter, every month due to cramps and other pains, I felt like I was dying for most of my premenopausal life. No medicine lessened the agony. The best answer for the discomfort was bed rest in a dark quiet room. The idea that labor pains could be worse than that agony was a major reason I decided never to birth children.

I cannot explain how it was triggered, but I have always been unnerved by the word and frightened of the sight of any kind of *snakes*. My brothers and brother-in-law Carl, Mamie's husband, thought the best method to address that problem was shock treatment. So they selected the encyclopedia for all things starting with an S. Then using surprise approaches, they repeatedly came up to me or called my name. I unwittingly looked each time they called me. They then flashed colorful pictures of all kinds of snakes in my face. That sent me into a major panic. I froze and wailed each time. When I slept, I balled up into a fetal position, and because I retained the pictures in my mind's eye, I had nightmares. For months, they continued with their picture-torment therapy. The experience was traumatic. Their untrained uncertified shock treatment experiment failed to cure me of my fears. If anything, it strengthened it.

For those unaware, an encyclopedia was the early substitute to Wikipedia sources currently found on the internet. They were alphabetized books, sold door-to-door and paid in monthly installments. We subscribed to *The World Book Encyclopedia* series. The books were hard-covered, cream-colored with a black spine and gold etching of its name and per book alphabet letter on the spine and cover. The book contained every subject known at the time, categorized and summarized. They were updated yearly. Because issues and events were constantly changing, the books were always out-of-date. To compensate for that, once a year, the company printed a book to address all the new things that had occurred and were noteworthy that year. One could buy that if a new set of encyclopedias could not be afforded. At the time, many things were sold door-to-door, including life insurance. Salesmen would make the sales pitch and make out payment arrangements to complete the sale. They even came back monthly to pick up the payment.

My oldest brother, Billy, lived with us before we moved to the 800 block of Florence Street. He worked at Sears Auto all his adult life until he retired. He was always around. In the early years, he was the only one of us who had a car. On Saturday afternoons, he often came to take the younger children to the drive-in theatre in Pennsauken, New Jersey. A drive-in theater was an outdoor movie venue. It included a massive movie screen located in the front of a large multicar parking lot, designated by white lines on the ground for each car. There was also a pole with a detachable volume box that was to be put onto the driver's side window so that those in the car could hear the dialogue and soundtrack as they watched the picture on the movie screen. The charge to get into the drive-in was based on a per-person headcount. To minimize the per-person charge, at some point, before we entered the drive in, some of the children would get into the car trunk. Once in the drive-in, those we could not afford to pay for came out of the trunk. We then bought one box of popcorn to be shared by all during the movie.

Like many families with lots of children, we had our share of weddings. Mamie was the first one of the children who lived at Florence Street to be married. Before that happened, she dated Carl Fullard. He worked at the mail distribution center at the time. He came by the house and courted her and bought us ice cream and introduced us to bologna and cheese sandwiches. Carl ate bologna as luncheon meat on a sandwich, and he fried it for breakfast or dinner. He also ate Vienna sausages out of the can; but the thing I remember most about him was that he loved to go for long rides and he took Mamie and us along with him. He did that before they got married and afterward. At some point, Carl became a manager of a

Roy Rogers, a Marriot fast food restaurant franchise. That restaurant was famous for its roast beef sandwiches. I remember going for long rides and stopping at one of the stores he managed—I think it was in Ardmore, Pennsylvania. We ordered at no-charge to us, whatever we wanted, when we got there. We were in child-heaven. We never really noticed that we were there for hours. Carl had stopped in to see how his assistant managers were doing, and he had gotten bogged down in work. At some point later in his career, Carl moved over to manage two Burger King franchise stores. We got to do the same thing there.

Mamie and Carl lived within walking distance of Florence Street for the first several years they were married. So we saw them often. Later they moved to Lake Shore Drive which was a ten-minute walk away from our house. They bought a dog and named him Benji. He was so cute. I remember just wanting to go over to their house to play with Benji all the time. I was in high school by that time. It seemed that just as they got the dog, it ran away. I was distraught. They got another one and named him Pepper; but fearing that Pepper would one day run away too, I never warmed up to him. Even at thirteen, I was a very naive child and I believed them when they said that Benji ran away. It was not until one Thanksgiving Day, when I was well into my fifties, that I learned that Mamie and Carl had given Benji away. Mamie said the dog was crazy, just like the people they had bought him from. Carl had passed away by then, so I could not hold him accountable.

Mary and I had short hair. Annie was the only one who had a beautiful body of thick hair down to her shoulders. In those days, girls and women had their hair straightened. In our house, after our hair had been washed and dried, usually on either a Friday or Saturday night, Mom had us take turns and sit down on a chair in the kitchen near the stove. She had, near her, a can of hair grease and a straightening comb. The straightening comb was heated on the stove's gas burner. Mom combed and parted the hair of whoever was in the chair at the time. She applied grease to the hair and scalp and then she took the hot comb off the burner, laid it first one side, and then the other on a rag to cool down, and then she straightened our hair. There were burn marks on the rag from where it was laid.

In my mind's eye and ear, I can still see and hear the grease sizzle as the hot comb was pulled through our hair. More times than I like to recall though, I felt the burn on my ear or scalp as the too-hot comb got too close to my ear or scalp. My mom was heavy-handed, and I do not think she enjoyed doing hair. It was her responsibility so that we could be presentable in public, namely school and church. It was good times when my sister Geneva got married, moved to California, got her beautician's license, returned home, and could take over the duties of doing our hair.

I think the hair experience permanently damaged Mary and me. Not so much Annie. Mary began wearing a short Afro shortly after she began college. She was one of the first black students to attend Rider College in affluent and culturally segregated Lawrenceville, New Jersey, in the late 1960s. I don't know if she was being revolutionary or she had bad memories of my mom and the straightening comb. As soon as I could afford to have someone professionally do my hair, I discovered the perm and the Gerrie curl. I have had one or the other in my hair from that point on. Annie also went to Rider College. She was two years behind Mary. She alternated hairstyles. She had a big Afro, and she wore her hair shoulder-length and straight. She did not have a short haircut until many years later.

As I mentioned earlier, due to school redistricting, I went to Fairview, a very white section of Camden, in the late 1960s for middle school. Yorkship was the name of the school. While I was initially concerned about the lack of diversity, I made some very nice girl and boy friends. I was introduced to new ventures that I had not experienced before. I was invited to parties. I was invited to go to skating rinks and bowling alleys. I was embarrassed that I had never skated or bowled before, so I always made excuses as to why I could not attend. Looking back on that time, my friends did not care that I did not know how to do those things. They were asking me to come for the companionship. I know this because many of us remained friends well into our adult years until we outgrew one another.

Many of the girls that I hung out with in Fairview graduated from middle school and enrolled in Cathedral Academy for Girl's in downtown Camden. Although each of my siblings had attended there, I did not know anyone who was going to Camden High School. I feared that I would be the only person without a friend walking through Pollock town to get to Camden High. Pollock town was another all-white section of Camden in the late 1960–1970s. It was so named because most of the residents were of Polish descent. This was also around the same time that Annie and I had converted to Catholicism. So Mom and Mamie visited the principal of the school on my behalf. The result was a full scholarship to attend the school.

Overall my high school years were a great experience. I had to walk six blocks to Morgan Boulevard and take a public service transit bus each day to and from school. My friends from Fairview would have gotten on the bus several stops ahead of me. We enjoyed each other's company for the duration of the forty-five-minute ride to school. Among other school activities, I was on the basketball team, student council, the school newspaper, and the yearbook staff. Girls' basketball, in those days, required us to wear skirt-like uniforms. I was a guard. Guards were not allowed to cross the center line. The rules and dress are very different now. I was enrolled in an academic curriculum. That was for people focused on going to college, so I was not allowed to take typewriting, shorthand, or bookkeeping. That was for people who were going to be secretaries. I was not allowed to take home economics classes because that was for girls who were going to be stay-at-home moms. Home economics offered courses on cooking and sewing.

The academic curriculum offered electives for languages. I took Spanish and Latin. The mathematics courses were algebra, trigonometry, geometry, and calculus. The sciences entailed biology, chemistry, and physics. English and writing filled out the basic curriculum. There were many other electives. I made honors each semester. However, in my junior year, Sister Eileen, a young pale-skinned tall and thin guidance counselor (one of two) advised me that I would likely not succeed in college. She strongly suggested that I consider other options. I did not heed that advice. The following year though, I did switch to a different guidance counselor. Father Mike began working with me. I was accepted into each of the five renowned schools where I applied. I received a full scholarship to attend Douglas College, Rutgers University in New Brunswick, New Jersey. It was an all-women's school. I was in the last graduating class of Cathedral Academy. There were seventy-five girls in my class. The school closed due to low enrollment. I learned later that Sister Eileen left the convent and pursued other career options.

My Educational Endeavors

For two summers, Annie and I accepted jobs at the same places. One job was at a uniform factory. The uniforms were matching shirt and pants commonly worn by delivery men. The job was one of the worst jobs I have ever had. The uniforms were washed and dried on the premises. We were then required to press them and put them on hangers. The benefit of the job was that it was around the corner and just five minutes from our house. We could come home for lunch and did not have to drive to get there. However, the disadvantages of that job far outweighed the benefits. We were required to stand for eight hours a day. My feet had improved, but I was still experiencing tenderness where my bunions were removed. I was miserable. I frequently burned myself with the steam coming from hot presses that we used to iron the shirts and pants. We had to work quickly. I was not adroit enough to position the hangers correctly when I pressed the clothes and hung them on the production line for final packaging. They were always supposed to face the same direction. Mine did not. The hangers on the conveyor belt became tangled. The production line got backed up, jammed, and would stop. Knowing that I was the cause of the problem, the manager came back to me and furiously pulled the uniforms off the line and dropped them at my feet. Consequently I did not last the entire summer at the uniform factory.

The next summer, we worked at a bomb manufacturing plant. It was a plant that put together timers for the bombs. This plant was in Cherry Hill, just off Fellowship Road. It took about an hour to drive there. Putting aside any concerns we had about creating bombs, we could sit. I could at least do this job and meet the basic job requirements. My problem with this job was that it was my first exposure to adult men and women who spoke openly about sex and who used foul language incessantly. The daily experience was so nerve-racking to me that I sat and prayed my way through each shift. I prayed ferociously for the people who cursed and seemed to be enjoying the off-color references and personal sexual experiences they so freely shared aloud. And I prayed for myself to make it through each day.

I tried to always gleam learning experiences from my jobs. From these, I learned that first, production-line jobs may appear simple but may require a degree of manual dexterity that everyone does not have. Second we all have an individual tolerance or comfort level about people, places, and things. If a situation exceeds your tolerance level, it is best to separate yourself from that situation and move on.

Annie graduated from Rider; thereafter, I got a summer job as a school counselor. I worked in positions like those I participated in when I was a child going to the HB Wilson Elementary School summer program. It was a better suit to my temperament than the production-line jobs I previously held. My coworkers were other college students, teachers, school administrators, and aides. I also met Joseph Whaley, my future husband, while performing this job.

Despite Sister Eileen's negative influence, I had a positive experience as a Catholic from the time I converted at age thirteen. It was so powerful that I decided to become a nun. My goal was to graduate college, join the Sisters of Notre Dame in Philadelphia, Pennsylvania, and serve the Lord in that way. I had done a little research and decided that I should complete college to allow myself to be exposed to the world to ensure that was the right commitment for me. While I did not enroll in any education courses, I considered the idea of becoming a high school teacher. Since I was not comfortable around people, I also considered becoming a cloistered nun dedicating my life to constant prayer. After my junior year, I did not discard the idea of going into the convent. I simply thought it was best to delay it. My commitment became less firm. I convinced myself that I should work a few years so that I could truly be sure that I was being called to serve in that way.

My first semester of college was not great. My first-year room-mate was not at all neat, and she socialized only with her friends. A person who I considered a dear friend, after two months of knowing her, was homesick and wanted to return home to Atlanta. She spent the first semester at Douglas and transferred to a college in Georgia for the second semester. Two of my other newfound friends, one from North Jersey, the other from the South Jersey shore area, spent most of their time in their rooms with upperclassmen they had just met. Due to bad grades, they ultimately failed and dropped out of school.

Douglas was, at the time, known as a suitcase-college campus. Most of the students were from New Jersey, and they went home every weekend. There was little opportunity to mingle when not in class. During my second semester, over time, I met six other people who became my treasured lifelong friends. We met in shared classes and activities. We met because some were friends of the person that I had become friends with.

When I began Douglas College, Annie was a junior at Rider College. It was just down the road from Douglas on Route 1. On Fridays, she picked me up in the shared car Frankie had bought us. We spent the weekend at home, and she dropped me off again on Sunday evenings. Annie did not always have money for gas. Neither one of us had jobs during the school year. She donated blood to get spending money. One day, she did not allow enough time between donations and she passed out. That was scary. Thereafter, she relied less on blood donations as her source of generating funds. With one exception, after Annie graduated, I traveled back-and-forth to school on weekends with one of my friends. Her dad picked her up each weekend and offered to drive me home as well. Sometimes her uncle, who lived in New York, visited the family in South Jersey, and he stopped by and gave us a ride. Good for us, this did not put him out of the way. After a few years, my friend received her own car and we rode together to South Jersey. Transportation back-and-forth to school was never a hindrance.

The one exception of riding home and back to school with my friend came one Sunday after a holiday weekend. I cannot really recall which holiday it was, but I remember that my North Jersey siblings had come to celebrate the holiday at our house. It was time for them to return home. Since they were going my way, I asked my brother Charles if I could get a ride with him and his family. He agreed to drive me back to Douglas. Charles and his wife, Doris, and their three children and I piled into his car. Exit 9 on the New Jersey Turnpike is the exit for Douglas College. At some exit prior to Exit 9, Charles said he had to make a rest stop. Rather than park, he pulled up to the front of the building and went in. We all waited in the car for nearly an hour, wondering what was taking him so long to go to the bathroom. When Charles finally came out, he advised us that he had gone into the restaurant to get something to eat. It was the early 1970s and the rest areas along the New Jersey Turnpike had restaurants where one could sit and be served a full meal. It apparently had not occurred to Charles to park or to ask if any of us wanted to partake in a meal.

I graduated from Douglas College in the late 1970s with a bachelor's degree in economics and finance. I missed honors by 1/100th of a percent. Bruce Gordon recruited me into a middle management program at a telephone company. I later learned that Bruce had attended Camden High School with my brother George. Although it was my intention to stay at the telephone company for no more than five years, I remained with the company in its various merged stages for thirty-three years. The draw to me was that I had numerous jobs within the company. I worked in personnel, sales, marketing, treasury, product management, and as a lobbyist. While pursuing career goals during the day, I earned my master's degree in finance and business management at Widener University, taking evening classes. When I retired from the telephone company, I had benefitted from a wealth of job and promotional experiences.

I had many growth opportunities as a manager at the company. My early years were challenging. I was an introvert in a middle management program that pitted me against peers who wanted to be the first to be promoted. The program goal was to make it to district-level management in five to seven years. If an intern was determinedly not capable of doing so along the way, they were terminated. To make an impression, my peers were always the first to give their opinions and to volunteer. They frequently used the approach of repeating what another manager said to make it sound like they were adding value. They loved to attend company functions to mingle with the company's officers. I was not typically the first to speak up in a meeting. I usually tried to absorb information, process it, and then speak to provide insight. I relied heavily on facts to support my ideas. I tended to shy away from mingling situations. I had to find my way. There were trial-and-error periods before my path was cleared.

I began as a management intern, reporting to a director, in the labor relation's department of personnel. We negotiated with seven unions across Pennsylvania to resolve workplace disputes between associates and management. I had never done any of the jobs, but I was expected to have command of all the details of each union contract. More than that, I had to adapt quickly to changing situations and counsel managers on the spot when they called in to get guidance about how to handle active cases. When union presidents came in to attempt to settle in-person negotiable cases, before allowing the cases to go to arbitration, I learned, from the meetings, not to react or show any expressions. For all, except one contract, the union presidents were older white men who had previously worked in-line jobs. Either to intimidate or simply because that is how they spoke, they used the foulest language I had ever heard outside of my early summer job experience at the factory that manufactured parts for bombs. They were often trying to get the general manager or any of us in the room to respond in kind, falter in judgment, and make an emotional decision.

My first career stumbling block came in my second year in the program. Interns who made it through the first year were assigned to a supervisor. I was no longer under the guidance and direction of the director of labor relations. I now reported to a supervisor in his organization, a black female who had capped out in her career. On the surface, she was very sweet. I shared everything with her. I invited her to my home and introduced her to my family. I made the rookie mistake of thinking she was my friend. At performance review time, my blinders were removed. Among other things, many of the private insights I had shared with her were identified as performance short-comings. That experience helped me to brush off workplace naivete.

I learned the hard way from my early years at the telephone company. From that point on, I was friendly but guarded with personal information when I was with workplace associates. Still I managed to develop two meaningful friendships that I have maintained for over thirty years. I learned to mingle to pass the tests that upper management laid before me, and I became a trailblazer when I was promoted and became the first female black director in New Jersey. I learned over my thirty-three years with the company, now a national company, that color was not a determining or even relevant factor in developing interpersonal relationships. I had to learn how to achieve corporate goals with all my coworkers. Among other things to be successful, I needed to be flexible, confident, influential, have strong decision-making skills in quality, quantity, and in quickness. Particularly I had to be very knowledgeable about the subject matter for which I was responsible, making it a reality to me that I had to learn to react on instinct. Facts mattered, but one would have to read into the facts to make the best decisions.

As with all jobs, it soon became clear when it was time to move on. From time to time, management was called upon to do the jobs of the associates during telephone company strikes. In some years, I was excused and allowed to continue to perform my regular job. In those cases, I was doing something the company considered critical to its ongoing operations. Still over the years, I did line work during four strikes. Some strikes were longer than others. Some conditions were easier than others. A typical strike duty shift was sixteen hours. I learned various jobs for strike duty: operator, frame man which involved stringing circuits to activate dial tone for landline phones in a central office. And twice I was a resident customer service representative. I handled customer complaints, established billing arrangements, and changed service for landline customers. While I never wanted to perform any of these jobs on a regular basis, I could handle them as an emergency assignment. It was the last call to strike that caused me to accelerate my retirement plans.

Each of my other strike assignments had been indoors. The last call to strike was different. The needs of the business had changed. Many of the inside jobs were now mechanized and fewer people were needed to do them. I was assigned to be a lineman. Linemen climbed poles and strung wires from houses to streets and across streets to connect landline phones to central offices that delivered dial tones. We were always well-trained before we were sent to do the jobs assigned to us. In this case, the training had two phases. The first part was considered pretraining. It was three months of training at your own pace online. The second part was field training near Bowie, Maryland. The good part about this training site was that I got to stay with my sister Mary who lived fifteen minutes away from the training facility. The bad thing about this experience was that I had to wear steel-toe boots, an equipment belt, a construction hard hat, and climb poles. I am deathly afraid of heights. I survived the first two days of field training. We were doing on-the-ground prepa-rations, be that as it may, on the third day; as I climbed the pole for the first time, my body and the pole shook uncontrollably. I made it halfway up the pole and I could not get my body to go any further. I could not go up or down. I managed not to cry in front of the others who were also there to be trained, although the interminable shaking was totally out of my control.

There was no strike that year. I did not have to feel too bad that I flunked out of lineman training. Anxious to avoid the possibility that I could be called upon again to be retrained if there ever was another work stoppage, I decided that it was time to call it a career. Two years after this experience, when I was fifty-seven years old, I volunteered for an early-retirement package being offered because the company was downsizing.

My Adult Life Exploits

In 1974, I reconnected with Joseph Whaley while working at the HB Wilson Elementary School summer program. We had first met years before. He was the boyfriend of one of my Cathedral Academy classmates. I was not looking for a relationship. During that time of my life, I still believed that I was going to be a nun. In fact, for the first three of the six years we dated, that was still my intent. Over time, I came to understand that I could serve God in many ways other than as a vocation. After thirty-five years of a blessed marriage and adopting our son, John, our life goes on.

As the three youngest children, close in age, I always felt closest to my sisters Annie and Mary. After everyone else grew up and left home, we were there together. Annie and I stayed in South Jersey. Mary was married and lived in Boston for a short time. Then she divorced and moved away.

Annie was on the go all the time. Even after she married Gary Freeman and had two children, she was not homebound. Most times, she simply took the children wherever she went. If she needed to go to the store late at night, she took her children with her. She was a teacher, and then a librarian. From all accounts, she was excellent at both. She was handy and would try to fix almost anything. Among other things, she could install a lock in a door, cut the fabric and create new seat covers to refurbish a chair, and decipher computer problems, but there were other sides to her as well. A telephone conversation with Annie never ended, especially if there was a decision made on the call. I would think that we were finished because each of us said goodbye and hung up the telephone, but then Annie would call me back again and again. Each time she would be indecisive about the points that we had agreed to during the previous call. She waited until the last minute to complete lesson plans. She arrived late for most family events. And though she was sweet most of the time, if someone seriously annoyed her, she would curse like a sailor.

Annie was a great companion for me. However, the one thing we did not enjoy doing together was shopping. Annie was a bargain shopper of clothes, shoes, furniture, or anything that she wanted or she felt anyone else needed. She would travel near and far to seek out bargains. Her face would light up as she talked about her findings. This is something we did not have in common. I did not like shopping in general, and I certainly never wanted to go out of my way to do it.

I relished my time with Annie. I was relieved when she called on my birthday, February 20, 2003, to say she had been in an accident. The car was totaled but she was all right. I thanked God. Then exactly one month later, my heart was broken when Mamie called me and said, "Annie is gone."

Joe and I cried that night as he said what I deeply felt, "I thought we would grow old together." Annie was fifty-three years old when she passed away due to a heart attack. I stopped celebrating my birthday after she left me.

Mary was an adventurer. As a child, she had international pen pals. She used to read books and communicated aloud and wondered about all the places in the world she would travel when she ever had the chance. She had an insatiable curiosity for faraway places. She easily struck up conversations with strangers and asked a stream of endless questions to satisfy her desire to know about any subject she was interested in. As a result, it was not a surprise when in the late 1970s, she decided to travel to Iran to teach business classes. Until then, I had never heard of Iran.

Shortly there afterward though, Iran was prominently in the news. Students were rioting. They wanted to get rid of Shah Pahlavi of Iran who had been in power and was pro-American. The Shah's government was ultimately overthrown. A Fundamentalist Muslim group called the Islamic Republic, led by the Ayatollah Khomeini, took control of the country. The new government was anti-American. Americans were stranded in the country. For days, we could not get in touch with Mary after we had not heard from her. Finally she called and advised us that the American team with which she was teaching was safe. She was flying to Paris and would be home soon. We were thrilled.

Mary was a bit of a gypsy. She taught for the private sector and in public schools. Her skills were transferable. Over her career, she had lived in Union City, New Jersey, Boston, Massachusetts, and Atlanta, Georgia, and in various cities around the District of Columbia metro area. In some of those cities, she stayed with siblings; at other times, she lived alone in apartments.

Mary was a free-thinker and altogether nonconventional in her outlook on life and in her religious beliefs. This made some of our siblings, who leaned toward religious fundamentalism, very uncomfortable. To soothe any potential problems when interfacing with their children, Mary did not share her views with them.

Mary treasured individualism. She wore unique vibrant-colored clothes and novel jewelry that one would not see on others. She furnished her home and accessorized with pieces that were one of a kind. She budgeted her money but spent wisely, as she would call it, on things that she valued. One of the things that she did not like to spend money on were cars. When Mary bought a car, she kept it for years. When she was in Atlanta, she finally bought a new car. The dealer asked her not to trade in her old car and advised her that he would pay her to keep it. Mary kept that new car, a 1987 Ford Taurus for more than ten years. She reluctantly agreed to buy another vehicle to replace the Taurus, even though she was using a screwdriver to turn its ignition.

Mary settled in Bowie, Maryland, to live and teach. After many years of sharing domiciles with siblings and apartment living, she decided that she wanted to own a home. She found a three-story town house in a community that suited her perfectly. The backyard abutted a state park filled with trees, flowers, and deer that did not shy away from humans. She frequently called me on Saturday mornings, while she was eating breakfast, to say that a deer had just wandered near her deck. She was breathless in her excitement about such things.

She loved to have visitors. Whenever Joe and I went for a weekend, she had each day planned with activities. She loved the DC metro area restaurants, museums, tourist events, unique stores, and places to venture. She desperately wanted to share each place with us. When we returned home, we had to rest up from our weekends with Mary. She had many diverse, well-traveled, longtime, dear friends. Many of them were international. She spoke about them often, and when they were in the area, we met them as well.

Two years before she succumbed to cancer, she received a diagnosis of stomach cancer. The doctor explained that it was treatable and he was prepared to move quickly to contain it. Mary delayed and pursued holistic treatments from a certified doctor. She followed the doctor's guidance, ate healthy foods, and decried that by doing so, her body would be more energetic and able to self-heal. For months, she deflected family questions and concerns about her treatment choice. Sad to say that the delay of treatment allowed the cancer to progress through her body, her lungs, and esophagus. Shortly after attending my sister Josephine Goggins' funeral in December, Mary returned to traditional medical care. Within a short time, she was put on oxygen. She could no longer climb the stairs and enjoy the three-story home that she so dearly loved. In February 2010, Mary was hospitalized and never returned to her beloved town house again. She passed away on March 16, 2010. She was sixty years old. Her memorial was held on March 20, the same day that Annie died seven years earlier.

I was appointed as Mary's executor. As such, I called many of her friends and they spread the word to others who had known her over the years. As I took care of her estate, I got calls from her past students who praised her as a teacher and, more meaningful to me, as a person. One young lady shared her story of when Mary was her instructor. She recalled working for the railroad union and did not have money for personal items, so Mary gave her clothes to interview for jobs. She marveled about the way Mary was an example and the way she cared about her students. For months after she passed, I was still receiving similar calls from past students, expressing their grief and sharing their stories about Mary.

Chapter 18

In Remembrance

Sibling 9: Robert Jackson (Bob)

Born January 3, 1945, Bob, sibling 9, was quiet and easygoing. He was never able to do much physical work. Even in Georgia, he was limited and did chores only around the house. He gathered wood from the woodpile. He carried it inside for use it in the pot-belly stove for cooking and use it in the fireplace during the fall and winter months. He did not work in the fields. As we gathered for community games though, Bob was as active as all the other children. He especially enjoyed playing baseball. The item we used and called a ball was simply a bunch of rags rounded and tied tightly together. Everything we played with in Omaha was homemade—the bats, gloves, and ball.

Last summer, I attended and spoke at the funeral of a childhood friend who grew up in Omaha. His family lived less than a mile from us, and his father was our barber. After the service, as we reminisced about our childhood, one of his brothers recalled the time we played ball in the pastures and Bob caught the ball in his pocket. The incident was funny because we spent a considerable amount of time looking for the rag baseball. After nearly fifteen minutes of searching the pasture, someone jokingly asked Bob to check his pockets. Sure enough, he had unknowingly caught it in his pocket. We were ages nine to thirteen and that was so funny to us. We laughed at the event last summer as if it had just happened, even though it had occurred sixty years ago.

Bob was small and thin in stature. He had a series of medical, mental, and learning disability challenges. He had heart disease, brought on by an enlarged heart with a hole in it. We knew nothing about his heart condition prior to relocating to Camden. Bob was not overly active. He had some physical limitations, but he was not sedentary. It didn't hinder him from trying to do many of the things that his other siblings did. He participated in all our social activities, along with other boys our same age group.

Bob lived at home with Mom, Dad, and the younger siblings. Before he passed, he was enrolled in a nonprofit training program with Goodwill to learn a skill. To my knowledge, he never enrolled or attended public school in Camden.

Bob died on September 15, 1967, a month to the day after I left the country on a two-year assignment with the US Peace Corps in Kenya, East Africa. He and Gustin, my youngest son, were born on January 3, thirty-nine years apart. Bob died at the age of twenty-two. It was tough dealing with a family death when I was eight thousand miles away, especially when it was a total surprise. He had not been ill. I had said goodbye and I will see you in a couple of years. Never did I give a thought that those would be the last words we spoke to each other. My Peace Corps supervisor drove ninety seven miles from Nairobi to tell me. He had a plane ticket in hand for me to return to America. I now had to take a lonely eight-thousand-mile flight back home to be with my family as we put his body to rest.

Bob was a very special person. The only way I handled his death was to be with my family. He was the first sibling to pass. I never saw Bob's body nor did I attend the wake or funeral. It was not easy for me. I grieved quietly and alone. I felt the loss down to my core. Ultimately for me, I had made a commitment to the Peace Corps, so

I had to pull myself together, regroup, and move on with life. After a week at home with my family, I returned to Kenya and resumed my assignment.

Sibling 4: Charles Jackson

Charles danced to his own tune and loved life to its fullest. He was the only sibling who recreationally drank any significant amounts of alcoholic beverages. He did not hold it especially well. He was a social drinker. I lived with him and his family during summers prior to and after my academic suspension from college. While we did not actively hang out together, I spent some time observing his social tendencies. Charles dressed like he was straight out of a *GQ Magazine*. When he stepped out socially, he always wore a trilby or a Stetson fedora hat, cocked suavely to one side. He and his friends enjoyed flirting with single women as they patronized the local bars. Charles was married with a daughter and two boys. He took care of his family financially but loved hanging out with the boys. He worked hard and played the same way. When at work, he was all business, and when he played, it was for pure enjoyment. Charles was a manager at Pep Boys and later became an owner and operator of an Esso gas station in Jersey City for many years.

What I really loved and respected most about Charles was his honesty. He did not mince words. He told it like he perceived it to be. He left the ears that heard it to draw their own conclusions. He had an engaging personality but never led one on to believe something other than what he meant.

Charles lost both of his legs due to diabetes. He passed away at the age of sixty-three, on December 13, 1998, from the disease after many years of suffering. His wife, Doris, survived him and passed away in 2015. She left behind a daughter, two sons and grandchildren.

Sibling 13: Annie Freeman (Ms. Ann)

It was 1951 when Annie, sibling 13, was born—Ms. Ann as we affectionately called her as an adult. I vividly remember the year and the day. Annie never knew anything about our living arrangements in Georgia; therefore, I often accused her, teasingly, of being the blame for our move from a place with electricity to one without it. I jokingly said, "You are the reason we were told to move." We had to make way so a white farmer could occupy it. The place had been recently renovated, with electricity added, and suddenly, it was too good for us.

I knew each time I called Annie, we both would have an enjoyable conversation. She knew me and could match my stories word for word.

Her personality was infectious. She had one of the most awe-inspiring beautiful smiles I have ever observed. She had an engaging, contagious personality to match, and she was fun to be around. Both she and Mary Lou, sibling 12, overlapped in attendance and graduated from Rider College in Lawrenceville, New Jersey.

Annie taught elementary education in the city of Camden and earned a master's degree in library science from Glassboro State College, renamed Rowan University. Teaching and being around children were Annie's calling, and she did so with all the energy and joy that life brought. She engaged and conversed with every child she met. She spoke with their parents if the opportunity arose. She loved all children and was always very genuinely kind and caring when she interfaced with them. Those who did not know Ms. Ann could have easily had the impression that she was a homemaker, raised a family, and dealt with things inside the home only. She was that and much more. She knew quite a bit about gardening. She maintained plants in and outside of her home.

I am not sure where Annie inherited or gained the talent but she was a jack-of-all-trades. She could upholster a piece of furniture in little or no time. Upon completion, it would be professionally done, updated in style and in texture. During the summer break, she visited my family and bought her two children. They were about the same age as my two older boys. Upon visiting my family, she suggested ways of sprucing up our home. She went beyond suggesting, she became an interior decorator, bought fabric and refurbished several pieces of furniture in just a short while. She looked at our dining room chairs, then said, "These chairs need a makeover." And in an hour, they looked new. She had refurbished them using fabric that matched the décor of the room and carpet.

I was floored when she told me she changed the motor oil in her car. There was nothing in Annie's 4'11" stature that portrayed a Mrs. Fixit skillset, but she was indeed handy. She was as comfortable reading technical manuals to solve computer problems as she was in preparing a meal or sewing a dress.

I was away in college when she was in fifth grade. We did not spend any time together until we both were adults and married. Perhaps one of the reasons we communicated so easily was that we were both born in June. In fact, one of the significant dates for the family happened on her birthday, June 10. It was the infamous date in 1958 when we left Georgia in the back of a Greyhound bus.

Annie was an amazing woman and a beloved sister. She passed away on March 3, 2003, of heart failure as she and her daughter, also an educator, drove to work at the school she loved so dearly. Her death was a total surprise. It was heart-wrenching and very difficult to accept. I missed the conversations we had and the smiles they created. She will live in my memory and heart forever. She was just fifty-two years old. Annie was survived by her husband, Gary; a son, Gary; and a daughter, Adrianne. Adrianne give birth to three children, posthumously making Ms. Annie a grandmother.

Sibling 5: Josephine Goggins (Jo)

She was perhaps next to the quietest of the eight sisters, yet she was known for her laughter. In my family, all the children learned to cook. Growing up in Georgia, Josephine was known for her cooking and was probably the best cook of my eight sisters. The family never had a cook-off, so this is the writer's personal assessment and is not intended to offend any of my five living sisters. Josephine was very vocal about taking care of children. She didn't want any part of it. She had an attitude about "all those children" that she and the rest of us had a hand in raising in one way or another.

Josephine had nothing against her younger siblings. She just took exception to the amount of work that we invested while our dad just enjoyed the pleasure of producing them. In looking back, it was likely our father's attitude that caused the contention. He displayed minimal responsibility, care, interest, or interaction with any of his children. His caretaking duties were pushed off on Mom, Josephine, and the rest of us to share in their rearing.

Josephine was resistant to take care of all those children that Mom and Dad produced. Surprisingly she had nine of her own. That is the most of any other sibling in our family. In the spirit of uniqueness, Jo's ABCs started and stopped at alphabet M. Each of her children's names start with the letter M. They are Michele, Michael, Morris, Marsha, Malynda, Marvin, Margarite, Mark, and Martin. She and her husband, Gil, raised a tight-knit and loving crew.

She sang in the choir at her family's home church growing up in Georgia. When she moved to Jersey City, Josephine continued to participate in the church choir; this time, at Mount Olive Baptist Church. She appreciated the Newark-based gospel legends like Cissy Houston, Dionne Warwick, and the musical group the Drinkards.

James Cleveland, the Caravans, and the Gospel Clefs were also a few of her other favorites. Josephine's singing talent was so respected by the president of the Newark-based Savoy Record Company that he offered her a contract with the company. She did not accept it because she had recently married and was pregnant with her first child.

After living many years in Jersey City and another ten years in Camden, New Jersey, Josephine moved to Baltimore, Maryland, in 1978 with her family. While there, she met and remained close friends with Delores. Delores and Josephine became traveling buddies. Among other places, they attended many Jackson family reunions together. Josephine was active in her church in Baltimore. Unfortunately because of other life choices, Josephine did not complete high school. However, she began working at a private school in Baltimore, and over time, she became head of food service in that school.

When she passed, she had twenty-three grandchildren, four great-grandchildren, and six great-great grandchildren. Josephine was affectionately known as Jo to her family and friends and as Nana to her grandchildren. She was joyously received into heaven on December 19, 2009. She was just seventy-one years young.

Sibling 12: Mary Lou Jackson

Mary, sibling 12, was a dreamer. She had a fascinating imagination. She was an avid reader as a child. She would sit alone and read about all kinds of adventures and subjects. She communicated with pen pals in Germany and France when she was in grade school. She looked forward to traveling to new and interesting places when she grew older. She mind-traveled to various countries when she was a child and shared those adventures with us as if she had been to those countries and had experienced those adventures.

As an adult, Mary was ambitious. She strived to do the best job possible at every work assignment she undertook. She never accepted second best. Mary was a risk-taker and enjoyed new and challenging opportunities. She married and later divorced a Ghanaian. Mary traveled a great deal. She visited Ghana, the Netherlands, and France. She worked in Iran. She traveled with Geneva to Haiti and the Ivory Coast. She always enjoyed being exposed to different cultures and mind-expanding ideas. She loved museums, traveling throughout the US and abroad. She loved the Metropolitan DC area. Most of her friends were multicultural professionals from foreign countries, and they resided in the DC area, relishing their diversity and shared community. Mary could converse intellectually about many topics.

In the mid to late 1980s Mary Lou accepted an assignment in Atlanta running a Job Corps program. During her tenure, she lived with my family until she secured her own place. Later she relocated to Metro Washington, DC, and every year, she always remembered my sons' birthdays and called, and many times, sent gifts to them.

She was an active member of the Unity Church. Unity teaches its members to have a positive perspective on life, to see good in everyone, and that you can make your life better by the power of positive thinking. It emphasizes healing by spiritual means, although it does not object to its members using traditional medicine to address illnesses. Unity does not promote dogma or rituals. It is a proponent that there is goodness in all religions that have God as its Pilot. Its members freely accept the religious beliefs of others.

Mary was a spiritual being. She believed in Reiki and nontraditional medical treatments, so it was not surprising when she was diagnosed with cancer in 2009 that she turned to holistic medicine as her first choice to treat the illness. She spent a year with a holistic doctor. During that period, she appeared energized and rejuvenated. When queried about the cancer, she gave the family assurances that she was fine.

During the Christmas holidays in 2009, while she was with Geneva, she was rushed to the emergency room of a nearby hospital. The diagnosis was that she was not in remission. In fact, the cancer had spread throughout her vital organs. Still until February 2010, she continued to teach at Bowie High School in Maryland. She so loved her students that she did not want to rest. But, her body could not take it any longer. Mary was hospitalized and after a year-long battle with cancer, at the young age of sixty, she succumbed to it on March 16, 2010.

Sibling 3: William C. Jackson (Billy)

Billy, sibling 3, my oldest brother, acted more like my father than my dad after we arrived in Camden. He enjoyed spending time with us. He realized that we were new to urban life and had some adjustments to make. He tried to make our lives as normal as possible. He and I had a very close relationship. Perhaps he enjoyed seeing me mature with aspirations which is something that he was denied as a child.

He was my hero. I was a dreamer. I wanted to do things nobody in the immediate family had ever talked about previously—like going to college. When I came home from college during breaks or for the summer, he'd come to me and say, "Let's take a ride." He took me to visit his friends. He would show me off as his brother in college. He was very proud of me. He acted as if I was his son.

Billy was the brother who deserved every accolade that I earned. He was there to encourage me when I needed it. I lived the life he deserved, but I lived it with his support, joy, and pleasure. He seemed prouder of me than I was of myself when I went off to college. There just was not any amount of money or concrete thing I could do to compensate him for what he meant to me and how much I learned from him.

When I visited Mom after I finished college, I always visited Billy too. He was married and sought my approval of things he had purchased, especially his fishing boats. His boats were never new.

They always looked and operated like they needed repair, but that would not keep him from getting excited and inviting me to go fishing with him. It didn't matter if I wanted to fish or not. I went because he asked and because I just could not say no to my hero.

The onboard motor of his boat was not always in the best shape. He asked other siblings to go out on his boat but none ever did. They were leery of Billy's boating prowess and the viability of his boat. They laughed at us as we towed his boat to the South Jersey Bay and launched off. What they did not know is that Billy and I fished and enjoyed ourselves. When the time came to return to shore, the engine failed to start. I put my faith in God that it would do so. Eventually after several tries, the engine turned over. By faith and the grace of God, we were able to make it back from that and other scary boat adventures.

On another subsequent visit north to attend a family reunion, Billy, my three sons, and I went deep-sea fishing on a public charter boat. We caught sixty bluefish. We landed more fish on that outing than I have ever caught in my lifetime up to that point or after. Each fish was at least three feet long.

We had an option to have the charter crew fillet the catch for fifty cents a fish, but Billy thought that price was too high; so we packed them in huge waxed boxes and took them to his house to fillet them ourselves. We were not experienced in filleting fish and it was getting dark by the time we left the charter boat. We spent more on waxed boxes and ice than it would have cost us to let the charter boat crew fillet the fish. We filleted maybe ten of the sixty fish before darkness arrived. Then we tried to give them to all who would accept them. The next day, I drove back to Georgia with my three boys and a cousin who also had attended the reunion. I iced as many of the fish as I could. Upon reaching my cousin's home in Atlanta, I gave all the fish to her. My vehicle smelled like fish for weeks. I tried to minimize and eliminate the stench using many remedies, but it lingered on for some time.

Billy had many friends. He had an engaging personality. He loved to laugh and tease people. He particularly enjoyed annoying small children by repeatedly pinching them on the arm and giggling.

He did that to each of my children and those of his siblings. That became a very familiar and unwelcoming trait of their Uncle Billy. Billy worked at Sears Roebuck for his entire adult life. He became an entrepreneur several years before he retired. For a while, together with his son, he provided cleaning services to business customers in the South Jersey area. Billy passed away on February 16, 2013. His wife, Viola, preceded him. He left behind a son, Billy Jr., and a grandson, Christopher.

Mom (Rosie L)

Mom never sat us down and said, "Children, this is my dream for your lives." Instead she taught us to love one another. She did not mean to limit our love to brothers and sisters but extend it to mankind. She directed us to be respectful to others, even if we were disrespected. She never preached the Bible to us. She lived it. It was her guidebook to life and eternity.

Upon being asked for money, Mom had a saying, "This ain't gimmy, Georgia." This meant nothing will be given to us, it must be earned. Mom was a very proud loving person. She worked and earned the money she was paid. She never sought a handout, and she taught each of us to never look for a handout or to expect something for nothing.

Mom did not have an easy life while she lived in Omaha. She had fourteen children over a twenty-four-year span. Before 1951, she worked in the fields, did day work on other farms, and worked as a domestic at Fort Benning Army Base to make money to feed and provide for our needs. As part of our farming family, every able-bodied child over age six was assigned chores. We worked as laborers in the fields or took care of the younger siblings and cooked. She established our moral fiber. She demonstrated strong ethics and taught them to us. In every job she performed, it was as if God physically stood watching over her.

She challenged each one of her fourteen children to seek a more prosperous life. She stressed that we should never forget that some-one helped us. She directed us to go and do likewise. While none of us intentionally set out saying, "Mom wanted me to do this or do that," the lessons she taught took root and the opportunities availed themselves.

Mom not only read Scripture, it inspired her. She fully under-stood that one could not sit back and wait for things to happen. One had to step out on faith and make a way for himself or herself. God will be there to support you.

Mom never completed grammar school. However, she provided guidance and inspiration for each of her children to do so. Because of that focus, ten of her fourteen children completed college, and five of them pursued and acquired secondary degrees. Mom's children were a sense of pride to her. She let us know it, and she shared her pride for us with friends and everyone else who she encountered.

Mom was raised in the AME church as a child. Her family was a member of the St. Paul AME Church in Omaha. However, she attended Mount Moriah Baptist Church for much of her married life in Omaha. When she moved to New Jersey, she joined the First Nazarene Baptist Church and was active in its missionary ministry for over twenty years. After the missionary ministry was disbanded, due to a changeover in church leadership, Mom left and became a stew-ard in Harris Temple AME Church on Florence Street in Camden. Her presence and contributions became so appreciated that she was recognized as an elder. Her picture became the first lay image allowed on the church's wall.

During her years in Camden, Mom was a very active member of the Eastern Star. She attended many functions throughout the Delaware Valley.

Dad (Frank)

I was predestined to walk in my father's footsteps behind a mule. He was a dirt farmer. His father was one. His father and his family had farmed similarly since slavery. There was nothing that indicated my future would be any different, except my mother's vision. Daddy did not seem to have a long-term view. He took each day as it came. He did not understand that a change was needed from his old ways of thinking and doing things for his life to improve.

Even in the '40s and '50s, Daddy had not transitioned to be his own person. Whatever he was told, he believed from anyone other than a person of color.

If he directed us to do something, we had to drop whatever we were doing and immediately focus on the task he instructed us to do. A slow response was viewed as an act of disobedience and resulted in us being whipped. We observed a softening of this behavior much later with his grandchildren, but with his children, as we grew up, Dad rarely engaged in conversation nor was there idle chatter between us.

After our move to Camden, he exerted little or no influence over me. Aside from mowing the lawn and picking up around the house, the boys had no outside chores that he needed to oversee. Because he never promised us anything in exchange for doing work or for any other reason, there was nothing in common that he had with his children. Because of our little interaction with him, there is not much for me to discuss or talk about. He did, to their great annoyance, rely on the girls to prepare his meals and to serve him upon request.

As an adult, out of respect, I tried to show appreciation to him. Unfortunately it was difficult to find common ground. He was a loner, almost like a stranger to me. In 1978, I reached out to build a rapport and have him visit with my boys. So I invited him to visit us in Miami. It was also an opportunity for him to see his brother Grover my namesake, whom he had not seen in thirty years.

My dad was the opposite of my mom. When she came to visit, she did not stay put. Prior to arriving, she had contacted relatives and friends to announce her plans to be in the area and had made visitation appointments for the duration of her stay. The moment she entered our home, after a brief hello, she was on the phone confirming the dates and times she would visit each of the people who she had contacted prior to her arrival. The next day, either my wife or I dropped her off to her scheduled appointment on our way to work. On our return home later that evening, we picked her up. This was the daily routine until she returned home to Camden.

Since Dad and his brother had not seen each other in three decades, I wanted them to reconnect. Both had some very strange ways and my best efforts were for naught. I lived in a mixed neighborhood and my Uncle Grover refused to even visit me. Given my work hours, I could only take Dad to visit my uncle after work and on weekends. They spent a very limited amount of time together during Dad's visit to Miami.

The visitation constraints seemed okay with my dad. While I was at work, he found the liquor and tobacco stores. Neither my wife nor I smoked or consumed alcohol. A nonsmoker's senses heighten to the smell of cigarette smoke. We could smell it immediately upon entering our home. It is tough for a child to lay down rules to a parent. But we made it known that we did not allow either smoking or drinking to be done in our home. In the end, my opportunity to connect with Daddy was not a successful venture. He was as uncomfortable visiting with us as we were in having him visit.

Dad passed away, a little over a year after my mother, at the age of seventy-nine, on November 17, 1985. I remember him as neither happy nor sad. Reflecting on our relationship and his role in the family, if I had the opportunity today, I would ask him these questions:

- What was his motivation for fathering fourteen children when he had no financial means of caring for them?

- What was his goal in life, for his children?
- Did he give any thought to their future or the lack thereof?
- How had he planned to provide for them?
- Did he even consider there would be societal changes? How had he planned to deal with the changes?
- If he could make just one change during his early years, what would that change be? What did he do to contribute to his children's development and growth? What was the most significant contribution?
- If he could point to a moment in time, what would he consider his proudest moment and why?
- What was one sacrifice he made knowingly and purposely for the family and why?

Of course, I would get no satisfying answers to those queries, given the kind of person my father was. I would like to believe that he meant well. He just lacked the capacity to demonstrate his compassion and made some rash decisions that communicated a lack of concern.

Daddy was the chairman of the deacon board at Saint Elmo Baptist Church in Omaha. When we relocated to Camden, he joined Nazarene Baptist Church; however, he rarely took the time to fellowship with the church's congregation or to attend any church worship services. I wonder whether my dad asked God for wisdom as Solomon did as a young man. Perhaps God demonstrated wisdom and intelligence through Mom as God had done through Abigail, Nabal's wife, as written in Scripture, (1 Samuel 25) of the Bible. God blessed our family. He brought people in our lives to guide us and to prepare us. God protected us, just as He protected Nabal through David and his men. He shielded Nabal and his household from harm, although Nabal made a poor decision when it counted the most.

Mom was Dad's partner. She kept our two-parent family together for fifty-five years until her death. Our protection was the foundation of *love*, built on biblical *faith*, "The assurance of things hoped for, the conviction of things not seen" (Hebrews 11:1, ESV).

With physical and spiritual *strength* of mind, our character and our willpower developed. When all was summed up, *determination* by each participant was required to deliver us across the finish line, triumphant.

Chapter 19

The Siblings' Legacies

We Are the Jacksons

A person's legacy is defined as how they are remembered, contributions they made during their lifetime, and other attributes. A legacy is created by what a person did or said during person's lifetime. It reflects how others, with whom you have interfaced, remember your contributions or perspectives. A legacy may be written or shared orally. The legacies herein are my documented observations of each Jackson sibling based on my firsthand experiences with them. To avoid the awkwardness of writing my own legacy, my sister (sibling 14) did it for me.

Sibling 1: Leola (Lee)

Lee has a very kind and gentle heart. She is known to tell it like she sees it to both her benefit and to her detriment. I would not say she is hot-tempered. Rather she is her daddy's child. Lee earned everything she has gained in life. She is the mother of five children, four daughters and one son who is the youngest. Her husband passed away of a heart attack in 1970 while the children were still young, even before puberty. Three of her children earned college degrees and one of the three did so with honors. Three of her daughters married and had families, but her son is still single. Family was there to support Lee as much as they could. The fact that she was the oldest literally made it difficult to receive financial assistance from her younger siblings. They were either in college or had recently finished when she was in need. Lee never remarried. Her strong will is the character trait she needed as a single parent to raise five children. She maintained a household, entered college as an adult, and graduated from Saint Peter's College in Jersey City, New Jersey, with a bachelor's degree. For the next fifteen years, Lee was employed by the Jersey City Board of Education. She later worked as a social worker at a local hospital. She retired from full-time employment in 1994.

During her retirement years, she has kept busy serving mankind through her church's homeless ministry. Lee volunteers to provide meals and clothing to the homeless on a weekly basis to all who come. The service is free for the asking. In addition to her volunteering, she enjoys spending time with her eight grandchildren, seven great-grandchildren, and two great-great-grandchildren. She still has time to stay in touch with her siblings and talks with Rose at least once or more per day. Although she said her memory comes and goes, I talk with her at least twice a week. She communicates as one with a sound mind as we settle the world's problems. She is always current on the latest political scoops. Lee is the family historian. She is the first person we call for detailed information on and about uncles and aunts and their offspring. Information most requested is specific ages, ancestors, and lineage.

Lee successfully raised a family. She set an example for them— never to be satisfied nor make excuses for their circumstances. The uncertainty of life will catch one unaware and unprepared. We will be measured on how we respond to the challenges presented to us. This is a legacy to be extremely proud of. I am thankful to our Lord and Savior, Jesus Christ, for blessing Leola, my beloved sister, who overcame the challenges of life despite the odds.

Sibling 2: Rosie (Rose)

Rose was always a person who worked within the system as a team player. Early in her life, she applied Mom's challenge to her make a difference in the world. Rose learned early on that she must be part of the team for her voice to be heard. Otherwise she felt she would be just another voice, crying in the wilderness. As a factory worker, she became involved in union activities. In the community, she became a very active member of the NAACP and Jersey City's Democratic Political Party. As a practicing Catholic, at that time, Rose discovered in Jersey City the political power that existed in and through the Catholic Church. Therefore, she shared her views and concerns through the church leadership. While she never had any interest in running for political office, she learned and used her influence to affect change for the betterment of the entire Jersey City community, regardless of the ethnicity.

In 1964, Rose participated in civil rights activities. She attended the 1964 March on Washington and helped to organize many local civil rights events. She focused her attention on many injustices and the plight of many underserved citizens. When the factory where she worked closed and relocated, Rosie used her connections to get a job as a security guard in the local high school. She later enrolled in St. Peter's College in Jersey City and graduated in 1982. After graduation, she accepted a job and taught at the same high school. Due to her social activities and involvement in community issues, she knew the decision makers and the positions of power and was able to open doors for others.

Her connections enabled Mary Lou to get a job as a business education teacher at a New Jersey City High School that opened in the fall of 1971. Rose was known from her block to Jersey City's City Hall and to the New Jersey State Capital because she became involved in issues that affected minorities. She lobbied for higher wages for migrant farm workers in the state and voters' rights for all citizens, whether locally or nationally. She was a member of the city's Civil Rights Commission and was involved in discussions with local organizations, businesses, politicians and met Dr. Martin L. King Jr. on his visit to the area.

Rosie is the mother of three children, two daughters and a son. After she retired as a teacher, she relocated to Maryland where all three of her children live. She enjoys the blessings of having four grown granddaughters and several great-grandchildren. Rosie volunteers in her community and is committed to holding elected officials accountable for the community's survival.

My sister and I talk by telephone daily, discussing all the fake news of that day and our solution to the current day's issues. I believe Rose's calling was to work for social and economic change. She has remembered our mom's charge to her to make a difference in society by helping the many who are less fortunate.

Sibling 3: William (Billy)

Billy loved his family and made great sacrifices for us to thrive and become successful. For that, I am eternally grateful. At age twenty-five, when many young men and women thought about marriage and themselves, he unselfishly looked out for us and made personal and financial sacrifices to make it possible for us to have a better life once we arrived in Camden, New Jersey. This move created more opportunity than we had as a child growing up in Stewart County, Georgia. Billy helped the family purchase a home. For a short time, he also stayed with us and contributed to our family's well-being until he got married. He was a surrogate father to me. He was my big brother, and we both enjoyed our roles. He took me to see professional baseball games, to the New Jersey shores to fish. Though I was often wary, fishing on his boat was our favorite thing to do. We had some great times fishing, whether we caught any fish or not.

Occasionally the mechanics on his boat didn't function the way they should have, but our spirits did not dampen. We relied on our hopes and prayers. We continued to fish and dealt with any complications associated with our survival or mobility after the fishing was over.

Billy married a preacher's daughter, and they had a son. Billy's wife passed away of breast cancer, and he never remarried. Billy shared his home with his adult son and grandson until he passed away in 2013.

Billy loved God. He loved his family. He was employed and worked at the same company for his entire career. And he fished for enjoyment, in that order.

Sibling 4: Charles

Charles was a smart businessman and a great salesman. For much of his early adult life, he managed a large automotive parts' store in Bayonne, New Jersey. He transitioned to own and operate an Exxon gas station that sold gas and employed a mechanic to make automotive repairs. It was a thriving business and one of only a few black-owned and operated gas stations in Jersey City at that time. Charles took his business seriously. He worked diligently to make it successful.

Primarily Charles was a family man, and he played as hard as he worked. He was very personable and was a snappy dresser. He enjoyed drinking. He delighted in partying, dancing, and listening to music when he went out with the boys on weekends.

Charles and his wife had three children, two sons and a daughter. Their daughter was the middle child. At last count, they had three grandchildren. Both Charles and his wife are deceased.

Sibling 5: Josephine

I will always remember Josephine as the sibling who seemed joyful, fulfilled, and laughed a lot. I saw Jo as an observer who could be drawn into a conversation, but rarely would she start one. She was a very private person. She was quiet and never talked or bragged about things she did. She avoided shining the light on herself. God knows she had many reasons to do so. I only recently learned, upon requesting input from my siblings for this book, that Josephine was instrumental in financing our migration to Camden. She never talked about it to any of us. She never mentioned anything about her role in our venture north.

We found it amusing and we often teased Jo about her nine children whose first names each began with the letter M. Unlike the Jackson's household, there were no duplicate sibling names, like Mary F. and Mary L., but the first two letters of the names for the last six children each began with the letters M-A. I enjoyed visiting her home with so many gleeful little children running around and not a care in this world. Contrast that to our rearing in Georgia, we all ran around but also had responsibilities and chores. Like most children, they were very active. They were always very polite and friendly. Her family unit reminded me of the distant memory of our childhood when we had the opportunity to run around, just being carefree children. Josephine did a fantastic job raising her children to be responsible, morally strong, close-knit, and loving adults.

She was the head of food service in a private school in the Baltimore area. She helped to support her family, along with her loving husband, Gil. She praised the Lord by using her voice to sing in her church's choir. She served the Lord and Savior faithfully in her daily walk, work, and worship.

Sibling 6: Mary Frances (Mamie)

Mamie bridged the gap between the older siblings and the younger ones. After our mom passed away, she became the mother figure for Mary, Annie, and Chris. Her home was always open, and my family used it on each of our visits to the South Jersey area. Before she moved, after living thirty years in Voorhees, New Jersey, her home was a frequent family gathering place during holidays. Unlike some of my siblings, perhaps she and I remember the most details about growing up in Stewart County (Omaha), Georgia. Her initial family research about the family captured my attention and interest. Our independently written summaries of the family's history appeared as though we plagiarized each other's story. This is curious because my stories had been written several years before she dictated and I transcribed her stories from a cassette tape or before she had seen anything that I had written.

Mamie is very kind-hearted and willingly helps those in need however the need arises. She has had many jobs including educator and day care administrator. Her job of thirty-five years and career before she retired was with New Jersey social services in the family services division. She is keenly aware of the state agency services that are available to families who need assistance. In support of her church and other charities, when shopping, Mamie is constantly on the lookout for items that someone may need at some point of time, in the future. She often purchases goods to set them aside when the need arises from strangers and family alike. Among other volunteer contributions, Mamie plans and organizes her church pantry ministry. She is an active participant on the food ministry which feed members and others for special events and repasts. She teaches Sunday school and prepares the Eucharist for communion Sunday.

Mamie graduated from high school in Stewart County. Blacks received a separate and certainly not-equal education in those days. We often joke that while seven of us earned degrees and graduated from private and public colleges and universities in New Jersey, Mamie is the only one who graduated from college as magna cum laude. She was not even confident that a higher education was something she should pursue, but Mamie succeeded from the minute she entered Camden County College. Her story is one of my favorites to share. I believe Mamie will be remembered by future generations for her hunger and thirst for detailing the family's initial genealogical history.

At this stage in her life, Mamie is a widow whose days are brightened by her son and two delightful grandsons, ranging in ages from twenty-one to four years old.

Sibling 7: Geneva

Geneva seems to prefer to remember only positive events and activities. When I am speaking with Geneva and I make a comment that doesn't sound complementary, she says, "That's not nice." I'm one who can talk about all subjects without it affecting me emotionally, one way or the other. Perhaps Geneva's conscience is blocking some of the things she said as a teenager in Omaha. This is a true story. I will never forget it. I will always associate it in her legacy. I think it's funny. As a teenager, Geneva was falsely accused of something and Dad whipped her for it. She got so angered by the injustice that she heatedly told him that she would poison his food as she cooked it. How she came up with that idea, I don't know. What I do know is that for a long time, Dad wouldn't eat anything she cooked.

I get tickled to think about our Dad, a grown man, who frequently disciplined his children by beating them, was scared to eat his daughter's cooking for fear of being poisoned. That was one meal she didn't have to prepare. It may have also been the last time he whipped her. Now you know why I tend to remember all the good, the bad, and the ugly.

Geneva has a great deal of patience with children. Before she retired, she was an educator and a media specialist who taught library skills to elementary school students in inner-city Camden. She won lots of awards and received much positive recognition for the progress and ongoing success of her students. Geneva does not always portray the same indulgence with family members, particularly if they do not agree with her or have her same mindset about an issue.

Unlike with her interactions with children, she is not persistent in expressing her view. Rather she is ready to move on from you to pursue interests that she perceives as more peaceful.

Geneva has lots of friends. She enjoys talking on the telephone with them and socializing with them. She is an active supporter of the Girl Scouts. She is in several church ministries, including the Shepherd's Committee that sends cards to sick and shut-in members, the trustee board that cares for the church building's upkeep, and the pastor's committee, a ministry that supports the pastor's outreach efforts. Geneva's personal ministry is to freely give her time to serve seniors and others in need because they have no family nearby. She visits them and often drives them to shop, to doctor's appointments, or other places they need to go. She is also an active member in her sorority. Geneva has a daughter, who lives with her husband, and two children in a metropolitan area surrounding Atlanta, Georgia. Geneva and her daughter are very much alike in temperament and the willingness to freely serve others.

Sibling 8: Grover

Grover is a dreamer. He is always looking for ways to do positive things to help others. He remembers clearly how generously others have helped him and his family. He wants to pass it forward.

He will give his last dollar and do it without hesitation if he feels that the person needs it more. He is eternally grateful that his wife is his sounding board before he gives to charity. She appreciates his soft-heartedness and burning desire to pass it forward. However, she is always there to balance the level of sacrifice with their family's welfare. This does not mean that together, they have not made decisions that turned out to be foolhardy. They have. They may have gotten taken advantage of, but their spirit was in the right place when the decision was made to give from their hearts.

According to other siblings, Grover tried to distance himself from them during much of our travel north. He was totally embarrassed by having to carry the sheets that wrapped up our meager belongings. So it was no surprise to many of us that he purchased three suitable pieces of luggage to replace the tattered bags of his homeless houseguest who traveled to visit him and Millette by Greyhound bus. It was not a rarity that he and Millette bought her a cellphone to keep in touch in an emergency and paid some of her bills. Nor was it unexpected that he helped create and fund a 501(c)3 to allow his Kenyan friend to open a ministry to support educational programs for children whose parents have died from AIDS and alcohol abuse in his homeland.

Grover coordinated the homeless ministry for his church, First Baptist Church of Atlanta, more than twenty years and served as one of its deacons. The ministry serves up to 175 homeless individuals on a weekly basis.

It is clear why Grover's true occupation was always meant to be sales. He loves being with and around people. He is curious. He enjoys networking. Being a friend to him means that he will always stay in touch with you. Whether he met you twenty years ago or two years ago, if he established a bond with you, he will reach out to you. You can be assured that when he is traveling to your town, he will call you to have lunch. Given his time in sales, Grover likely has a friend in every state in the union.

Many years after he retired from his technology company, Grover still seeks marketing opportunities to pursue. He has an unquenchable entrepreneurial spirit. He is working on an Internet based effort now. Before this current venture, there were many others. To Grover, retirement does not mean that you stop working.

Grover's legacy should be, "Doing what's right today means no regrets tomorrow." His favorite motto when he realizes that someone has taken advantage of him is, "As for you, you meant evil against me, but God meant it for good"(Genesis 50:20, ESV).

Grover is uncomfortable with conflict and will go out of his way to avoid it. However, he will never compromise wrong for right and will always defend what he perceives to be right. He lives with his wife and two of his three sons. Their first son, Gerod, is a special needs child. They spend many hours participating in Special Olympics and other events to keep him active. His middle son lives in northern Virginia, a suburb of Metropolitan District of Columbia, with his wife and two children.

Sibling 9: Robert (Bob)

Bob passed away so young until most of us just remember him only during his childhood before we left Georgia. In New Jersey, he will always be remembered as the brother who was quiet with a wry sense of humor.

Sibling 10: George

George is an extrovert. He is very calm and approachable. He enjoys being with and around people. He is warm, open, and smiles generously. He is in his comfort zone as a salesman. He uses the business training and skills that he received when he was employed in all facets of his life. He is instrumental in planning and organizing our family reunions. He cajoles and finds other ways to convince family members more resistant to participate to do so. He expects 100 percent attendance at the family's reunion events. If he must settle for financial contributions from those who cannot attend, he is willing to accept that. He will use the financial contributions to help someone else attend or to defray the cost for something to help all who are attending. If a sibling upsets another, George is one who may get called upon to listen to both sides and then try to mitigate the situation using inclusive and calm words to reduce the tension.

George is a religious Fundamentalist. He is openly curious about the religious beliefs and practices of others. He engages in conversations with people who do not share his beliefs, whether religious, political, or other. He is very receptive to new information but holds strongly onto his own beliefs and will more than likely attempt to persuade you that his thoughts are the right ones. George believes that he has been put on this earth to make a positive difference in people's lives. He became a big brother while attending Hampton Institute, now known as Hampton University. He continues that personal relationship up to the present day. His little brother is now grown and has a family of his own. George has been a Sunday school teacher for many years. He is active in the prison ministry.

George is a neat freak. He likes organization, cleanliness, and things to be done right and to be put in their proper places. This is evident inside of his home. It is always well-kept and no dishes are found in the sink. His home is spotless. The neatness tendency is also on display by way of the beautifully designed flower gardens he tended in the yards of the homes he has owned over the years. The family often teased him about his yard, saying that it is flawless, having every blade of grass in its proper place. He spent a fortune on plants and flowers as well as ten-hour days keeping it up. Although he had retired from his corporate job, he created another full-time one to maintain his yard. George's desire for neatness extends to behavior traits in those who are relatives or active participants in his life. He does not welcome drama or people who attract it.

While George recognizes and accepts that life is not always orderly, he would clearly prefer that his personal life be tidy. A working motto for George may be, "Teach a person to fish and you will never have to feed him." After relaxing and tending his yard for years, George downsized and moved to a condominium. He then took on another challenge. He determined that he could best make an impact on today's youth by becoming a substitute teacher in the Hampton area. His philosophy is that he brings a corporate approach and the value of his experience to the classroom. He believes that if teachers could share such real-world experiences, dress and act more corporately, students would respect them and respond positively to their efforts to better manage the classroom. Six of my siblings, including many nieces, nephews, and other family members were educators. Despite attempts by them to dissuade him, George enthusiastically seeks out opportunities to substitute. He presses his clothes the night before and, unlike most teachers today, dresses professionally in his custom-tailored fashion attire and proudly heads off to his daily assignments. He aims to be a role model for the students in how he dresses, handles himself, and in his speech. Although many students have not yet welcomed his freely shared lessons, learned experiences, George offers them anyway. His goal is to reach one or two students with his message to feel that he is being successful. He has been subbing for five years now. His goal has yet to be realized.

George lives with his wife who has recently retired. They have one daughter who is a professional entertainer and lives in North Jersey.

Sibling 11: Otis (OJ)

Otis displayed strong artistic talent when he was in junior high and high school. He could create a pastoral scene using colors, etch in pencil architectural buildings, or sketch in charcoal a portrait of anyone with keen likeness from memory or at a sitting. He was also an elocutionist. He may have had his public speaking skills earlier than high school, but I only noticed them then. While he did not continue to develop his drawing talents, he clearly mastered his ability to speak in public. He freely and easily speaks extemporaneously and eloquently. For many years, whenever we needed a family representative to speak at events such as benefits, weddings, family reunions, or funerals, Otis was always the one to call upon to do so. For a long while, it was assumed that he would one day become a lawyer or a politician.

Before he married and had a family of his own, he cared for our parents and younger siblings. He provided for them financially and handled business matters as needed. He was the youngest male child at home after I left for the Peace Corps and George went into the army. While most of us grew up in small similar gender age groups, Otis was not blessed to do so. Nevertheless, he became a self-made man. He is an astute businessman. For many years, he thrived being self-employed as an independent insurance broker. He was noted for his strong product knowledge and personable customer service.

Otis has a close-knit family. He is very proud of his wife Mary, daughter Jolene, son Jay, son-in-law, daughter-in-law, and four grandchildren. He has strong religious beliefs and is an ordained minister. So too is his wife and son. He is probably our most outwardly sensitive sibling. He has a strong moral character and a positive outlook on life. He is well-known by many in his community of influence and has a wealth of friends who he considers family. He has a bright welcoming smile. He did not become a politician but he has developed the skillset that would have made him a very successful, engaging, influential, and cajoling politician. He can debate with the best orators on just about any subject. He is most intelligent.

Sibling 12: Mary Lou

Mary Lou was a dreamer. Since she was a very young child, she ventured and visited many countries throughout the world by having pen pals and an unquenchable thirst for reading. When she became an adult, she accomplished her desire to travel, met new people, and appreciated many different cultures. Her love for traveling took her to Iran, Greece, Europe, Haiti, Ghana, and the Ivory Coast. During her travels, she befriended many individuals from all facets of life. She made her home in the culturally diverse metropolitan area of Washington, DC, to be closer to her friends. She believed that there was always something culturally viable that she could learn from them. Mary was well educated and well-read and maintained an immense curiosity about all facets of people, places, and things, making her a person who was never without a query. If she asked a question and it was answered, there would be a follow-up of several additional questions. The receiver of the questions would get exhausted from responding long before she got tired of asking the questions.

Mary did not believe in traditional religion. She did, however, believe in God and in the goodness of mankind. She was a positive spirit while she was here on earth, having been a high school teacher, recruiter, and business instructor, all with a big heart. She loved imparting new and useful information to her students and wanted to share with them her worldly traveling experiences. Her dedication and aim allowed her students to have the skills needed to be successful in their real-world encounters. She taught academics, practical and common sense skills. When she worked as a recruiter and instructor for the Job Corps, she gave female students some of her clothes so that they would look business-like for job interviews. She invited students to her home and to the homes of her relatives when they traveled so they would feel comfortable or be offered hospitality and a home-cooked meal.

She cared about sustaining the environment. Long before it became popular, Mary avoided buying and using plastic materials. When she had no other option but to buy it, rather than discard the empty container, she set it aside to later take it to a centralized recycling center. She bought and used natural laundry and cleaning products long before conservation was common. She was sensitive to the ecological impact that such products would have on the environment. Mary was fascinated by the natural reserve that backed up to her yard in Bowe, Maryland. She was thrilled to spot wild plants and deer that came near her backyard to nibble and marveled at all of God's creations. Mary was single at the time of her passing.

Sibling 13: Annie (Ms. Ann)

Annie had a beautiful smile and a warm and engaging personality. Annie accentuated the positive. She did not go around looking for fault in others. She had many friends and was active in her church in its hospitality ministry. She was an educator in the classroom and, ultimately, as a librarian. She provided materials to quench their thirst for reading. In the role of educator, she was beloved by students and parents alike because she actively cared about the well-being of her students. If they needed clothes, she helped to get some for them; and if they needed supplies, she provided them too. She did all that she could to create a positive learning experience and environment for her students while at school.

Annie was close to her family and freely traveled to see her niece in Ohio and sisters and brothers in North Jersey, Maryland, Massachusetts, and Georgia. She always stayed in touch with them. She was a willing traveler, and her two children were always in tow with her. It was rare that she went anywhere without them. She was a night owl, and if she needed to get something from the store late at night, she took them with her. She did so rather than wait for the next day. I think this approach made her children flexible, even-keeled, tolerant, and ready for whatever would come next.

Although she was married, Annie was a very independent person. She was never afraid to tackle something new on her own. Long before YouTube and Pinterest became popular, Annie explored books and used the trial-and-error method to make creations and to correct mistakes. She learned to fix computers, overcome computer application problems, change the oil in her car, sand, finish, and upholster furniture, frame pictures, and successfully complete other do-it-yourself projects. She had an eye for design and never hesitated to offer advice about how to reposition pictures and furniture in family members' homes for better representation. Annie left behind her husband, Gary, a retired policeman, son, Gary, and daughter, Adrianne.

Sibling 14: E Christine (Chris)

Chris looks for ways to do positive things to help others. She has been an active volunteer in the Big Brothers Big Sisters Program.

Although she is involved with other activities at her church, Chris is a devoted steward to the pantry ministry. She offers a smiling face, an open heart, and aims to return the blessings she receives to each client that she schedules, greets, and serves. Before taking on this role, Chris shared her blessings at the soup kitchen at her previous church home. She attends Bible study class. She is a longtime officer in her church's Saint Vincent de Paul Society. The vocation of the ministry is to, through person-to-person contact, provide service to those in need regardless of social background, gender, political affiliation, ethnicity, or creed.

Chris does not gossip or engage in pettiness. She is more inclined to look past a fault in search of a solution to a problem. Her favorite scripture is Matthew 7:1–5.

> Jesus said to his disciples: "Stop judging, that you may not be judged. For as you judge, so will you be judged, and the measure with which you measure will be measured out to you. Why do you notice the splinter in your brother's eye, but not perceive the wooden beam in your own eye? How can you say to your brother, let me remove that splinter from your eye, while the wooden beam is in your eye? You hypocrite remove the wooden beam from your eye first; then you will see clearly to remove the splinter from your brother's eye."

Chris is happy to have her husband, Joe, who shares her values as an active partner in life. They have taught adults to read via adult literacy programs. They assist strangers and family to fill voids in order that they may succeed. Some say this occurs sometimes to their detriment. Chris and Joe overlook that perception and note that it is a common family trait to find ways to pay forward the many blessings they have received. They share their many blessings with a son John, daughter-in-law, a granddaughter, five grandsons, and other extended family.

Endnotes, Exhibits, and References

1. Road marker in front of Stewart County Courthouse in Lumpkin
2. Stewart County, Georgia, map with associated landmarks, Omaha, Florence, and Lumpkin
3. Florence and Background Battle of Shepherd's Plantation
4. Lumpkin Courthouse and county seat
5. Fort Jones and Fort McCreary road markers regarding the plantation's Creek Indians attack
6. James Fitzgerald the rider to warn the militia of the Creek Indians attack on Shepherd's Plantation
7. Family's Genealogy William L. & Phyllis T. Bryant, my father's great grandparents and Austin and Josephine Givens, my mother's great grandparents
8. See family's genealogy: Bryants, Worrell, and Jackson and Givens, Davis, Williams and Jackson
9. Picture of Madline, my mother's grandmother
10. St. Elmo Baptist Church, Daddy was a member and chairman of deacons
11. Aunt Ann Harris' daughters: Ruby, Edna, and Alice
12. Fitzgerald Family Cemetery located a quarter mile from the "The Big House" the family residence
13. Cotton bud and opened bud ready to be harvested
14. A typical field of cotton that we planted and picked yearly.
15. Typical clustered framed housing that was located on the Fitzgerald farm called the quarters
16. Mom and Dad at their fiftieth wedding celebration
17. Place with electricity; we were told to move out so a white farmer could move in; my birthplace
18. A place we use to obtain white dirt to whitewash the inside walls of places we stayed

19 Picture of Grandpa Frank Sr. and Grandma Hattie
20 The Silver Meteor Train, my oldest sister, Leola travelled to Newark, NJ
21 Family black pot sitting in Grover's garage
22 The town of Omaha, the physical area
23 AFL/CIO meeting with Martin Luther King
24 Civil Rights Committee of the AFL/CIO
25 Rosalie Boyles, Honoree
26 Omaha Post Office, old and the new
27 The Fitzgerald's big house residence
28 Copy bill of sales personal property, dated January 4, 1951
29 Mount Moriah Baptist Church, our first school
30 The Omaha Training School, first county-provided school, now a private home
31 Omaha Post Office, old and the new
32 Omaha Elementary and Junior High School converted into the Omaha Brewing Company
33 Philip Crayton drove us to the Greyhound bus station, married our cousin, Mom's side of family
34 A view of JCSU Biddle Hall administration building from the west gate
35 Omaha established 1891 sign, pointing to the post office
36 Mom and Mrs. Fallings, Mom's traveling partner
37 Bishop Johnson, pictured and exhibited at President Jimmy Carter Presidential Library
38 Jack Holbrook, "Webster County," *New Georgia Encyclopedia*, July 6, 2017.
39 Road marker recognizing Bishop Johnson contribution and significance to the people and area
40 St. Mark AME Church in Plains, Georgia (Archery), today founded and pastored by Bishop Johnson
41 John Haag, "Hall Johnson (1888–1970)," *New Georgia Encyclopedia*, July 6, 2017, http://www.georgiaencyclopedia.org/articles/arts-culture/hall-johnson-1888-1970
42 Omaha road marker and year it was established
43 Geneva (center), my wife, Millette, and me
44 Mary Lou: Teacher tells story of Iran stay
45 My birthplace, too good for us, it had electricity; we were told to move for a white farmer.
46 He motivated his students to perform beyond normal expectations.

47 Steve, Margo, Lorraine, and I met in junior high and attended the same college at the same time.

48 The old Singer Company building located in Lumpkin across from the Stewart County Courthouse

49 A glued silhouette of President Kennedy in my yearbook along with this quote.

50 Thirteen of the thirty-five PCVs who served with me on top of Menegai Crater, August 1967

51 Map of Kenya, Nakuru, cities and towns I worked/visited during the two years I lived there.

52 Menengai Crater viewed from top

53 Map of Africa with the country of Kenya, on the east coast and the Indian Ocean

54 My job description as a PCV

55 Me on my motorcycle

56 Menengai Crater viewed from my front yard

57 Our residence, the house

58 Menengai Crater and coffee farm in the foreground and me dressed in my front yard

59 Rolf, the German, my friend and housemate in Nakuru, Kenya

60 Standing next to the huge container that collected rainwater for our personal use

61 Thompson Waterfalls

62 Just one of my many visitors, atop of Menengai Crater

63 An African fishing boat with sails at sunset in Zanzibar

64 Sample herd of animals

65 Sample herd of animals

66 Sample herd of animals

67 Pictures view of the crater

68 The YMCA swimming pool in Moshe, Tanzania

69 The YMCA, the place we spent the night.

70 Mount Kilimanjaro before reaching the last cave before the final 3:00 a.m. climb to reach the top by 6:00 a.m. sunrise

71 Mount Kilimanjaro, day 2 climb

72 Two Americans who often visited us in Nakuru during a weekend of sightseeing near my house

73 Judge Joann Bowens, Dr. Gerry Smith-Wright and me out to lunch in February 2018

74 Pictured at my wedding are Joann, former Fulton County judge, and Dr. Gloria, retired college professor

75 US Department of State offered me a position to return to East Africa, Tanzania

76 My first apartment and view of Hoboken, the Hudson River, and Midtown Manhattan

77 Information was shared by her best friend, Charlyn, during a visit to Houston in 2015

78 Job offer from Gulf Oil company later purchased by Chevron

79 My lovely bride

80 Rev. Crawford W. Kimble Sr., Charles, my best man, and myself

81 My bride, her father and mother, and my mother

82 Mrs. Lucille Vinable, the sister of my mother-in-law and my lovey bride

83 Mrs. Hattie B. Waters and my lovely bride, the day of our wedding on August 5, 1972

84 Position offered from a Houston bank to return to Houston

85 Roosevelt Cox with his wife and two of his three daughters

86 Florida International University adjunct professor offer and performance

87 A friend since 1972, worked at two different companies together, retired from the one we joined in 1977

88 Mom's funeral program

89 Dad's funeral program

90 Ramada Plaza by Wyndham Atlanta Downtown Capital Park

The Jacksons
Front row left to right: Grover (me), Leola, Mom, Dad, E. Chris & Rosie
Back row: Otis, Josephine, Mary Frances (mamie), George, Geneva,
William (Billy), Mary Lou, Charles & Annie
Missing Robert (Bob) who passed 9-15-67

My family—Millette, my wife, Grover (me), Gerod, Graig and Gustin touring NYC during the Bryant's Family (2007) Reunion

About the Authors

G rover started his professional career on Wall Street as a corporate banker, then spent the next thirty-seven years in the technology sector. Coworkers often asked him about writing a book upon hearing many of his childhood stories about farming in Georgia.

Mary F. Fullard has always been curious about their genealogy and drove their parents and anyone who would listen and answer or respond to her many unending streams of questions.

But the familiarity with the community did not quell her thirst for more knowledge about their descendants. The evolution of the Internet and websites such as ancestry.com became the solution to her quest for answers that she found by doing research on the Internet. Her professional career was in state government, public sector administration, early childhood education.

E. Christine spent her entire career in the telecommunication industry and was the first black woman to serve in the position as director for her employer in the state of New Jersey. Initially she had zero interest in participating in writing a book, but after sharing that it isn't about her, rather it's about future generations she showed interest. She edited the initial text, then Mary suggested she write her own life story. She wrote it as well as chapters 18 "We Commemorate" and 19 "The Siblings' Legacies" and did the initial edit of the entire book. Together the three of them are first-time authors but have together written a book of *A Journey of Love, Faith, Strength and Determination*.

CPSIA information can be obtained
at www.ICGtesting.com
Printed in the USA
FSHW011548230221
78869FS